IN PURSUIT OF
Chocolate

A JOURNEY OF DISCOVERY

ALEXANDER VAN 'T RIET

Le Noble Publishing

Published by Le Noble Publishing 2018

First edition; First Printing

© 2018 Alexander van 't Riet

All rights reserved. No part of this book may be reproduced or transmitted in any form or by any means, including but not limited to information storage and retrieval systems, electronic, mechanical, photocopy, recording, etc. without written permission from the copyright holder.

ISBN 978-0-9967769-1-2

Table of Contents

Prologue 5

Running up the Corporate Ladder 9

Marriage and Family Complete the Picture 13

Family Closer Together - a Move to Austria 17

Where Everything Changes 19

The Route to our Journey 21

Volunteering - for us and Others 25

The First Stop: US Culture and Final Preparations 29

The Galapagos - from Extreme to Extreme 33

Peru - More than Lost Incas 51

Australia - No Volunteering but Wildly Educational 81

Leaving Australia 103

The Cruise-a-fixtion 103

Viet Nam - Where History comes Alive 119

China - Impossible to Capture 161

Nepal - Serene Reincarnation 201

Cambodia - Hit Hard 247

Closing the Book 289

Appendix 295

Prologue

SITTING AT THE KITCHEN TABLE with mom at four in the afternoon was one of those rituals. Regardless the season, the temperature, wet or dry, tradition put us on the brightly-colored plastic kitchen chairs. Over a glass of tea and a dry biscuit we'd have "the school day in review", a chat about everything and nothing.

I was 8 years old, lived in Holland, and loved those moments. Sometimes they were hasty, before running out to kick a ball with the neighborhood kids. Sometimes it was more leisurely and we'd engage in serious conversations.

One afternoon my mom must have been in a good mood, because I remember getting a piece of chocolate on top of my biscuit. This was usually reserved for Saturdays, birthdays, and when grandma and grandpa would visit. I treasured the little square, letting it melt slowly and sticking the final bit to the roof of my mouth, trying to savor it as long as I could.

I don't know why, but in that instant something 'clicked' in my brain. I looked at my mom and said "you know mom, happiness is not something absolute. Having a little more each time is much better than getting what you want in one go, or having it all the time." My mom gave me a puzzled look, wondering where that came from.

Okay. I paraphrased. I can't remember exactly what was said. In fact, odds are that time has substantially distorted my memory of the event. But the root of the thought -I know- came there, with my mom, at the kitchen table sitting on those brightly-colored chairs.

Over time, the concept became entrenched in my thoughts. Like a shortcut in the park created by the frequent passages, where grass is worn down and only a hard sand path remains, time marked my belief that 'small improvements are best'. Repetitive observation of this phenomenon came back time and again.

I noticed it in the joy I felt when Coke was promoted from a birthday drink to a weekend luxury. Likewise for potato chips. Many other improvements followed (nicer house, nicer car, new clothes). Later, while I was in University, I learned there is a curve showing the effect of "marginal diminishing returns". Basically, the more you get of something, the less value it will hold. According to my economics professor, few items escape this phenomena.

Later, we moved to Belgium and the USA. Family finances improved and by the time I was eighteen I'd come home from college in my own car. Hungry and thirsty I'd attack the fridge and happily gulp down half a liter of Coke while chewing a Snickers without reflection. Little joy, it merely bridged the gap until dinner. For the record, my mom would be sitting at the kitchen table with a cup of tea and a biscuit asking "how was your day?".

Being very blessed, I finished university, worked, traveled a bit and got an MBA. Jobs and promotions followed quickly and easily. Despite evasive measures, my wife "hooked me" and we got married. Dual careers worked harmoniously. International moves took us from Belgium to The Netherlands, from Ukraine to Switzerland and France. We were very, very blessed. Two healthy kids, boy/girl (the king's wish), and our finances were well in order. We had the wind in the sails; a house with a pool, cars, lovely holidays and we never worried about the bank account at month-end.

And then I got worried. With the kids having this type of life, what is their chocolate? One of them eats milk chocolate, the other prefers dark chocolate - they are allowed to be picky. When I was young, I needed to be friends with the two neighborhood kids who owned a soccer ball. Now, my kids have a basket full of basket-, soccer-, volley-, tennis-, and baseballs. It's troubling. They don't have -or care- about pocket money. Actually, they don't mind it, it's just that they "want" little, because they have so much. We gave them a weekly allowance for a while, only to have it handed back to me on Father's Day! Sweet, but troubling. What happened to "a little more each time brings happiness"? If small improvements bring joy, and the curve of marginal returns exist, we have a serious problem brewing.

Through circumstances described later, we ended up leaving everything behind and traveling for eight months around the world. Nothing but four backpacks on our shoulders. We hopped countries and took on volunteer projects in far-away places. While society seems to live precariously –via social media– on other people's daily (non-)events: "look my dog just sneezed", "look this is what I ate for lunch this afternoon", "look I am at the Charles de Gaulle Airport,…", I decided this book was not to contain a detailed snapshot of everything we did. Instead, there are specific stories of our travels. In part it is diary-like, but that is mostly for chronological effect. The stories are meant to entertain while giving a flavor of what it was like to travel the world travel with a family. Hopefully it provides a view into how we passed our time, an idea of the places visited, insights into the things we encountered. The focus is on the lessons we learned and volunteer work we did.

Overall, the main story of this book is about the dichotomy between 'having (more)', 'joy' and being 'content'. The first sections describe the run-up and how, at sixty miles an hour, we hit a T-intersection; a brick wall of sorts. The latter part is about our travel and the sense and (perhaps) nonsense of volunteering. From my perspective, the book is the start of an unfinished trilogy. The pages in your hand cover the pre-trip and trip part only. Today we find ourselves in the post-trip phase. Time will tell if the overall experience will be a saga, a tragedy or comedy. I will leave you to be the judge if what we did was a wise move. It certainly contrasted with the norm and the rest of our lives up to that point. For now, I invite you to hop-on and enjoy our ride. Let me start by setting the scene.

Alexander van 't Riet

Running up the Corporate Ladder

LIKE ANY GOOD DISNEY MOVIE where you know good will defeat evil, we need a bit of an introduction to the main characters of the story. Unlike Disney movies, there were no villains or bad events, so we can keep it short.

Growing up in Holland, my life was fairly easy. Loving parents, fun weekends and no major upheavals outside of the daily fights with my brother. Now, for those not familiar with the Dutch, we are direct. Extremely Direct, capital D. And we take enormous pleasure in being this way. Just like a Scotsman will wear a kilt more often abroad than at home and the Irish will spend each possible night abroad at Paddy's Pub singing songs they'd never dare sing at home, the Dutch will claim to be 'culturally sensitive' but secretly ensure they are slightly more direct than is acceptable in their environment. But let's not stereotype.

In my early teens, my father was transferred to Belgium. My brother and I ended up as the only foreigners (and non-practicing Protestants) in a Catholic boys' school. It was tough. Three years later, the director of the school summarized it nicely. He told my dad "I am glad to observe that the school has had an impact on your boys, as did your boys on our school". In my case, the change came after many pages of punishment writing. In one particularly bad semester, my Dutch directness seems to upset most of my teachers and I wrote a record of 164 pages. For the non-math people, this meant an average of well over two pages per school-day.

After the 'correctional' and strict Belgian school, we moved again. This time to the USA. I ended up as a senior at an exclusive Atlanta high school, with little command of English. In Belgium, we studied Dutch and French, so what little English I knew was learned during a two-week course in England right before we crossed the Atlantic. My newly acquired and very limited Oxford English only led to embarrassment. I asked the girl sitting behind me during my first math quiz "do you have a rubber I could borrow?" Since it was the first time I opened my mouth in that class, it needs no explanation that I was seen as the oddball by my American peers.

I survived, however, and went on to college. I graduated with degrees in economics and business. After a short break, I returned to The Netherlands for my MBA. I was keen to be around my fellow countrymen again, only to find out that between the ages of 13 and 19 I missed out on some critical Dutch Directness Development. Luckily, the gene had only gone dormant, and during the MBA it perked up nicely. It was also in these two years that I met one of the other main characters of this story. My (now) wife Heidi.

Heidi was born in Wisconsin but raised in North Carolina. She came to The Netherlands to get her MBA having determined that she didn't want to be an electrical engineer. As it turns out, her willingness to start new projects and her zest for life takes her (and us) to places and situations not fathomed or easily anticipated. Language, currency, and a bare apartment (think concrete floors) took her totally by surprise as she landed in The Netherlands. She adjusted quickly, however, got her diploma, and never lost her will to start up and explore something new and nutty.

After graduating, we both coincidentally moved to Brussels, where, I, wanting to be independent, rented a room in her flat (being a true Dutch cheapskate). Proximity rules, and despite my unwillingness to commit, we were soon inseparable. We enjoyed life and our budding careers. Heidi's interest in trying new things and solving puzzles meant she was soon heavily into IT and the 1990's trendy BPR work (business process re-engineering). I moved from one role to the next in my company, jumping jobs on an eighteen-month cycle.

High energy levels, a Dutch lack of respect for hierarchy, and willingness to go against the grain worked in my favor in those early days. Once my boss and I had a run-in which led to a "I won't speak with you" standoff. It lasted 5 weeks. Imagine that - over a month and not a single word; no 'hello' or 'good morning', nothing. Mind you, this is pre-internet. Intercompany mail was typed up by secretaries and sent in big brown envelopes. The climax came when I decided to take my personal computer to the office. I felt I needed the computing power to do my job, but my job level did not justify a company machine. The situation blew up when I threw a little hand grenade into the HR office. I asked, in writing (typed up by my secretary to ensure the entire office would know about it), if my

In Pursuit of Chocolate

computer was insured for theft and fire when in the office.

To push things over the edge I walked up to my boss's boss. I looked the European president straight in the eye and told him It was no longer possible to work with my direct superior. That Saturday, I got a call from a good friend "Hey, I see you are switching jobs again, why didn't you tell me?". I was stunned and asked him the source of his information. He told me he read it in the newspaper. Convinced that someone was playing a joke on me, I went out to get the paper. There in the classifieds, I read my that company was looking for the National Sales Manager for Belgium. Oops.

Needless to say, I was in the office earlier than normal on Monday. Standing at the President's secretary's desk, I requested audience, which I got at the end of the day. It was probably one of the longest office days I have ever had. Clearly my friend was not the only one reading the newspaper. I noticed colleagues carefully tip-toeing around me, having lunch early before I could ask if we should go together. Finally five p.m. arrived.

Worried, I made my way to the executive suite. I knew that firings often happened at the end of the day. The president sat me down and asked me what I wanted to discuss. This caught me off guard. I mentioned the job posting in the paper. "Yes" he said with his heavy German accent "*und*?". "Well, urh, I was wondering what that means for me" I stammered, not really having prepared for this eventuality. He told me he had listened to me. Obviously, things weren't going well between me and my boss. He also told me he had to back his subordinate, so he needed to find a replacement for me, and quick. Simple, boom, done. Next, he told me he liked me, and he'd find me an alternative role in the group. In fact, he did better, he got me a promotion - a bigger car, larger office, increased salary. Two lessons learned. First, as a boss, never undermine the people who work directly for you; second, don't let people who work for you scare talent away.

And so I went, up the ladder, skipping from one division to the next, from one role to another. Bosses became peers or subordinates. If a summary was needed, I'd say fast, faster, fastest. The job and the career progress meant more and better chocolate every year. The epitome of the speed of change was that I probably had the shortest full-blown expat move in history. For two months I had worked from the continent on a new role in the UK. Finally, it became official and I picked up the little stuff I had moved to England.

Various stories exist as to the state of my relationship with Heidi at the time, but clearly the gods intervened. As we dropped off my company car, the local HR manager told me there was a potential role for me in Belgium. "But the movers are packing as we speak!" I told him, stating the obvious. "You're just one of the candidates" he replied, "so you have to move. Decisions will be made in a couple of weeks". Two weeks later I called the moving company: "I'd like to move 24 boxes, a bike and a stereo back to Belgium, can you quote for that?". They remembered my name.

Back in Belgium, I bought a house, and Heidi moved in. We lived as a happy couple and put a lot of elbow grease into the house. Careers continued to grow and were dynamic. By 30, I found myself sitting in a management meeting observing the landscape. I noticed no one around me was less than 45 years old; in other words, fifty percent older than me. This made me a bit paranoid about progress slowing down. I heard the echo of an HR management course from my college days, explaining the difference between job enrichment versus job enlargement. I feared it would take me half my life to move one more step up on the corporate ladder. Anxious, I started considering moves to other companies and jobs.

Soon after, both Heidi and I changed jobs again, and we assumed our lives would settle for a while and decided to get married. Given the geographic spread of our families (from Australia to the USA) we arranged the wedding a year later, giving everybody ample time to plan their journeys. We treasured the thought of quiet preparation time, and were glad to avoid the "we have to get married now, or The Company won't move us abroad as a couple"-scenario. Note, for years I have maintained that *that* (and tax-complications) was the primary reason for exchanging our vows. I explained it to anyone who would listen; "I don't need the church or a government to approve who I live with". Truth be told, our marriage was one of the better moves I (and I like to think we) ever made.

And we lived happily ever after...

Marriage and Family Complete the Picture

OF COURSE THAT WOULD BE too short a Disney story. Yes, we did end up getting married, a lovely period spread over two continents and three countries. In the six months after deciding to get married our lives only got crazier. Heidi was unexpectedly transferred to the Ukraine, and although I decided to quit my job and go with her, I stumbled upon the job of my dreams. We couldn't refuse either opportunity. I ended up spending most of my time in Scotland while Heidi learned Russian. I barely saw a kilt, but I learned the difference between cold and warm rain, the difference between single malt and blended whiskeys. Heidi learned to deal with freezing temperatures and how to bargain her way out of policemen-invented traffic fines. The wedding preparation was challenging, but we managed by commuting every weekend. Our house in Brussels became our weekend retreat. Though we tried alternating travel the entire way, we found that meeting in the middle and one time-zone jet lag each was preferable. We savored every moment that we were together and with friends.

The good news about our wedding being spread out was that Heidi got to wear her dress three times. I see this as positive. I consider wedding dresses right up there with fireworks when it comes down to the quickest way to rid yourself of money. At least she got to shimmer and shine 3 times! Our legal wedding was just outside of Rotterdam in The Netherlands, the party took place in a small Chateau in Belgium (actually, two parties on two consecutive nights), and the church wedding happened in the USA followed by a reception in a golf club.

As our lives were high-paced (and fragmented), Heidi and I started a tradition – a tradition we still have in place today. Every six months, we sit together for dinner (just the two of us) and answer one simple question: "is this still working for you?". It has served, and still serves us well. It allows us to pull the emergency brake before things go off the rails. We had our dinner and concluded all was well.

Our dual careers progressed nicely. Whereas I hopped from one company to the next, Heidi followed the long and steady career path in a large Fortune-100 company. With her love for new experiences, Heidi convinced me to become a parent, and we had two children. We were blessed with a boy (Leendert) and a girl (Alicia), both healthy, with all fingers and toes accounted for. Our son was born in Belgium, and by the time our daughter was born two years later, we lived in Switzerland. I ended up an executive in a company in the north of the United Kingdom and commuted on a weekly basis from Geneva. Door-to-door it took over six hours; it is that one spot in the UK that is at least a two-hour drive from any international airport.

As time went on, we moved from Switzerland across the border into France. Our new house was what the French call a "coup de coeur" (literally: it makes your heart beat; it is something you have a crush on). It was not just a house, it was home. Home from the day we moved in. The kids went to the local school, and though I only spoke Dutch to them and Heidi only English, French became their mother tongue. This was not completely surprising, since our nanny (the closest person you can find to a Mary Poppins in real-life) spoke French to them and school was in French. Unsuspecting visitors always get a bit of a shock sitting at our dinner table. Without blinking, one single conversation takes place in three languages; How was school? *Het ging wel. Tu peux me passer le beurre?*

I continued my weekly commute to Her Majesty's Kingdom, and got to know most the flight attendants on a first name basis. I typically left late Sunday evening, returning home on Friday. But the weekend was ours. We protected it like a lioness her cubs. People knew. During the week I was available anytime (midnight calls were not uncommon), but from Friday at five until Monday at six am, people knew better than to even think about calling me on work related matters. Work and weekends were treated as mutually exclusive. In all those years, the only exception to this rule were longer business trips to Asia or Latin America. For these stints I was gone over the weekend and work was fair game. I can remember only two other times the weekend rule was violated. Both times I had a thought I did not want to lose so I quickly captured them on my computer.

Despite my weekly absences, home life was manageable and both Heidi and I were happy with the set-up. Our biannual review dinners kept us calibrated, and all the travel-time allowed me to reflect a lot on what I saw around me.

Happy people, grumpy people, rude people, indifferent people. Trust me, if you fly enough, you see them all. Just like sports and drink, travel opens people up, makes them show their true colors. In those conditions they show a bit more of their true selves be it open, warm and friendly or intolerant, pushy and selfish.

At times the travel was a bit extreme. On one eleven-day trip to Asia Pacific I only slept three nights in hotels, spending the other nights in airports on ugly midnight and red-eye flights. I once flew to the USA, got snowed in, made a connecting flight, and was delayed enough to entirely miss my meeting. I re-boarded the plane I came in on! For three days I never left the boundaries of the airports and airplanes.

There was a stage that I traveled so much that I lost track of where I was. I once had to dial hotel reception to ask what city I was in (it was a hotel chain, so there was nothing unique in the room to give it away). That year, I flew the equivalent of 80% of a flight attendant's miles. In distance it equated to a trip to the moon and 1/2 way back. All good fun.

At the beginning of new jobs, the inhumane travel hours meant that I on-boarded quickly. I regularly emptied my inbox, even reading most reports. I suspect that many a subordinate feared the moment that my flight touched down. Once on the ground, I'd get online and a tsunami of mails would fly down the fiber optic lines.

Once I reached steady-state in a job, however, I'd begin to read books or find something else to do. For the first years I read business books. Soon, the business classics became repetitive and no longer captured my interest so I read a wider range of books. Perhaps it was age, but books like *Tuesdays with Morrie*, *Man's Search for Meaning*, *The 100 Year Old Man Who Climbed Out Of The Window And Disappeared*, and *Unbroken* became more and more appealing.

My reading interest ran parallel to my interest in the subject of 'joy' and 'what makes people happy'. In part, this was undoubtedly triggered by questions and remarks of acquaintances. This circle of friends, slightly removed from our inner core, seemed to see it as their mission to "bring us to our senses". They wanted to convince us that our lives were not normal, in fact bizarre, and that we needed to become more "regular" if we were to be happy. Their mental model did not allow for our happiness, being apart so much and on the move all the time. Having said that, our closest friends understood us and our lifestyle. They knew that we were truly happy with our lifestyle (in fact, some had fairly similar lives; and when we called them they would be 'offline' or in an airport).

After all of that reading and reflection on my own life, one thing became clear: happiness is not something to pursue. It is something you decide. It has no timeline; it has no target. The moment you want x-amount of chocolate by y-time, you will be disappointed. Distance yourself from it and life is much better.

For now, suffice it to say life was like racing around in Willy Wonka's Chocolate Factory.

And they lived happily ever after....

Family Closer Together - a Move to Austria

LIFE WAS GOOD. WE WERE healthy and living in the picturesque Haute Savoie, France. From the mountainside, we overlooked Lake Geneva (lac Léman for the French). The Mont Blanc was just around the turn. It is an affluent region with the 'proper' demeanor of the Swiss mixed with the laid-back lifestyle of the French. Ski slopes and the Chamonix glacier were less than an hour away.

We found ourselves in our picture-perfect house with a stunning view, a swimming pool, an SUV and a convertible in the driveway. Did I mention life was good? We had plenty of space and the wine cellar was nicely (over)stocked. Winter weekends were spent skiing, summers on the terrace with friends and family, Champagne in hand, next to the barbecue.

In free moments I learned how to fly a small plane and get a boating license. With a friend I climbed the Mont Blanc. Actually, we had to settle for Mont Maudi -which is right next to it- because the weather turned on us, forcing us to abandon our primary target.

One summer day I found myself water-skiing on the lake, a big smile on my face, only thirty-five minutes after landing from gray and dreary England. Trust me, not much beats being pulled by a classic James Bond-like wooden Italian speedboat, seeing the Alps reflection on the water with only the wake disturbing the mirror- like surface.

We traveled, rode in a hot air balloon competition and bungy jumped for the rush. We celebrated birthdays in a private tent on the beach in Dubai and in a ferris wheel in Vienna. Work offered great opportunities to travel and crazy events. I rode on the back of a GP motorcycle with a ten-time GP winner at the wheel, roaring around the Autodromo of

Estoril, Portugal; I drove a bright red F450 Ferrari with a test pilot around the Ferrari track in Italy; we had a private tour and dinner at the Louvre.

In short, we were not the richest in the world, but it felt close. There wasn't much we liked and couldn't do or buy. Probably the only thing we lacked was a bucket list. We lived it instead.

Then, in one of our "is this still working for you?"-dinners, Heidi and I came to the conclusion that it wasn't. It was time for dad to be at home more. The kids were growing quickly, and being home on the weekends wasn't good enough. While before, when the kids were 3 and 5, I felt like the 5th wheel, things were changing. Having more fatherly presence (and being more involved day-to-day) seemed like the right thing to do. We decided to find a solution where we could spend more time together as a family. Basically, I needed to find a job closer to home. We considered moving to the north of the UK, but eliminated that option rather quickly.

And wouldn't you know it. Stars aligned. Within six months a job opportunity popped up which could work out for a better family life. We'd have to move to Vienna, but that didn't seem like hardship since Heidi worked 'location free'. Just as we were about to move, however, Heidi's long-term employer changed its views on having her work from afar. A slight hiccup, but family-time trumped income, so we accepted her career-break. After twenty-three years with the same company, she wasn't unhappy with that choice. We packed up part of our house, mothballed the rest, and headed east to Austria.

Vienna is fantastic. We only knew it from a quick visit and the New Year's concert on television, but it had always given us a positive impression, and this musical city lived up to its reputation. Within 6 months, imperial Vienna crawled under our skin. We loved it. The gala balls, the access to music and the theatre, the old buildings, the warm summers and the snowy winters with Christmas markets, it worked for us. Strolling in Vienna one expects Mozart to jump from behind a curtain or the corner of a building at any time (though of course we learned he hailed from Salzburg). During the first year, we spent more time in theaters than the five years before and found a great group of friends. True to form, within a couple of months Heidi plunged into something new and became very active in the school. In fact, within twelve months she was elected chairman of the school board. Overall, Vienna turned out to be a great move. And although I held a global role which required extensive travel, we spent much more quality time together as a family, so all was good.

And they lived happily ever after…..

Where Everything Changes

AND SO WE GET TO the intermezzo. That moment which bridges the gap between two parts. For us this is the intermission, the part where in less than 18 months we go from high-income-straight-line-dual-careers-to-the-top, to sitting on a couch together, both without work wondering "now what?".

We'll leave the drama, the emotional roller-coaster, the reflections and the explanations for what they are. Suffice it to say that it might have been that luck simply ran out. The Black Swan from Taleb appeared to create havoc in our already Extremistan world.

I suspect that my direct Dutch approach may have contributed to our new situation. What works early in a career might not be the best in later years. In my case, asking the CEO - in front of the management team in a Michelin star restaurant - if he knows how many widgets my division has to sell to finance the meal might not have been one of my better moves. My remarks to him about the nonsense of having caviar served out of a block of ice (with frozen vodka glasses sticking out from the side) while flying first class over the Atlantic might have contributed. Be that as it may, in the turbulence of a company restructure, my job as family breadwinner suddenly transformed into garden leave. And it happened abruptly.

This was my last workweek: Monday - board meeting in Vienna. Tuesday - early flight to Asia and a team dinner upon arrival. Wednesday - opening a new factory outside Shanghai, China, complete with firecrackers for fortune and prosperity. Thursday - business review in Kuala Lumpur, a quick dinner followed by the night flight back. Friday morning - 05:50am arrival back in Europe. Quick stop home, shower, drop the kids at school and straight to the office. Friday - 12:00 lunchtime appointment with the boss. We were scheduled to discuss next year's capital plan. At 12:30 I was out of a job, on garden leave. "Thank you", please leave the keys and your badge at reception.

Wow, what happened? Let me read that again…

Driving home I got on the phone with Heidi. The timing was not only sudden, but it was hideous. She was driving the kids home. It was the last day of school before the summer break. Luckily the kids were chatting and oblivious to what I blurted out over the bluetooth. The following morning, we were bound for Turkey to celebrate my dad's eightieth birthday. It's a big event and Heidi's parents were traveling in from the US that afternoon. In parallel, my brother and his wife were traveling in from Perth, Australia. Rats, how to handle this situation?

We took a deep breath, concluded no one was served by informing them of the changes. The last thing we wanted was for the holiday to turn into an explaining - or worse - a grieving party. We decided to follow the behavior Nick Leeson. Go to a resort, play golf, have a drink at the pool and pretend nothing happened. You might notice that I skipped the first stage of grieving - anger. Heidi made up for that one. Somehow she carried more anger than I did. I was glad we did not run into my boss en route to Turkey - I think she would have slugged him. It did not seem to bother me to much at first; surprising little in fact.

During the course of the week I had a few follow-up phone calls to manage a 'correct' exit. By the middle of the week we informed everybody about our new situation. In hindsight, it was perfect. The fact that we decided to keep it quiet for half the week meant we could carefully coordinate and script the message. First the kids, next my dad and brother, then my in-laws. Given we had taken time to reflect meant that the message was sugar coated to the kids, and without too much emotion to the rest of the family (thus ensuring it did not become the center of attention for the rest of the week). It became no more than a sporadic side conversation, which suited me fine.

Denial, a perfect step in grieving.

But now, how will they live ever after…?

The Route to our Journey

AFTER RETURNING FROM TURKEY, HEIDI and the kids flew, as planned, to our house in France. Since I was now jobless, we decided I'd drive the car from Vienna and spend the summer holiday with them. Now that had never happened before! It would be a good time to figure out what to do next.

A bit puzzled, perhaps dazed, Heidi and I reflected: "now what?" The kids were happy in school in Austria. We had savings in the bank so there was no direct financial stress. But NOW WHAT? I started having nightmares, which I'd never had before. Nightmares about missing planes, meetings spinning out of control, budgets being missed. Having nothing to do threw me completely - I didn't know how to act.

Heidi and I ran scenarios in our heads. I've always prided myself on being able to project forward, seeing what would or could happen next. In fact, I have lovingly been called 'compulsive' when it comes down to anticipating what's next. And it's true, I see a glass on the edge of the table which someone will elbow off; I have some cash stashed away when I ride my bicycle, just in case; I pay attention to the nearest fire escape in buildings and planes; I foresee the reactions of team members when I bring tough messages. I claim not to be a control freak, but when I say this, Heidi always raises an eyebrow.

But this time, reflecting on what's next, I got crickets - blank, *niks*, nothing, *nada*, *rien du tout*. The only image which came up was Heidi's nightmare: both at home, me hovering around asking every half hour "whatcha doin'?". In one of my better dreams Heidi gives me the suggestion to go and have a midlife crisis "buy a Harley and go on a long road trip…"

"Okay, this is crazy" I said to myself. The family is in good health, financially there is no direct worry, and we have time on our hands. Let's enjoy it, be happy! For the next two weeks, pondering, I clean the crap out of the garden. No really, I cleaned the crap out of it, and had the blisters to show. Several weeks of cleaning, hammering, painting, *et voilà*! In the previous ten years the house and garden had never looked as pristine as it did that summer. Okay, done. "Now what?"

It was time for our six-monthly dinner. The kids were at summer camp, we had plenty of time. We went to a local restaurant. This evening, in the restaurant, with the house in tip-top shape, the third week of garden leave, a crazy thought popped into my head. Whatever the cause, a spark ignited a thought, and as with a combustion engine, once the plug lights the fuel, there is no going back.

My brain racing, I casually suggest to Heidi, "what if we'd pack it all in and travel around the world for a year?". I want to say that her initial reaction was lukewarm, but I'd be lying. If looks could kill, I'd be a dead man. Now, I must confess, the kids had been gone for three days, and Heidi was feeling down. It is that empty-nest feeling she always gets when the kids are both from home for a few days; their empty bedrooms too tidy. She only wanted to go out for a quick dinner because she didn't want the fuss of cooking at home. She certainly did not anticipate a serious conversation on world travel. I explored the 'travel around the world' a bit more, but it becomes a monologue, me pulling on a dead horse. Nice try, I might as well have been talking to a brick wall that evening.

The next morning I arrive downstairs and Heidi has obviously been up for a while. My best guess is that she is on her third cup of coffee. She gives me this I-am-up-to-something look and states "IF we are going to make this trip, it is better to travel West around the world, than East". Wow, what did I miss? Clearly the spark ignited in her and all her pistons were firing. Within no time I realize roles are reversed; she is starting to convince me that this travel-the-world thing might not be as outrageous as it appears; "we save the rental of our house, I can homeschool the kids, you always wanted to show us Asia…"

When explaining it to other people, we typically say it took us a week to make up our minds. Reality obliges me to cut that timespan. With the kids at camp we had a lot of free time. We could kick the thought around and discuss the implications freely. We surfed the internet, explored the possibilities. I estimate that forty-eight hours after the initial suggestion it was effectively decided. *Fait accompli*. It was not so much the opportunities that drove us, but especially the thought of **NOT** going which clinched the deal. We'd both sensed that if ever there was a moment, this was it. We were all healthy, no fixed jobs, financially secure and the kids were the right age to appreciate the trip - there was simply no better moment. Not taking 'the road less traveled' at this moment of our lives would have implied a lifetime of regret and "we had the chance then, if only…".

Had our lives been frantic before, it paled against the following weeks. Research taught us that wise people planned a life time to do a sabbatical year. People meticulously figured out where to go, what to visit, how to travel, where to stay. We wanted to leave sooner rather than later, hop on a plane and be gone. Having never even entertained the thought of a world trip, we certainly had no notion of what to do, where to go, what to consider. Early on I made it clear we were not traveling to rate the beaches and hotels around the world. We needed a purpose.

The reasons for this were many-fold. First, beaches and I don't blend. For the life of me I do not understand the attraction of beaches. Laying around doing nothing, burning your feet on the sand, looking at people in bathing suits made for the bodies they want to have, but don't. I don't get it. Add to that sand filling your swimming trunks (making you realize why they make sandpaper from beach sand), your mouth (sand with your banana - yummy), your towel, shoes and car all sums up to discomfort if you ask me. I just don't get it.

Second, the attraction of hotels had long since gone for me. During our trip, we met a family making a similar journey, but they stayed exclusively in Intercontinental Hotels. Really? Outside the financial attack on our bank account, I cannot fathom why one would want to travel the world that way. Surely travel is about experiencing different places and cultures, not about auditing a hotel chain, seeing how well the group is able to have a uniform feel, look and service around the world!

From the comfort of our living room, Heidi and I decided that we wanted to give our children a world experience, but also to demonstrate to them how fortunate they were. We were keen to show them 'how people around the world live'. Not like being in a people zoo, but focusing on building an appreciation for what we had, to give them a baseline for gratitude, to make them realize how privileged they are "No, not everyone has chocolate!". Soon after, the concept of volunteering entered the equation. Darn, more material to research! Over the months that followed we learned volunteering comes in many shapes and forms; good, bad and ugly. The next part of the book covers the locations where we volunteered. I'll skip the volunteering remarks for now. Don't worry, it will return.

While we wanted to leave sooner rather than later, practical matters and reality did slow us down a bit. We had a three-month notice period on our rental contract in Vienna. A *little* preparation was required. The next ninety days were a whirlwind. We on-boarded the kids, packed all our belongings in Vienna and moved them into storage in France, moved to temporary accommodation, started a website, researched volunteering agencies, pre-selected projects, visited doctors for various immunizations and medications, planned homeschooling, booked the first flights and accommodation, founded a company in Dubai, took up residence in the United Arab Emirates, started school applications for the kids, researched and selected global travel and health insurance, etc.

Meanwhile the usual household activities kept going, amazingly we stayed more or less sane during the process. If it wasn't for Heidi's organizing skills I am sure I would still be sitting in Vienna, trying to figure out what to do next. But, all in all, it took us only three months, and everything was done and dusted. We were ready to go, ready to step on a plane, leave everything behind and start the first leg of our journey.

And they traveled happily ever after…

Volunteering - for us and Others

BEFORE PROCEEDING, I'D LIKE TO come back to the sub-theme of the dichotomy between 'having (more)' and 'being content'. This strongly influenced our trip.

Being convinced that 'more' is not always 'better' helped us make critical choices. Since joy is often derived from a positive change in a situation, a delta that one is aware of, it follows that seeking and understanding this delta creates insight into happiness. After all, one often only appreciates the joy of having the functionality of both arms after one of them is in plaster after an accident.

We knew that we lived in a luxurious bubble, and Heidi and I were keen to calibrate our children in a way that made them appreciate what they had. A nice illustration of how fortunate most of us are: "if the world was represented by 100 people". Basic statistics show that 13% would not be able to read, only 7% would have a college degree, 23% would live without shelter from wind and rain, 16% would be undernourished or starving, 13% would have no clean drinking water, 22% no electricity. We, in Vienna, in the international school environment, were pretty much on the other extreme. Simply put, we were short of nothing.

To help our kids understand their world better, we wanted to place ourselves in an area of need, and thus experience the delta. We also hoped to give back to the world, so we opted to volunteer during our trip - to do something good. And hey, doing a bit of work and making the trip less costly was a nice side benefit, right?

Think again.

Doing the research, we soon found ourselves lost in the jungle of the volunteering world. First of all, there is a vast spectrum of volunteer projects around the world. There are short- and long-term projects, conservation and environmental programs, educational and (orphan) care efforts. And, of course, there are the relief and emergency programs. Within these projects, various skill sets are required. One can go for a year as a medical professional to Africa, or as a high school student to a rescue camp for monkeys in Costa Rica. The choice is endless.

This is not surprising. The number of international volunteers was estimated north of 1.6 million people in 2008. The industry is enormous and growing fast, with thousands of agencies encouraging the voluntourism boom. The statistics are staggering and opinions and views on the fantastic contributions (or disgusting rip-offs) fill pages on the internet. Full-length books are written on both. As it turns out, according to the US Department of Labor statistics, Heidi and I perfectly fit the target profile of the volunteering world; Caucasian, well-educated and middle-aged.

Having no medical degrees eliminated many options. As we mapped out a rough schedule, we decided we preferred projects in several places, each two to three weeks long rather than one six-month stint. We felt a two-to-three week timeframe was enough to break biases and get a small appreciation for the place, but not too long that we'd take years to circle the globe. That trimmed the options further. The next filter was our profile.

Traveling with the kids and not being ambulance chasers meant that 'disaster volunteering' could be scratched of the list. That left us with conservation and educational/care programs. I know many people have great experiences saving the monkeys, seals, dolphins, elephants, condors, sea turtles, and the rain forests, but somehow I cannot get myself to really care. The dinosaurs are gone, and I do not miss them. Even more recently the Golden Toad (1989), the Zanzibar Leopard (1996), the West African Black Rhino (2006), disappeared from the earth. While an extinction is sad – just like many endings that are truly final – I somehow do not share the passion to volunteer in that area. Okay, that may be a bit harsh, but I'd rather put my effort in helping fellow humans than nurturing a baby canary back to life.

The good news? There are thousands of options for volunteers interested in care-giving, human support and the educational projects. We continued to troll the net and reached out to people with experience.

In a discussion with an uncle who was committed to bringing water-wells to arid African countries for many years, I got some valuable insights and practical warnings. Beware. Do not assume that the direct efforts you put in actually helps. "Beware that the contributions you make fit in a larger, systematic scheme" he warned. Wise words. He gave the example of a well they drilled to ensure the women of a village did not have to hike all day, every day, to carry water for basic family requirements. You would think this was a good cause were it not for the fact that the village grew as a result of the well. No one was prepared for that. In fact, not long after the drilling was done and the volunteer agency left, a local war-lord claimed the source and put a fence around it. This subsequently lead to regional fighting (a mini-war). In short, the intrinsically good effort of bringing water to a dry far-out village brought havoc and devastation. Of course, the conclusion is not that one should avoid bringing water to these remote villages. That's too black and white. However, it does point out that providing direct help and drilling without thinking about the long-term, broader consequences is not the solution either.

To make the final selection on our volunteer projects, we returned to our primary goal: showing the kids the world and how fortunate they/we are. For us, the projects needed to (1) give them a sense of how people lived locally, (2) expose us to local customs, food and habits, (3) provide a platform to learn and discuss, and (4) contribute and make things better (or at least not worse) for the surroundings in which we volunteered.

Notice that three of the four are about us. Only the last one focused on the environment we'd be working in. We were comfortable with that. The warning of my uncle resonated, and subsequent research had dimmed lofty ideas of changing the world in two weeks. In my opinion, in most the cases, the biggest benefit of volunteering comes to the volunteer, not the people on the receiving end. I am not saying this to be controversial, nor that it is a bad thing. I just stating my view, my observation. A young volunteer traveling alone for the first time, seeing how fortunate he or she is, learning to care for others, learning another language, becoming more independent, learning how to use condoms (yes, the environment and age group creates this opportunity), are all positive effects. It does no harm. If they contribute in the process, even a little, the world is a better place for it.

Now at this stage we also need to clear up a couple of other common misunderstandings about volunteering. First of all, volunteering in not a cheap way to travel and see the world. Unless you are committing for a long stint (6 months to a year) and/or have a specific degree (medical), you might as well stay in the Intercontinental. Averaging a two-week stint in Africa, Costa Rica, Philippines, Thailand, Australia, Fiji (excluding travel, visa, vaccinations, insurance and spending money) will typically be between $2000 and $3000 per person (it is surprisingly location inelastic)! Divide these US dollars in twelve effective days (one day arrival, one day departure) and you are over $200 a night. Assume you go with a friend, and you are at $400 a night per room. You can find a fantastic hotel, beach front, with pool, breakfast and piña coladas included at that rate (certainly considering the consumer price index of most countries where the volunteering takes place). Reflect a bit, and you realize that if you opt for a 4 star resort, you'd also be sponsoring the local economy - providing work for the staff, helping out an otherwise deprived area (possibly providing an income to a family so kids can go to school).

Second, volunteering projects are not as organized as you might think. Yes, how to get there is well communicated and clear, but once on a project don't expect it to be a well-oiled machine. The agencies will promote "you get out of it what you put in" which is their way of saying "make it happen, don't expect a clear (work) plan". Again, not necessarily a bad thing, since it leads to learning opportunities, but realize it is an expensive education - for you. The fact that there are no lesson plans, often no books, pens or paper means educating is tough. It is a drop on a hot plate. Often it is not part of a larger structure, and thus the effort evaporates quickly.

One last comment on the financial matter before I go on. One university research project has shown that the more expensive a volunteer-tourism project is the less responsible it tends to be. Go figure. Beware. Do your research.

Now where did all this leave us? Ah, we knew it was all about us, we were keen to do projects in various locations, and aimed for two weeks per experience. So we booked. We used one single agency (Love Volunteers) run by lovely people from New Zealand who effectively provided broker and selection services for us. They placed us in Ecuador on the Galapagos Islands, in Cusco, Peru, and also in Asia: Ho Chi Min, Vietnam, and Pokhara, Nepal. No regrets there. They did well.

Finally, the story of our journey can start. Our quest to learn about joy and happiness, the appreciation of life starts. The following pages are snapshots of our journey. Memorable moments for us, hopefully some interesting insights to those considering doing something similar. It is a distillation of what we did, experienced and reflections made over time. Enjoy.

The First Stop: US Culture and Final Preparations

A VERY EARLY WAKE-UP CALL gets me out of bed at our hotel in the center of Vienna. Leendert and Alicia are still asleep. Heidi helps me strap on my old Nomad backpack. As I walk out the door, my son barely opens his eyes. I hug him and look over at Alicia before quietly closing the door, leaving the three behind. Because of the chaotic planning we weren't traveling this leg together. They fly later via Washington, I travel through London to meet them in North Carolina.

A typical Austrian luxury taxi brings me to the airport. It is strange to leave Vienna on my own. Twenty minutes later I stand in front of the check-in counter. For some reason I can only get the first boarding pass. No big deal, I will collect the onward pass in London. I grab coffee and a croissant and seek an outlet for my phone, my umbilical cord to 'the net'. Business habits die slowly. I check at the gate if I can get my connecting boarding pass. I ask, because I am a strong believer in "you don't get what you don't ask for". To my amazement I can. A good omen I am sure.

The flight boards late and we hit more delays 'waiting for air traffic control' to unleash us. As usual, there are air restrictions over London. I'm relaxed, a two-hour layover offers plenty of time to make my connection. As we near London, the captain's voice crackles over the intercom, telling us we are in a holding pattern for at least 30 minutes. The reduced layover time worries me slightly since I know Heathrow's security checks can be a bear. But hey, it is what it is.

Boarding pass in hand, I sprint through the terminal and convince a lady from BA to walk me past the long queues. About those queues, allow me to rant for a moment. What is it about countries that can't get the immigration process fixed? Especially for transit passengers. Little is more infuriating and frustrating than being on a plane for hours, or being in a rush to make a flight, only to find yourself queuing to pass a pseudo-immigration. Why does this bother me so much? Am I against safety precautions? No. What bothers me is the stupidity of it. First, there are ample counters available. This indicates that whoever designed the airport was able to predict the travel flow quite well. All assets are there. I see computers sitting idle, tax payers' investments collecting dust. It's nuts, but the booths are not staffed. At beginning of the long queues people are employed to 'manage' traffic flow. If you put those same people behind the computers, you wouldn't have to manage the long lines - everybody would be better off.

Second, from an image perspective, we all know 'you only have one time to make a first impression', yet somehow, someone decided that the first impression for people entering the country is to have them wait in line. Waiting with no benches. Just young and old standing in human warmth, sweaty and close together, half of them holding their bladders. Most people try to ignore the over-tired child and attempt to stay calm as a security officer tells them to switch off their phones as "this is a restricted area, sir". Ahhh. If Mr. Officer would sit in one of the booths, the lines would be shorter and I would not feel the need to call the airliner to see if they can book me on the next flight! Sorry, I digress.

Due to the special assistance, I zip past security to the gate. I survive another security check where I promise that I am not and never have been a terrorist. Answering correctly, I am allowed on board. I settle in the next-to-last row and notice the plane is one of the oldest excuses for a flying machine I have seen for years. Seats are crammed together, and 3 small TV screens are stuck on the ceiling, spaced out above the middle aisle. The seats are packed so tightly that my knees touch the seat in front of me even though my butt is against the back of my own seat. This is *before* the passenger in front attempts to recline. What a start of the world voyage! I endure eight hours of solitude with practically no movement, my knees pointed outward. The unfriendly air hostess compliments the interior perfectly, as does the food. Boy, the American international airlines can learn from their Asian and Arab counterparts!

I land in Raleigh, North Carolina, and though we are the only international flight coming in, the lines are long. Eight counters, 3 officers, and only one dealing with non-US passport holders. Welcome to America! It takes the better part of an hour before I pass the border into the land of the free. I switch my phone on while waiting for my bags. First message?

In high Oxford English: 'We are terribly sorry to inform you....', from BA. My backpack did not make the connection in London. The message advises me to go to baggage services to fill out some paperwork.

As I exit customs, I see my mother-in-law. We complete the "lost and found" forms and head home.

Later, I return to the airport to pick up the rest of my family. We await the bags from Washington. Despite the 'complete' signal, none of the backpacks appear. Clearly we are jinxed. Two airliners, two layovers, all bags lost! More paperwork before the reunion. The evening is filled with the usual excitement after a long separation. We catch up and talk about our upcoming journey. Over a wonderful Southern barbecue we laugh about our website which is called "followourbackpacks.com". Given the first day of travel, this seems ill-advised if one wants to know what we are up to!

When we wake up the following morning we find our backpacks piled up at the back door. One bottle of shampoo leaked, impregnating a set of clothes with flowery smell, but the rest arrived in good order. First lesson: use more ziploc bags! We pass the time preparing for the trip and enjoying family time. Heidi's internet shopping efforts are stacked in boxes along the basement walls, leading to multiple fashion shows. Unpacking feels like Christmas. The biggest hit are the mini iPads for the kids. Little do they suspect they are being offered for schoolwork while on the road.

Our timing in North Carolina is perfect. Fall is a delightful time of the year. We indulge in the Southern delights of sausage, eggs, biscuits and gravy for breakfast. We make an excursion to Southern Pines, best described as a cute American village with a bit of a bohemian feel. We wander aimlessly over a local market passing the folding tables filled with homemade artifacts. Upon hearing "oh, that's so cute", I repeat endlessly "if it doesn't fit in you backpack, it ain't coming along". Having thus resisted any non-functional purchases, we make our way to lunch, strolling under impressive magnolia trees. We partake in more Southern delights. The food is wonderful, and the sweet potatoes and coleslaw go down well.

Now skeptics might ask "USA and cultural?", especially since Heidi is American and no stranger to the country. However, I'd say 'yes', a definite yes. And we are in luck. The State Fair is on - what better way to see the local culture?

The State Fair can be split in two distinct sections. The traditional part – which I like most - is where farmers show off the prettiest apples, the biggest pumpkins, the hottest peppers (measured on the Scoville scale).

They shop for animals, tractors, trailers and general farm equipment. One section is dedicated to education. It shows how to grow your own vegetables and features a stand on the importance of hygiene. The latter includes a 'wash your hands station', which, using black lights, shows how badly you normally wash your hands. Yuck!

The second part of the State Fair is 'rides and food'. An interesting combination. This is where one is bombarded with sounds, and smells. Bright neon signs promote typical American 'fair' food. It ranges from corn-on-the-cob, to burgers, to massive turkey legs (of such dimensions that kids can barely carry them). The food section is an overwhelming sight: large buckets of fries and Mexican food followed by 'Deep Fried Mars Bars', funnel cakes, 'Deep Fried Macaroni and Cheese' and the culinary delight of 'Deep Fried Twinkie-Twix wrapped in Bacon". That last one alone explains the average obesity problem of America. What amazes me is that people manage to keep all of this food down. Not only because of the grease or the quality of the food, but because the food goes together with the rides. The rides are fantastic. They toss you from left to right, drop you in straight free-fall or hang you upside down multiple times in a row. I am awed by the human body as I observe that what gets eaten stays inside despite all the movement.

We have a blast, spending more time than intended, being suckered in too many rides. But hey, for that one time we are at a State Fair, let's experience it! The day flies past, and before we know it we return home to prepare for the next stage of our trip. The backpacks are prepared for real this time. It proves beyond a shadow of a doubt that Heidi has planned well. Everything, including all the newly arrived clothes fit neatly. We have a total of four backpacks and three small carry-ons (iPads, sweaters, socks, etc for the flight). The real adventure is about to begin.

The Galapagos - from Extreme to Extreme

IT'S A LONG TRIP FROM the USA to Ecuador. To my surprise, I notice on the flight overview that we are flying east. Somehow, I always assumed South America was south of the USA, but it isn't. It is more southeast meaning we move an hour closer to the European time zone. We arrive in Quito, where Leendert does some self-declared 'extreme sleeping'. The first night he chalks up ten-and-a-half hours. The next day we tour the town and visit an impressive gilded Jesuit church. Noteworthy facts: (1) the entrance fees are double for foreigners - this is neatly posted up front, no excuses; (2) you're not allowed to take pictures inside, God forbid you would show friends that you visited something impressive and get them excited to come and visit; (3) behind and under the church is a nice catacomb and burial place. Upon exiting, we run into Jill who is staying at our hotel. We have a chat, making a friend.

It starts raining, and we learn the weather in Quito can be volatile. One moment it is nice and warm, the next unpleasantly cold. We're not dressed for it. We visit the volunteer coordination center and escape the cold while we learn about the transfer to the Galapagos. We'll fly and then island-hop to get to our destination: Isabela. We are told there are no banks or ATMs on the island, "so take cash". The Ecuadorians also tell us to stay away from the juices. They are blended with local water - apparently a sure and speedy route to getting sick. In fact, our local coordinator says she only lets her kids drink Coke and Sprite on the islands. She does allow them to drink bottled water, but only if the bottles come from the mainland. "Definitely don't touch the local liquid!".

We coordinate with Jill to ride to the airport the next morning, and exchange information. We tell her about the water/juice warning, and she informs us we need to buy an additional 'access permits' for the Galapagos at the airport before departure. We build in extra time. That evening we munch on local delights. Leendert is keen to try Guinea pig. For dessert, we feast on *'colada morada'*, a red drink made from purple corn and various berries (blue-, straw-, etc). The unique drink is made once a year during All Saints Day (*Dia de los Muertos* - 'day of the dead') and is complemented by a thick gingerbread man. The latter is to be dipped in the thick drink. We genuinely feel the trip has started as we are getting exposed to so many new things.

The next morning the alarm goes off at four a.m. Backpacks were packed the night before and within seventeen minutes we slip our arms through the straps, ready to go to the airport. To our surprise, the hotel has freshly baked breads and *café con leche* waiting for us in reception. For the kids there is hot chocolate. Wow, what service given the ungodly hour!

A taxi-van arrives in front of the hotel at 4:25. Since Quito is far from the safest city in the world, the gates must be liberated of numerous locks before we walk out into the cold air. Despite the hour, the kids are in great form; babbling and talkative, still excited by the newness. The flight has a stopover in Guayaquil. We stay on the plane for the 40-minute layover during which I read the in-flight magazine. I find that with a lot of effort I can read a bit of the Spanish (it helps to have the English translation next to it). This pleases me, as I am a bit freaked knowing our host family on Isabela reportedly has no English skills.

As we arrive on the Galapagos, we march over wet 'de-contamination carpets' between the plane and the airport 'terminal'. The local park commissioner is concerned with visitors inadvertently bringing foreign life-matter onto the Galapagos Islands. The carpets ensure our shoes are free of any diseases. Next, a bus takes all passengers for a 15-minute ride to the other side of what turns out to be a rather small island. We stop at a narrow channel and everyone hops onto little boats, luggage tossed on the roof. We have to pay for the crossing. Talk about a captive market! We observe the birds and bright red little crabs on the black lava rocks. Not anything too impressive, but it serves as a warm-up for things to come. The Galapagos is, after all, unique and known for its nature. This is where Charles Darwin got his inspiration for the theory of evolution and *The Origin of Species* (which he wrote years later after returning to the UK). The boat ride is less than four minutes and one has to wonder why the airport is on the breakaway piece of land and why a simple bridge hasn't been built. Collecting our backpacks, we hop in a pick-up truck taxi avoiding the much slower bus option. The first part of the trip takes us uphill over arid terrain. As we get approach the summit, the landscape suddenly changes and becomes green and lush. Great excitement fills the cabin of the truck as Alicia spots the first tortoise. Within 5 kilometers we all see tortoises, except for Leendert who manages to miss them each time.

We check into our hotel in Puerto Ayora. It is an apartment semi-detached from a house. The owner, 'Yojo', is a jovial young man who tells us all about the town. When we tell him we are to travel out on the first boat the next morning. He suggests we don't. "Relax, take your time, you are on the islands!". Not wavering we tell him we are volunteers and have people awaiting us on Isabela. "Don't worry" he says, "my sister lives on Isabela, I'll pass a message on through her". Less than ten minutes later he pops his head back into our room and informs us he directly reached out to our contact person and the matter was settled. We can take the later boat. Good news, we get to sleep in tomorrow.

We spend the afternoon around Puerto Ayora. We buy our tickets for the boat ride the next day and have lunch. It could have been any small coastal town; Spain, Greece or Italy. The menu has fish & chips and pizza. In a small grocery store we buy some fruit and a small, but expensive ($20), bottle of suntan lotion. I guess the price is not surprising given that everything must be flown onto the islands.

We visit the Darwin Center, a lovely setup in the mangroves where we have our first close encounter with big tortoises (this time Leendert gets to see them too) and massive yellow iguanas. While we have a drink, birds collect around us and we observe for the first time one unique feature of the islands. The animals do not see humans as invasive predators. They have no fear of man whatsoever. One finch happily sits on Leendert's head, resulting in many pictures and a video.

Afterwards, I offer the kids the bananas we bought earlier. I notice they are a bit greener than usual, peel them with some difficulty, and hand them out. Within 30 seconds the kids are back. "Dad, you said the banana's in the tropics would be yummy. These definitely are not". Putting a stern face I tell them to be happy with what we provide, and force them to have another bite. As I hear the sound of them biting, I, too, nibble on a piece. It is hard as rock, dry as cork and tastes like cardboard. Hmm. I let the kids off the hook as I look at the bunch of bananas on the kitchen counter. A bit of research teaches me that I attempted to make them eat raw 'plantains'. Even today, I live with the consequences. We rarely see, buy or eat bananas without reliving the Puerto Ayora experience.

For those not familiar with plantains, they contain more starch than the bananas we usually eat. According to Wikipedia they are "always cooked or fried when eaten green". Wikipedia also reports that the pulp is hard and the peel so stiff that it has to be removed with a knife. In my defense, the plantains are from the same Musaceae family as the well-known yellow bananas, so maybe my mistake can be forgiven.

After the plantain experience, I am pleasantly surprised when later that evening Leendert orders something off the dinner menu stating: "I don't know what it is, so I will try it". It seems the craziness of our trip is having an impact already. New things are fun! Against better advice we decide not to be concerned about the food quality here on Santa Cruz; we eat the salad and drink the juice despite Quito warnings. It strikes us as too touristy a place to live by the 'cook it, fry it, peel it or forget it'-mantra. During dinner, we start feeling very drowsy. The four a.m. wake-up call is finally overriding the "we're in a new place" adrenaline boost we've been cruising on all day. It's a good thing we were exhausted. It protects most of us from the late night singing of the tourists in bars or the early morning rain hammering the roof. As we rise the next morning and grab our electronics we notice that what was slow internet yesterday, has now completely abandoned us. We end up truly stranded as it remains unavailable the entire day. The feeling of non-connectivity for twelve hours is amazing. While sitting in a simple hotel/guest house, this electronic aberration makes me feel like we are truly 'roughing it'. Total silliness, bordering on idiotic. Surrounded by a stove, coffee pot, people, running water, a fridge and an old, old TV, the simple lack of connection to 'the Net' makes me feel as isolated as Robinson Crusoe. Perhaps I am also influenced by the fact that I just finished the book *Floreana*, which describes the first settlement on that namesake Galapagos island. It depicts how the early families barely survived, living off the land, totally dependent on what nature provided. Either way, I realize we will have to live with this new reality. On the less-inhabited Isabela Island, bandwidth surely won't improve.

As the rest of the family awakens, Heidi updates the cost spreadsheet and crafts a study plan for Leendert and Alicia. Breakfast is served in our room (just like Robinson would have it in his days, I am sure), and we head for Tortuga Bay. It turns out to be a two-and-a-half kilometer walk. The first two kilometers follow a beautiful two-meter-wide stone path through the mangroves. The cactus trees are particularly interesting. They are true trees, with insides which look like a cross between a honeycomb and stringy fibers. The structure allows them to store massive amounts of water. The last five hundred meters of the walk are over a soft sand path. Then, suddenly, a wide, white, flat beach with fine sand stretches before us. Sea iguanas stroll aimlessly from the dunes to the water. It is idyllic in many ways. The kids start wading ankle-deep in the ocean. Soon they are knee-high in the water, and within fifteen minutes their clothes are drenched.

We play for a short time at the beach and return to the pier, ready for our sea trip to Isabela. On the dock we submit to a baggage check for animals/plants, compliments of the same paranoid park commissioner, and wait amongst sixty odd people for our boat: the Juliet. Heidi opens the seasick medicine bag, and the kids get acupressure bracelets, some oil behind the ears and one earplug in the non-dominant ear. Heidi prefers to err on the side of prevention. In small batches people are packed on small yellow boats and depart. I take a critical look at the boats and find them awfully small for a long oceanic trip....

Finally, it is our turn. We are loaded on board and amazed that the luggage is loosely placed up front. Surely not? Four minutes into the boat ride - and the request of the captain of payment of an additional fifty cents per person - all becomes clear. These yellow boats are merely water taxis taking us to the main boats. The Juliet is a larger boat (note, the 'er' at the end. The vessel is not large, only larger). It has three 175hp engines. Once all twenty people are installed and life jackets distributed we turn towards the open sea. The polyester boat slams on and into the waves. Within ten minutes the first passengers get seasick. The captain's mate (almost asleep in a corner) has the skill of opening one eye and passing plastic bags just before someone barfs, unsympathetically closing his eye right afterwards. The passage takes over two hours and most of the other passengers get sick or are at least very pale. Part of the discomfort is the waves, part is the smell and the noise of the engines, part is that we are sitting quite packed, shoulder to shoulder, making it stuffy and warm. Though Heidi and Leendert look a bit green in the middle of the trip, both hang in well.

There is a general sense of relief once we finally pull into Isabela harbor. We transfer again into small taxi boats, which, this time for $1, bring us to terra firma. We go through 'customs' and another $20 later we finally arrive on Isabela Island.

Julio, the local English teacher waits at the wharf. While our luggage is transferred, we chat with him and watch sea lions play in the water below the dock. Great entertainment for the kids. Alfredo drives us in his pick-up truck to what will be our abode for the next two weeks. Alfredo turns out to be our host and, as anticipated, speaks no English. The accommodation is a hostel called 'Los Flamencos'. One room for all of us, two singles and one double bed with just enough space to walk between them. I look at the brown tiled floors, inhale a distinct sewer odor and notice that it will be tough to find space to store our backpacks. Our residence for the next two weeks is truly modest. Not only in physical space, but everyday facilities appear basic too - exactly what we had hoped for!

The room itself is clean enough, but the bathroom contrasts sharply to what we are used to. The shower has no fresh water. A brackish melange pours from a hose with a single, thumb-wide, stream of water. The temperature is controlled by the outside temperature. Needless to say, showers became military style. Upon closer inspection it became clear that only a cold water tap of the sink was attached to the water mains. This did not affect us much as we had little need for hot water and we'd use bottled water to brush our teeth. Probably the trickiest adjustment was to toss toilet paper in the (open) bin. The sewer system of the island can't cope with toilet paper; it could clog up. I fear that in moments of not paying attention we might have violated this rule once or twice, but we learned the new habits quickly. The consequence, of course, is that four people's soiled toilet paper lays in a small bin, open to the air, nicely impregnating both the bathroom and the adjoining bedroom with the expected odors.

Over the next two weeks, we'd become accustomed to the rather basic food. Food was abundant, but limited in variety. Breakfast, lunch and dinner consisted of rice with either pasta or potatoes. In extreme cases, both. Each meal was supplemented with pieces of bread. Carb lovers heaven. Each meal, every day: rice, potatoes and bread. Typically, lunch was supplemented with a piece of fresh fish or squid. *Una sopa* (soup) would invariably be a starter before lunch and dinner, resembling tasty dishwater. Some days, to our delight, a green vegetable would make it to our plate. Looking back, I remember great joy being derived on the few occasions that lentils, green beans or a small piece of meat was served.

That said, each time we'd clear the dishes after a meal, I realized that the kitchen was magic in action. It was a miracle what came out of it, given the way it looked: old, dilapidated, black and unclean. The lady of the house tried her best, and clearly, she was an alchemist. She was a good cook given the ingredients she had and the environment she was in. Thinking back it is a wonder we did not spend more time in the toilet than we did. To really do us a favor, the day before we left, we were served "toad-in-the-hole". For those not familiar, it is a piece of bread with a hole in it, in which an egg is fried. We devoured it with great joy.

El Día de los Muertos is also a day that stands out from a culinary perspective. For breakfast we got a hamburger and a coffee cup filled to the rim with *colada morada*, complete with nice chunks of fruit. The purple-red drink grew on me while in Ecuador. Evidently we were stationed at a good source. One by one, our hosts' family members came around with plastic buckets. They'd pick up voluminous quantities of this homemade brew, transporting it back to their families on the back of motorcycles. I am not 100% sure if that the visitors were all relatives, but I suspect they were. Just like nobody can ever beat my mom's meatballs, I am sure the heavy morning traffic at the house was driven by the island sentiment that "mom's *morada* is best".

But let me get back to the day of our arrival. Julio introduces us to the host family and promises to come back later, after dinner, to give us a tour of town. The kids jump in the hammocks outside, and Heidi and I unpack our backpacks trying to figure out where to put everything. We visit the local supermarket to buy some drinks and water, carefully selecting the brands from the mainland. Around dinner time we walk into the living room and find Alfredo and his wife. Neither one speaks a word of English. We have fish and rice for dinner and are introduced to bright orange lemons. Leendert really loves citrus fruits, even eating whole lemons, so he thinks he has landed in vitamin C heaven.

That evening Julio gives us the thirty-minute walking tour of town. It was the extended tour. We saw all the roads, all the shops and all the attractions in that half hour. Sandy roads, big ship ropes for speed bumps, a tree in the middle of the main street, a couple of roadside restaurants. By nine it is dark and quiet on the island, all the tourists having returned to their cruise boats. Tomorrow at 7:30 we are expected to report for volunteering duty. Heidi and Alicia will go with Julio - I am to report at another school with Leendert and ask for the teacher we'll be assisting. In all honesty, I am a bit nervous. Helping to teach, in a school of eight-to-twenty-one year olds, a school where the principal does not speak English, what on earth have we signed up for?

Day one of school. Unforgettable. We have breakfast; a scrambled egg, rice and a piece of bread with pineapple marmalade. A cup of hot water is offered for tea or instant coffee. Alicia complains about bugs on her bread. I tell her to wipe it off and eat it, giving her 'the look'. I do not want her to be picky. I abhor spoiled brat behavior. To her credit, she listens and opens her bun. It is infested, and not just a little. It is Hitchcock-like infested. Oops. A dark wave of ant-like vermin streams from the bun, making me wonder how it is possible to have that many critters in one piece of bread. No screams, just frightened looks from Alicia. The hostess seems more shocked than Alicia, and she takes the plate and replaces the bun. It takes Alicia a moment to recover. Even today, she never takes a bite out of a bun without carefully opening it and peeking inside.

At 7:15 we are off to school. Alfredo drives us with his pickup truck to show us to our respective schools. At the first stop, 400 meters down the road, Leendert and I get out. We walk through the gate, over the courtyard searching for our teacher, Mathilde. Within minutes she finds us. We stand out a little, being the only Caucasians present. Mathilde is a charming lady, originally from Isabela, and she speaks a bit of English. She is far from fluent but does a good job as she translates for us in the principal's office. The head of the school speaks no English. A teaching schedule is easily fixed. We will join Mathilde on her beat as she is the head English teacher of the school.

We join her and walk into the first classroom. The setting would make a great picture for a volunteering brochure. The room has solid concrete walls on two sides, the opposing walls are waist-high wood, leaving the rest open to the elements. The roof is corrugated metal. Old furniture dating from the seventies is placed in rows and is in desperate need of a paintbrush. There is a white board on the wall but I see no pens or erasers.

The class consists of twenty-four kids in uniform. It never ceases to amaze me how uniforms meant to harmonize and have people dress 'properly' can lead to such variety. We see pristine white shirts neatly tucked in, stained shirts with missing buttons hanging out. Some kids have pressed pants, others dirty pants with ripped seams. Not much 'uni-form' detected here! Leendert and I are introduced. Each student stands up to say "good morning my name is…", and Mathilde explains that the kids are preparing for the school's "open days" which take place later in the week. Some students are to present a short story on a chosen country. Mathilde suggests Leendert and I take the six kids presenting at the open days and help them practice their speeches. We agree and are ushered outside. So much for an easy landing strip. On small benches under a tree, the pupils read their stories from index cards. We work with them on pronunciation. After the first student is done, I suggest to Leendert to split off so we can divide and conquer. Leendert - by nature more quiet and reserved - takes on, without objection, a group of three students. His willingness to try makes me proud.

From an educational perspective, I immediately see opportunities for improvement. First - academics - the texts have both what I assume to be typos, but more importantly grammatical errors. For now I decide not to create upheaval and refrain from correcting the short texts. Second - discipline - when you help one child, it appears to be the norm that the other kids run and horse around so there is no joint learning; even if it is just three of them around the table. Third - structure - none of the students take notes, or for that matter carry paper or pens. They are fairly carefree and seem to have no intention of editing or improving their presentations.

After class, during the break, we discuss with Mathilde what's next. She explains the schedule while proudly showing the "English lab". It a room in a side building which probably dates from the late eighties. It too has seen better days. Plywood cubicles used to give students personal practice space. Today, the wall fronts are wobbly and bent chairs sit idly behind the few old remaining headphones. I'm sure most have seen no repair or maintenance for decades. I doubt there is a link to any recording device. A rack hangs from the ceiling, but an intended projector is missing; Mathilde believes they might get one soon. It is a sad sight; the lab is no more than a room with dilapidated tables and chairs in disrepair.

We walk to the next class. The kids do the same initial stand-up introductions as in the first class and present the work done in the days before. Based on an old American text book full of simple pictures they learn to describe their own house. The dated book shows a four story American house; basement, first floor (dining room, living room, kitchen, garage, etc), second floor bedrooms, office and bathrooms, plus an attic. The house is filled with the household articles from the early seventies: a record player, a tape deck, a black and white TV, cupboards, etc. We listen to the kids, tuning our ears to the Spanish accent "thees iz my e-house, …I live in the e-house with my parent, four brother and two sister,… My e-house has a kitchen, My e-house has e-bedroom, …. My e-house has a bathroom, …My 'favorite site' in the e-house is the living room". Note, with the exception of family members, all are singular. As we'd learn over the next days, this was not a language issue. No translation errors, just correct statements of fact; large families living in humble one-bedroom bungalow houses. While the pictures in the book look dated to us, they must look like huge space stations to them.

That first day we go to four classes, spread over two schools (the two schools are walking distance apart). Believe it or not, the second school is a 'rougher' state school - with less discipline. In the beginning, Mathilde shoos some kids away from the door, kids who formally are not part of the class. The action is about as useful as trying to keep flies away from food at a lunch table on a hot summer day. Likewise, without much success, she tries to tell the students not to hang in over the window edges from outside. Clearly, seeing the 'white teachers' is a better attraction than their own curriculum. While in the first classes Leendert assisted, by the forth one, it's getting old, and he sits in the back of the room doing his own homework. The novelty has already worn off. Frankly, he is getting fed up with the laughter, eyeing and giggles of the girls who continuously try to attract his attention, all having fallen for the tall blond teenage stranger. At the end of the last class, one of the girls walks up to me, shakes my hand and gives me a peck on the cheek saying "thank you". This sets precedent and allows her to treat Leendert the same way. It takes me a moment before I realize I just got used by a seventeen year old girl to get to my thirteen year old son. Leendert doesn't quite know where to look as she kisses him on the cheek.

After school Mathilde says she is very happy with how it went. "Tomorrow we'll continue in the same way" she says confidently. She also inquires if I am willing to help her with her English. "Of course" is my immediate response. I am delighted to give her some lessons in the afternoon, realizing that improving her English will do far more good for the local school than I can ever do directly in the couple of weeks that we are present.

In the afternoon, there are no classes. We enjoy a siesta and wander to the beach. The kids play in the sand and the waves while pelicans dive next to them kamikaze-style. Sea lions play nearby and stingrays and iguanas pass in the surf to say quick hellos. It is incredible to be this close to nature.

The following days are pretty much a repeat of the first; a bit more challenging perhaps as the novelty wears off, but easier because I know what to expect. One difference: five minutes after class starts Mathilde hands over her white board pens, wishes me "good luck" and walks out. Gone - not to be seen until the end of class. I have to rely on creativity as all Spanish speaking authority has just left the building, leaving me to control the rascals. It is a phenomenal experience. Back home, in work life, I'd give presentations to audiences of 150+ managers and executives without blinking. There, people knowledgeable about the content, even deep subject matter specialists, would be in the audience and it wouldn't faze me to enlighten them with my views. Journalists would write articles afterwards for industry magazines. That was cool, I was cool. Now I find myself in front of twelve teenagers, zero exposure (risk) to the outside world, talking about a subject on which I am definitely the expert in the room (in the land of the blind one eye is king), and I am nervous and stressed out! If it wasn't for the presence of Leendert, I am not sure I would have tackled the situation as well as I did. Strange what parents are able to confront in the presence of their children, just to set a good example.

The next weeks are delightful and spiked with great moments. The students continue to show up for class and most seem to like the sessions.

Since no educational program or plan is in place, we can free-wheel it. Figuring everyone likes music, I download some music on my iPad and, armed with a copy of the text in English and a translation '*en Español*', I introduce them to *Don't Worry be Happy* from Bobby McFerrin. It is an instant hit. In parallel, Leendert and I do our best to learn some Spanish. Our efforts are well received, and we get applause for our efforts.

Teaching on the Galapagos was thrilling. Mathilde's instructions were often no more than "continue what you are doing please; this is a two-hour class, you are doing well". At times she would be in the back of the class room for the first five minutes, at times she would disappear into a black hole right from the start. Often, but not always, she would reappear just before class-end. She would still teach the sporadic session herself. I remember one such session. I supported her and noticed class discipline was totally absent. I felt for her. Teaching seemed more like a screaming contest than anything else. Take it from me, trying to out-yell twelve rowdy teenage kids is a lost cause. I began to understand why she was happy to hand over the reins that first day.

True, in the classes I was teaching, kids would climb in and out through a sliding window as well. True, kids would horse around in class. True, one kid decided to lay across two chairs for a while, and I think he actually was asleep. However, overall, things were well in hand most of the time. In one session I had the classic 'spit ball' flying through the air, blown through an empty pen tube. Impounding the pen used, I captivated the class' attention with my sternness. I took a risk there, and, probably because I was a foot taller and double the weight of the biggest student, never became a spit ball target myself. This was good fortune, for I don't know how I would have reacted had they taken aim at me.

Class schedules on the island were incomprehensible to me. A northern European at heart, ten o'clock is ten o'clock. A schedule is a schedule. Not there. Time and again Mathilde would show up with some complex story about scheduling errors and changes by the school; my Spanish was not sufficient to understand her, her English not good enough to explain. One day I arrived knowing there was a 9:15 class, but I had no clue which grade or which room. Mathilde? Nowhere to be found. I went to the principal's office, and in my broken Spanish I made her understand the dilemma. She looked at the scheduling board on the wall behind her desk. Staring at the overview she looked more puzzled then me. She walked me to a class, and said she'll call Mathilde. She obviously did not succeed. That morning I didn't pretend to teach. The kids were playing cards, so I grabbed the opportunity to teach them the face card names, numbers and colors. Halfway through class one of the kids pulled out a two liter PET coke bottle. It was filled with an unknown concoction. I had no clue if it is within school rules to drink in class or not. However, with Mathilde absent I guess I make the rules. Given that I stopped two students from writing with permanent markers on their desks, I figured I was in the positive overall, even if they are not supposed to consume beverages in class so I let them. Leendert and I tried some of the yellow-greenish elixir. We comment in Dutch, and are glad there are some dry crackers to absorb the taste. The milk-like substance might be a delight for the students, but for us, it is easy to refrain from seconds. Not even a week on the islands, and how far have we come from the "don't drink the local juice"!

As for Mathilde, I had a love-hate relation with her. I didn't appreciate her constant disappearing acts or the fact that she would not assist and contribute in her own classes. Her absence and lack of planning really irritated me. I guess the 'island time' mentality did not blend with my control habits. For those classes where she did show up, they were so much better and educational for the students. Having said that, we shared some wonderful times together. The private English lessons were as educational for me as for her. Mathilde would come to the afternoon sessions with specific questions, and I would learn about her and island life. At first it was hard. It was hard for both of us. Having a two-and-a-half hour conversation with someone with a low command of the language, someone you have little to nothing in common with, is not easy. She, like her parents, was born and raised on the island. For four university years she lived with her aunt in Guayaquil, on the mainland. However, city life was not for her: "too many people, too much pollution". As soon as her studies were done, she returned to Isabela. Her life was, is, and will be on the island.

She explained she was originally a Spanish teacher. In fact, she did not want to be an English teacher at all. Simply because she had taken some English classes on the mainland, the school appointed her - she was the best English-speaker available. In our afternoon sessions, she disclosed how the municipal school where Heidi was teaching and the government school (ours) were competing for students. The tension was substantial between the institutions, since the nicer municipal school (which was sponsored by the locals) kept dropping school fees to entice new pupils to attend. She explained the local politics and how the rivalry between the various schools played out. For example: the municipal school refused to select top sports players from other schools to participate in the coveted inter-island competitions. Reportedly, they only let their kids go to the competitions on Santa Cruz Island. I guess there is a universal rule - as soon as you have more than two homo sapiens together there will be politics! How strange that we have called ourselves homo sapiens, literally meaning 'wise person', yet often act so foolishly.

One afternoon Mathilde invited us over to her farm. Her brother had a car and drove us from town into the Highlands. There, we were welcomed by the sweet smell of citrus blossom and her husband's sweaty hands. He'd been working hard to get the property looking nice. The residence consisted of an outside kitchen, one room and corrugated metal roof. The sounds of the classroom echoed in my ears: "I have e-house, e-kitchen,......".

The house was surrounded by fruit trees. Mango, papaya, guanabana (pronounced gua-na-va-na), lemon, bananas (regular, small and black) and tons of oranges. Soon Leendert and Alicia were picking oranges. Mathilde's husband gave me a knife to eat a fresh orange and I cut one into pieces, juice dripping over my hands. He showed us how to do it properly. He peeled off a thin part of the top of the orange with his sharp knife. Then he cut a coned hole in the top. He shows us how drink the juice out of the top, getting more juice by simply squeezing it. After drinking the juice he discards the rest of the orange, tossing it on the ground, like one does peanut shells in laid-back bars in Europe. I have never tasted better juice than that day. For the rest of the afternoon, Mathilde plays guide in the area. We taste fruits as she shares stories and points out the unique beauty of the island such as the Sabre tree (a tree fully covered in thick thorny spikes). She explains how large parts of town were built by convicts in the late 1940's and early 1950's. In fact, the island was mainly a penal colony at that time, which is no wonder given its remote location. I dare not ask what brought her parents over originally, but I do learn they were 'early settlers' who owned loads of land. Land which is now farmland split between her and her brother. She takes great pride in the island's history, its nature and all it has to offer.

The two school weeks were an interesting introduction to us developing as volunteer teachers, and for the personal development of Leendert and Alicia as well. Leendert, not liking to be the center of attention, was definitely in the wrong place. Since he was fifty centimeters taller than most of the girls (who were five years his senior) and the only blond person in the school, he started out as nothing short of a circus attraction. Luckily, during the break on one of the first days, things changed. Girls collected around us, happily giggling while footballs flew about. As one ball passed, the leader of the girl-group grabbed it and sat on it. She clearly had no intention of returning it to the players. She was definitely the alpha-female of the group - if there is such a thing. Soon her plan became clear; and it materialized rapidly. If she was to return the ball to the boys, they had to ask us, or rather, Leendert, to participate. It took a few minutes, but she got what she wanted. The boys ask Leendert to join. No sooner is Leendert on the pitch than all the girls are participating too. For the next two weeks Leendert runs around on the school yard with the kids. Girls still go out of their way to impress him; both with show-off moves and passing the ball frequently to him. Luckily, the 'circus' element eventually wears off. Within a week he blends in magnificently; plays, passes, and is goalie. The playground activities become a catalyst for young friendships.

During class, however, Leendert continues to be somewhat of an attraction and hence a distraction. More often than not, I promise to have him participate towards the end if everybody pays attention during class. This works. Leendert (reluctantly) participates at the end of the classes, and once he does, the girls instantly find new interest in English: 'beautiful eyes', 'tall', 'handsome', etc.... Leendert is not charmed and does not quite know how to act, but seems less bothered as time passes. The last days have a different feel to them and Leendert teaches the kids a bit of French. The girls tell us they are '*triste*' and 'sorry to see us go'. The bolder ones ask if we can take them with us. Needless to say, by the end of our time on Isabela the girls take out their mobile phones, and many a selfie are taken.

All too soon, we must plan our departure. The next stop: San Cristobal Island. To get there one normally starts with the two-and-a-half hour boat ride back to Santa Cruz, followed by a three hour stopover, and another two-and-a-half hour boat ride. With a clear memory of bouncing over the Pacific on the way in, and knowing that we'd have to do it twice, we are not keen to tempt fate again. We opt to use the small airstrip of the island and fly to San Cristobal. The flight itself was not a noteworthy event, were it not for *la colección* (the collection) we witness the day before at school.

That day, we see girls walking around with a shoe box, clearly doing a collection. They circumvent us, but by the second time they cross the schoolyard I wave them over. In broken English and fluent Spanish they explain what is going on. We can't make heads or tails of it, but luckily Mathilde walks up. She translates. The girls are collecting for their friend who has gone to the hospital in Guayaquil. She is seventeen and has a nine-month old baby who has fluid in her lungs. The collection is to give mother and child some extra support. It is their first time off the island and, due to the complications with the little one, their stay is extended. Money for food and care is an issue, hence the request for alms. Looking at Leendert, I ask in Dutch "should we put some money in?". He nods his head. I slip a larger note in the box, hidden inside a one-dollar bill.

Since part of Leendert's schoolwork happens to be about ethics and ethical dilemmas, I deemed this a perfect moment to pursue the theme. I ask him "Why did you want us to participate in the collection?". He replies with a simple "It's the right thing to do". Having jumped the first hurdle, I ask him "What might be a reasonable amount?". He reflects and inquires what others might put in. I said between one and five dollars, most likely. "Okay" he said "that seems reasonable". Not letting him off the hook so easily, I ask him how much he thinks our flight to San Cristobal costs. He didn't know, but we establish it is about $250. "So let me summarize", I said, "you think that giving $5 to a girl who has a critically sick baby is 'reasonable', knowing we ourselves spend $250 on a flight, just to make sure we don't risk the chance of being seasick for a couple of hours?". A puzzled stare is followed by the question: "So how much should we have put in?" And thus the boomerang flies straight back at me. Not only do I now have an ethical dilemma on what is the right amount, I have a parental issue. I asked him a question, and the return question is as least as difficult. Note, he did not ask "How much did you put in" (that would be easy to answer); he asked how much *should* we have put in. After a bit of conversation, I answer him honestly, "I don't know either; that's why it is an ethical dilemma". A learning moment for the both of us.

One cannot be on the Galapagos and not be impressed by nature. Our mornings were filled by the formal school setting; afternoons were dominated by nature's school and teaching. We snorkeled with hammerheads, sea turtles and two-meter long sting rays. We not only saw sharks, we swam with them. No, not scary Jaws-like great whites, just gracious two-and-a-half meter, slick looking, white-tipped reef sharks. One afternoon, while diving, we see a dark cloud floating towards us about two meters under the water line no more than five meters away. At first I thought it was an oil-spill, perhaps algae. But then, suddenly, as three white fish descend towards the cloud a hole appears in the middle. It is as if Moses parted the seas. Once the aggressors had moved through, instantaneously and effortlessly, the gap closes again. It turns out the black blob was a school of fish. The densest cloud I have ever seen. One black patch moving with the tide, barely swimming, only a sporadic fin in motion. Absolutely stunning.

We explored the Sierra Negra, the second largest crater in the world; we navigated lava tunnels. We saw blue-footed boobies, spotted owls, wobbling penguins and night herons. On the various islands we learned how tortoises evolved differently over the ages (longer necks, different shell shapes) and we saw flamingos at an arm's reach happily poking their crooked beaks in the muddy water. We watched pelicans dive for fish in the ocean, red-necked frigates plunge into mountain lakes to wash salt water off their feathers, and sea lions surfed next to us in the waves. We ran into iguanas as docile as apartment cats, a group of seals passing on the beach so close that one decided to sniff my daughter's knee. We walked over deserted beaches and rugged volcanic terrain formed by boiling lava between half a million and four million years ago. The boiling stone instantly solidified because of the contact with the cold sea water giving it its unique sharp and pointy profile. This type of lava is also known as A-A lava, as one screams Ah-Ah when walking on it bare feet. All of it was magnificent, impressive and unique.

After two weeks, I heard Alicia say "I am getting sick of these iguanas". She said this as we weaved toward the harbor passing those strange salt-spitting, reptilian creatures. Too much of a good thing perhaps? Did it only take us two weeks to get overdosed?

All good things come to an end

The islands were great. We loved it. Guides and locals greeted us as "*Los Professores*". We saw amazing nature and met incredible people. The hospitality was impressive, as was the curiosity of the local kids. We were invited by new friends to their home for dinner and treated like kings. Sitting on the beach, one of Heidi's students came to look what '*los hijos*' (the children) of '*la professora*' were making. Soon after, they were all building a sandcastle together. It went on until sunset. In the hostel we met a Vietnamese traveler, who, when she learned we'd be in Vietnam during our trip, she extended an open invitation. We hung out with hippy backpackers and heard their stories over tepid beers. The variety of people was as extensive as the nature.

We lived together in a small, smelly room. No potable water from the tap, a small fridge which electrocuted us slightly each time we opened it. Two lizards, affectionately dubbed 'Joop' and 'Jan', became a friendly duo visiting our ceiling each night. Oh how different a setting to the six bedroom home we left behind only a few short weeks ago!

As we left for our flight, the school girls stood along the road toward the airstrip to giggle and wave goodbye to us (or rather, to Leendert!). The four of us, the pilot, and one other passenger, completely filled the small plane. We took runway seventeen into the skies giving us a nice view of the town and the full island as we turned east. At 5500 feet above the clouds chapter 'Isabela Island' closed for us. A short forty-five minutes later we descend, pop through the mist and land on San Cristobal, another Galapagos island which we aim to explore for several days.

The hotel owner picked us up. We have two rooms, right next to another. We are slightly startled; fresh running water comes out of the taps, each room has a working shower. Led-lights in the ceiling allow us to read at night and there are bedside tables with lamps! Wow! We find ourselves in luxury heaven as we have more built-in closet space than our backpacks can fill and we have access to uninterrupted wifi connection for our electronics. Oh the joy!

That evening, we walk to the center of town. We know we are close to downtown as we encounter the one and only traffic light on the island. Two weeks ago, we would have seen this as a small little coastal village. After two weeks on Isabela, it feels like a metropolis. The food tastes amazing. We appreciate the variety which contrasts sharply against the general monotony of our Isabela cuisine. In the morning, the feast continues: a bowl of fruit-yogurt-muesli and we eat like kings: small omelets, fresh empanadas stuffed with cheese. After two weeks of only instant coffees the abundance of freshly brewed *café con leche* never tasted so good.

The next day we catch up on mundane things. We make travel plans, get cash, get a haircut. A barber lady cuts my hair while keeping one eye on the TV, obviously able to multi-task between a soap-opera and chopping hair. She does a good job and finishes in about seven minutes. She overcharges me, but I happily hand her the five dollars, wondering why in the west the same haircut has to take nearly an hour and costs 8 times as much.

The following day, we leave on a big airplane and return to the mainland of Ecuador. As we cruise through the air at over 800km/hr for more than an hour-and-a-half, it strikes us how remote the Galapagos Islands really are. It takes until that moment - leaving - to truly appreciate how unique a place it is; how unique it is that there is life on the islands. Sea life makes sense, but the long journey animals have made on randomly floating debris of vegetation (or logs of wood) to get there is simply astonishing. It is no wonder Darwin was so utterly impressed by what he found having sailed the seas to get there. As the Galapagos Island chapter closes for us we are grateful to have had the opportunity to not only visit, but to have lived on this unique archipelago.

Alexander van 't Riet

Peru - More than Lost Incas

OUR NEXT PROJECT TAKES US to Peru. We have several early morning flights, the ones which guarantee insomnia caused by the paranoia that you won't wake up for a 4:15am pick-up. Even after a night of three restless hours of sleep the kids do a good job stumbling out of bed and slinging their bodies into a taxi. This particular day we are well in time at the airport, and as things go when you are early, delays pop up, so we have even more time. In our case two-and-a-half hours of hanging around. The kids question why we have to travel at these ungodly hours during our trip. I explain we are not on a 'holiday' and that we are making an 'educational journey', but I too have to admit this is a lame excuse for the timing choices. To undermine this argument even more, our plan is to visit Peru as tourists first, before going to Cusco for or next volunteer project. The actual truth is that we are on the current flight because we made a mistake booking; we booked a connecting flight which departed before we landed from the Galapagos. Luckily, the folks at the volunteering organization were able to get the flight we are now on as alternative, the local airlines having pity on us 'poor volunteers'. They generously allowed us to change our non-changeable tickets without paying any fees, provided we took the way-too-early morning flight. And so we arrive in Lima, Peru.

We book a van and a guide and roll down the Pan American Highway (which goes north-south, ultimately becoming Highway 1 in the USA). We visit Ica, Pisco and fly over the famous Nazca lines in a prop plane piloted by a kamikaze insisting we will get the best view when the plan is in a sideways freefall. We spent many early mornings in a zombie-like state, shuffling in and out of vans, trying to cram in as much as we can in the time we have allocated. Despite the cruel schedule we set for ourselves, the guided tours in Peru are well worth the effort. I feel the urge to make a small pitch for the Peru tourist industry, as this Andean nation caught me completely off-guard.

Cruising down the coast, the family asleep with inflatable horseshoe-shaped sleeping pillows around their necks, I learn that Peru is not all green, lush and hilly like the pictures of Machu Picchu seem to suggest. A 70km wide strip along the coast is nothing but desert. This part of the country gets about two millimeters of rain a year and is a rough living environment. As if that is not enough, the area is frequently hit by earthquakes. The last one struck in 2007 causing extensive damage. We pass abandoned towns and villages. In two places, the sandy landscape suddenly transforms into impeccably maintained agricultural land. Both spots have rivers running down from the Andes. Supported by pumped ground water, they effectively form the vegetable garden of Peru. On our excursions south we see flamingos, salt deserts and a rusty red beach. We visit islands near the coast with amazing fauna; dolphins, sea lions, pelicans, and many other birds. While the rest of the passengers are ooh-and ahh-ing at the sea lions, I realize we have had our fill of them on the Galapagos; oh how spoiled we are!

Our guides take us to a visitors center, where school buses empty out right behind us. Surrounded by students running around barely looking at the exhibits, we learn how Peru has a unique place in the sea world. Due to the climate and the sea currents along the Peruvian coastline, vast amounts of sea plants flourish. This, in turn, provides food for fish, and subsequently fish-eating animals. Migratory birds pass by. We learn that seventy percent of the oxygen creation on earth (think Co_2 reduction) comes from marine plants (not from trees as I was taught as a youngster). We read how dolphins can swim at speeds of up to 50km/hr - and at depths of 500 meters - and how otters stay warm because of a double layer of fur trapping air creating a layer of insulation between them and the icy water.

The micro-cimate in this part of Peru is unique. Strong, cold winds blow across the plains. As the hot desert air ascends it creates a vacuum pulling the airflow from the (cold) sea across the land. We learn that Peru is an exporter of both copper and salt and that the desert roads we drive over are made of salt! It looks similar to the highway in France after the snow plows have tossed their mix of salt and sand on it. We get on our knees and lick the road for proof. Yuck, yes, motor oil and salt (the things tourists do!). It wouldn't surprise me if the guides have a bet going - see who can make the most tourists get down on all fours and lick the highway.

We visit Ica and taste the local *eau de vie*, sweet wine and cocktail mixes. We are introduced to Pisco and its production: the usual foot stamping of the grapes, pressing, boiling and distilling. It's fun, but it pales against our next experience: dune buggies. Advised to dress warm and take sunglasses, we jump into homemade dune buggies. The machines could have come straight from the set of *Mad Max*. Colorful steel frameworks, big wheels, and huge American V8 engines. No protection beyond 4-point seat belts; it is magnificent. We fly over the sand - it is dune bashing at its best. We try our hands (and bellies) on dune surfing. All in all, we make three stops, each at a higher dune. The group of surfers gets smaller at each hill, but we hang in, flying down the last sandy slope with only three other daredevils. Days later, we were still trying to get the sand out of our pockets.

At another information center, we learn more about the local culture. I recognize that I slept through most of my history classes in school, probably spending my time finding arguments to prove to the teacher that history does NOT repeat itself. To my surprise I hear the Incas are a rather recent element of the Peruvian history. The development was as follows: the Paracas period (900BC-200AD), Nazca period (200-600AD), the Wari period (500-900AD), the late intermediate or landlord era (1000-1450), and finally the Inca Period (1476-1534). The earlier and lesser known Nazcas were at least as impressive as the Incas. They made the famous Nazca lines, mummified their dead, did brain surgery, and built impressive systems of underground aqueducts using subsurface water for irrigation. Some of the ducts still function today!

The Incas walked away with a more dominant place in history books simply because the Spanish conquest - or rather looting and murder - took place during an era of record keeping. We know about the Incas because writings document what the Spanish found. They tell us about the gold, the building techniques (fitting complex blocks together without mortar), the use of record keeping using Quipu (strings with knots), etc.

The conclusion of my tourist pitch: Peru is a country worth visiting. I won't comment on Lima as we did not spend much time there and it struck me as a typical city. Big, chaotic, and with traffic much like Holland during rush-hour in the Utrecht-Amsterdam-Rotterdam triangle. For those not having had the pleasure, it is a gridlocked expanse with sporadic movements forward. I should note that I have not commented on 'the other side' of Peru. We did not cross the Andes to visit where the jungle stretches into Brazil. Reportedly this is also spectacular. Unfortunately, we only have eight month for our entire trip, so we had to make choices. The tough life we live...

CUSCO

In an uneventful trip (my favorite kind) we fly with StarPeru from Lima to Cusco, an Andean mountain town in a valley at 3400 meter elevation (about 11,000 feet). This is where our next volunteer project will take place. Standing around at baggage claim gives us the first introduction to the altitude. I feel a bit light-headed and my breathing is definitely impacted. Eventually the bags arrive. We meet Carlos, our local host, outside. As I sling my backpack on and walk towards his van every node of my body is firing "slow down". I notice the rest of the family is also out of breath when we arrive at the car which is parked only a hundred meters from the airport exit doors.

Carlos speaks good English, and he speaks a nice blend with Spanish as we drive the ten minutes to his parent's house, where we will stay. We are welcomed by the entire family and after we unpack we sit down at the dining room table to drink some coca-leaf tea. This reportedly helps with the altitude adjustment. Following tea, we relax and Alicia promptly falls asleep on her bed. We lunch on rice and chicken (with a potato, not unlike the Galapagos). We drink water with a touch of orange juice, wondering if the water here is 'okay'. Towards the end of the afternoon Carlos takes us for a walk into town to visit the language school where we will be having our Spanish lessons every afternoon for the next two weeks.

The walk starts out in a rather industrial area, along the principle access road of Cusco, a town of 600,000 inhabitants. It is a strange physical experience. Altitude affects our bodies and the weather conditions are like something I have not experienced before. There is a bit of wind, which feels similar to the cold Swiss *bize*. It cuts through everything. However, out of the shade, the sun rays burn hotter than in Dubai. You can actually feel it burn on your skin. Luckily Carlos had told us to put sunscreen on and to wear our jackets! After the first 500 meters we walk past a large Inca statue. Huffing and puffing we work ourselves towards the center of town. Leendert suffers from dizziness, Alicia is hot and Heidi shows the first signs of a Quito-like headache. O boy. My symptoms are limited to minor light-headedness and my lungs are kicked into overdrive. They seem to pump little additional oxygen into my bloodstream however, and the slight uphill requires disproportionate effort.

Luckily, the promenade is worth it - the center of Cusco has a beautiful square with several churches from Spanish colonial days. One older building gives a snapshot into what is to come: it displays a 500-year-old black Inca wall, stones of different sizes, neatly placed together like a puzzle, without mortar. You could not stick a knife blade between the bricks if you tried, that's how snug it all fits. Impressive!

We reach the language school. Since it is Sunday, it is closed. It only now dawns on me that this was a 'show you where the school is' trip. Really? All that physical agony for nothing? We loop back towards the main square and take a much needed break in a juice bar. It has a huge collection of juices. Some fruits are known to us, many are not. Some are mixed into bizarre combinations; avocado and milk to name one. I always wonder as I dissect these types of menus. I wonder about the crazy combinations someone tried which didn't make it to the list. Given what's on the menu, one has to wonder what people are willing to try out! Revitalized, we continue on our merry way, glad the walk back is slightly downhill. We eat dinner with Carlos' parents, who are lovely hosts, and catch a fair amount of their Spanish. The meal is a repeat of lunch; rice, chicken, and one potato supplemented by a piece of cake for dessert. It reminds us of the Galapagos, but then high class. After dinner the kids and Heidi, who are suffering from the altitude, go to bed. I stay behind and butcher the Spanish language talking with the old couple and another volunteer worker until late in the evening.

The next morning, at 7:30 we wake up to get ready for school. Leendert was already in a semi-awake state. Alicia, on the other hand is deep, deep asleep. By eight a.m. we munch on round flat bread buns (no yeast), typical of the Andean region. They are served with jelly and scrambled eggs. We're all starting to adjust to the altitude, so we eat happily.

After breakfast, Carlos walks us to our new school. The traffic is not too dense, but crossing the roads we learn that in Cusco, pedestrians had better beware; cars, though small, have priority. It will take some adjusting after being on an island nearly devoid of motorized vehicles!

The 'school' is dedicated to 'children' from the age of ten to over twenty. All students have mental handicaps. Most also have physical handicaps. It is quite a sight and a site. There is a large (unused) building in the center, an old gymnasium with a sports field next to it. Next to the gym stretches a long wooden shed. The shed has a loose fitting door every five meters. Carlos walks to the last wooden door and pokes his head in. The chain of plywood lean-tos turns out to be the school! In the first class, a group of girls are 'knitting', this is where Heidi and Alicia will help out. Two doors down, Leendert and I meet Wilburn, the '*profe*' in charge of the class we'll be helping.

A description of the environment is in order. The classroom is a wooden structure, plywood walls with an uneven dirt floor. A metal corrugated roof with holes functions to keep most of the elements out. There is a small window consisting of four squares of plastic. One is missing half its pane. The interior furniture consists of three old and mismatched low wooden tables. A collection of small wooden chairs stand on the soil, most so small you would only expect them in a preschool building. I notice one wall has a whiteboard. Over the next days we learn that the white board only serves to prop up the cross beam of the roof. For stability it is resting on a wobbly chair. It was never used for its intended purpose - pen and erasers are missing.

Our class has thirteen students, mainly with mental handicaps. The *'profe'* tells me they are between 14 and 22 years old. Although they are normal Peruvian height (short compared to us Northern Europeans), they definitely look uncomfortable on the kindergarten seats, knees higher than their buttocks. The *'profe'* explains that most of the students are gentle, but some have a more aggressive and physical streaks. Given the variety of disabilities, they each work on different things. The teacher shows me how we can help. My first task is to assist Victor to write the letter O on a piece of paper. Victor is 18 and his assignment is to trace a pencil over the letter O today. A sample has been written 12 times with an orange highlighter on a large page in a notebook.

I am puzzled how to help and the teacher shows me. I effectively have to hold Victors' hand and help him trace. It takes some time but I figure how to stand next to him and repeat the *rondo* movement with him while giving him verbal encouragements. As I look over my shoulder is see Leendert struggling with the girl he is supposed to help. His role is similar to mine, so I show him what to do. He catches on quickly, as does the girl he helps.

To keep Victor on task is tricky, or rather impossible. He has too much attention for everything going on around him. First of all there is me, helping him out. My shirt is of interest *bonito*, as is my hair *bonito*. Second there is the girl next to him who continuously wipes a dirty rag in the face of another classmate for no apparent reason. Third, one of the pupils crying, although it is unclear why. On top off that Wilburn, the *'profe'*, keeps walking in and out of the classroom, which is definitely not normal. Finally, there is the girl next to Victor, working very hard with a thread and beads, and beads are shiny and *bonito*.

But other than that, there is little distraction. "Okay", *bien*, "O", *rondo* I hear myself say, tracing his hand over and over, over the orange highlighted letter in the notebook. I continue to trace and re-trace the 'O' for about twenty minutes, at which point my mind starts to wonder: Why is he doing this? Why am I? Is this useful? How could this improve…?

Suddenly, my contemplation is interrupted. Something agitates the group. It is as if the beehive has been kicked. It soon becomes clear; the girl who had her face continuously rubbed with the cloth has a bleeding scratch mark. The red liquid upsets the entire class. It gets worse. The crack of the door widens as wind blows it open, and the group sees the activity outside the classroom. Flu-shots. It is as if the hive tumbled over. Kids out of their seats, trying to run around, but there is no space in the packed room, there are tears of anguish. Wilburn walks back in - he was helping outside. His entry instantly helps settle the group a little bit. Our class is next in line for the shots. In batches of three, they walk from the shed to the nurse standing outside. I handhold some of them as they are poked with the small needle. The range of reactions is as can be expected from such a mentally diverse group.

About twenty minutes later everyone is back in class and quiet returns. I continue with Victor and build rapport with a couple of other students. I succeed. Thus, I promote myself to a second job, alternating holding Victors hand for the 'O' and the girl across the table who is working the 'i'. *Sí, a bajo y punto.* I quickly realize I have set myself up for trouble - both want one hundred percent of my time. Neither is able to trace on their own, nor capable to decide where to trace without assistance. In the end I manage to help both without a total meltdown of them or myself. I wonder how on earth Wilburn handles this without the support of volunteers.

At 11:00 a bell rings: recess. As we walk around, we catch up with Alicia and Heidi. Several kids walk up to us and give spontaneous hugs. I am glad of the difference in height between us and Peruvians, as otherwise it would have been rather tricky. They are strong huggers. One girl attaches herself to me. She grabs my hand and remains latched on for the next thirty minutes, squeezing most of the blood out of my fingers. Only by offering my other hand do I get her to let go and switch every once in a while, thus avoiding osteonecrosis in my hands.

We walk circles around the main –dilapidated- sports building. We create some laughter and generate smiles by interacting with the kids. We have to manage an incident as one kid walks up to Alicia and throws, from half a meter distance a hand full of grass and sand in her face. Now what is the right protocol and response to that? Parental protection moves me in one direction, the pity of a mentally challenged child linea-recta into the other.

By the time we are on our third tour of the building, I can't help thinking of the guys in the movie Shawshank Redemption, endlessly walking around in circles. Nothing new to see or experience, just walking round and round; and this is only day one! Luckily, the monotony gets broken when we see big pans arrive. And when I say big pans I mean huge pans, the ones you see in refugee camps. Large cleaning buckets and huge bowls appear from inside the various class rooms. We see how the content of the two pans gets redistributed with a big ladle into the smaller plastic buckets.

At 11:30 the break is over and I pry myself loose from the girl still holding my hand. We re-enter our classroom, and help the *'profe'* distribute the food. The food is scooped for a second time, from the large plastic bucket onto plates. A metal bowl is used to make the transfer. Lunch is served. It consists of rice complemented by strips of potato (think thick soggy french fries). Over this carbohydrate foundation some tuna is sprinkled. In all honesty, I am not sure it is fish, but it is what my nose seems to detect. Just before eating the *'profe'* asks for silence. Most kids fold their hands and a short player is sent to the heavens. Wilburn thanks God for the *día* and all the good He has graciously given us, reminding us of people that are more needy. More needy? Really? I give an evil eye to the picture of a white Jesus with blue eyes that hangs on the wall. No further comment. I'll protect the guilty.

There is one spare plate and it's offered to Leendert who politely replies he is not hungry. I consider digging in for a moment, if only to demonstrate to Leendert that we should experience the local life as it is. Instead I hear myself explain to El Professor that the people in our *casa* are expecting us for lunch (which is true). I have a short conversation with Leendert on how this school lunch compares to the meal at the *Collège* in France and The International School in Vienna. As the words escape my mouth I realize it is more of an insult to his intelligence than a necessary statement from my side.

We finish school at 12:30 and rush to our host family for lunch. Lunch consists of a green vegetable soup followed by rice with a corn-based sauce and half an egg. Once our plates are cleared we speed to town. We are gung-ho to start our Spanish lesson and are running late, so we decide to take a taxi. We cross to the other side of the town center for about one dollar.

Heidi signed us up to take Spanish as a family. Now that should be fun. The four of us sit with Miriam, our private teacher, in a small room with no windows. Both kids impress me with their ability and agility to learn, their interest and tenacity. We parents are clearly out of practice when it comes to being in school. Towards the end of the afternoon, concentrating becomes harder. The impact of the altitude, the plethora of new impressions, the first day of school and the four hours with Miriam take their toll. We're all worn out by the end of the afternoon and are relieved when the little bell marks the end of class.

We stroll back home (fortunately downhill) in a daze. The fresh air does wonders for the mind however, and stretching our legs feels good after being cooped up in that small classroom for hours. We make the mental note to take coats along tomorrow. Temperatures drop quickly in this high altitude Andes town after dark. I am glad there is no wind. Dinner is, like yesterday, a repeat of lunch (rice and the corn-based sauce) without the soup and egg. Luckily, there is an additional packet of the flat bread-buns on the table, which we devour while talking with the hosts.

Routine sets in

No matter where in the world, no matter what age, day two of school is always less intimidating than that first day. You know more or less what to expect. We show up at 8am, reportedly when classes start. While we can't claim 'island time' here in the Andes, clearly this school, too, is on a flexible schedule; some kids are there, but the majority trickle in around 8:15.

The day is a repeat of yesterday. We draw simple letters repetitively, do basic math up to 10 or 20 depending on the capability of the individual. We knit hats for the Christmas festival. Leendert finds his comfort zone helping kids with numbers. The good news is that math is made easy by counting bottle caps. In general this works as long as you stay away from zero. Ten plus zero is a tricky concept, as is ten minus zero. As we work the numbers I find it extremely challenging to explain such a simple concept as 'zero', 'nothing', 'no change'. No matter how hard I try, no matter how many times I demonstrate and give examples, "emptiness, void, nought, nil, zip, no effect, nada, squat, and zilch", nothing appears to help explain that little mathematical circle. I just get empty stares, smiles or guesses in return for my hard efforts. No wonder the Romans didn't have a zero!

At one point, Wilburn walks out of the classroom for a while. Caroline, a short girl who is manifestly the bully of the class, seizes the opportunity to become more than difficult. She hits other kids, pulls their bracelets, throws the math caps, steals pens out of other pupils' hands. I try to make her stop, but once she has something in her mind, there seems to be no way to adjust her course. Given the language barrier, I can't even talk with her… ahhh. Frustration for both of us. In the end I find no other solution than physically putting myself as a human shield between her and her targets. This solves the problem partially and temporarily. She is short but incredibly strong and I am thankful when Wilburn re-enters the room. Miraculously her aggressive behavior stops. All at once she sits nicely in her little chair and quietly draws a picture. Wilburn gives me an 'I know' look and throws her the evil eye. He picks up where he left off.

Around 11am the kids eat. Today, the food bucket is half-filled with rice and topped up with warm milk. It is more than a drink, but not quite lunch. Apparently, it does deserve the same prayer as yesterday, so hands are folded and He, the blue eyed poster on the wall is thanked for the *día* and the *comer*. There is some extra food, and, as before, the '*Profe*' offers us some; Leendert accepts. I do too. The milk comes with a packet of quinoa tea crackers. Not bad. We feel more integrated as we slurp down the food from the plastic mugs.

After the cups are emptied, the kids get their morning recess. Some are tasked to wash the beakers. This is done at outdoor sinks, next to the sport field and toilets. Just like yesterday, several kids latch onto us and we promenade around the building. Heidi informs me that her teacher disappeared after ten minutes, and that she is not sure what to do with the food that was being provided. Needless to say, I see a sigh of relief when her teacher reappears.

The following class hour is rather mundane. Our class knits and puts beads on chains in preparation for the Christmas festival. Except for a little intervention to untangle a piece of wool it does not really require any outside support. As I help out it remains tricky for me to get a feeling of progress, purpose or sense. Then it dawns on me. Our contribution is not so much the 'teaching'. Our real gift is to the teachers. Our presence gives them the flexibility to walk out for a moment, to have another grown-up interaction, to spend a bit of extra time with each student.

By 12:30 we leave the school grounds. At home a clear vegetable soup awaits us, followed by pasta. Spanish class consumes our afternoon. Evening dinner, – yes, you anticipated- a repeat of the pasta lunch, no soup, but yes on the flat breads.

The third morning is fully routine. No stress. We start with breakfast and walk to school. We feel local. As we approach the entry gate, one of the kids from class sees me and shuffles as fast as she can towards us. Running is difficult due to her handicap, but she outpaces who I assume

In Pursuit of Chocolate

to be her granddad. She catches up with us and grabs my hand. It is nice to get this 'I-recognize-you-and-like-you' moment of affection. We walk the remaining two hundred meters to the gate and I notice the chaperone granddad follows us. He probably wants to make sure this 'white person' does indeed go into the school grounds. We wave a friendly goodbye from a distance as I cross the school playground with her towards class.

Classes go well. Both Leendert and I are now comfortable with the kids, and we get hugs upon arrival. Leendert has moved from 'statue-mode' while receiving hugs to returning the embrace. The activities in class are a repeat act, though we do get some excitement. Right outside our classroom, in the open air, three big cakes are being prepared. Kids take turn to help. It is a laborious task. Batter is mixed and in parallel two dozen egg whites are whisked by hand with a plastic fork; I guess speed is not essential, and this keeps the team busy.

The batter is made in a big bowl, under teacher supervision. Wilburn spends much time outside and Leendert and I entertain the ten remaining kids. At one point 'difficult Caroline' acts up again and I am glad it happens just as Wilburn peeks into the room. He physically takes her outside, and she is punished by having to stand silently facing the gymnasium wall. By mid-morning we let Leendert and Alicia skip class, sort of. Their escape is into the gym where, high on the bleachers, they get to do their own homework: the study of the Inca empire.

I chat with Heidi, who reports that she saw the school principle threaten Caroline 'the bully' with 'the nettles'. As it turns out, if someone like Caroline is behaving badly, the physical punishment is touching their hands with nettles. My first reaction is disapproval, but upon reflection I find that I change my views. In fact, I pass through understanding to approving. If mentally one cannot get through, if you can't isolate the young adult as punishment (there really is no place to put them and you run the risk of them wandering off), you need to let them know not to hurt other kids, and you do not want to hit them (for a host of reasons), the benefit of a non-violent, short pain of a plant starts to make sense. I am sure that pedagogically there are better solutions, but for the moment they escape me.

Towards the end of the morning, I too, help make the cake batter. Stirring the dough is hard work (very heavy and sticky) and my effort is most appreciated. At set intervals, liquid is added making stirring a bit easier, but it is still hard work, enough to work up a good sweat. Towards the end, a small bottle of *espirituoso* is emptied into the mixture. The teacher smiles and winks, *receta especial* (special recipe) she says.

The rest of the day goes well. I trace a model Christmas tree multiple times on a large piece of thin green corrugated carton. The kids will cut these out later. Wilburn shows how to get as much out of one single sheet of carton as possible for cost saving purposes. He can fit the various designs together such that there is hardly any scrap paper left. I oblige and can't help flashing back to my French label-printing company, which specializes in printing sheet optimization. They employed specialists and computer programs for this activity. Wilburn could have a job in a heartbeat in their pre-press department.

At the end of the morning, the completer-finisher in me sends Heidi and the kids home alone. I stay a bit later to finish pre-cutting the carton Christmas trees. At our guest house we are well in time for a lovely green spinach soup followed by cauliflower as main dish. From there we rush out to our Spanish lesson. On the way we make a quick stop to book our return flights to Lima. The good news is that the fares are better in the travel agency than on the Internet. Go figure!

We have a good Spanish class. We escape the small, windowless room in the old building and walk to the local market. The vegetables and produce look amazing. We try some local puffed wheat which tastes just like Smacks cereal, a piece of local cheese, and buy some jello. The handiwork on the market (cloths, clothes, bags) also looks beautiful. We buy a wooden spoon as a gift for the lady of the house - we saw her break her spoon the day before by hitting pieces of ice.

A couple of glasses of juice perk us up for the remaining Spanish class. Afterwards, we attempt to suck some cash out of the wall to pay for dinner in a restaurant. We try four different ATM's, but none is willing to offer *dinero*. Darn. Finally, in a dark and dubious small alley we find cash machines that accept our cards. I look paranoid at the single escape route as Heidi punches in her pin codes. The paranoia is luckily misplaced, and loaded with bills, we enter a restaurant recommended by our local volunteer leader Carlos. It is a quiet place and the food and service is excellent. We eat Alpaca steaks and go for a bottle of Peruvian wine, which is quite tasty. The table conversation is about the school we teach at, about how lucky we are. Much contentment, laughter and some teary eyes, the ones only intense happiness can create. We get home well past 11pm and we agree to let the kids sleep in the next day. Only the parents will go to school in the morning.

The next day students 'write' their letters and I keep them from picking on one another. Carton and wooden Christmas trees are cut and painted. The good news is that the Spanish immersion classes are beginning to pay off. As I help the '*profe*' with the distribution of milk and cookies we make light conversation. I comment that some kids share a mug. He explains some mugs had been broken, and there was no budget to replace them. I make note to buy some later that afternoon. The day becomes a sponsor day. The cake we prepared the day before is now for sale. It costs one sol per piece. We not only buy four pieces for the family, but we also tell Wilburn that we will purchase all the remaining squares at the end of the day. As the school day closes I walk away with eight additional pieces. Happy to have donated the additional cash, we also score with the host family who appreciate the dessert we bring home.

That afternoon, we continue Spanish class and do a bit of planning for our trip to Machu Picchu. We visit a place recommended for buying train tickets. The guy offers us not only the train tickets but also van transfer from our hostel to the train station, entry tickets, a private guide for entry into Machu Picchu, and transport back. All-in-all a slightly more expensive deal then doing it in parts, but the hassle-free factor is attractive.

Once we commit, he asks us to pay in cash, saying his Visa equipment is not working. He insists on being paid right then and there. We try various machines and luckily we have enough cards to draw on the different bank accounts for the down payment. As we hand over our soles, he tries his machine "one more time" for the remaining amount. Guess what? It miraculously works. Only at that instant do I recognize the *spiel*. The vendor needs the cash to buy the entry tickets. The way he operates, asking for cash up front, lets him avoid a cashflow issue (and moves the risk to us). He could have just asked!

The entire ordeal takes much more time than anticipated (it is well after 8pm when all is settled), so when we arrive at our host family we are apologetic for having missed dinner. Luckily the cake had bought goodwill. We walk around the block to a local diner serving only *pollo* (chicken). We order a whole chicken and are pleasantly surprised with a bottle of Coke and a big plate of French fries which accompanies the order. They tell us to help ourselves to the salad bar. All that for under the cost of a single burger in the west, not bad! Local families come and go and we appreciate that we have this chance to live outside the touristy center of Cusco.

And so we arrive at the last day of the school week. Quick breakfast, a brisk walk to school; writing, coloring, bottle cap math, avoiding total meltdowns. "The usual". Our class is full – only one child is absent today which means 14 kids fill the very cramped space. Moving from one student to the next requires crawling over the pupils in between. I honestly don't know how the teachers survive without outside volunteer assistance. Since the kids can't work solo, they need constant attention. With only four minutes per child per hour, this is an impossible task, especially if you compound it with the remaining activities that fill the day. Using my newly acquired Spanish skills (heavily blended with French words) I succeed in exchanging thoughts with Wilburn. He repeats time and again that he is appreciative of the help we bring.

The late-morning a snack is provided in the usual bucket. This time it is filled with a white vegetable soup and it comes with supplemental bananas. Personally I never trust white soups. Especially white vegetable soups. Aside from cauliflower what vegetable can make a soup white? However, as Wilburn offers a serving, yet again, I join out of politeness. Afraid to figure out what's in it, I assume it is a local delicacy and scoop the liquid out of a small plastic Tupperware-type bucket into my mouth, having to admit it isn't half bad. A leftover banana is shared between us.

At 12:30 we walk home and have lunch: rice with some beans and - we think - mushrooms. It's white. Hmmm, is there a theme for Fridays? Next we jump in a taxi to the bus station bound for Pisca. We are to meet Miriam for a field trip. In the twenty minutes we wait - she is definitely on island time - we are accosted by at least fifteen people offering rides. Once Miriam arrives we hop a local bus taking us up onto the mountains above Cusco.

The top-down view of the city is impressive. In what appears the middle of nowhere, the van drops us off. We find ourselves at Cochuahuasi, a privately run animal sanctuary. This place specializes in saving injured and endangered animals. The real attractions are puma's, wild cats and condors, but it has space fillers like various types of lama's, a typical Peruvian dog (which has no hair and a body temperature of 39 degrees), turtles, a stork, rabbits, and guinea pigs. The condor is an especially impressive animal which captures our attention. We learn that: (1) while it is a meat eater, it only eats dead, red meat - the bird has no claws and therefore cannot attack or kill; (2) with a wingspan of 3.20 meters, it is the largest bird in the world; (3) condors can live eighty or ninety years; (4) they fly at 70km/hr and are often injured by flying into above ground electrical cables; (5) they only lay one egg every two to three years which impedes the growth of their population. So much for today's biology lesson. The team at the sanctuary makes one of the condors fly towards us, and it lands just a couple of meters behind us. Trust me, when this monstrosity comes at you, you hope that the caretakers are right and that it is not an attack bird!

Later, we learn about Alpaca wool, specifically how they are stained using plants and parasites. We visit an operational Lama/Alpaca farm and see traditionally dressed women sitting on the ground weaving Peruvian scarfs by hand. We chat with one of them who tells us she has the pattern in her head, no samples are used. A cloth of 45cm wide by 140cm long takes about one month to finish. She expresses her gratitude in having the chance to sell her beautiful wares.

Unfortunately, that afternoon Leendert is not feeling well, suffering from stomach cramps. Miriam is nice enough to arrange a cup of *mate* tea (coca leafs), but the situation does not improve much, and on the way back in the bus Leendert is in bad shape. Further proof that Leendert is unwell is that he is not interested in dinner that evening. The lady of the house offers him another tea, which he drinks, but not with pleasure. I pray he recovers quickly as we are planning to go to Machu Picchu tomorrow; a trip which I have been looking forward to for months. In fact, months before, sitting on the couch in our house in France, we had decided to splurge on this part of the trip. You only visit a place like Machu Picchu once in your life, and we were going to make it count. We were going to do it in style, so we booked the Belmond Hotel. Horrendously expensive, but the only hotel at the gates of Machu Picchu. Leendert better get well soon!

Machu Picchu

At 5:50 Alicia and Leendert remove themselves from the blankets and sheets. The process is smoother than anticipated and Leendert reportedly recovered from his stomach ache. We slip out the front door and walk to the main street for our taxi pick up. Though they are supposed to be there at 6:20, there is no sign of the promised private van by 6:35. We start to worry since there is a train to catch. Per Murphy's Law, my phone is dead so we decide to split up. I wait at the rendezvous point, Heidi walks back home to charge the phone and dial from a landline. Five minutes later, the van arrives, so I run back to get Heidi, who just got off the phone with the lady in the car sitting next to the driver. We get in and start the trip.

Into Cusco town we go. We experienced what is best described as a 'switch-a-person' game. First, we drop off the lady who Heidi had called on the phone. Next, we stop at the market where it appears the brother, mother and nephew of the driver get in. We drive a few kilometers further, and the mother and nephew get out. The game continues, and the driver explains his brother is *cansado* (tired) because he has worked through the night. About 15 minutes further into the trip, our driver gets out, and the 'tired' brother takes over the wheel. Now that seems like a good idea!

Needless to say, for the next ninety minutes I watch the brother's eyes and the frequency of his blinking like a hawk. The roads through the Andes are far from monotonous, winding left and right, up and down. The 'brother' stays fairly awake. Luckily, he does not pull stupid stunts like most others around us: no passing in blind turns, no clipping close to pedestrians, no speeding through towns oblivious to road side activities. The kids listen to music with Alicia having an earplug in her non-dominant ear to avoid car sickness. Placebo or not? Who cares, as long as it works! Heidi and I enjoy the landscape. We gaze at the incredible peaks, some covered with snow, and observe the local bright colored Peruvians making their way along the road, seemingly to nowhere. Lots of women with traditional hats, wearing cloths around their shoulders, with babies or parcels wrapped inside. Peru seems to be a country devoid of strollers. Perhaps it is the landscape or road conditions, more likely the cost. Either way, no babies are transported in luxury 8-wheeled padded chairs with seat belts like we observe in the west; in Peru a simple cloth will do. Under one year old up front, over one year old in a pouch on the back. Simple as that.

We wind through the Andes, and ninety minutes later the van arrives at the train station. We get our passports checked (I don't know what for) and make a short stop in the station restaurant. While we wait for two cokes, two cappuccinos and a couple of sandwiches, Heidi scouts the *baños*. The cokes are partially to help settle the stomachs of the kids, because their intestines seem to be acting up again. The bathrooms are deemed acceptable, so we take turns visiting while the others protect the backpacks. We slurp down the (great) coffees and colas, grab the warmed Paninis and hop onto the train which drives up, of course, minutes after we had ordered our food and drinks.

The 'vista train' is beautiful. It has luxury seats, a half glass ceiling and assigned seating. Soft background music fills our ears as the train sets off. To our surprise the average speed is well below 25km/hr. We enjoy the views of the snow-capped mountain ranges and take lots of pictures. At one point in time Leendert asks for his iPad and I tell him I won't even dignify the question with an answer. I also let him know that I'll get back to him later about this request in a one-on-one. When later that day I do, and he admits that while he was getting a bit bored with all the steep mountains, in hindsight looking and observing this unique part of the world is probably better than getting lost in his iPad game.

On the train we get an unexpected, positive surprise. Coffees, lemonade, two pastries and nectarines are served as we chug along. We find ourselves in heaven; luxury seats, good food, great company and lovely scenery, what more can one want? We have stunning views of the mountains and catch glimpses of the famous Inca trail sprinkled with hikers making their way to Machu Picchu. We see great peaks and the river right next to us. About 1.5 hours later we arrive in the train station of Aguas Calientes (translation: Water Warm) – a town known for its hot springs. As we exit the station, a lady awaits us with a name sign and we walk through the little town and some tourist markets to the main square. A short wait, and our guide helps us on a bus. She stays behind, but confirms that our guide will be in the Belmond Sanctuary Lodge at 13:00 for our afternoon tour of Machu Picchu. So far, so good.

The bus-ride is a scary twenty minutes, zig-zagging up a small steep road. Only at special bays can downward bus traffic pass. Once on top, we exit the bus and to our delight see that we are at the entry of the Machu Picchu site. We also find ourselves smack in front of the hotel. Ascending the steps of the hotel we make ourselves known and the bellboy relieves us of our backpacks as he ushers us politely to the front desk. A quick glance at our passports (did I mention they love checking passports in Peru?), and we are told 'please follow me, so we can make your check-in more pleasurable'. We follow the clerk into the lounge, where we park ourselves on comfy sofa while she tells us about the hotel.

In headlines: we can have lunch as of noon, there is a day room available (including showers) for our use till our room is ready, the train station in Aguas Calientes has a lounge for our convenience (for when we depart). If we would like a drink right now? How many bags do we have? Might we want to make a reservation for dinner this evening? Do we require additional oxygen in our rooms to avoid altitude sickness? Would we like a guided tour of the hotel's orchid garden and spice garden? Would we like to partake in the Pisco tasting later this evening? Might we be interested in the Inca presentation? Would we be willing to follow her to see the location of the outside jacuzzi overlooking Machu Picchu, and would we prefer to do so before or after we finish our welcome glass of champagne? … with apologies that our rooms will only be available as of one o'clock.

My heart leaps with joy. This is exactly what we had hoped for. Bathing in luxury for a day and a half. The stark contrast with the accommodation of the last weeks could not be greater and makes it twice as pleasurable. We enjoy the outside, look at the whirlpool, repack our backpack in the day-room, and walk through the Orchid garden with a 'picture menu of flora' in hand. Soon it is noon, and we move to the restaurant for lunch.

The food is worldly and outrageously good. What's more, it comes at a leisurely French pace. Therefore, at one o'clock, I walk into the reception area to find Juan, our guide, and tell him we are not quite ready to go yet. He joins us at the lunch table, while we finish our main dishes and glasses of champagne. The waiter is attentive and hilariously funny. One of his best wisecracks is to offer us freshly ground pepper on our mains, stating with a straight face that "today it is free of charge". Knowing the backdrop and the obscene amount of money we transferred from our bank account to the Belmond for the pleasure of staying there brings tears to my eyes, twice.

Our guide, on the other hand, seems slightly less on the ball. Without trying to be funny, he explains that we should drink a lot of water. Water is good for altitude sickness "as it is H2O, and it is the lack of 'O' - which he informs us stands for oxygen - which creates the sickness". Leendert gives me a puzzled look, and for a moment our table discussion switches to Dutch, out of politeness.

After our impeccable lunch, we are ready to walk to the main gates where we get to show our passports. I might have mentioned Peruvians and their passport obsession, but the use in this case seriously escapes me. We climb up a stone stairway and peek through a clearing between the leaves. Heidi comments it is breath-taking. No kidding – at this altitude! I quip she should grab a glass of water. We get to the first and probably the most famous photo opportunity spot. I notice we breathe more easily than most tourists around us, a benefit of having acclimated in Cusco - the town is substantially higher than is Machu Picchu. We soak in the view and enjoy one of the seven construction wonders of the world.

Rain, sun and rainbows alternate continuously over the next three hours. As might have been anticipated after our guide's lunchtime comments, he is okay, but not great. Perhaps I am a hard judge, but I expected him to be an expert. Having read a book about Hiram Bingham who 'discovered' the site (or at least promoted it) - as well as two other Inca chronicles, I know the basics; for that I don't need a guide. The kids, too, have read up on the old culture, so we expect some deeper insights, not just what can be read in the tourist fliers. It is not to be. Nevertheless, the guide does lead us through the various points of interest, and he becomes the replacement of our selfie-stick. Clearly he is experienced in taking pictures, and we end up shooting over six hundred pictures.

By late afternoon we return to the Belmond and are informed our backpacks are in our rooms and 'tea is being served'. We order drinks and scavenge the buffet (salmon, caviar, scones, chocolate dipped strawberries, etc…). Following tea, we quickly put on our bathing suits, wrap ourselves in thick, heavy bath robes and walk up the path to the jacuzzi. Only two other people are around; one to bring fresh towels, the other to take (and bring) the orders of drinks – Champagne and Lemonade.

The water is very hot so we find ourselves popping in-and-out for the next hour, drinking our drinks, chatting and overlooking Machu Picchu. We miss, but don't miss, the Pisco tasting but make it in time for the Inca presentation. Heidi and I upload the pictures and reduce the number from 600 to 150. That evening, the kids believe they in heaven; *"fois gras* for a starter!". They jump for joy as the plates are presented; *fois gras poêlé* is their favorite. We enjoy sea bass, alpaca steak and French wine. By 10pm Heidi and the kids are ready for bed. I stay up, grab the computer and go to the lounge where, slowly sipping a Bailey's, I am intensely happy that Heidi agreed not to set the alarm for tomorrow. If we wake up early, great, we'll enter the Machu Picchu site at sunrise. If not, no big deal, we have a leisurely breakfast and then enter…

Trouble at Machu Picchu

But then again, not everything goes according to plan. At four in the morning I hear soft knocking on the door. Popping out of bed I find a distressed Leendert, holding his tummy. He is not a happy bunny. From his posture and white face I can see he is in serious pain. Instantly the thought 'doctor at Machu Picchu' flashes through my brain. Heidi remains asleep as Leendert crawls into my spot of the bed after an attempt at the toilet. His usual six-pack is hard as a rock and he needs to pull his knees up to his chest to get even a little bit of relief. Time and again he needs to go to the bathroom [with apologies for the graphic detail of the next paragraphs].

On the porcelain bowl, he tries to get rid of whatever is bothering him, but not much more than gas exits his body. His entire belly is rock-hard. Still in the bathroom I talk to him. He relaxes slightly, only to suddenly switch around and put his face in the place where you normally don't want it. He attempts to throw up, but, again, ninety-nine percent is air. The only thing escaping his cramped body is pretty awful sound. It's one of those moments as a parent that you wish you could take over their suffering and pain. Once the waves are over, I cool him down with a washcloth, wiping the sweat from his face. Ten minutes later he is back in bed and despite the dark of the night I notice he has more color on his face than before. Unfortunately, the rest of the night does not get much better for him. We have several repeat sessions, with me wondering how much air a child's body can store.

Heidi, meanwhile, has joined the festivities and commenced an internet search. It appears that the 'gas problem' some of us are experiencing might be part are known as HAFE (High-altitude flatus expulsion), more lovingly known as "the toots". Needless to say, the increased quantities of rectal gases can be rather annoying and painful in the bowels. We also learn that causes of flatulence can be one of three: (1) the difference in pressure (simple physics), (2) CO_2 transferring from blood to intestinal gas, or (3) a systematic dietary change. Since the first two occur soon after rapid ascents, I rule these out. The dietary change has, however, been part of our lives and is - according to my clinical diagnosis - the culprit. Yes, I know doctors will get upset since I might seem to confuse their eight years of medical education with a quick Google do-it-yourself-internet-doctor, but we are not talking brain surgery here. Either way, we all seem to enjoy the '(alti-)tude toots' to a certain extent. Leendert will just have to manage as best he can. Given that the color is back in his face and that he is out of the pain zone, we leave him in our bed with the TV remote while Heidi and I go downstairs for a morning coffee and croissant. It has been raining for hours and is not letting up at all. In fact, it is pouring so hard that the glass veranda of the restaurant can't cope with the deluge of water. It drips down from the ceiling, and the staff is apologetic, continuously mopping and placing buckets strategically around the room.

By 9 a.m. we return to the bedroom, awaken Alicia, take Leendert and have breakfast together. The rain turns to a drizzle. Leendert only eats two pieces of dry toast and acts the part, Alicia mentions a headache. I lean on the family; "you are in Machu Picchu only once in your life. We are in a unique and superb place. Enjoy it!". It sounds slightly like; 'the beatings will continue until morale improves', but it seems to work. Everyone agrees to at least try walking to the Sun Gate, up the Inca Trail.

As they go up to change, I stop at reception and to arrange to keep one room for a late checkout. This is my safety net just in case Leendert needs to return after 500 meters. We pack a small bag and go to the entrance gate. The heavens still sprinkle us abundantly. There is a queue to get in, but we walk through the shorter "foreigner" line. On certain days, the Peruvians get in at a reduced rate (or free), which explains the other longer lines.

We wind our way up the muddy path and realize how lucky we were the day before with the weather and the limited crowds. The people in front and behind us today are mostly wearing colorful thin plastic poncho's in an attempt to stay dry. Heidi remarks that it looks as if a box of Quality Street sweets has been spread over the Machu Picchu site.

We move away from the main site and start walking the Inca Trail. The hikers we encounter are on their final mile. Going the opposing direction they look at us with disdain. I can hear them think "losers", and part of me wished we had tried the hike.

The trail is about three meters wide, and is impressively well laid. The stone path is made of big rocks, in parts carved out of the mountain-side. We get wet, but it is far from cold. Soon Alicia and I remove the zip-off part of our pants. Leendert is touching his belly, still hurting, but hangs in. After thirty minutes Alicia is reporting pain in her heel. Sometimes she has growing pains. Her bones growing quicker than the tendons can keep up. Nervous, as the same pain put her on crutches only months before, Heidi decides to take her back. I'm happy we didn't check out and have our late check-out room. Leendert decides, against my expectations, to go on. We trot on for another 25 minutes. Leendert hands me some of his coca-candy which reportedly helps settle his stomach. At times we catch glances of the Machu Picchu site between the clouds. We shoot pictures, glad to have taken the underwater camera. At the Sun Gate we take the required 'selfies', turn, and start the descent. Leendert perks up, feeling better and better. We end up having some great father-son time. Lots of laughter as we hobble down, both commenting on being happy we decided to go on despite the general conditions.

Back at the hotel, we decide to head down the mountain. We want to avoid the late rush, walk around town and use the hotel service lounge in Aguas Calientes while we wait for the train. Having settled the bill, a bellboy helps us to the bus stand, twenty meters from the hotel entrance. As expected, there is a queue as the first wave of people leave to catch the train back to Cusco. The bellboy tells us to sit on a bench near our baggage. He walks off towards the queue and disappears. A bit confused, we look around. The kids take their last pictures of the hotel and I try to figure out what the bellboy is up to. I spot him. He went to stand into line for us, complements of the Belmond! Once his turn is up, he walks over, grabs our bags and we hop on the bus. Wow, the Belmond at Machu Picchu. If you can afford it, do it!

The trip down the mountain is quick and frightening. I try to balance looking outside, soaking up the view, and ignoring how steep the abyss is fifty centimeters to the side of the tires. I don't like small sandy mountain roads when I am not at the wheel!

We spend the next 2.5 hours in Aguas Calientes. Despite the acclaimed hot water springs, I am convinced the sole existence of this town is to offer Machu Picchu visitors a place to sleep, eat, buy souvenirs, do their laundry and get a massage. None of these are of interest to us, but we settle for a pizza to kill time. Sitting on the patio we notice a lady lighting an outside pizza oven with wood, so expectations rise. Unfortunately, thirty minutes later we get served a poor excuse of Hawaiian pizza; bored and disappointed, the kids argue if it has pineapple on it or not. We settle the bill which is inversely related to the size of pizzas and meander through the tourist stalls of town, waiting for the train departure. The train takes us all the way back to Ollantaytambo (yes, I had to look that up) where a driver waits for us. Driving back we are in good spirits and play a letter game (name an animal, a food, a place, famous person, etc. "with a …. 'P' "). Back in Cusco we settle back into the simple accommodation of our host family's home and get ready for our regular school day tomorrow.

The second week - with a twist

Incredible how, again, within one week we have grown accustomed to a new reality. It feels as if we've been here for ages. Classes are a repeat of the previous week; help to write, assist counting bottle tops, hold hands tracing big letters, sharpen colored pencils, wash hands, scoop milk and rice in cups, do artsy–crafty stuff. The kids help half the time and do schoolwork in the gym. In the afternoon we subject ourselves to Spanish class and irregular verbs. We use the mid-afternoon break to pop by "Plastic 2000". It is an impressive store with anything imaginable made of plastic. We find buckets, mugs and boxes to donate to the school. Dinner is as dinner is, a repeat of lunch, but with bread and jam on the side. Simple routine days. It's quite nice, actually.

Wednesday should have been a routine day, but it was not… After the usual bread, instant coffee, egg, jam, and maple syrup breakfast we walk to school to find it in a state of general arousal and excitement. Large pieces of paper are being decorated with texts. Posters are tacked to wooden frames. Teachers are hustling back and forth. I notice more parents than usual hanging around. It takes a while before we understand what is going on - a protest march is being organized. Once the signs are finished, the kids are gathered in the schoolyard. Wilburn asks me to keep an eye on the kids as he needs to run out for a moment.

As I stand with the kids, I try to find out what the protest is all about. They are taking action because their new school, which they have been awaiting for years, is still not finished. They are going to march, but I am unclear where. Looking around with two challenged Peruvian kids holding my hands, I catch myself scanning to see if the entire class is present and accounted for. I check if they are holding the signs the right way up. Most are. Next, I ask myself (and Heidi) if we should be part of this. Am I really about to join the first protest march of my life? Should we protest while not knowing quite what the demands are? Is it not a bit weird to walk in a march if you don't know where it is physically going? For a moment the thought crosses my mind - 'can a foreigner be arrested in Peru for protesting?'. I decide that asking attention for the conditions in which these kids are taught is more than reasonable. Creating awareness is definitely not a bad thing. And let's be clear, I am here as a volunteer to help these children; who am I to choose how that is best done? Let's not worry if our contribution is supporting a loftier long term cause or helping them walk safely over the road to wherever the protest takes us.

The march starts, and one block down the road we pick up a second batch of students. It is unclear if the organizers want us to be on the sidewalk or the middle of the road, but as the march grows in size, the group consensus seems to be to go across the whole street. Soon, oncoming traffic comes to a halt. Traffic from behind goes at the pace of the slowest physically challenged student. And that is slow. To my surprise, I don't hear much more honking than is usual for Cusco.

Walking in the middle of the road protests might appear no big deal, but you may underestimate the solid training mentally handicapped kids receive when they are young. I notice that each of my three hand-holding subjects (on one hand I have two) have all been well trained. They know that traffic is dangerous and that they should walk on the sidewalk, not on the street. Keeping them in the middle of the road is a challenge. Luckily I get pulled from both sides keeping me more or less in the middle.

We march for less than a kilometer and stop in front of a building. It turns out that this is the new school-to-be. The brand-new building sits exactly between two roads. Logistically, this is good news. Traffic finds an easy alternative going one block around. Except for one small incident of a stubborn driver trying to get through, all goes well. The driver fails miserably by the way. A few teachers, parents, myself and a committed group of students stand fast, unwilling to budge. Ultimately, the driver backs up to find an alternative route to his destination, wildly waving his arms outside of the window.

I am puzzled why we are standing in front of the building, since no one seems to be on site except for a lone painter. The protest continues however, whistles blowing, road blocked. I seriously regret not having put on sunscreen this morning. The high-altitude sun burns my head and face. More and more people seek slivers of shade, but my three musketeers, now convinced that standing in the middle of the road is the cool thing to do, hold the line and refuse to move despite my efforts to guide them off the street to a less sunny spot.

The sunlight is sharp, but the temperature is manageable. Some parents, well-prepared, offer the kids drinks, fruit and jello. A local lady smells a business opportunity and sells watermelon. Heidi's motherly instinct takes over, as does the entrepreneurship of the local lady. The result? Heidi gets some of the water-filled fruit for the desperately thirsty-looking kids, the lady a great price as she notices her client is not a local.

After about an hour a man with sunglasses (rarely seen in Cusco) and a briefcase (also not seen here) shows up. He interacts with what seems to be the spokesperson of the school (or at least the one most vocal). After ten minutes he is on his way out. He passes us and asks if we are volunteers. Our 'yes' get answered with "thank you, you do good work, it is much needed". Not much later, a sunglassed duo shows up with a recording device and camera. The noise increases and the signs and protest slogans are waved more vigorously. A news reporter talks to teachers, parents, a student and then walks up to us. Heidi speaks to him for a short while, explaining in her broken Spanish the plight of the students.

To our positive surprise we see some of the school leaders entering the site and talking with representatives of the construction company. They are given a completion date of December 15th. This pleases the leaders and formally ends the protest. We walk back along the road; to the relief of my kiddos we can walk on the sidewalk. I talk to Wilburn - my Spanish has improved to the point were we can have basic conversations, and he conveys his happiness with the outcome of the protest. I inquire as to what prevents the move into the school, since it seemed finished. He tells me the handover is blocked by the electronics. Specifically, the interactive white boards and computers are missing. Really? That is the hold up? What on earth do they need those for? I comment "why not move now and worry about the electronics later", Wilburn nods; *exacto*, that's what they want. The concern is that with the upcoming political elections the buildings might be 're-purposed'. Hence the demonstration.

We return to the existing school yard at recess time. After the ritual hand-washing which marks the end of the break, a bowl of rice is served. The new plastic buckets and spoons we provided are immediately put to good use. There are plenty leftovers, since some parents took their kids home right after the protest. For me, having grown up in Europe with parents who lived through World War II, it is ingrained in me that food may not go to waste - saying no to a bowl of rice seems a waste, so I eat some rice as well.

For the last half hour in school I glue Christmas trees on carton Christmas cards. I have a second lunch at home; rice, potatoes and a little bit of green vegetables as usual. I don't know if it is altitude or something else, but after lunch we are all tired. None of us is in the mood to rush over to Spanish class. I guess the novelty has worn off. We all take a nap, deciding to regain the time by taking a taxi to town rather than walking 40 minutes. Once in class, as usual, Miriam does a great job capturing our interest. This time we learn interesting facts about life in Peru. One of them is that there are no dishwashers. Nowhere. Not even in a city the size of Cusco. You should have seen Leendert's eyes! The simple fact is that the cost of the equipment and especially the potential issues of maintenance afterwards are such that it doesn't make sense. Everyone washes by hand.

The last week in Peru - a second twist

Today started overnight. Suffice it to say that Leendert had a rough night again and the both of us spent the dark hours between his bed and the bathroom. It was a repeat of the morning in Machu Picchu but much more violent and painful. For me, it meant less than three hours of sleep, spending most of the night sitting on the cold edge of a bidet holding and caressing Leendert's head resting on my shoulder. I've heard that child birth is painful, I know from experience that kidney stones are unpleasant, but sitting on the edge of a cold bidet for a full night gets close to the same category. Having said that, I suspect Leendert's discomfort may have surpassed them all. Given the painful night, Heidi stays home the next morning with the kids and seeks a doctor's advice for Leendert. I consider skipping school, but duty calls, so I walk to class on my own.

School is uneventful other than the teachers making apple pie. It seems appropriate since tomorrow is Thanksgiving. I try to explain the concept of Thanksgiving to the teachers, but I am fairly sure I fail. My limited Spanish could not convey the reasoning of why all Americans would eat turkey, pumpkin and apple pie on one particular Thursday in November.

Five minutes before the official end of class Wilburn tells me to go home and "see how Leendert is doing". I am grateful, and do as instructed. As usual in these matters, Heidi made the right call. They visited a medical center and Leendert got the full check-up. It turned out he had both an intestinal infection and parasites. I feel guilty for having pushed him to eat the school food, as well as for pushing him so hard at Machu Picchu. Probably neither was the wisest choice.

The good news is that the drugs are very effective and Leendert recovers quickly. By lunch he eats a bit, ready to attack Spanish classes in the afternoon. Miriam decides to split us from the kids, and Heidi and I get separate lessons. Miriam pops back and forth between us. During the break, a game of bingo helps us cement the Spanish numbers, and afterwards we go on an excursion. We walk into town and visit the chocolate museum. It is quite interesting and overflowing with educational facts. Here is what we learned:

Cocoa beans come from a yellow/orange fruit which looks like a large melon (a bit like a wrinkled American football). It grows on the stem of the tree, not the branches. The beans have a soft mango-like meat around them, which protects the (white) core. This core holds many large pits (in the middle, like a melon). Once the fruit is picked, the white pits are removed and placed for up to seven days in wooden crates on trays lined with banana leaves. This creates fermentation and enhances flavor development. Next, the beans are laid in the sun to dry. Afterwards, they are roasted, again to alter and improve the taste. Well dried, they are now easy to peel. The outside of the cocoa bean (the peel) can be used for tea (which we try and find quite tasty). Last, the nut is pressed which creates a cocoa paste. Pressing this further leads to cocoa butter and ultimately cocoa powder. We learn about the key people responsible for the inception of the chocolate industry: The Dutchman 'Van Houten' invented the cocoa press making it a mechanical and industrial process; the Swiss based 'Nestle' was the first to add milk to cocoa powder (until then it was just mixed with water); and the Brit Cadbury and the American Hershey, made the product available to the masses, rather than just the elite.

The cocoa bean has its origin in Latin America and was transported by the colonials to other regions. The French and English took it to Africa, the Dutch carried it to Indonesia. Today 35% of the world cocoa beans come from the Ivory Coast. One last chocolate factoid, the Aztecs (in Mexico) used cocoa beans as their currency. During their reign, an egg cost about three beans, a rabbit 20 beans, and a chicken 300 beans. Clearly it was a luxury item (and it still is). The museum is a great introduction to chocolate and makes us keen to go to the 'chocolate making' class which we book before we leave. Needless to say, we buy a couple of bars-purely for research purposes.

In Pursuit of Chocolate

And so we get to our last day of volunteer work in Cusco. As we gather our things and have our flat bread breakfast, it feels different. Somehow, knowing that it is the last day at school changes everything. I can't decipher if it is sadness about leaving or happiness for a respite from the fast-paced days we have been living - morning teaching and full afternoon Spanish lessons was tougher than we had anticipated. It is also different because today it is the 'exhibition day' at school. The hard work of the pupils from the last weeks will be on display.

Walking into the school yard one senses that something special is going on. The students are hustling, cleaning up the ground, taking tables and chairs out of the classrooms, preparing the display areas outside. I finish the last elements of the Christmas cards before helping with the external set-up. By 9:30 everything is in place and music plays through a mobile speaker. The director of the school graces us with a long speech through a bullhorn, only to be outdone by the gym teacher who takes the microphone next. Only a few parents attend the ceremony but the orators don't seem to mind, discernibly enjoying the airtime and hearing their own voices.

The next hour is spent looking at the products made by the different classes. We talk to the students and chat with the coordinator from the volunteering organization who came to visit. We purchase some of the cake, which is fabulously fluffy. Alicia likes one of the knit hats, so we invest ten Soles. After the event, we move everything back into the classrooms and I reflect with Wilburn. From our class we only had three parents visiting, which, to me, was somewhat disappointing; but it was better than some other classes. The end of the fair also turns out to be the end of school day, and for us the end of the volunteering project. For some reason, Wilburn ushers me back into the classroom and attempts to do the same with Leendert and Alicia. We look puzzled. He also wants to know where Heidi is. It takes me a moment to figure out what is going on. Inside, on the table, I notice plastic cups, a plate of the fluffy cake, a bottle of regular Coke and one with Inca Cola. Note: Inca Cola is a yellow Peruvian soft drink which the Coca Cola company tried to displace but failed. In the end they accepted defeat and bought a large stake in the Inca Cola company. But I digress. We find Heidi, and over the next minutes all the teachers, the director and the school security guard gather in the small classroom. They planned a 'going away party' for us. Crowded around the table on the small kindergarten chairs they give us an official 'thank you'.

We're all very touched. Leendert admits later, as we walk from the school after the obligatory hugs and kisses from both profe's and remaining students, that leaving is a bit sad. Making our way home we pass the new

–almost finished– school. I notice I am genuinely happy for the teachers and kids we leave behind. We take a quick snapshot of the building and continue home, quietly praying the new school will open soon.

The remaining days in Cusco are filled with tourism. We visit Moray, an Inca agricultural lab (now Unesco site) where the Inca's created microclimates in a terraced thermometer-shaped area. They experimented with various plants (potato, corn, etc.) and tried combinations of various natural fertilizers (alpaca, guano, sheep, etc.). It served as their agricultural university and research center. We go to Maras, a salt mine which has a natural water source spitting steaming hot water which is three times saltier than the ocean. We see many old Inca sites. We have cooking classes where we make a local drink called *Chicha Morada*, *Crema de Moraya* (a soup), and as a main course *Aji de Gallina* (a chicken dish with peanut sauce)… all over rice, of course. We re-visit the chocolate museum, dine out in restaurants and feast on guinea pig, deciding it definitely tastes like soapy chicken.

On our last night with our host family we cook for them. We prepare a typical Dutch dish *"hutspot"* (a mash of carrots, onions and potatoes) with meatballs. Cooking turns out to be somewhat of a challenge because (1) at the Cusco altitude water boils at a much lower temperature, hence cooking carrots take ages, (2) the burners are small and I am cooking for many people in two large pans, (3) we don't have a 'stamper' (a tool to mash the potatoes), (4) there is no beer or wine in the house to support the cook, (5) basic spices like pepper and curry are not in the house. Luckily, Heidi is able to run out to the local store and remedy (4) which means I can gulp down some lovely Chilean red wine pretending the other issues don't exist.

The last supper is a hit. I tell the story of *"hutspot"*, which is one rooted in Dutch history. The headline is that during the Spanish occupation in 1574, the city of Leiden was besieged for a long time. All of a sudden, the Spanish gave up and left. According to one story, their departure happened so suddenly that they left food in the pots on the fire. The starved city feasted on the meal left behind. The tradition in Leiden still calls for white bread, herring and *hutspot* to be prepared every year on the third of October. As I tell this story to our Andean mountain hosts, we feel a kind of a kinship. It was that same century (in 1531) that the Spanish arrived in Peru. They plundered its wealth (gold) and started the religious inquisition. They introduced diseases which killed ninety percent of the Incas in less than eighty years. Let's just say that the old head of the household, who still speaks Quechua, loved the story of the Spanish being defeated (I am sure partially because I told the story in my broken Spanish, which added insult to the Spanish). Lots of reflection, laughter, and joy over a very simple meal.

The next morning we gathered our backpacks, exchange gifts, hugs and kisses and leave for the airport. As we pass 'our' school and realize this episode had come to an end, we have mixed feelings. There is a sense of excitement about the next part of our voyage but also a sentiment of sadness leaving behind the kids behind we had cared for for the past two weeks. Peru was wonderful. I promised myself I would promote it whenever I had the chance. So go!

Alexander van 't Riet

Australia - No Volunteering but Wildly Educational

AS WE LEFT PERU WE jumped in rapid succession from Florida to California to Fiji to Australia. It felt like we were soaked in luxury in all those spots. Great meals with vegetables of every color of the rainbow, big fluffy beds, thick bedroom carpets, shopping in Palo Alto, the Golden Gate bridge, coconuts and cava in Fiji. The only thing we missed was the ninth of December. Not because we drank too much of the hallucinatory cava, but because we traveled West, and thus flew through the date line. Fiji Airlines performed the magical trick of getting us in a split second from December eighth to the tenth. Logically I understand, though "losing a day" remains a strange concept.

It probably doesn't come as a surprise that our visit to Australia was not driven by a volunteering project. Don't get me wrong, many environmental conservation and wildlife protection programs exist, but we weren't attracted to those. This chapter provides contrast to other places we visited and gives a short snapshot how family life, education and joyous moments blended into our journey. After a short stop in Sydney with friends, we find ourselves in the north east of Australia, the area of the Great Barrier Reef. This is where we pick up the timeline again.

For ten days, we settle into an apartment, two bedrooms and two bathrooms. Oh, how wonderful. We finally hit a long-anticipated 'break in Port Douglas'. At last a breather in our otherwise hectic lives. Ten days without packing and repacking backpacks. Yes, I know what you are thinking; how dare they complain, being on the trip they are? But let he who has had this arduous life of continuous family travel 24/7 for nearly 60 days in a row throw the first stone!

I think I actually caught Heidi do a pleasure-dance this morning as she looked into the fridge and realized that all items in it were hers. What made it even better was that she could scan for gaps, and plan for a grocery run. Interesting how what strikes us in "normal" life as a chore can be transformed into moments of absolute bliss under different circumstances!

I will spare the reader from a detailed report of our month in Australia and focus on some specific days of fun events and the schoolwork we did with the kids. Hopefully it provides a flavor of how we blended education with our overall journey.

Visiting the Wildlife center - Biology day

You might remember I am not the biggest animal lover. Nevertheless, after a lazy morning in Port Douglas, Heidi convinces me to go on a tour at the local wildlife reserve. We fetch the kids from the pool, make quick sandwiches and we are off. We arrive in time for the tour and purchase bags to 'feed the roos'.

The reserve consists of three habitats: the grasslands, the wetlands, and the rainforest. A guide first takes us through the rainforest where the various birds are pointed out. Next, she gives a presentation on koalas. Fascinating animals. We learn that koala in Aboriginal means "no water", a befitting title since they get almost all their liquids from the pound of Eucalyptus leaves they eat daily. We hear they don't really have natural predators and that they are awake only for two to four hours a day. In these few hours they eat, burp and flatulate (a result of only eating Eucalyptus, a plant which is toxic to humans and many other animals), and they mate. Busy happy hours by the sounds of it, and it makes me wonder if I do not want to be reincarnated as a koala. Too bad it is a myth that the Eucalyptus gives them a permanent high…

The animal lovers in the family get pictures taken holding a koala, and I am happy to support the park by paying the supplemental charge. Interestingly, Queensland is the only place where one can hold a koala. Each koala is restricted to being manhandled a maximum of half an hour per day. A reasonable proposition, since for a koala this could be 25% of its waking hours, and cuts directly into his eating (and farting) time - a fragile balance.

Later, the guide shows us a non-venomous olive python and a small crocodile. We get to touch them both but decline the photo-op; there is a limit to my willingness to 'animal donations'. The guide talks about the power of the croc's mouth. It is the strongest jaw-force of any animal, enough to crunch ice. Interestingly, it's opening force is minimal, which allows the keepers to be safe using only minimal retainers. In our case the little croc has only a small piece of tape wrapped around its snout preventing it from opening it up and doing damage. The guide assures us that even though this is a small animal, the damage can be severe. She has nasty scars on the back of her leg which remain after two rounds of plastic surgery and says: "those I got not from a croc but from a simple Australian lizard".

It never ceases to amaze me how casual the Aussies deal with run-ins with nature. They always seem to brush off incidents as one-time events or something caused by human error: "I shouldn't have moved my leg, the lizard thought it was prey". The guide reminds us that the chance of being killed by a croc is much smaller than being killed in a car accident. I find this a funny parallel, since I consciously decide to be close to a car, but not a croc – the latter pretends to be a log in the water and appears suddenly out of the blue having decided you are a tasty lunch. Cars don't have that same unpredictable behavior (though I have to admit in some counties I've visited over the years, the predictability of drivers might make crocs a safer bet).

We move on to the grasslands tour. Heidi and the kids hand feed the marsupials, many sizes and versions of Wallaby and Kangaroo. Of course, this is a big hit; the kids have shiny joyful eyes while they caress the furry jumpers. A bit further we see huge pelicans and finally top it off with the park's huge 'pride croc'. The reptile has laid its 4.20-meter body on display on a little beach right next to the fence. I make mental calculations of fence-to-jaw strength and decide the fence is much weaker than a block of ice. Noting the number of people in the park, I conclude the statistical chance of becoming his mid-afternoon snack is minimal, thus catching myself becoming more Australian. Clearly, I already make excuses for potential damage done to my body by nature. And thus we log 'Biology' day.

Physical Education day

It took no effort to get Leendert out of bed this morning. In fact, as we debate if we should give the kids a 'first wake-up call' or give them an additional ten minutes of sleep, Leendert appeared from his bedroom all dressed. In the thirteen years I have known him, I never, and I mean NEVER have seen the lad get into his clothes straight out of bed without an external force acting upon him (school, his mother,…). Needless to say, he is excited.

We inhale a quick breakfast, and at exactly the agreed time, a coach picks us up from the front of the house to bring us to the harbor. We walk down the docks to the 'Calypso' and register. Leendert and I complete a form, as the two of us are booked for an introductory scuba dive. A moment of concern arises as I answer 'yes' to the question "are you taking any medication?". Luckily it fades into the background as a diving doctor is called. He does not foresee that the anti-parasitic I have been taking since Sydney (a left-over from Peru school food) will interfere with my dive.

As the vessel moves onto open waters, Leendert and I join the group of diving neophytes and get a sixty-minute theoretical class from our spirited instructor, Lachie. We learn about air pressure, the need to breath (go figure!), how to expel water from a mask while under water, how to recover the mouthpiece if lost and some of the basic hand signals (underwater, 'thumbs up' does not mean all is well – that means 'I need to surface - now').

At the end of the lesson there is a short test. We pass, and off we go. Leendert and I are scheduled for the second of three dives. Following the briefing, we go to the second deck where we find Heidi and Alicia. They have been chatting with the Captain, also named Alicia. Alicia II – the captain - gives us a head's up that it is smart to get our "stinger suits" on as we are about to arrive at the first dive/snorkel stop.

We work our way to the first deck and get handed black – slightly damp - body condoms. This full body armor covers us from ankles to the top of the head (yes it has a hoodie). It covers the arms and includes gloves. While the actual chance of getting hit by a stinger this far from the coast is small, we see it as a free travel insurance. No need to tempt fate when it comes to encounters with Australian nature.

I chat with the instructor and we arrange for Leendert to have a neoprene body suit. Yes, the water is warm, but the last thing we want is for him to be uncomfortable like in the Galapagos (where he nearly shivered to death during a dive since he has almost no body fat) – call it double free insurance. About ten minutes later we plunge into the ocean and snorkel our way to the reef. The water is nice and we enjoy the forty-five minute discovery swim. Back on the boat, Heidi and I muse that the corals are not quite as vibrant as we remembered them. Part of it is that the coral is dying, part may be that our memory has selected the best parts from our visit 13 years before and lastly that the water is a bit blurry. Still, the exploratory swim with the kids is great.

Hoisted back on the boat we sail to dive spot number two. Leendert and I are fitted with the harness and bottles and are ready to descend. We climb in and hold to the guiding rope. There is a strong current which does not make things easy. Lachie conducts the three practical tests we need to be able to pass: (1) taking the mouthpiece out, holding it 'face downward', placing it back in and evacuating water, (2) removing water from the face mask while submerged, and (3) losing and retrieving the mouthpiece while under water. We both do well, though I forget to exhale slowly on exercise number three. Little feels more uncomfortable to me than breathing out under water, while searching for an oxygen supply. It seems to me infinitely wiser to keep every ounce of air in the lungs while scouting for a source of air, but we're instructed that 'holding your breath' is the one thing not to do under water. It feels counter intuitive, but we practice and learn.

We are in a group of six divers and follow a thick rope downwards. One of our co-divers is a Brit. While preparing on the boat, I had picked up from Lachie that in the previous dive the Brit had been a challenge to manage and Lachie was not too thrilled to have him on three dives today. As we descend, our royal citizen has problems following instructions. He is off on his own, doesn't stay with the group and randomly floats back to the top. Leendert, meanwhile, is as cool as a sea-cucumber, truly in his element. I notice that my fatherly predisposition to protect my young begs me to be behind him, so I can see what's happening. This is probably driven by two invalid assumptions (a) that I can intervene if something doesn't go according to plan, and (b) that I can run interference on the Brit's erratic movements.

The current is quite strong, and Lachie manoeuvres us aptly upstream finding submerged alcoves in which to take a breath (pun intended). He does have to leave some of us behind intermittently, as our English Sherlock disappears completely from time to time. Once, for about eight minutes, we hang about, luckily sheltered by wonderful corals which envelop us. The lost man is brought back, and we continue our dive. The Great Barrier Reef – one of the 7 wonders of the natural world - lives up to its reputation, it is full of fish, octopus, clams, and sublimely colorful.

Back on board, we find the girls had a grand time snorkeling and we dine on a cold buffet. Meanwhile, Alicia II sails the boat to our third and final stop. Leendert is keen to dive again and I overcome my personal reluctance. I agree to one more session with him, accepting that I'll have to inhale from a high-pressure metal container for another half hour. I really have no choice; I have seldom seen Leendert so enthusiastic. As we prepare it seems we'll dive with the same team as before. One exception, the Brit is sitting this one out. Lachie says that he pulled out at the last moment. We exchange glances - neither one of us sheds tears over his absence. I also let him know my preference is to swim behind Leendert. He says not to worry, he will ensure all is okay. I impress on him that it is more for my comfort than anything else; if I don't see Leendert, I worry, which degrades the pleasure I get out of my dive.

We have a tremendous forty-minute dive. Since we are only four, it is easy for Lachie to keep an eye on us. Given that we all follow instructions well and 'sign' when asked, we cover a large part of the reef, curving around some beautiful sites. As we cross with another set of divers, I look around and I notice Leendert latched on to the crossing group, an error easily made since all wet suits, bottles, masks and fins look alike. I signal to the other guy in our team that I will go and fetch Leendert. Bringing him back to the 4-man herd I give a quick glance at Lachie. I'm not sure if he can read through my mask what my eyes are telling him: "ha, so there! See? I told you I should be positioned behind Leendert in the chain!".

After our dive, both Leendert and I are keen to re-enter the water to snorkel. Alicia II confirms we still have time before lifting anchor, and she points us to the best location, just off the stern of the boat. We are awestruck by the corals, fish (including clownfish) and the warmth of the upper layer of the water.

The return trip is spent in great comfort. The boat can easily hold 85 passengers and we are with less than half that number, making it feel like a private yacht. A bit of sun, a bit of shade, a cup of coffee, some juice, a brownie, a chat with the captain, and the 90 minutes back to the wharf disappear like snow in front of a hairdryer.

Back at the dock, we shuttle back to the apartment. And what do the kids do? They jump in the pool! Who says you can get too much of a good thing? We call the kids for dinner and Alicia has a total melt down. The triggering event? She forgot her goggles at the swimming pool just twenty-five steps from where we are sitting. I guess one can have too much of a good thing. The day of boating and swimming simply wore her out. Only a quick shower keeps her -and us- from bed. We log a 'PE and Biology' day.

Meet the Aboriginal - Social Studies day

The liberating thing about having no set school schedule is that you can flex the education. Today was a good example of that. After breakfast, we packed up to go to Daintree, a natural park in a rainforest jungle. While driving towards Daintree the kids are in school, reviewing Spanish. Since we studied together in Cusco, the lesson is enjoyable as we test our memories. We drive past the beautiful coastline and through the sugarcane fields. Heidi points out the sugar cane railroad and moments later we see a locomotive pull carts full of cane: *Esta azucar en el tren; el tren es azul y amarillo.*

As we approach Daintree, we have to cross the river with the same name, which is done on a rope-pulled ferry. The ferry is only half full as we traverse the lazily streaming river. Once across, we follow the road another fifteen kilometers, passing signs warning us for crossing cassowaries, birds best described as colorful crossbreeds between an ostrich and a prehistoric animal with a big vertical head plate. Unfortunately, we see none. Arriving at the visitors' park, we are told an educational presentation will start in twenty minutes. Yawn. No real interest from any of us.

We walk over the mid-tree boardwalks listening to an audio guide; stories on the flora and fauna around us. We arrive at a platform and notice the cultural performance had already started. The reason why I say performance is that the man giving the speech is putting on an amazing show. He captivates the audience from the moment he opens his mouth.

Let it be said he was a tsunami of words, thoughts and ideas. All delivered with humor and a contagious laugh. It is good for young and old. He successfully transfers knowledge about the Aboriginals. Sean himself is of mixed blood; his mom was Aboriginal, his father was a Scottish body builder. His dad trained Sean Connery (James Bond), and liked the first name, hence his moniker. Five cultural facts we picked up about the indigenous Australians:

(1) Aboriginal men and women lived mainly apart. (2) Once children are born, they stay with the mother, the father has little to do with the upbringing. (3) The seaside aboriginals would only marry dry-land partners, thus avoiding inbreeding. (4) All knowledge was passed on orally (no written texts). (5) Secrets are only passed within the gender. Man to man; woman to woman. A bit of mystery exists on what he can share - 'I know but can't tell you'.

Sean shows different boomerangs and explains how and why an open

V- shape, a Y-shaped one or a cross-shaped version were used. The original boomerangs were much thicker and heavier than the ones we know. In practice, boomerang were needed to hit and hurt (knock-out) the hunted animals. He points out how the traditional ones were made from the bottom part of the tree trunk; that bending part where the base of the trunk is linked to the roots. Since that moment, I see boomerangs at the base of every large tree.

Sean talks about aboriginal food and gives examples of how women would prepare flour from poisonous fruits. They would crunch the fruit, soak it in the river, squeeze it, and soak it again. It would take three days until the deadly milky substance would no longer ooze out. I guess you had to trust mom's cooking!

Sean continues to share practical bits of daily aboriginal life. He shares how the fishermen would stand in the ocean and disperse a natural substance which removed oxygen from the water. The fish would not be able to breath and simply float to the top to be scooped up. He shows handmade spears. One uses a second stick. The second arm-length stick has a small hook which can be placed at the end of the first spear. Using the second stick as lever, Sean once threw his spear over 300 meters. And no, he didn't hit a target. In fact he didn't even try. The objective was different. Before throwing it, he'd pass it under his armpit, putting his "scent" on it. Slinging the spear from a downwind spot, it flies over the prey. The animal, would hear and smell trouble. The natural reaction would be to flee away from the noise, and thus straight to Sean, who stood ready to make the kill.

Sean demonstrates native songs and dance, which used to be his source of income, taking him around the world. He demonstrates a "beat box" – and how that is linked to the didgeridoo. He plays the hollow stick using circular breathing. This is no mean feat, considering he has had lung-tumors and now has only one lung.

He describes how the didgeridoo is made (termites eat the bottom part of the trunk hollow, and with coals the top part is burned out). He explains that the sounds made through the instrument are often calls from nature. Thus, by listening to the musician carefully, one can often identify the region from which the player originates. But one will never hear an aboriginal from Central Australia play. The reason? They don't have didgeridoos. The inland wood was too hard for termites to eat through the center.

After a well deserved applause and a couple follow up questions on musical instruments, we leave Sean behind. We climb a twenty-three meter high tower, stopping at three intermediate platforms to observe the various types of life at different levels of the rainforest canopy. We discover the layers consist of different plants, butterflies and birds. We stroll over the walking paths seeing – and peeking inside- the famous strangler fig trees.

Next we drive up to Daintree village. Heidi and I refresh our memory. Just like our last visit 13 years before, there is nothing to do or see in Daintree. We turn the car around and drive home continuing Spanish homework: *un segundo lecion de español*, followed by a lesson on plate tectonics. A quick stop at the grocery store sets us up for dinner. A simple kangaroo steak on the grill with corn and beans. We log the 'Social Studies' day.

Painting Dots - Art Day

It was our last full day in Port Douglas. Time flew by. The kids do some 'extreme sleeping'. I do not mind them sleeping in, since this gets them closer to Perth time, our next stop. Once awake, we shovel brunch into them and we hop in the car for a short drive to Mossman where Heidi has arranged an aboriginal art class. The artist, whose little gallery we enter, is a friendly guy, but hard to understand. He explains that he has been deaf since birth. Once we know this backdrop it somehow becomes easier to make sense of what he says. He rambles on a bit, but I am impressed with his ability to talk so Australian, "right?" (pronounced with that typical Australian "o" sound for the 'i').

He tells us a bit about the Aboriginal art, then hands us the three key colors of paint: yellow for the sun, white for the rain, and brown for the earth. A little demonstration follows on how to work 'the stick'. For this type of painting, you work with a wooden stick, not unlike a wooden barbecue skewer. One side is fat, the other is pointier. Leendert chooses to paint a boomerang, the rest of us get a small black canvas. For the next two hours, we are artists. Dot-dot-dot, paint cup, dot-dot-dot, paint cup, Big Dot, paint cup, Big Dot; change color, dot-dot-dot, paint cup...you get the drift. I figure on my small frame I put well over a thousand dots, not once having the feeling that it was pointless. In fact, all our works of art turn out well. Upon returning to Port Douglas, I search for varnish so we can fix the paint before we travel. The good news is that I found the varnish. The bad news is that it was expensive. The horrible news is that when applying the lacquer, the pictures developed a milky overcoat.

Damn. I am really upset; I was hoping to hang them at home in a prime spot. As I winge and complain, Alicia comes up and gives me a hug. I was afraid she'd be upset with me for ruining her artwork, but instead it turns out she is trying to console me. She looks at me lovingly, followed by the infamous words: "okay, now cry yourself a river, build a bridge and get over it!". Wise advice.

Later that day Heidi and I visit a local aboriginal art gallery in town as the kids do homework. The visit is educational. Having painted a small canvas ourselves we have a much deeper appreciation for these huge works. From the gallery owner we learn that the art was only 'discovered' in the 1970s. Before that time, the art only existed in ritual ground paintings in the sand. As soon as the aboriginal ceremony was finished they would wipe out the picture, thus losing it forever. Looking at the price tags, we also determine that some people are willing to spend enormous amounts of money, upwards of a million dollars, on blobs of paint smeared upon a canvas by Aboriginals. Evidently, primitive art is 'hot'. And as so often with modern art I think 'I can do that', telling Heidi the real art is not the creation of the artwork itself, but the selling of it!

As we stroll through the gallery we cross several works (worth more than a business-class trans-Atlantic flight) I would consider hanging on my wall and calling 'part of an inheritance'. In fact, given the choice, I'd take the painting over investing it in a glass of Champagne on board a Star-Alliance flight. We are intrigued enough to ask if the gallery ships to France. It does. In the end, we back off and decide against an acquisition. We log the Art day.

Christmas in Australia

From Port Douglas we fly via Melbourne to Perth. Perth is on the west coast of Australia, grown out of the mining industry. For several years my brother has lived in this remote corner of the world and we look forward to spending Christmas with him and his wife. For some families, Christmas might be a time period of forced family dinners, stress and conflicts (who to visit, in what order). For us, it always seems a joyous period, a real treat. I am excited as we shift time-zones. It is fun to see a familiar face at the airport picking us up. Despite the summer heat, a Christmas tree (with gifts!) stands in the corner of his living room. Judging by the boxes they took our coaching. No big gifts for the kids, we are backpacking!

Due to the time difference, some of us are up early the next day. I find

Heidi well before the dawn has cracked with a cup of coffee in the living room. We chat quietly and decide not to wake the rest of the household. It turns out to be a very relaxing morning as we adjust to local customs. Like good Australians we watch the 'test' Cricket match. My brother attempts to explain the rules and the lexicon that goes with it: balls, overs, maidens, ducks and a series of other nouns. I find it puzzling how you can have a game that can last up to five days, played by grown men and still call it a 'test'. In truth, one batter did get a ball in the balls, which certainly seemed testing for him. He missed the next ball tossed at him - of course - and was out (for now); in a few days he gets another shot at it I think. Go figure.

To me cricket rates right up there with baseball. A great excuse to go to a ballpark, eat and drink and spend time with the family, but don't try to convince me it is a sport. In my book, to qualify something as a sport, there are least a few criteria (1) there must be lots of movement; (2) the heart rates of the participants should go higher than those of the spectators; (3) sweating should be involved and not just because of standing in the blazing hot sun; (4) in case of a team sport, more than four people ought to be active at the same time; and (5) there should be referees and scoring involved.

You notice that by this standard cricket, baseball and darts are in the same category as chess; not a sport. Curling (as silly as it is) almost qualifies. It will not come as a surprise to the reader that this viewpoint and my willingness to share it has meant that I have had to navigate myself out of sports bars on numerous occasions. The funny part is that if it was not for point (5) bar fights would qualify as a sport.

Anyway, watching the game is a great pastime, and we enjoy the drink that comes with it. Personally, I am more exhilarated when later in the day a game of "Aussie rules Football" comes on. Talk about a sport! If you haven't seen it yet, find a clip on YouTube. Leave it to the Australians to define a manly sport. It has everything you might want. It is non-stop running and kicking, more than in soccer and without the *schwalbes* and theatrics. It is rougher than American Football, but without the padding. It is played by strong men taking one another down like in rugby, but without those scrums. Rugby scrums always confuse me. Scrums slow the game down, what fun is that? Also, the concept of getting these big 'blokes' to put their arms around one another to deal with 'props' and 'hookers' seems silly to me. My point is that Aussie rules football is the Sport of all team sports. Capital S. Too bad it is only played down under.

But that day there are more sports for our entertainment. That morning, the excitement climaxes as the annual "Sydney to Hobart" sail race sets off.

Sailing is a tricky one on the sports definition front. The careful observer will notice that sea-sailing doesn't pass my five-point sports definition. Interestingly, smaller sail boat racing probably does. A fun factoid about the Sydney to Hobart race; camera-men are on board until right after the start to get the best shots, then they literally 'jump ship' to be picked up by small vessels. Given that it's Australia, being the camera man is probably a high risk vocation (jellyfish, sharks, venomous I-don't-know-what's could attack before a rescue vessel gets to you).

The days at my brother's are full of joy. We eat and drink a lot and tell each other "we'll be healthy next year". We participate in a local tradition: a visit to the beach Christmas morning with a bottle of Champagne. Very civilized. No brown bags, just nice hampers with food and drink. Being on the Southern Hemisphere, it is mid-summer and the water is lovely. The waves are fantastic and we spend time body surfing, inhaling salt water and filling up our swimming trunks with sand. The coastal waters are splendid and we watch surfers and boogie boarders before making the trip back home. Not Christmas in the snow, but quite delightful.

One day we ride bicycles on Rottnest Island. Rottnest is off the coast of Perth, accessible by ferry, and known for the population of quoka. Quokas are small marsupials, like mini-wallabies. They happily hop across the arid terrain. Aside from the beautiful beaches, they are the key attraction of the island. It being Australia, we have several animal encounters. First, there are flies. Thousands of them. Invasive, persistent and relentlessly annoying. I feel I need an Akubra with dangling corks. We ride bikes and for the first time in my life I am happy facing a headwind. Had it not been for the wind blowing the flies away, we would have gone back to the ferry after the first hour, happy to leave the island behind.

Our second nature encounter happened as we cruised back to the harbor. A snake decided to entertain us. Three of us spotted it along the side of the road, but by the time Alicia arrived, it decided to cross the road. Alicia almost rode over the two-meter legless elongated carnivorous reptile, and believe me, I have seldom seen my daughter change color that fast. In the thirty seconds that followed Alicia pumped the peddles with such ferocity that she would have out-sprinted Lance Armstrong on the Mont Ventoux in his best days. For days following the incident she couldn't see a stick or hose along the path without thinking it was coming to get her.

We had a great time in Perth, and would have liked staying longer, but we were off to the airport on the 30th of December. The reason? My long-time desire to see the famous Sydney Harbour Bridge on New Year's Eve.

Ending the Year in Style

We spend the last day of the year in Sydney. As we came from Perth, the jet lag is in our favor. On the 31st, we let the kids sleep in ensuring it would be easy for them to stay up until midnight. Around midday we go to the famous Sydney fish market for late breakfast and are overwhelmed by choice. We order a 'basket' each, which was way too much food. Each bucket is a very yellow-brown affair: the base fries, piled high with fried calamari, shrimp and fish. We go outside with our 'piles of beige' and try find some shade. We can sit under some trees but that seems ill-advised since the ground indicates a fair amount of birds use the branches to position themselves for depth charges. The disadvantage of avoiding the bird's drop-zone is that we have to sit in the sun. We pick sun over excrement, which means the food is protected, but it is uncomfortably hot.

We nibble through the fish and chips, that culinary British delight left behind in the colony, but none of us enjoy the greasy food all too much. I guess fresh fried fish is not our thing for breakfast. As a side note: I get the importance of fresh sushi and sashimi, but why on earth advertise freshly fried fish? I wonder if it is really important that fish is fresh when it gets bathed in heated oil. Does it matter if it has been on ice for two or three days? I doubt that many people are able to distinguish the difference. Either way, less than half an hour later we are thoroughly overheated and our foreheads are getting as crispy as the food on our plates. We head back towards the hotel. On the way we pass a particularly nice looking French café and decide to re-do breakfast our way. We sit at a small table, order juices for the kids and coffee for me and Heidi. As luck would have it, the lady behind the counter is from Lyon, and we order our croissants in French. I detect a little sign of homesickness as we order '*un pain au chocolat*' and a croissant!

The afternoon is spent at the Maritime Museum. We walk over a gunship and queue to visit a submarine docked in the harbor. The entry system is well controlled; you get a card to go on, which you hand back at exit, thus the number of people on the vessel is limited: one out - one in. The submarine served as recently as 1999, and when it docked, it was left untouched. No alterations. As a result, it gives an authentic view of how the 68 men lived in the confined quarters. The submarine was also unique in that it was the quietest of the time. The propulsion was done electronically by batteries. Two big diesel engines could charge the batteries in twenty minutes good for a five-day submerge. The boat itself could stay under for up to six weeks. Some other factoids we pick up crawling through the tight little compartments: (1) the torpedo's could either be a direct shot or guided by a long unwinding wire – which would be cut a few hundred meters after it homed in on the target; (2) the engine room would be a scorching 48 degrees Celsius when the diesels were running; (3) normally, unlike in the movies, the crew in a sub is fully dressed (coats and long pants), since it is cold in the vessel. Water temperatures would cool it down, and the last thing the mariners want is to leave a heat signature under water; (4) showers were a luxury: one minute, once a week.

We take the gangway back to the dock, and about a hundred meters further we enter a perfect replicate of the *Endeavour*, the boat James Cook sailed along the Great Barrier Reef naming the capes. Originally the boat was built to ship coal down the UK coastal line, but the Royal Navy bought it for exploration in the late 1700's. The guides are dressed up in clothes from yesteryear and give intriguing explanations of what life might have felt like as a shipmate on board. It was not pretty, illustrated by the fact that James Cook assumed he'd lose a large portion of the men during the voyage (and he did). To allow for the initial crew on board he added an additional deck. The result of the refurbishment is that in ½ the ship one has to crawl on all fours to get around. To sleep, hammocks were suspended above the dining tables (but often crew would sleep on deck, considering it more comfortable.

For New Year's Eve we booked places at Pirrama Park Wharf. From there, we should have a good view of Sydney bridge and the midnight fireworks. VIP tickets in hand, we enter a secondary fence into a sectioned-off part of the park, straight onto a boardwalk. There are two levels. Tables are set up on the lower part, lounge chairs closer to the waterfront. The view is magnificent, but a strong wind makes the conditions less than perfect, bordering on uncomfortable. Enormous yachts pass as we collect our dinners from covered tents. We nibble on our food and await the light show. Thankfully, after dark the wind dies down. We enjoy a pre-show at ten p.m. and play games while waiting for the main event at midnight. The second show starts as we enter 2015. We see it twice, simultaneously. Yup, that's possible. One time we see it upside down! The wind has faded completely and the water is like a mirror. We see the colorful firecrackers go up, and in mirror image on the pitch-black water surface. Stunning pictures of the pyrotechnics with the Sydney bridge in full view. The grand-finale is spectacular. Check in the box for the bucket list.

Though it is a joyous way to exit one year and enter the next, I feel something is missing. Part of it was that I did not hear a formal count down, which to me is always a fun part. But that was not it. There is nothing wrong with the start of the New Year being announced by fireworks, and it wasn't the absence of popping of Champagne bottles either. I had a hard time putting my finger on it, but having hugged the family I realize what it is. It is just us! There are no other friends to share the moment with. Being the four of us together is not "extra" special to us, we have been doing that for months now! It caught me off guard, and I make a note to myself. For a good New Year celebration in the future, make sure you are with family AND friends!

Excerpts from Australia's best experiences

From Sydney we work our way to a town just outside Adelaide on the south coast of Australia. We stay at a friend's lovely Victorian-style house. It has big verandas and a modern kitchen. There are many large rooms filled with furniture, books, chairs and paintings. I like the house. It has a unique atmosphere best described as a blend of spacious while, at the same time, cozy and lived in.

That evening, as I go to the bathroom before calling it a night, I notice a big black spot on the ceiling above the bathtub. Upon closer inspection, it turns out to be a spider. It is close to the same size as the steak I shared with Alicia for dinner. Normally I would leave, close the door and have sweet dreams, but since it is in the bathroom used by Heidi and the kids, I decide it is best to get rid of it. From the past I know waking up to the sound of kid screaming is one of the most frightening experiences any father can have. Hence I choose to brave the animal.

I have no clue if this Angus-sized animal is one of those Australian man-eating, venomous, strangler spiders, so I need to come up with a plan of attack. Normally I don't mind spiders. I definitely do not suffer from arachnophobia, but I don't particularly like spiders either. Not trusting bigger animals in general, this one actually gives me the creeps, staring down on me from high up on the ceiling.

I determine a plan of attack. I'm thankful for having learned how to "snap" a towel when playing at the swimming pool lockers as a kid and I grab a towel off the rack. The standoff is now in full swing. The animal is positioned in the corner above the bathtub where it is hard to reach. The good news is that the bath towels are big, so I am able to cover the full distance and whip the piece of cloth to the corner. First attempt - miss. The spider moves deeper into the corner, strategically positioning itself for what I am sure is an attack. Second attempt - "snap" says the towel. Hit! I see the eight-legged beast fall into the bathtub. Before I can sigh relief, I see it bounce out! In one single move, it leaps over the edge of the tub and reappears on the floor. And it's coming for me! No beta blockers or other sedatives could have slowed my reaction at this stage, the shock put my body in overdrive. In a split second I toss the bulky towel over the moving beast. I notice to my shock and surprise that the heavy cloth actually continues to move towards me, propelled by the monstrosity beneath it. Barefoot, I jump on top of it and to my relief I feel and hear a cracking sound. Still anxious, I hammer it two more times with my heel. Only when spider juice oozes through the topside of the towel do I feel confident that I won the battle. Carefully lifting the corner of the towel, I look at the carcass. For a moment I consider keeping the skeleton as a hunting trophy to show the kids. However, parental duty and fear that it will scare and scar the kids, I peel the corpse and 'bones' with toilet paper from the towel and flush it down the toilet. Slightly paranoid, and my heart still pounding, I go to bed, peering at the ceiling corners, wondering what other Australian animals might be lurking between my sheets or appear during the night....

Three days later I learn I had battled a Huntsman spider. Known for its speed, mode of hunting and its forward looking eyes. See, I told you it was eyeing me! The animals are also called giant crab spiders because of their size, their leg span of up to 15 centimeters, and their general appearance. Looking it up later, I learn that if bitten 'a cold pack may relieve local pain'. Furthermore, and I quote, 'in an investigation into spider bites in Australia, [it] figured prominently' and they found 'not any severe or unusual symptoms resulting from confirmed bites'. Given it is Australia this does not comfort me: 'severe' and 'unusual symptoms' in Australia are on a different scale. You could have your leg gnawed off, and the local bushman might say; "ah, that's not severe, mate". Or, after being paralyzed, the first aid nurse could tell you, "that's not unusual, mate". No thank you, I've seen Crocodile Dundee, I don't feel bad about my towel attack.

Australia is heating up

One morning we decide to go for a road-trip. As we pull out of the driveway, I realize that I forgot my phone. Since it serves as our GPS, Heidi jumps out of the car to fetch it. As soon as I turn it on, I receive text messages. Many of them. The phone just keeps bleeping. They are from the Australian emergency services, warning us for bushfires in the 'whatever' valley, one that has some unpronounceable aboriginal name.

Before hitting the main road, we see the neighbor and greet her. We mention the bush fires and our intended direction for the day. I have planned a nice trip through four little towns, with stops at rose and lavender gardens, an old blacksmith, a cask-making factory, a whispering wall, and a vineyard. The neighbor looks over the rim of her glasses and suggests for us to change plans. She is adamant we at least change directions and go to the south; "but you should really forget the trip altogether". We drive off, listening to the radio on her advice.

The radio blurts out conditions similar to those I heard in Melbourne on Black Sunday six years earlier. I recall the drive through the blackened Yarra Valley a few weeks after the disaster and the ash clouds in the air. My memory carries vivid images of the open-air memorial service for the fireman who lost their lives. Today, the news echoes the conditions back then: 40+ degrees and one hundred kilometer an hour winds. Looking at the sky, I see familiar brown/reddish clouds, so I suggest it is best to just get groceries and make it a school day. For the rest of the day, the kids study while I sit glued to the TV. Fascinated, I stare at the flat screen, closely following the developments of the wildfires as they are reported by ABC news.

Three of the towns I intended to visit are by now in the fire zone. It's a good thing we returned for the phone and made friends with the neighbor! I am transfixed on the news and start learning about bushfire emergency plans. Exaggerated? I don't think so. The warning zone gets closer and reaches a town about 10-15 kilometers away. Sounds like a long distance? Not really. Fire with winds of 60km/hr travels that distance in about 15 minutes! That's not a lot of time if the wind changes direction. Some other fire facts I learn that day: (1) there is an 'ember' zone; this is the area where the sparks - after flying through the air for a while - are likely to cause new fires; (2) convection heat is the most dangerous; rather than the fire itself, it is this radiation heat, which causes most deaths; (3) the house we are in (determined by postal code) is NOT is a "bushfire-safe" zone; (4) for every five degrees uphill slope, a fire will travel twice as fast; so a fire normally traveling along at 5km/hr on the flat will go at 20km/hr on the slope of the garden of the house we are in.

As a good scenario planner, I work out the three best escape routes from the house and consider which car (or cars) to take and what to bring. Fate is with us. The winds turn by early afternoon and the danger zone moves away. By late afternoon I am confident enough to take the dog for a walk and leave the news updates.

A few days later, while driving over the local mountain range 'koala spotting' we get a real appreciation for the wild fire that ravaged the region. The lookout at Mount Lofty is still affected. The bush fires have created a cloudy mist over the landscape blocking the panoramic view. The view to the ocean is comparable to the soup I saw hanging over Los Angeles twenty five years ago, or the air pollution in Shanghai and Beijing today. Further down the road, the police makes us detour as the bushfires are still not 100% under control. We turn and encounter blackened terrain and smoking tree-stumps on the side of the road. A smoky smell fills the car and creates a rather eerie and scary atmosphere.

Kangaroo Island - a hopping place

After our stay in Adelaide, we take a ferry to Kangaroo Island. Can a name be more Australian? There are strong winds when we cross and the boat rolls as waves hit the boat. Fortunately no one gets sick. Soon after arrival, we find ourselves in a Toyota Landcruiser on our way. Our friends' one-story farmhouse dates from 1876 and consists of a series of rooms, one behind another. The house has old wood floors and white paneling throughout connect it into one lovely dwelling. Modern bathrooms were recently added - five years ago it only had an outhouse. It's beautifully furnished. The house is located at the bottom of a hill and has a large wooden deck in front. An idyllic spot with nothing but spacious rolling hills around. Crossing the road and traversing a single sand dune, one drops onto a kilometer long beach. While not private, nobody is in site, so it might as well be. It is stunningly beautiful.

We have lunch on the deck, a bottle of rosé and water from the tap. I learn the tap water is unfiltered rainwater. It is caught in a large underground tank, straight from the roof. Just rainwater? Isn't that dangerous? No? Okay, cool. How quickly we recalibrate. In the Galapagos we were worried about the 'wrong' bottled water, here we accept the rainwater off the roof in an instant. Somewhat strange to me. I guess we trust the Australian rain more than South American bottling companies.

Following lunch, Heidi and the kids head for the beach. I attempt to catch up with my diary, but get attacked by a sleepiness which has to be dealt with. Grabbing a lounge chair, I fall asleep, enjoying the shade and the sounds of the wind blowing past the house and in the tops of the pine trees. I barely wake up in time to go kangaroo-spotting at sundown. We spot well over a hundred kangaroos and wallabies.

The following day, we drive into town to drop our friend at the ferry and to book our return tickets for later in the week. I ask if there is a project in the house she needs to have done, but she replies "no, just relax and enjoy yourself". Yup, fat chance, me enjoying three days of laying on the beach. Luckily I have identified a project already, a garden bench which has about fifty percent of its paint flaked off. I decide not to tell her; it'll be a surprise for when they come back. In town, we get gas, and as we return, Alicia notices the back window of the car does not roll up anymore. It is stuck in the bottom of the door. Now I have two projects to sink my teeth into. Unfortunately, the local town has no real DIY store. The only hardware available is in the gas station. I love these 'one stop' gas stations. The ones which also serve as a fishermen's supply store, a bakery and the local post office. Interestingly, the station sells brushes but no paint. I am told I should head for Kingscote, a town about 45 minutes further onto the island: "they should have paint, mate". Before setting off to get paint I examine the car window figuring special tools or hardware might be needed to fix it. Better to find this out before returning from an hour-and-a-half trip to the shop.

Having worked in car body-shops in my youth, I know how car-doors come apart. After a bit of effort, the Landcruiser's door is stripped apart and I stare inside the door's cavity at the mechanism. It is clearly worn, having done its share of up-and-downs while the car clocked 445,000 kilometers. It is the middle of the day and the sun is scorching. Losing what feels like half my body weight in sweat, I work on the window. Ultimately I am triumphant - the window works again, boosting my self-worth tremendously. The door panel is re-installed and the electrical window button and the door handle placed where they belong. Even the speaker is positioned so that you can't see the door has been taken apart. Icing on the cake of self-pride.

What's even better is that while searching the shed for tools to repair the car, I also ran across what I needed for the garden bench, including white paint. Score! This saves me the trip to the DIY store in town. I strip the paint from the bench. As usual, half comes of nicely, the rest is a bear. And, as always, a bench made of individual planks has many more sides than you anticipate and hope for as you start. It is probably why people have been smart enough not to attempt this chore before. For a short while Alicia helps me out (as she is in her 'recess'). Her bubbly companionship is appreciated as it breaks the monotony of sanding the planks.

The next days are nice and relaxing: schoolwork, another coat of paint on the bench, planning our journey through Southeast Asia. We make a day trip west, then north. Heidi humors me. She lets me to go off the main road onto a typical Australian bush road. Fully off-road would be one step too far. The trick here is to drive neither too slow nor too fast; the former makes you lose your fillings as the roads are ribbed, the later means that the monstrous vehicle starts floating uncontrollably on the gravel. We observe beautiful nature, including large lizards, kangaroos, rainbow lorikeets and white and red parrots. To see better Alicia rolls down the car window I so proudly fixed, which is followed by a "clunk". The window slid to the bottom and becomes inoperable again. Ahhh! We drive back to the main road and continue the trip on bitumen to Stokes Bay. A few drops of rain splatter on my windscreen. I make note that we might have to find a way to seal Alicia's window if it gets worse. Luckily it does not. Once at the beach, we go to a tiny restaurant. We order at the counter, choosing between fish & chips, different fish & chips, and fish & chips. Actually, that's exaggerated – I have a variant: squid & chips. At the counter I check if they have screwdrivers: "No, not the drink, a regular one and a phillips-head; I need to fix the car". The food is brought out as is a screwdriver. Splendid.

The food is excellent; the squid certainly rates as some of the best I have ever had. Once the food is gulped down I attack the car. The learning curve carries overnight. In sixteen minutes - yes, I timed myself - the car door is stripped, the window fixed, and all is put back together, including the speaker. Feeling like McGyver having fixed the four-wheel drive with one tool only I re-join the family. Crossing the parking lot I see a man with a toolbox fixing his car; automatically I feel a kinship. He, too, is a survivor. We spend a couple of hours on the beach before returning home. We need to make a pit stop for the kids, which also provides a good moment to fill one of the tires. The local BP station, baker, fisherman's shop, post office thus serves to both add and relieve pressure.

That evening, we make good on a promise to the kids to go fishing on the pier. We set off just before seven. Two fishing rods and two lines with squid-jags on them. The temperature has dropped and a fierce wind blows. We regret leaving our coats in Adelaide. At the first throw, Leendert's fishing line gets tangled up on the tackle. I switch rods with him and sit down on the dock to unravel the knot when 'Roger', a nice local chap, walks up. Very appreciative of his presence we ask what to catch, or, for that matter, what to throw back. He enlightens us and asks if we'll stay for a while. Before I can answer Alicia starts bouncing up and down. With her second toss she caught a squid! "Here's dinner!". I look at Roger and hear my self say: "Yes, I guess we'll be here for a while".

Roger helps unhook the squid, Leendert takes a photo, and Alicia starts singing "I caught a squid". A song which continues throughout the evening. Sung correctly it has a long "i": "I caught a squiiiiiii-id". Roger walks home and gets his own fishing gear. We continue to pull things out of the ocean (mostly seaweed)–and I continue to disentangle the line. We hit another moment of excitement as Leendert has a squid on his line, but unfortunately he looses the ink producer just as he pulls it up over the water. Darn.

For the next forty-five minutes we only get colder as the temperature sinks. The wind blows harder and aside from risking to catch a cold, Leendert catching the dock, and the nice chat with Roger nothing happens. So in the end, with one squid and a singing Alicia we return to the car and drive home.

Squid part 2. The cleaning. Luckily Roger gave a short introduction on cleaning the tentacled beast. It's not so hard actually; cut off the head, watch out for the ink(!), pull out the long bony transparent 'spine', remove the guts, and peel off the outer skin. Alicia makes me proud being a great help doing this. We cut of the wings and clean the tentacles noticing the suction cups still work. Next, the body of the animal is sliced, which gives the rings you find on your plate in restaurants.

Squid part 3. Give it to Heidi. Heidi shows Alicia how to fry it. A bit of butter, a hot pan, oil, pepper and salt. A lovely little appetizer which we all enjoy. Especially the wings are very tasty!

Squid part 4. We return the next evening to the dock to catch more! It isn't long before Alicia can repeat her song… "I caught a squiiiii-id". As if the fish are enchanted by her voice, she catches two fish and one more squid. Sadly, the one person who so desperate to go fishing – Leendert - gets no more than a few nibbles on his line. He never has the pleasure of reeling one in. Unfortunately, we are leaving the next day, so he won't get another go at it. Credit to him, he keeps his spirits up.

The next morning we leave Kangaroo Island. We park the car on the lot where we found it only a few days ago, check in, and embark the ferry. I note that quite a few of the people coming off the vessel are gray-faced. The wind is fierce, and once we board the captain's voice rattles over the intercom. He shares that it will be a "bumpy ride" and points out that there are plenty of lined paper bags around. He almost pleads with the travelers: "please use them if you have to". Some of the people boarding are already pale.

We sail and it takes no more than five minutes before the ship starts bouncing and rolling seriously. A few minutes later the first people start using the bags promoted by the captain; oh boy, this will be a fun ninety minutes! I take Alicia to the front of the boat to stand in the middle of the cabin. By doing so she is in a less rocky place and with a good view of the horizon – my attempt at fighting sea-sickness. We pretend to be in a roller-coaster; a '*montagne Russe*' she tells me in French. The boat really pounds on the waves, sending vibrations through the entire boat. We hear loose items in the galley behind us flying around, the cabin starts to smell of the various paper bags which are being filled. Deciding it would be more fun and pleasant to our nostrils to be above deck, Alicia and I walk like drunken sailors towards the back stairs. We pass Leendert who plays on his iPad, oblivious to what goes on around him. Heidi sits quietly in her chair, eyes closed, pretending to take a cat-nap.

It is well past lunch time when we arrive back on land. Driving home it doesn't take long before our stomachs settle from the rocky boat ride. We seek something to eat and find a bakery. It is filled with kidney pies and sausage rolls; a small reminder that we are in a former British colony. They are quite tasty, and we enjoy them, each sampling the other's. That evening we sleep with our friends in Adelaide and get ready for our return trip to Sydney. From there we have a cruise-ship booked which takes us up the east-coast to Singapore.

Leaving Australia
The Cruise-a-fixtion

THE FLIGHT FROM ADELAIDE IS uneventful and the airport conveyor spits out our backpacks as per plan. It is not particularly cold, but it is gray and rainy in Sydney. As the taxi drives through the center I almost feel local; given this is the third time here in one month, it feels more than just a little familiar. About $55 later we arrive at Circular Quay where the 'Celebrity' from Carnival Cruises has moored.

In all honesty, this is the part of the trip I have not been looking forward to. Cruise-ships don't work for me. I'm not at ease with people crammed in confined quarters, queuing for food, watching lame entertainment, and angling for deck chairs – hoping to get the elusive four-in-a-row. Now, there are several mitigating circumstances which got me to accept to go anyway. First, it is a relative inexpensive way to get to Singapore as we booked a 'repositioning' cruise. This is when cruise boats move from one base port to another as the season changes creating a one-way trip. Second, the kids can probably find some other kids to play with. Third, it will also provide some quiet homework time. And last but not least, the boat has a gym. Post-Christmas workout sessions are desperately needed.

We deposit our bags and get slightly wet walking towards the check-in terminal. Alicia's flip-flops are drenched as she, like a good eleven-year old, seeks out the puddles. We enter a big hall and fill in papers before making our way to the first floor where the real check-in is done. Queue number one. I can't stop my mind spiraling to negative stereotypes I affiliate with cruises, but try to keep a smile on my face.

Over twenty stations are open for check in, so the line dissipates quickly. Fifteen minutes later we stand shoulder to shoulder with other passengers showing our booking papers. I hand over a credit card and in return we get our welcome pack. My mind goes back to a Disney Cruise we made a few years ago. It is only now that I realize how smooth and pleasant the check in was at that time; Mickey had made it a festive experience. Today is purely a functional but laborious international hotel check-in. A check-in at peak hour. Oh boy, keep smiling!

With passes in hand, we walk to immigration. We are going into international waters so we formally exit Australia. There are only a couple of people in front of us, so we zip past the passport control and turn the corner. Queue number 2: security check. A zig-zag line meanders around the queuing posts, and step by step we get closer to the screening lines. I notice there are almost no children and estimate the average age of the crowd is well over sixty. I smile at Heidi. Unsurprisingly, she reads straight through my poker-face smile and addresses my apprehension; "it won't be *that* bad".

We get through security and make our way to the gangway. Queue number three. We slowly shuffle forward. We get a squirt of sanitizing liquid on our hands. Leendert and I cringe as we both have open wounds; Leendert from a fall on the pier on Kangaroo Island, me from fixing the garden bench. We pass the entry post where our plastic room card keys are recorded and a digital picture made. Finally, we are ready to step aboard.

Oh no, sorry, first we stop at a table with info for the kid clubs & activities. Next a tray appears with welcome drinks. Being thirsty, I slam the drink quicker than I should have. It was intended for the family picture, all smiling, glasses in hand, in front of the huge reproduction of the ship – cheese! The photographer reminds me to "be happy, you're here!". Once digitalized, we learn that the cabins are still being prepared, so we are invited to have lunch.

In the bowels of the ship we use the maps on the staircase walls to find the restaurant. It consists of four identical buffets loaded with everything one might imagine (salad, pasta, rice, sushi, curry, etc). We settle at a table close to a window and enjoy the view over The Rocks and the Sydney Harbor Bridge while munching our food. Halfway through lunch the intercom informs us that the 'Staterooms' are ready for the guests.

We finish lunch and locate our 'Stateroom'. Now, the definition of a stateroom is 'a very grand room which is designed to impress. [It is] typically the most lavishly decorated [room] containing the finest works of art'. As we enter our cabin, it is not quite the stately affair and it certainly is far from impressive. For a moment, Heidi and I considered upgrading to a cabin with a window but decide to stick to our 'inside' State Room. Spending a boatload of money on an upgrade only to get a similar room enhanced with a small round porthole window seems silly. The room has limited art, but is spacious for a boat cell. It has one double bed in the middle against the back wall and two beds which fold down from the side panels at nose-height. The space is just large enough that you don't have to go outside to change your mind. The kids are happy; any bed that requires a set of stairs to get into is an instant hit.

We set off to explore the ship. While the vessel is an older one, it is well maintained and lush. I am glad that every staircase has a map. Yes, the one with a red 'you are here' dot on it. On any road or in a forest I have a solid 'men are from mars' directional capability. Put me in an enclosed man-made labyrinth like a big shopping mall -or this ship- and you'd better have Heidi chaperone me. I don't know what it is, but inside large constructions my compass goes out of whack. Make an appointment with me in a mall and, at best, I will be late, at worst I'll be at the wrong Starbucks. And where I struggle to backtrack to the car in a shopping center, it is uncanny how Heidi miraculously develops a sense of direction. Clearly she finds magnetic bearing-points which are scrambled for me. The good news on board is that each floor has many maps, and I have ten days to familiarize myself with the new habitat.

We visit the kids' clubs. I notice Heidi smile, but I can read on her face that she is slightly disappointed. I know she is comparing to Walt Disney's mouse-boat, an unfair comparison; a floating 'full house' compared to a 'one of a kind' experience.

The vessel is scheduled to cast off at five o'clock and the captain runs a tight ship. At exactly 5pm the ropes are lifted from the pylons and slowly the mastodon of a ship reverses past the Opera House, rear end towards the Sydney Harbour Bridge. We stand strategically on the back deck and – despite the drizzle - enjoy the most amazing views of the Sydney skyline as we start the journey.

Once at sea, we return to the cabin and find our backpacks have arrived. To our great pleasure we notice there is enough storage space for all of our stuff. The only challenge is our smelly shoes, but I can hardly blame the cruise operator for that. We'll battle it with Febreeze.

Being gung-ho to enjoy everything, we go to the 'introduction theatre show'. It fits nicely with the timing of our dinner reservation. Walking down the corridor, we notice that the ship it has a gentle rock to it; nothing bad, just enough to sometimes hold a railing. The performance in the theatre is a sampler of the shows to come in the next ten days. The theatre is huge and the singers, dancers, comedian and acrobats are of high standard. It's very entertaining.

Afterwards we head to dinner. A two-story restaurant awaits us. A friendly host ushers us to a round table set for eight. Two people are already seated and we introduce ourselves to Brian and Liz. They are in their mid-sixties and come from London. He wears a bone-and-wood necklace and is on the all-inclusive alcohol drinks-package. Judging by first impressions, he is clearly on course to get his money's worth. Brian has the skill of making me totally disinterested in him within the first five minutes. He tries to impress us with his language skills (all two of them), and he considers himself a comedian. He tries to convince the kids the empty chairs have people seated there, very, very small people. Oh boy.

The restaurant service is excellent, our waitress is a lovely girl from Kyrgyzstan. She will be helping us for the rest of the cruise. We enjoy our *escargots*, carpaccio, and salad starters when disaster strikes. Brian mis-swallows, turns red, coughs-up a bit of food which drops onto his plate. This, in itself, is not too dramatic, but it sets off an asthma attack which his inhaler cannot suppress. Within a few minutes both him (red) and Liz (pale) leave the table excusing themselves. I have to admit I am not sorry to see them go. It makes the rest of our high quality dinner more pleasant. We enjoy each other's company and find every dish tasty. The *crème brulée* even passes Alicia's high-standard approval rating.

On the cruise - ups and downs

We all sleep well. Perhaps the gentle rocking of the boat throws us back to our baby years. A nice quiet night with only the slight squeaking sounds of the wall panels to remind us we are inside a ship. In the days that follow we often wake up early and dive into the breakfast buffet on the aft of the boat before the crowds arrive. Nothing wrong with watching dolphins jumping along of side of the ship as you eat a fresh fruit salad. While Alicia and Leendert spend time making friends in the kids' clubs, Heidi and I visit the gym regularly. The workout space is neither empty nor overcrowded, which makes it a good environment to sweat in.

The first time in the gym, I end up on a treadmill. Heidi reluctantly follows suit. She doesn't like running machines but her preferred tools of torture, the free-weights, were being used by short squatty guys with tank tops. We notice that the elliptical machine and running machine provide a novel challenge. The movement of the ship not only affects the incline of the apparatus but also throws the body slightly off balance, to the point where I feel a bit nauseous. To avoid falling into the side rails while running, one has to run with feet apart, a wide stance run. It feels unnatural, but seems to intensify the workout. In about half the usual time I am at the end of my rope. Clearly the slight side-to-side movement burns extra energy.

Overall the days are filled with little. We spend time reading, me focusing mostly on the places we are about to visit. In parallel, I read the American classic *To Kill a Mockingbird*, a book Leendert reads for school. It is one of those books asking to be ripped apart after the first two pages. I want to find the writer and drown her. The author insists on introducing eight characters in as many paragraphs, most with full flowery descriptions, names and nicknames. Who is she trying to impress? Why make it so complex right in the beginning? I resist the urge to toss the text into the Pacific and struggle through the book just so I can discuss the literature (and subsequent book report) with Leendert.

In preparation of a review with Leendert, overlooking the blue Pacific, I ask Heidi the type of exam questions which he will be asked. She gives me some examples. The second one sets me off. It throws me in a time-warp, putting me straight back into my high-school years, reminding me instantly why I disliked reading literature sooooo much. The question? "How do you think the character 'Boo' feels and experiences the events taking place". It seems like a reasonable question on the face of it. However, what you need to know is that until now, the book has only alluded to this character. Pages of character description in the first pages, but no mention of 'Boo'. In fact, he has never directly appeared. Boo is 'believed' to be inside a house which features in the book. Really? Comment on his state of mind? You might as well ask how my dog feels about it! It is of little importance that I don't have a dog. Heidi attempts to explain to me that the question actually does make sense, but my frustration only grows. Slamming the book closed I feel as lost as I was in the largest Dubai mall, desperate to find a way out.

Sea days pass. Kids go to the clubs and doing school work for HWH (Heidi World High). Mom and dad reading, overlooking the vast horizons, enjoying a bit of sun and mostly air-conditioned lounges. Dinners in the restaurant are excellent and we are pleasantly surprised that the London couple remains absent from our table. Heidi comments that at first she felt a bit 'rejected', but reflecting on it we see it as a compliment that they did not want to sit with us.

As we sail north, the weather flips from rain and clouds to hot and sunny. The deck chairs at the pool fill with towels and mostly old and overweight bodies. By my estimate, ninety percent of the people get scorched the very first day, their skin color nicely complementing the lobster on our plates that evening.

Late one afternoon Alicia goes swimming with her new friends while I join as lifeguard. Looking at the people on the lounge chairs its obvious the only slim-looking people on the ship are crew members. Smiling servants from Serbia, Russia, Honduras, Jamaica, etc. I guess for them being on a floating hotel is not a bad option. Keeping a watchful eye on the kids I am amazed as a family with grandparents and two little kids enter the pool. The toddlers are in pool diapers. They enter the water despite the specific signs asking people not to do so with youngsters who are not potty-trained. The children are dragged around, and, as can be expected, inhale a fair amount of the salty pool water. Ten minutes later I see 'bits' floating in the pool and notice the three-generation family quietly getting out. Identifying what I assume to be vomit (not wanting to entertain the thought of the alternative), a crew member overhears me instructing Alicia and her friends to vacate the pool. Minutes later the pool has a rope around it. It is closed 'for technical reasons'. Unfazed, Alicia and her friends continue playing in the second pool and in the whirlpools.

The evening theater shows vary in quality. One night, there is an Aussie electrical guitar player with Italian roots. He puts on a nice show albeit aimed for a slightly older audience 'vooooo-lare, o-ho, cantare, oh-oh-oh-oh…' Especially the songs from the mid- 50s go over well, totally in line with the age of the audience. The ratio of hearing aids to people in the theatre is close to 1:1 and the electric guitar is obviously appreciated for its loudness.

One evening Leendert and I take a peek at the rock-and-roll party on one of the decks. It starts with dance classes which we skip, deciding just to observe the 65+er's attempts at the 'twist'. Obviously hip flexors are not as loose as they once were. The twist is followed by a quiz – listening to Elvis Presley's *Blue Suede Shoes* and having to write the title on an answer form while everyone is singing along. We shared a Coke Zero and soon return to our cabin, deciding our books make for better entertainment.

Being bored one evening, I go to see a stand-up comedian. I remember all his funny jokes. My memory is very good for funny jokes. For those interested, I have a collection of every one of them in the appendix of this book. Headline? Had I not been sitting in the middle of the theatre, I would have made an early escape. After thirty minutes, however, I had my fill and was ready to have all the people next to me stand up just so I could get out. And what do you know? For the one and only moment in the show the comedian demonstrated good timing; he surprised me by announcing he was telling his last joke! What joy that brought.

Another day, I went to a presentation on the ship itself and how it operates. The Captain and crew members do a good job, and I admit, it was full of fun and interesting facts. The ship has two major propellers which have a total of 25kHP. On top of that there are redundancy engines worth another 14kHP. For maneuverability, the ship has side thrusters in the keel of the ship, three up front, three in the back giving about 15kHP. The vessel sails at 18 nautical miles per hour (its max is 20nM), and, at regular speed, would need about 3,5 nautical miles (over 6km) to come to a full stop. In an emergency situation, the stop could be made in 0,5nM. The captain explains that if that happened you would not want to be on board. A 'emergency stop' could be made, but the vibrations would be enormous and it would most likely ruin the engines.

At sea, the ship consumes about 150MT (think 10 truck tankers) of fuel a day. Depending on where the boat is the fuel type can be adjusted, and optimized on availability and emission regulations. In fact, even the oil from the kitchen which can no longer be used for culinary purposes is re-used as fuel. My skeptical side hears "we burn what we can get away with", but I must give it to the marketing team - nicely packaged.

On the positive side, the vessel has a full recycling plant, both for water and food waste. Fresh water for drinking and bathing is created in the on-board desalination plant and wastewater is cleaned before being dumped in the ocean. The cruise liner claims that their waste stream is cleaner than their intake. Glass, carton and cans are sorted. The cans are crushed and once back on land, sold. To motivate the cleaning crew to work diligently on the environmental matters, the revenue generated by the recycling effort is shared with them. The economics and operation of the ship intrigue me. Somehow this floating ecosystem, partially self-contained, partially variable (new ports, visitors, etc) must be a phenomenal thing to plan and schedule. I like the business side of it.

The cruise - Stops

One of the good things about cruises is that they stop, and like a dog getting the chance to get out of the house, cruisers get to run around on land every so often. One such delightful day for us is at Airlie Beach.

Unfortunately, the cruise liner cannot dock at Airlie Beach Harbor itself, so smaller boats transfer people from the ship to the shore. Luckily the seas are calm, which means boats can load and unload from both sides of the ship which make it a smooth process without queues.

We ride on an ocean worthy lifeboat to the terminal. The sun is beating down on the closed craft, and it is unbelievably hot. I suppose if your survival depends on it, being in a water-tight tumble dryer type vessel is a good thing. For the casual trip to shore, it is not. There is practically no airflow, and soon sweat streams down my body. Leaning forward, my arms leave sweat imprints on my shorts, I feel the perspiration stream down my legs into my sandals. Heidi hands me a beach towel and asks with a smile on her face "how on earth are you going to survive in Dubai". I respond "Air-conditioner".

Half an hour later we climb ashore and stroll through the local market (obviously timed with the arrival of the cruise-ship). Heidi and Alicia buy the overpriced sun-hats and we make our way to the recommended public pool. The pools are well maintained, sizable, vomit-free and they have proper changing facilities. There are plenty of trees offering comfortable spots in the shade. We spend just under two hours there of which the kids spend all of it in the pool, me about half that. Of my half I am a solid ninety percent under the waterline, complements of the kids who take great joy in pushing me under. Not only do they get older and stronger by the day, they clearly become tacticians and start to master the skill of teaming up. With one grabbing my legs and the other climbing on top I literally have no leg to stand on. I lose most battles. We spend priceless moments together, albeit me mostly devoid of oxygen.

After two more sea days we get to Cairns. Somehow we are all weary. For the first time since the start of our voyage none of us seem keen to go out and do something. It strikes me a bit strange. We just laze around all day, have not packed or unpacked for several days. We only meandered -without rush- from deck to deck, eat and drink when convenient, with no commitments or things to do. Why do we become lethargic now? We should be rested, full of energy! Guess cruising wears us out.

We make land, partially because we prepaid a rental car, and go explore. The Cairns map showed the car rental agency is located on a road close to the ship, so we decide to walk despite the 32 degrees and high humidity. It turns out that the road of the rental place is close, but the office is at the opposite end of the same street. This gives us a brutally hot thirty-minute walk. As we enter (nice and sweaty) the guy behind the counter admits that even for the locals it is hot. He just learned on the internet that while it is only 32 degrees it feels like 39. Nice. Once the air conditioning brings our body temperatures down, we are all in great spirits. The temperature, the freedom of movement, the purpose of going somewhere, what a nice change of pace! Originally we planned to drive to Mossman Gorge, but as that feels like a long way away, we settle on visiting a local fish farm to try and catch barramundi.

The route to the fish farm is easily found, and forty-five minutes later we turn into a private property. We wonder if we are in the right place. It feels like the middle of nowhere. An older gentleman greets us and confirms we are in the right spot. I parked the car under a giant tree and ask if that's okay. He smiles and jokes "that's actually the VIP parking, but I guess they won't mind". We follow him up to a rather small pond, perhaps ten meters wide, eighty meters long, pay the $50 a fishing rod and the kids have a go. The old guy manages our expectations: "it being the middle of the day, the catch might be meager" and "if the lures don't work, we'll switch you to regular bait". Alicia casts in, and wouldn't you know it, by the second toss she catches a sizable one (though it jumps off the hook at the very last moment). This fires the kids up. At one time Leendert's rod bends making it almost U-shaped, but he is able to keep reeling (and thus keep the line tight). The old man walks up, helps with the fish-net and pulls up a gorgeous barramundi. We are allowed to take the fish home, but in our case, that makes little sense. What would we do with a dead barramundi in our cabin? The owner of the fish farm gives us a puzzled look and asks if he can have it for his dinner. Of course, we agree. I consider asking for a discount, but decide against it. A few moments later Leendert captures an even bigger one (reportedly), but it is so strong that the line snaps. Both fish and lure disappear.

The fishing hour passes quick and we chat with the old-timer, who proudly shows us his botanical garden. Not long after, we say our goodbyes. Driving back to Cairns we stop at a shopping center. Leendert gets a pair of sneakers. The shoes we bought one size too large four months ago are now too small. It is stunning how quickly teenagers grow! I consider new shoes for myself as well I don't need replacement due to size or wear, but since I have only been wearing 2 pairs since our departure (a set of sneakers and a set of sandals), both are so pungent that when I walk through the ship the carpet curls at the edges. The cabin closet, where they live at night, needs more than industrial strength ammonia. Unfortunately, we don't find any shoes I like, so we resort to buying another bottle of Febreeze. Hopefully that will breathe a few more weeks of life in the shoes. At another cruise stop we visit the town of Kuranda. Parking in town is easy. We slap on sunscreen and go for a three kilometer trail walk around town. After the confinement of the ship for all those days it is nice to stretch our legs and walk. The trail winds along the river; some of it sand, some paved, and some wood boardwalks. Except for two other couples, we have the jungle to ourselves. The rainforest walk is exactly what one would expect; warm, humid, and noisy with cricket-type animals. We love it. The cricket sound comes in waves, and at its peak, the intensity is such that you can't have a conversation. We enjoy the freedom, the massive trees, the bird calls echoing back from the canopy and the beautiful hanging vines. Soon the kids are using the vines as swings.

As we loop back into town we stop at a bar for a drink and to make use of their advertised internet connection. The sign proves slightly misleading. 'Internet available' means that for a fee we can use their internet. We pay the fee since we feel we need to sync our devices. While paying, I notice a stunning picture on the back wall. It shows "Barron Falls". The lady behind the counter informs me it is just a few kilometers up the road. Given that we have a bit of spare time, we return to the car and pursue the road leading us to the Barron Falls. A short boardwalk takes us to an observation platform. Before us stretches a rather impressive gorge. From the top of the wide cliff a meager stream tumbles over the edge of the rock face. Second misrepresentation of the bar in Kuranda. No impressive waterfall; nothing more than a trickle of water dribbling down a rock face. Other visitors are similarly disappointed. Overlooking the gorge, we overhear a father explain to his young son "it's the dry season, that's why there are no waterfalls". It gets an immediate bounce-back: "so why on earth are we here? This is sooooo lame!". Secretly, I can only agree with the young boy and remark to Heidi it is a good thing we didn't spend too much driving time to this attraction. Still, water or not, in my mind, the drive a little walk and the view is far better that the ship.

Life on the boat - Continued

The ship continues its way north along the Great Barrier Reef towards Darwin. Life is now a routine. Heidi and I quietly leave our Stateroom in the morning, leaving the kids asleep while we have our cappuccinos. We observe life on a cruise as it passes by. At a quarter to seven in the morning an older man is leaving the café where we are having our coffees. By now he has downed his second Heineken, and I guess it is time to relieve himself. He obviously is on the all-inclusive package. By seven-thirty he returns and the waitress brings him his next Heineken; clearly, a standing order. He continues. He finishes bottle number four while we sip our second round of coffees and then he stumbles out. It is eight a.m.

I'll spare you a day-by-day report from the cruise. I'll summarize to provide a flavor. We're on a boat, with lots of people. If you ask me, repositioning cruises are mostly for the newlyweds and the nearly-deads. I guess the newlyweds are enjoying one another in the privacy of their cabins, because the vast remainder is on deck "on the spit" trying to win the "I am the most sun-burned" competition. On deck, the people seem to multi-task getting scorched with eating and drinking as much as they possibly can. The latter makes me lose my appetite as time passes.

For us the days are mostly filled with homework, reading and the occasional workout. The 'vomit pool' is still closed as the cruise ship is not allowed to dump water (or take new water on) while sailing through the protected Great Barrier Reef area. This puzzles me given that they told us that they "dump cleaner water than they take in", but there you have it. One morning Leendert and I go to the cinema. We see a movie with Tom Cruise, who saves the world from aliens by experiencing Bill Murray's 'Groundhog Day'. Lovely escapism for a couple of hours.

To make you fully appreciate my experience of the cruise, I have added unedited excerpts from my diary. The entries capture the feel of the days and my state of mind. Notice the text becomes shorter as the cruise goes on:

<u>Sunday 18th of January</u>: *The second boat day of the set to reach Darwin. I will summarize the day as I have all the time in the world. The nice part is that I have the time to really go into detail: we're on a boat, with lots of people. Newlyweds still unseen, the rest of the crowd continues to bathe themselves in sunscreen while lying on lounge chairs basking in the sun.*

Like ourselves, the old guy is a regular in the café in the morning; like yesterday he is drowning himself from the inside with Heinekens. We read our books and over cappuccino's plan our non-eventful day.

The day slowly creeps by with homework, a workout, Heidi at the hairdresser, the kids in their respective clubs. The rest of the passengers all aim to get most out of their expensive all-inclusive deals. Two have apologized by now for being tipsy and drunk with the excuse that "it is free". My favorite line today came from an individual at the bar directed at the bartender. At eleven in the morning he said: "can I have a whiskey and diet coke… make sure you give me the best whiskey I can get on my drinks package". The bartender served a large glass with ice, a double shot of 12-year-old single malt Scottish whiskey, topped to the rim with diet coke; a straw completed it off.

Believe it or not, I am beginning to wish I were on a Disney Cruise... If only Pooh would come and save me....

<u>Tuesday 20th January</u>. Another calm sea-day. As I have all the time in the world having been captured by this floating mall-hotel, I'll take the time to describe all interesting things that went on today at the risk of writing too lengthy a report.

Coffee in the café with the beer guy, homework, workout, theatre show, sit on deck, a drink. Finish reading book. Looking at overweight, tattooed, old people and wondering what newlyweds are doing their second week in.

Two highlights: (1) Heidi asking me if the cruise was as horrible as I anticipated it. I answered "no, it is not" (think about that one for a moment....) (2) Elliot Finkel (a older Jewish New Yorker piano player) gave a classical matinée concert. It was brilliant. His explanation of what he was playing as well as how he played was inspirational. Clearly he is in love with both the music and the instrument he plays. A joy to see for the entire family.

And there it is. A day at sea.

<u>Wednesday 21st January</u> Let me see, where do I begin. Ah, yes, it is another sea day. Read yesterdays report minus the last two paragraphs. The evening concert was done by a lady playing the electrical violin. Of course, Alicia (a violin player herself) was delighted, but I would have walked out had in not been for Alicia's pleasure. Evidently, the performing lady's claim to fame was participation in Britain's Got Talent. Note that she didn't win. She attempted with much hair swinging to energize the crowd. It did not work.

She couldn't stay on the beat and I think I detected some frustration in the eyes of the ship's band (who generally are very good). About 30 minutes in to the performance Leendert summarized my sentiment best "how much longer is this going to last?"... Luckily Alicia enjoyed it.

There it is. Day at sea. Tic-toc-tic-toc. Tomorrow Bali!

Bali - Day robbery and Lessons Learned

As we pull into Benoa we have a pleasant surprise. Our expectations were well managed the night before by the cruise director. We'd anchor far from shore and tender onto the mainland. But early in the morning we slowly sailed past fisherman standing on sand banks and the cruise-liner crawls its way to a fixed dock thus avoiding an uncomfortable forty-five minute lifeboat ride.

Another Celebrity ship is at anchor in the harbor, and we see them being tendered. The difference is huge. Two principle differences: first, we gain about 4 hours on land and second, we can hop on and hop off the boat at any time without long lines.

We didn't sign up for any tours. Having visited the presentation on Bali the night before I knew a bit about the do's and don'ts. After breakfast, we descend the gangway walking into a sea of taxi drivers. We tell them we are interested to go to Kuta Beach. The prices start at thirty-five dollars (US), and after a bit of negotiation we end up taking a small van for fifteen.

The ride in the taxi with open doors is about twenty minutes. Kuta turns out to be a maze of small beach-front shops, many tourist bars, and the odd seemingly misplaced temple along narrow paths leading to the ocean. Typical one-room shops with text-covered beach t-shirts, flip-flops, sunglasses, sarongs, and the ever-present Rolex watches. We walk a bit on the beach getting offered five dollar massages and surfboard lessons.

The kids put their toes into the seawater. The temperature is good but the grayish beach is soiled with plastic cups, bottles and other tourist waste. None of us are interested in hanging on the beach so we decide to see a bit of the town instead.

We work our way back to the main street where sales people accost us and give us scratch-cards. And wouldn't you believe it? We won! Our choice of either $1000, a $250 gift voucher, a free stay in a hotel, or an iPad 3. What luck! The guys appear genuinely happy explaining they don't get that card very often and that it helps their commission.

The 'only' thing we have to do is to go to a brand new local hotel about 15 minutes away; no strings attached. Taxi is paid, no obligations, and a free lunch is tossed in 'for our trouble'. I look at Heidi indicating 'scheme', but the fact is that we have nothing to do, Kuta appears boring and that a taxi will take us back to any place of our choosing, which makes us say "why not?". In the van I manage the kid's expectation and tell them it is unlikely we walk away with the $1000 prize.

The taxi drives through the small streets of Kuta (which is not a bad way to see town), and the experience begins. In the taxi, we are coached into what to say at the hotel. We even get to practice on a form how to fill it in. Twice. A transformation takes place. Long story short, by the time we get to the hotel our last name is Heidi's maiden name, we have spent two weeks in an Australian resort and now are in Bali for two weeks. We reside in the USA; the kids don't speak Dutch and we have a two-week package deal in the Hoky Villa's; reportedly a swanky local hotel. To top it all off we are both working… (oh, boy).

As can be expected, the ride is longer than the announced 15 minutes – we go over a toll-bridge and it takes well over 25 minutes, partly because of traffic. We arrive at the hotel, which is clearly not the new-build establishment that was announced.

The place is nice enough, and we are offered tea in a lovely open lobby overlooking the grounds, pool and beach. The lobby has free wifi, which keeps me and Heidi busy. Finally, 'Andrew' a Brit who's lived in Bali for many years comes to sit down and talk to us. I re-live my days as a Time-Share salesperson and note how little has changed since the late 1980s!

Andrew makes conversation trying to figure out our holiday preferences – also known as 'collecting the bullets'. He calculates the money we spend on average on holidays – 'creating the value domain'. Next, he tries to establish the personal link through compliments – "obviously you guys know what you like, you appreciate the nice things in life". Following the script perfectly, he calculates the running cost of a timeshare – the 'value proposition'. True to plan he invites us to show the place we can buy into. Absolutely no change to the old sales pitch I did as a university student. I can't wait to hear him make the inevitable 'bridge'. This is where he demonstrates that the investment in the timeshare is way lower than the value; it is at that moment that he proves we are draining our wallets by not buying.

We walk and talk a bit, and the kids learn how difficult it is to live a lie. Our fake profiles almost break us up. Andrew noticed the bracelet Alicia has on her arm from the cruise ship's kids club, and as there is a big cruise ship right of the beach of the hotel he inquires if we are sure we are not on that boat. The family holds the line and answers we are not. This is true and a perfect example of a half-lie. Alicia explains later "we didn't lie; we do not stay on that ship; we are on the one that is docked around the corner!".

Now a couple of things don't work for well for the salesperson Andrew: (1) he does not realize I used to have his exact sales job, (2) he is talking to people with the right profile for his product, but given he has the fake profile he can't match us to his sales pitch, (3) I asked him twice about the total investment amount and he plainly refused (I know his script stipulates he needs to show the demo room first to whet our appetites, but it pisses me off beyond the point of recovery), (4) as we go to the 'demo' room we have to hop in a taxi (as the 'new hotel' is just up the road), but a procession blocks the road and we sit in traffic for another twenty minutes. Now we are beyond annoyed. We have spent over 1.5 hours and Heidi gets edgy, frustrated she accepted this scam. On top of it all, when we arrive at the

In Pursuit of Chocolate

newly built apartments, it is disappointing. They are nicely finished, but not in a nice location. The compound faces the inner side of the peninsula, overlooking water but the view is straight onto a concrete bridge rather than the ocean. If we would have had any interest, it would have dissipated right there and then.

Luckily, Andrew realizes his efforts are not going to turn into a sale. We drive back to the first hotel, for us to collect the prize and have free lunch if we want to. We shake hands, get two t-shirts and I ask the kids to check out the restaurant while Heidi and I collect the prize. Ah, yes – the winning gift depends on the special code on the front page… let's see. Ahhhh, so close, it is 'C', you didn't win the iPad or the $1000, but we do get the $250 booklet with gift vouchers for Bali.

By now Heidi is not even interested in the free lunch. Since lunch is 'free' on the ship 'we might as well go back'. The good news is that the taxi is paid for, and we direct him back to the ship terminal, paying the $1 for the toll bridge. The taxi driver is a nice guy and in the conversation we learn that for forty-five dollars we can rent him for a ten-hour day. Good to know for next time!

Back on the ship we have lunch and quickly return to terra firma, to the terminal building. Why? Wifi connection! On land, we sit between hundreds of other people doing the same thing. Finally, some connectivity. Sucking in and spitting out megabits of data I realize we missed an opportunity. We should have had the 'Taksi' driver take us out to some nice locations. He could have been our guide for the two hours that remained. But so be it. We had, one day on land, and we were robbed of our precious free time.

The next day we set sail for Singapore. Time passes while we go north. As you know, all good things must come to an end. The derivative of that is that all bad things do, too, in the end, after a long wait. For me this terminal moment is at 6:30 when the cruise ship docks in Singapore. For the last time we work our way down to the breakfast buffet and do the "scoop and move". We eat that final 'free' waffle and pancake, drink the last cappuccino.

The ship disembarks, and as we get set foot on land the words of Martin Luther King drop into my mind: "Free at last, free at last, thank God almighty we are free at last".

The Singapore arrival port is well run. Immigration is smooth and quick. Alicia gives a friend one last hug, and we hop into a taxi towards our hotel.

In Singapore, we pass the 100-day mark of our trip. We visit friends, soak in the luxury of Louis Vuitton, Gucci, Armani, Rolex, Cartier and all the other name brands on Orchard Road. We tour Little India and give a 'flavor of town' to the kids by walking most of the way. The temperature is bearable in the shade, uncomfortable in the sun. Luckily the overhangs of the buildings and trees provide lots of shade. When the heat gets to be too much, we walk through the buildings. They are like an intertwined air-conditioned mall. We enjoy the scenery; the old colonial style buildings with multi-colored facades; the smells of incense and curries; the shops crammed into small deep spaces selling clothes, cloth, and jewelry (mainly gold). The gold shops are striking - they have many attendants but no customers.

We enjoy the real-life non-cruise ship scenes. The restaurants where cooks chop chicken in the open air and people eat with their fingers off banana leaves, where customers drink light-brown liquid which gives me thoughts of diarrhea just looking at it. Heidi informs me this is called "lassi", a healthy yoghurt/fruit drink. We look at an odd temple, stumble through one or two shops and enjoy the liberty of walking around freely, with no time constraint.

Next, we whizz off to Chinatown in a taxi. What strikes me is that Chinatown is different than I remember it from my first visit in the 1980's. It seems so clean. In my memory, it had a more 'Little India' feel to it; chaotic, smelly and dirty. Today, Chinatown is totally different: the shops, albeit small, are nice and clean; the products neither cheap nor low-end. A fair number of tailors are present (interestingly they are all Indian looking), and several ask me politely (not at all pushy) if I am interested in a suit…

And thus we end the month of January with a small sampler of South East Asia. There is so much more to come!

Viet Nam - Where History comes Alive

AFTER THE SINGAPORE SAMPLER IT is time for us to dive into Southeast Asia full-heartedly. By mid-February we find ourselves in Viet Nam, in the charming coastal city Hoi An. The town, known for its silk weaving and silk paintings, is about half way up the coast, between Hanoi and Sai Gon. The 'silk painting' terminology confused me at first, until I realized that the beautiful paintings in the shops are not made with paint and brushes. They are stitched pictures, made with very fine silk thread. The historic center of Hoi An is picturesque and full of shops. For centuries the cloth trade has been important to the area and even today tailor-made clothes are a big part of the economy. Every shop we walk in, we happen to be the "lucky first customer" and are presented with "a very special price". Suit? Shirt for Madame? Leather shoes? The town also matches the marketed image of Viet Nam; ladies in bright colors with straw hats; baskets carried on either end of long bamboo sticks leaving the impression of being walking scales; older folks on bicycles, some of them loaded with goods up to twice their height, width and at least four times their weight. The newer addition? Younger kids with wild haircuts on mopeds with mobile phones stuck to their ears.

One day, after the sun passed its peak, the four of us jump on bicycles to pedal around. Now, if there is a more typical tourist thing to do in Viet Nam than jump on a rickety two-wheeler, I'd like to hear about it. The four of us on bicycles, this is tourist brochure material! Before getting to the quiet little roads between bright green rice fields, we have to deal with the urban traffic. At first this is terrifying. The constant honking, tooting, and ringing of the various vehicles and the number of objects which pass simultaneously on either side can be a bit daunting. Add to that the oncoming traffic going counter stream, sometimes three-wide, at fluctuating speeds, makes for a lively, albeit frightful, amalgam. But it all blends together: people stopping to chat, cars in a rush, hand/bike/motorcycle-pulled carts, and wild teens on scooters. Suddenly it falls into place. It clicks as soon as you realize that only three simple rules apply: (1) ignore what is behind you, assume that people will adjust, (2) pass anything slower than you on either side without hitting oncoming traffic - when possible make sound to alert when passing; (3) don't hit anything that's stationary or slower-moving in front of you. Nothing to it!

Another good local experience for men is to get a "Hot Tuc". For the non-Vietnamese speakers amongst you, this means a facial shave (what were you thinking?). I took the risk of not getting detailed advice on where to go, and I was happy to ignore warnings about hygiene. Hey, how bad can it be? I stroll over the streets and find that many shops are closed. It is the middle of the day and many barbers are asleep on their own chairs. The thought of waking one of these guys , only to have him stand with a sleepy head, a disgruntled mood and a sharp knife at my throat is not one I take a liking to, so I charge further into town, waiting to find the right spot. Slightly lost, I find a place to get my shave.

As I walk in, fed up with searching, I am committed. The moment I enter I notice there is no running water. As I slide into the chair with confidence pretending to be a local foreigner. Laying in what can best be described as a 1970 dentist-chair I subject myself to the treatment. Carefully, the young man puts foam on my face, straight out of a tin can. He drops some oil on it which stings (nicely) and smells a bit (less nice). I close my eyes, not wanting to see the open knife he uses. Every strike gets wiped off on a cloth which he placed on my chest. Not more than fifteen minutes later I walk back onto the road, my two-day beard (mostly) removed. It set me back 50,000 Dong ($2.00), because I forgot to negotiate. He clearly did not take me for a local! To be honest, the 5-blade disposable Gillette knives would have done a better job, but boy, few things in life feel more luxurious to a man than getting a shave! That's Al Capone stuff!

Our time in Hoi An is very pleasant. One morning, after the mango pancakes and eggs, we ready ourselves for another bike ride. We pack the small backpack, slap on sunscreen and select 4 bikes from the hotel collection, carefully selecting the best of the bunch. Most have wheels without major wobbles, adjustable seats, brakes that seem to work pretty well and a functioning bell; none of them have all - it is an optimization game. Pedaling down the road we note there is no wind and the temperature is agreeable. With the roads being as flat as Holland, cycling is easy and pleasant. We ride around without any specific route, weaving in and out of an array of passageways. Bitumen, cement, stone- and sand paths all pass under our wheels. We cruise over small dikes and hit numerous dead ends. The cul-de-sac bike paths end in rice paddies, making for nice pictures with bright green backdrops; most are well worth the u-turn.

The area we bike through is known for its bamboo and coconut leaf villages. Uniquely boats, formed like upside-down bowls (imagine half an orange, but two meters in diameter) lay by the side of the road. The boats are made from woven reed with something that looks like tar on the outside. As we push the pedals and pass the local houses we hear 'hello', 'hello', 'hello' from the under 10-year olds, who excitedly wave their hands and run up to the bike path. Passing on these little roads allows a glimpse into daily lives. It is just before the local New Year, so "spring cleaning" in advance of family visits is in full swing. Houses are washed with water, fences and facades are being repainted.

Just like we hang Christmas ornaments in the west, the decoration for New Year in Viet Nam is extensive and nicely repetitive. In this part of the world, one has large mandarin bushes 1,50 to 2,00 meters high and full of mandarins, their version of our Christmas trees. They also have one meter high yellow flowering plants and an impressive set of red lanterns on the porch. Every house looks festive. Peering past the mandarin trees into the open doorways allows a peek into Vietnamese life. The interiors of the houses are very similar. Straw mats on tiled floors, sometimes a few large wooden sofas or chairs, always a TV. Every house has a wood-carved Buddhist altar the size of a bedside table. The altars have bright, multicolored, flickering lights on it. Offerings to the gods accompany burning incense. The number of offerings Buddhists make is enormous. First of all, there is paper money (just colored paper), which is burned as an offering for the forefathers. But it goes much further. They burn paper hats, houses, Ferrari's, and iPads (yes, all paper). Anything one could imagine an ancestor might need in the afterlife is burned.

Also noteworthy is the music. There is music everywhere. Just as the USA is in love with "I'm dreaming of a white Christmas" around year end, the Vietnamese are hooked on ABBA's "Happy New Year". Every hour we hear it at least once, if not twice; the karaoke version is particularly popular.

While in Hoi An, we do the things tourists do; Vietnamese cooking classes, more biking in the rice fields, enjoying the local food, visiting a marble mountain and grotto, learning about silkworms, and - of course - hanging around at the pool doing school work. OK, most tourists don't do that last one. The time flies. By the third week of February we have seen what there is to see in Hoi An, and are ready to go to Ho Chi Minh City, also known as Sai Gon. No, not a typo, written correctly it is two words.

We fly StarJet, the Vietnamese budget airliner, and Heidi splurged on extra leg space. It sets us back $4.00 each, but it means we have a very comfortable flight. Once in Sai Gon, we take a taxi to District 1, Ho Chi Minh City. After the little town of Hoi An, HCM is hectic. But traffic is light, according to the taxi driver, since it is the last day of the year. Still, scooters are buzzing all around us like bees around a hive. It is a sight to see. Several scooters have five people on them: two parents (with helmets), two kids (no helmet) and a baby, sandwiched between the two kids.

We check into the apartment-hotel and gasp at what Heidi found for us. For the same price as two hotel rooms we have an apartment with a large kitchen, dining area, living room, a separate office desk, two bathrooms, two large sized bedrooms and a washing machine. The place is light, clean and has a balcony. Wow, after weeks of backpack life this is heaven!

New Year in Sai Gon

We unpack, settle in and decide to walk into the center of town for some food. While we had expected everything to be closed for Chinese New Year, the city is humming. We amble towards the Mekong river, passing the Intercontinental, the Hotel Saigon, and the opera. We settle for a lounge type café, sinking deep into the sofa's and order quesadillas, bento boxes, and fancy tourist drinks. We enjoy the western food, swapping plates and drinks. It turns out the bar is part of the Westin, which explains the pricing. Still, relative to Europe, it is good value.

On our way home we walk past the river, the fountains, a cathedral and many embassies. The city has a western feel to it, vastly different from Hoi An. Though we had planned to return to see the fireworks together, Alicia reports that she is not feeling so well. That one time we eat in a western restaurant, she gets hammered with food poisoning! She ends up in bed turning as white as her sheets. The next hour she ping-pongs between bed and bathroom. Poor soul. Finally, she falls asleep. It being Tet (Chinese New Year), Leendert and I take the elevator down to go and experience the celebration on the street.

We make our way back to a square close to the Mekong river and worm our way around the scooters to settle on a small piece of grass next to a fountain. The crowd is not like I'd expected. None of the abundance of laughter, joy, drinking, noise or music usually affiliated with new year celebrations; just people (often couples) sitting on their motorized wheels quietly waiting. Kids eat cotton candy and popcorn.

At exactly midnight we enter the year of the Goat as the first firework goes off over the river: Oooh, and Ahhh, from the crowd. The display is impressive and lasts exactly fifteen minutes, reaching its climax in a spectacular grand finale. As soon as it is over, scooters rev, motorbike rattle, a mass exodus starts. I see no hugging, no shouting *chuc mung nam moi* (Happy New Year in Vietnamese), no exuberant or cheerful smiling towards others. Just exodus. It is very subdued, almost anti-climatic. Leendert and I walk home, surprised by the mellow mood around us. Once back in the apartment, Leendert crashes on his pillow. I am still very awake and spend some time on my iPad. By two in the morning I too go to bed, ready for a good night of sleep. It is not to be. By 2:30 I am back out of bed. Alicia continues to feel unwell and has a bad episode, this one requiring bathroom, a shower, pajama replacement and fresh sheets. Now that makes for an interesting start of the New Year.

Chinese New Year - Family Time

Not surprisingly, Heidi and Alicia are the first out of bed the next morning. I find them covered under the duvet sitting on the couch as I walk into the living room. They are chatty, but Alicia is still pale. Suddenly we hear a loud drumbeat. Staring down from the balcony we see a show on the driveway in front of the Hotel. As it turns out, it is tradition that a New Year's inauguration ceremony takes place to bring good fortune to the business. Leendert is still asleep, so the girls and I go down without him. Our backsides get numb from the hard-stone VIP seats on the hotel steps, but we enjoy the show with the other guests.

The drums and cymbals start up and attack our eardrums. The following sixty minutes is an exhibition of color, dance, athletics, acrobatics and tradition. We witness a two-person dragon dance, while kids offer real and fake money into its mouth. The dancing dragon mounts a series of metal posts spaced about a meter apart, increasing in height to over two meters. The dancers jump effortlessly in perfect sync from foot-sized pylon to foot-sized pylon. It scares the living daylights out of me just looking at it. Finally, one of the performers climbs into what must have been a more than twelve-meter high pole, specially erected for the event. He performs a dragon-dance and personal acrobatics on the stick, proving he could work for Cirque du Soleil. His act ends high on the pole - it is a very,

very impressive show. A quick applause, and the team breaks down the climbing pole and is off to the next business location 'to bring fortune'.

Back upstairs we persuade Alicia to go back to bed. As if a tag-team, Leendert appears moments later, completely oblivious to the escapades of his sister or the drum show which just finished below his bedroom window. Ah, nothing like a teenager's deep sleep.

With Alicia pinning us to the apartment, Heidi does some travel research, Leendert schoolwork, and I read up on the history and geography of Viet Nam. I learn that Viet Nam conflicts were not only an event of the late sixties and seventies. In fact, they started in the early 1900's against the French. It grew in the aftermath of WWII as the situation with Europe got grimmer. First kicking out the Japanese (after WWII), then the French, the political unrest culminated in the Americans getting involved as they were fearful of a Russian 'domino effect', the threat that the entire Asian region would fall into Communist hands.

By early afternoon Leendert and I go on a walk-about in search for a meal. At first he has little interest, but soon the "I am really hungry" starts. We walk past the Notre Dame Cathedral and the Unification Palace. In the end we loop back to the central part of town because Leendert fancies a 'western meal', and we end up in an Argentinian steak house. We devour tasty bacon-cheeseburgers which, although we ask for a 'medium-rare', is only served medium or well-done. I guess they don't trust their source of meat. The father-son time is delightful and I make sure it lasts as long as possible. I say 'yes' to a free shot of drink which turns out to be Vodka with Caramel. A dangerous drink; sweet but not too sweet, with no alcohol taste whatsoever. It is offered while I pay millions of Dong. I am sure this drink will have suckered many a foreigner into a zero too much as tip.

Upon our return, we see Alicia has perked up; to our amazement she even declares to be a bit hungry, the ultimate proof she is getting better. The restaurant options are not phenomenal on New Year's Day, so we pick up a bucket of fried chicken, coleslaw and mashed potatoes from the KFC across the road. It was the convenience only, I cannot find another positive remark about it.

On the second day of the new year, we are invited by Anh's family. Anh is the Vietnamese lady we met way back when in the Galapagos. Luckily Alicia is recovered. She has color back in her face and some definite bounciness in her steps when she wakes up. Heidi and I grab coffees, which is easy given that the French have not only put big boulevards and some magnificent buildings in Sai Gon, but also imparted on this town the

French coffee culture. Starbucks is a small brand, but similar local chains fill many a street corner, offering roasted bean brew in all the classic ways.

In preparation of our visit to Ahn's family, I read up on customs, culture and etiquette of Viet Nam. New Year gift baskets are important, so we go to the shop and select the nicest one we can find. It includes wine, chocolate, tea, crackers and – of all things - *la vache qui rit* cheese. It is in a pretty basket, wrapped with a yellow ribbon. And so we are off to our first Vietnamese New Year.

As mentioned earlier, Viet Nam is not a typographical error; Viet Nam is two words. From what I can discern, the Vietnamese language, in general, has only mono-syllable words and sounds. The tricky part is that even the simple 'hello' pronounced "seen chau" can have 5 different meanings depending on the tonality. But wait, it gets harder. Practicing the accent is not enough. A single 'hello' does not seem to exist in Vietnamese. There a different expression for the female and male versions for: your parents, your grandparents, your siblings, a person up to ten years older than you, a person more than ten years older than you but not as old as your parents, etc, etc. I guess we'll greet the folks with an English "Hello" to avoid insulting anyone.

Reading through the do's and don'ts, I learn that whatever you do in Viet Nam, don't touch heads or shoulders (that brings bad luck). Shake hands with same sex only (as man only react if a lady offers her hand). Expect older people just to bow. Respect the elderly (they sit first, they eat first, etc). Never put your chopsticks upright in the rice bowl (looks like incense burning, associated with death and graves), scoop soup with your left hand, try all foods before returning to your favorite, put your chopsticks next to your bowl (only on top when finished). Be aware you can 'save face', 'lose face' or 'give face'. That last one was new to me. To 'give face' simply means you can grow the emotional 'face' bank-account by giving compliments. This grows the stature of the receiver.

We leave well on time, but the taxi driver and GoogleMaps don't agree on the destination. It takes much longer than expected to get there, not helped by the fact that the taxi driver asks directions several times only to loop twice back to the place we came from. We finally arrive at a gated community with a barrier and a uniformed guard who lets us in. We cruise the last few hundred meters through the neighborhood noticing luxury cars parked along the streets. About half an hour after the formal invitation we stop in front of a house where the front door stands wide open and many slippers clutter the entryway.

Anh's face appears as soon as we make our way onto the garden path, and she welcomes us in. Rather than us apologizing for tardiness it is she who apologizes for the number of people present as well as the noise level. We leave our shoes at the front door wondering if we will ever find them back again in the enormous pile and walk into the modern house. The living and dining area are filled with at least 30 people. We pass men sitting at a table and are ushered toward what looks like the kitchen table. Anh introduces her parents and grandmother. We shake hands with those that offer, we bow politely to the old guard. We are invited to sit at a table filled with food, stretch film still covers the bowls. I feel bad for the late arrival. Soon Anh asks if we want to split up. Besides this 'women's' table there is a kids' area as well as a 'men's' table. The kids are happy to stay with mom, but after I learn that at least one of the gentlemen at the 'drinking table' speaks English, and I detect that my presence is expected there, so I shift back to the living room.

The food is indescribable, mainly because I have no clue what most of it is. I recognize the somewhat regular chicken and they explain that the blackened chicken on the plate next to it a local delicacy, having been submerged in liquid for a long, long, long time. Which liquid never becomes clear to me, but I taste it and admit it is 'unique'. Smiles all around. Besides the chicken, there is fish, soup, meats of various kinds and of course vegetables. The men take great delight in making me try everything. One delicacy is a bowl of small soft, black chunks. If I understood well, it was chicken liver, only to be eaten with copious amounts of garlic. Soon, I realize the food is merely a distraction for the real purpose of being there. Drink with the family and have a jolly good time. Beer flows at a tremendous pace. It flows in combination with Chivas 18-year old whiskey. The latter is drunk straight, mixed with the beer, or in the beer with soda water. Ice is continuously added to the one-glass concoction. The seven men around the table, mostly uncles, all want to honor me with a toast. I happily participate, doing my best to remember in which order they lift their glasses so I can return the favor. I am glad that for the toast the custom is to share a shot glass rather than each having his own, for otherwise I am not sure I would have survived the second day of the year of the Goat.

As the drinking continues, a guitar appears at the table. Music is a custom, the guitar a family tradition. We are told that in the days around New Year the family moves as a tribe from house to house, bestowing good fortune wishes and songs upon the hosts. Days are filled with eating, drinking, toasting, and singing. Uncle guitarist leads the way and songs of romance, the history of Sai Gon and "the good life" are performed.

Note, the songs are about Sai Gon, not Ho Chi Minh. The locals don't like Ho Chi Minh as the name was dictated by Hanoi. There is a push for us visitors to sing as well, and in the end, I oblige, aware that it can hardly be considered 'returning the favor'. Luckily 'guitar uncle' does a splendid job syncing chords to my off-tune singing. Applause, more drink, more toasts and more songs follow. It was only a matter of time before the inevitable happened, two ladies singing the song we overdosed on in Hoi An: ABBA's "Happy New Year".

We talk with Anh and I enjoy the company of the uncles; some of which demonstrating much more physical contact than I had anticipated. Patting on legs, holding hands and waving together, hands in the air. I sing "King of the Road" solo, which gains me the pleasure of one uncle making a fist, holding it to my cheek and kissing his own hand. A compliment I believe. Not wanting to infringe on the hospitality too much and knowing the tribe still has another family house to visit, we bid our farewell. We almost succeed. We can't leave without dessert! Huge pieces of grapefruit appear and several 'encore' songs are sung. It is late afternoon when a taxi is ordered and we say our goodbyes.

On the way back, we ask the kids how they entertained themselves upstairs with the other youngsters. "We played drinking games with cards" was their response. Heidi and I are astonished. They told us they learned that in Viet Nam you are only allowed to play cards in the five days surrounding New Year. Outside those few days it is considered a felony resulting in imprisonment. They also confirmed the liquid in their game was water (aha, it is only practice drinking!).

Back at the hotel, the kids do homework and I relax letting the alcohol drop me in a sleepy zone. It doesn't last long. Heidi (school principal) suggests it is an excellent time for Physical Education, and PE-dad needs to take over. In fear of getting fired from Heidi World High, I do as instructed and go down to the pool with Leendert and Alicia. It turns out to be one of those pivotal moments in life when as dad you get knocked off the top spot. That afternoon my 13-year old son not only out-swims me breast stroke, but freestyle as well - and not by a small margin. Cognitive dissonance allows me to blame it on the Chivas 18, but deep down inside I know I'll be trailing for the remainder of my years. Deciding the alcohol needs to be sweat out, I jump in the steam room with Michael Phelps Jr. (I should have said 'van den Hoogenband junior', but I fear that would alienate some of the non-Dutch readers). Leendert is quite keen to join, not in the least so he can ask (and re-ask) if I really couldn't keep up with him. Salt in an open wound. I guess that even after all these years he does not know how competitive I really am.

The following day we breakfast on Pho, the traditional Vietnamese soup. It comes in different versions, all of which I find tasty. We start the first of many social/history excursions. Today we visit The War Remnants Museum. The museum – and its history - can fill many pages, but I'll focus on the most striking elements. The War Remnants Museum was formerly known as "Exhibition House for US and Puppet Crimes", and while the official name has changed, the overall undercurrent of the impressive (mostly black and white) picture collection leaves no doubt as to the formal view of the Hanoi government. The main message is that the citizens of Viet Nam were a peace-loving people who were attacked by the bad Americans. We walk through the garden of American fighter planes, flamethrowers, Horowitz's, Tanks, Huey's, reconnaissance Cessna's, and transport helicopters. Following the instructions on the tickets, we enter the museum and climb the stairs to the top of the building. We start three floors up and work our way down back to the exit.

And, yes, it is work. The top floor provides background, which leads the visitor from the WWII era into the Indochina war. This is the battle of the Vietnamese to rid themselves of the French. Earlier I mentioned the donations of the French to Sai Gon; the coffee houses and the French buildings. Now I can add another French curiosity to the list: the guillotine. This instrument was used by the French in the region until the 1960s. The South Vietnamese used it to execute VC prisoners (mainly North Vietnamese, but effectively any Communist would do).

But back to the American involvement. To avoid a scenario where all of Asia would fall into communist hands, the Americans decided to support the non-communist President Gno Diem. He was a nasty piece of work, and after several years the US was forced to drop support for him. The Communist threat, however, did not disappear. Walking through the exhibition, it feels that for every well intended political step taken, the atrocities accumulated. Through the colored spectacles of the Hanoi government we learn the reason the US went to war in Viet Nam. They wanted to secure the supply of Tin and Tungsten to America. Wow, that was news to me! We also learn that President Johnson claimed the Vietnamese started the war by attacking a US warship, which, according to the exhibition, was never proven. Either way, the event formally ignited the American War. Yes, in this building the Viet Nam War is referred to as the American War; funny how perspectives depend on where you grow up!

As we move one level down, the tone of the exhibit gets harsher.

Before entering this floor's main room, I buy a Coca-Cola from a little concession stand. I savor the taste and enjoy the irony of swallowing this all-American drink straight out of – can it be more poetic - the iconic red can. Strengthened by the sugary drink I usher the family into the next room. The space captures the bravery of the Vietnamese people resisting to an impressive and daunting enemy. A depiction of pure heroism against the backdrop of horror of the American war machine. To support the Hanoi point of view on history the second floor displays the 'Requiem Exhibit'. It shows the illustrations by both local and American war photographers powerfully depicting the stories of the common men in the trenches. A heavy, quiet atmosphere fills the room; visitors are all impacted part by the horror, part the intensity, part the sadness of the events.

But wait, we can do better (or should I say worse). The next chamber builds on the previous rooms. It depicts the cruelty, barbarism and savagery of the Americans killing the hard-working farmers "who only wanted to live their lives happily and support their own families". Do not get me wrong, the killings at My Lai and some other massacres were horrific, but then again, which war is clean?

The next area is dedicated to Agent Orange, Napalm and other colors of the chemical warfare rainbow. Having heard about these but not being all too familiar, I looked up the data afterwards. Agent Orange (so called because the drums from Dow and Monsanto had two identifying orange bands on it) was claimed to only defoliate the jungle thus exposing the enemy. In fact, it was extensively sprayed on crops as well. This was to hurt the VC by ruining their food supplies. Napalm already existed before the Viet Nam war. It is a 'burning gel' concocted at Harvard (nice to have top-end universities). The product burns at up to 800 degrees centigrade. Napalm is sticky and almost impossible to remove from skin. It is 'effective' because it causes surface and sub-tissue burning for an extended time. Needless to say, the photograph of the well-known naked 'Napalm Girl' features dominantly in the room.

Roaming the not-so-subliminal orange-walled room, one is faced with a long series of pictures of disfigured and maimed people, victims of chemical warfare. It starts with burns and infections, graduating to nasty skin deceases, expanding to amputees, and then to the ultimate crescendo of deformed babies born after the war. To drive the point home one of the last displays holds a series of jars in which deformed fetuses float in a suspended state.

It goes without saying that while we make our tour we carefully monitor Alicia and Leendert. The former is not too touched by it, summarized in her statement "it's gross". The latter is intrigued, taking his time to read the little plaques next to the pictures. I guess at Leendert's age there is that strange love/hate relationship and that sense of interest for the gore and the disgusting. When talking with him about what he sees he swings back and forth. At times he reflects like a grown up "but what they did does not make any sense….", at times he reacts like a youngster, quipping "that must really hurt when your leg gets ripped off like that".

When we finish the second floor, we have seen enough, each for our own reasons. Alicia is bored, Heidi, as an American, feels beaten up, Leendert is tired of reading, and I am overloaded on how cruel mankind can be. We have little desire to visit the ground floor which is dedicated to 'the army of today'. It is supposed to be more up-beat, but I can't see how, so we give it a miss. Crossing the museum's front yard, we see another small doorway. Clearly there is more to see. This is an area where 'tiger cages' are simulated. To make a long story short, Tiger Cages are coffin sized cages made from barbed wire. These cages where used by the South Vietnamese to keep VC political prisoners (preferably in the sunshine). The rest of the displays in this area show how these earlier mentioned peace-loving Vietnamese farmers interrogated their VC brothers: waterboarding, removing finger- and toe-nails, hammering metal pins in heel bones, knocking teeth out, etc. I am happy to take Alicia back out of this side area back to the front yard and to the ever so interesting flying machines: "oh, look, I think it is a Cessna".

As we walk back to our apartment we debrief a bit. We agree on a couple of things: (1) it is amazing how cruel people can be to another, (2) war is to be avoided, (3) chemical warfare is awful [as opposed to normal warfare?], (4) there was a fair bit of propaganda – or at least another view point. The excursion was the first part of a lesson in 'recent history'. Part two of our social / history lesson is planned for tomorrow. Cu Chi!

A trip to Cu Chi

For those not familiar with Cu Chi, they are the famous 'Cu Chi tunnels' known from the ….War. Early in the morning we crowbar the kids out of bed, which doesn't go over well. Alicia is close to a tantrum, Leendert mopes; "I just want to sleep!". The sun barely pops above the horizon when we arrive at reception where a guide waits with a van. We opted for a fast boat up the Mekong river (reportedly outpacing the buses from town to the same spot). It's a full day trip: the boat ride, a tour of the tunnels, lunch and some tourist stops on the way back.

As we pick up some other folks, the kids slowly step into the land of the living. They are still unhappy but some of it wears off once we board a boat with a 200HP engine on the back. The comfortable boat shoots us up the Mekong and the crew offers us fresh lychees and tasty croissants with ham and cheese. Smiles return on the faces of the kids; *vive la France*! We drink juice and iced coffee. Now these iced coffees deserve specific mention. The name in Vietnamese is *Cà Phê Sua* (ca-fe su-a). It is a popular local coffee made with sweetened condensed milk (the 'sua' part). Let me caution you - it's highly addictive. Once you try them you will be hooked! Tasty, cold, sweet, but not overly so, it's good at any time of the day. Heidi and I each have two.

With bright orange life-vests around our bodies we speed over the river for over an hour, zigzagging between vast ponds of water plants. Once docked, we enter the Cu Chi complex. The entry where our tickets are checked consists of a large tiled tunnel, not unlike one would see in a modern metro station. I quip that the Cu Chi tunnels are not half as bad as they are said to be. Heidi gives me a disapproving glance.

Behind me I notice the first buses arriving. Given the New Year break, the roads are clear of traffic and the busies made good time, not really being outpaced by the boats. Still, the crowds are mostly behind us and they are more than manageable. Our guide leads us to a sitting area to give a bit of a background to the site.

The Cu Chi area is about thirty-five kilometers due north of Sai Gon (referred to as Ho Chi Minh on this site as it is a formal government property). It was a major military battlefield from 1965 to 1975. The Americans had bases here and it was here that 16,000 VC lived underground. According to Billy Joel's "Goodnight Saigon" the M16's ruled the day and the AK47's ruled the night. A big map indicates the respective 'controlled' areas. Not far away is "Trang Bang", where the well known 'Napalm Picture' was taken. The guide shows the general layout of the area and explains the tunnel system with the use of a scaled model.

The forest surrounding the tunnels was full of booby traps. The tunnel system had rooms on three levels; the first level is two meters underground, the third goes down eight meters. The complex is hidden with only few small access points. Diagonal aeration channels were hidden by termite hills. Chimneys of the kitchens had three "smoke collecting rooms" before exiting meters away from the living quarters. Smoke would come out in small amounts through little mounds, and only during early morning hours when the mist lingered.

Keen to beat the crowd, the guide skips the video which we will see later. We leave the welcome area and walk to our first stop. A green-uniformed Vietnamese guy picks up some seemingly random leaves, disclosing a square hole in the ground. He put his legs in, slips down and puts the wooden leaf covered lid back on. I am not even 1,5 meters from the spot and I can't detect where he vanished. He pops back up, demonstrating not only how to disappear but also how to reappear. Next it is up to us to give it a try. While not everyone in our tour group is willing/able to try, both the kids, Heidi and I copy the disappearing trick, finding out that it is only possible to get in and out of the cavernous hole the way the green-man showed. Hands straight up in the air, making the top of your body smallest. Any other way is impossible; I tried and got stuck.

We move on and see a booby trap with sharp bamboo shoots sticking up; the war classic made famous by Rambo. We see the actual size of the Cu Chi tunnels; so narrow that even Alicia and Leendert would get stuck. A VC workshop shows how unexploded bombs, shrapnel, and tires were recycled and reused. Two fun details on the shoes they wore: they are made from tire rubber, so they last forever, and they were often made with the heel wider than the toe. Reportedly this would confuse the enemy, because the footprints would point in the opposite direction from where the person was heading. I only see one mistake in this logic. If the Americans tried to avoid the enemy, and walk away from Charlie, they would actually catch them from behind. Wouldn't they be approaching from the back, before the Vietnamese saw them?

We continue the tour and see how rice paper is made for the typical Vietnamese spring rolls. It seems totally out of place, but I guess Charlie had to eat too. Next, we walk past a shooting range where – if you so wish - you can shoot with M16's, AK's or even machine guns. You pay by the bullet, 10 rounds minimum. Luckily no one in our group has any such desire. We continue our tour and listen to the sounds of war in the background. Obviously some tourists feel the need to blow metal into a Vietnamese soil wall 200 meters out.

We carry on to a hut showcasing all various forms of booby-traps: 'See-Saw', 'Window', 'Rotating', 'Fishing trap', 'Doorway'…. It's amazing how inventive people can be when it comes to harming others. Very simply, you don't want to unintentionally encounter any of these metal and bamboo pinned contraptions.

Further down the track we arrive at a spot where tunnels have been created post war. They are a larger version than the original ones but ensures we can 'enjoy' the experience of being underground. People with high blood pressure and heart conditions are advised not to participate. The entire length of the demo-tunnel is 100 meters, but there are earlier escape routes if needed. The guide descends and the kids follow in a blink. They disappear like true 'tunnel rats', the nickname of the American soldiers (mostly smaller-build Puerto Ricans) who were brave and stupid enough to risk their lives entering the tunnels for combat. Heidi and I follow with backpacks and some apprehension. A couple of things we learn quickly: (1) don't enter tunnels underground, (2) definitely don't enter tunnels underground with backpacks on your back, (3) especially don't enter tunnels with backpacks on your back when you don't like heat, dark and you are slightly claustrophobic. Needless to say, the kids complete the one hundred meter adventure while Heidi and I are more than happy to escape after forty meters at the first exit hole.

The good news is that we all got an impression of what the underground life was like. I was happy Heidi brought some iced-towels to clean ourselves up after resurfacing! It's a good way to rid myself of dust and angst-induced sweat. We go underground once more in an even larger tunnel. Here we observe an underground meeting room, a kitchen and the water hole (an underground well for fresh water).

Completing the Cu Chi tour we watch the video on the tunnels. This is the one the guide skipped at first. I had read that they were scandalously choreographed. Truth be told, the guide tried to steer us away from it but the group seemed to think "we paid, so we say 'yes' to see everything". We watch the film, which was produced in 1976 and could have belonged in yesterday's museum. The film conveyed that same message that the 'American aggressors' were all to willing to shoot the patriotic peace-loving farmers, their babies, their animals and even their pots and pans (Really? How barbaric is that - shooting kitchen equipment!). Especially the list of names hailed in the movie - those who had received the "honorary award for killing Americans" - was a bit hard to listen to. Having blue-cover passport-holding family members and knowing that close relatives walked these jungle grounds as military personnel risking their lives, does make it an emotionally loaded visit.

Note: despite all the above, the overall impression we got in Viet Nam is that the real Vietnamese look at the War as something long forgotten. Their love for progress combined with the current leaps in the economy and the semi-free economy far outruns the governmental stance projected by Hanoi on this War which took place several decades ago. One cannot escape the feeling that these exhibitions are a time-warp; they have not yet caught up with the current lives of the locals. The latter are open and kind in approach, live in modern day Viet Nam rather than in history. But enough about the War, let's move on....

We have lunch at the waterfront of the Mekong river, and hop into a modern minivan to make our way back to Sai Gon with a few stops. 'Hieh' (pronounced 'Hi') is our guide for the afternoon.

The first (short) stop is at a rubber plantation. Hieh explains no latex, the base material for rubber, is being harvested at this time because it is the dry season. Once the rains start in June, the trees produce up to 15 liters per annum. Neither Heidi nor the kids are familiar with a rubber plantation, so picking at the latex stuck on the tree makes for some entertainment (in fact, both kids keep kneading a little ball for the next hour or so).

From there, the van takes us over small roads to a middle-aged entrepreneur who has discovered the value of crickets. In big plastic-lined boxes he raises millions of crickets. We see the process from egg laying (the female has a little stick on the back of her body to poke a hole in the ground to lay eggs), to feeding, to shipping boxes. Depending on the season they sell for up to $8/kg. The main use of the little critters is bird feed. The main markets are Hanoi and export to China. Secondly, the little jumpers also make a tasty dish for humans. The best ones, per true connoisseurs, are the pregnant females, since the eggs bring protein and additional flavor.

We are invited to sit on the front porch and partake in a tasting. A full plate with freshly cooked-up jumpers stands invitingly in the middle of the table. We dig in with our chopsticks, finding that the garlic stir-fried insects are quite tasty. The other tourists are more apprehensive and comment on our zest for life. Leendert and Alicia seem to have forgotten that we only recently had lunch, and eat well more than their fair share. The group members are amazed, parents proud.

That evening, over dinner, we discuss the upcoming volunteer work. Alicia comes up with a classic remark: "I hope it is an orphanage, because if it is a school it is just like normal". I copy back her answer, pointing out that she just called working in an unknown Vietnamese school as volunteer teacher "like normal". We all have a good laugh.

A dip in the road - Travel Sick

In the morning the kids wake up around nine. They go swimming while the parents go to find breakfast. When we return, we find the young ones showering and packing their backpacks, unprompted! At noon our

In Pursuit of Chocolate

ride arrives to pick us up. We walk down, and in the elevator Heidi belches out "I wanna go home". Within a split-second Alicia chimes in as well. Okay, I didn't see that one coming. There is no doubt that the comfort of the place we are going to won't be like this hotel, but going home? Really?

The moment passes quickly as we arrive on ground level and we shake hands with two ladies from the volunteer organization. They walk us to a taxi and tell us the driver knows where to bring us. They have another place to visit, more volunteers to collect. We settle in the cab and Heidi tries to undo a bit of her previous "go home" statement. I think it caught her by surprise as well.

While I could hear in her tone she truly meant it, she back pedals expertly stating that she is just "fed up with packing". I have the weak comeback that for the next two weeks we'll be in one place, so there won't be any packing and unpacking required. Meanwhile I pray the hostel-like conditions we are facing won't be too horrible.

We drive through town for about 15 minutes and stop in front of our new home. A big metal gate is the only barrier between the offices and the outside street. The office itself is open to the elements. We remove our shoes and are guided up the stairs. The first floor contains a small living room with couches which are more lived-in than those of a bankrupt fraternity house. Oh boy! We continue the climb. On the second floor is our room. Four metal bunk-beds are placed against the walls and remind me of the spartan French summer camp beds the kids enjoyed last year. Thin foam mattresses and one steel cabinet are the only other items in the room. We are told the air conditioner is only to be used as of 9pm. The bathroom is a small rectangle, toilet, sink and shower with no partitions or curtains. The shower has no resting place for the shower head, it dangles down on the ground. There are no towels. I dare not look at Heidi, fearful I might read her mind.

The ultimate make-or-break question is posed: "Do they have internet?". Instantly recognizing the importance of the question, I walk downstairs to ask Koen, our contact. Thankfully, he informs me there is internet and he gives me the passcode. Walking back up the stairs I see marked on a whiteboard that the entire room is allocated to us (the numbers of the other ½ of the bunk beds have no name behind it). Good fortune I tell myself. Sharing the bunk beds with others would have been a non-starter. Once back in the room I share the good wifi news as well as the fact that the room is entirely ours. Immediately the thin foam mattresses are tossed around; we stack them and get double thick mattresses, the top bunks become luggage storage. Later, we run to a local shopping center and buy towels and other basics. We settle in and I pretend to like the environment to uplift the family spirit. I am partially successful.

Dinner is served at six in the evening and we meet other volunteers; predominantly 23 to 30 year olds. "Dinner is served" is perhaps overstating it. There are pre-formed metal prisoner-like food trays with plastic lids stacked on the table. Each tray has a number. On the wall hangs a piece of paper where we can find our names and allocated 'food numbers'... *voilà* the system. We eat together in the bare room. It has a tiled floor and a white neon light high on the wall casting cold light on the plastic folding chairs and on our food. On our tray we find some veggies, a small piece of meat, and, depending on your number, spring rolls or a fried egg. This culinary delight is supplemented with rice out of a rice cooker in the center of the table. We sit with our trays on our laps since there is not enough space on the table to hold all our plates. We eat while making initial nervous conversation with the other strangers.

The group consists of two young Germans, four Japanese students and a very skinny, older Irish lady who has never had chopsticks in her hands. She struggles with every bite and I pray she either finds a fork or learns to eat with chopsticks, otherwise she risks becoming even skinnier. The conversation limits itself to the usual "when did you arrive?", and, "how long will you stay?" The Japanese mainly listen.

After dinner we rinse the dishes. The kids retire to the room and I sit in the 'fraternity lounge'. Heidi joins, but gets little enjoyment out of the company and she soon goes up. I chat with the newcomers and two youths who have been here for a while. Both seem worn out, clearly past their volunteering honeymoon. A Swiss girl is doing okay, but only enjoys half of the work, a French girl stopped teaching today because she could no longer take it: "the kids don't listen, they aren't interested, and there is no program….". I'm not too shocked, since listening to their descriptions, it sounds much like the Galapagos to me!

The remaining discussions focus on daily life of young volunteers: happy hour, 'girls night out', the girl who ran around with her pants pulled down last weekend. The new German arrivals inquire where they can best buy cheap local beer. Oh, boy. I have a suspicion we are in for a rough two weeks. I return to the room, just in time for goodnight kisses. The airco is now blowing full blast, making the room bearable. Kids are fine, but I detect a certain unpronounced "what am I doing here?" in Heidi. I am confident that in a few days we'll be back in a routine and all will be fine, or at least that's what I tell myself.

Our new reality - Getting Started

I had a surprisingly good night of sleep, the air conditioner making it wonderfully comfortable. By deduction, however, I derive that the rest of the family had a rough night. They, in stages, put more and more clothes on during the night, afraid to turn the air cooler off completely. It's tough to find a balance.

We enter the kitchen for breakfast and find an open box with white bread and two open jars. One jar with jelly, one with peanut butter. The spoons poke out from the top. We dive in and make ourselves an instant coffee. Heidi and I shake our heads at the crumbs and spills left behind by those who have already eaten and left the house. Yup, definitely a frat house feel.

Not much later Koen arrives and starts preparing the introductory presentation. It is close to eight-thirty when he is ready to lead us through the basics: the available projects, rules of living in the house, and general safety considerations for travel in Viet Nam. We recognize that the presentation and videos on the volunteering work are primarily designed to manage the expectations of "virgin" participants. It warns of the lack of classroom discipline (nothing we haven't seen before) and gives a bit of history of the orphanages. One new and painful story is related to the orphanage for handicapped kids. While the war remnants museum told us all about how agent orange caused the deformities, Koen tells us many are attributed to women taking drugs attempting to abort unwanted pregnancies, . The story requires a side explanation to Alicia.

We learn what we are allowed (and not) to do in the house and at the projects. We sign papers that we will respect the organization and the people we encounter on the projects. There is a clear undertone which addresses concerns around sex and child abuse. Koen is at a loss when it comes down to the paperwork of our kids. I smile, tell him that we will sign as guardians. Yes, Koen, we'll take the responsibility our kids won't abuse the kids in the orphanage and school. Yes, we indemnify you in case something happens to them. Scribble scribble, sign sign. Next we go around the room, all inductees introduce themselves and share what they would like to do and how they see themselves contributing. During the coffee break Koen and his assistant put the volunteer puzzle together, allocating projects to individuals. After the break, he suggests a program for each of us. We're up first. It is proposed we visit the Pagoda today (to take a peek), and start work in the adjoining orphanage tomorrow. Starting Thursday, we will teach in a regular school. The school project is, without a doubt, one of the better options. It is reportedly a real school with classrooms and teachers, as opposed to a loose assembly of people who might (or might not) want to learn. The latter is often the case in Buddhist Pagodas. Our initial pagoda visit is to bridge the gap to the school assignment. The school re-opens in 2 days, because it is still on TET (new year) break.

The projects are quite far away; ranging from 45 minutes to 1h30' bus rides from the hostel. How spoiled we were with our ten minute walks to the schools on Isabela and in Cusco! In the afternoon, we are chaperoned by one of the long term volunteers to the Pagoda. She shows us where to take and change buses. Adding a 10 minute wait at the first bus stop, the total commute is two hours. By the time we arrive, it is 4pm and we have depleted the two large bottles of water I threw in the back pack. Boy it is hot! Wary, Heidi and I agree that we'll return by taxi.

The orphanage holds abandoned and physically and mentally handicapped kids. It is not unlike what we saw in Cusco. Limited space, many young children running around, basic conditions. But things are different when we get to the next-to-last room. There, lying on their backs, are about ten kids with the worst hydrocephalus cases I've ever seen. Google images for 'water-head babies' and you get the picture, no pun intended. Despite their young age they carry heads the size of basketballs, no hair, slightly cross-eyed and skin pulled so tight that they can barely blink. It is hard not to think you have entered a Hollywood set where the next film about extra-terrestrials is being shot. The dreadful sight obliges a person to stare, while your legs want to do nothing else but to turn around and run away. Our guide tells us we are more than welcome to enter "say hello" and familiarize ourselves with the work "or would you rather visit the temple first".

I am not displeased when I hear that Alicia suddenly takes a keen interest in Buddhist temples. "Yes the temple would be nice." I too sigh relief. We walk away from the horrible scene and enter the temple. Heidi and I monitor the kids and discuss what we just saw – we are also heavily impacted and emotionally affected. Luckily the temple is a perfect change of scenery. What a temple! It is an architectural marvel based on its uniqueness alone. My phrase 'this is exactly like something I have never seen before' comes in handy. This temple is a combination of a Disney-like grotto, a tiled pagoda, a prayer room and a Buddhist statue exhibition accented with disco balls and ornamental lotus flowers. I have seldom seen something more eclectic.

Half an hour later we return to the orphanage and take a second hit of the 'painful to see'. We linger until we notice the experienced volunteers are getting ready to go to the bus, homeward bound. We also exit grab a cab instead. More expensive, but we see little benefit in sitting in a full bus for ninety minutes. No, we prefer to pay the 200,000 dong extra (nine Euros) and enjoy an air conditioned environment while debriefing with the kids. Given the rush hour the cab also takes about fifty minutes, but the time is put to good use chatting. Family therapy, and we all try to come to terms with what we have observed. We are all thankful for being healthy, and glad to be helping out tomorrow.

We have dinner and, physically and mentally exhausted, are in bed by nine. Tomorrow we need to be at the bus stop at seven, so no dragging feet.

Second day at the Pagoda

The next morning we dive into the nutrition-free white bread, the peanut butter and jelly and rush out at five to seven to catch the bus. We make the connection and walk from the bus station to the pagoda through the narrow streets. Upon arrival, we find that none of the other volunteers are present, nor any of the team leaders for that matter. Our trip was smooth and quick. We sit on a bench and wait. About twenty minutes later other volunteers from our house arrive, but still no coordinator is to be seen. Finally, just before nine a lady walks up and shows us to the 'big' play room.

We place our backpacks on top of a cabinet (out of reach) and dive in. A pile of Lego, some toys and a cluster of plastic balls attract us first. One child immediately engages with me and soon with Leendert: we end up tossing light weight plastic balls.

After a while, one of the ladies waves me over to a kid who is strapped into a full body contraption standing him upright. She indicates I should hold him while she undoes the bands around his shoulders, waist and knees. I support him under the arms and notice he remains as stiff as a plank, his disfigured legs not moving when the bands are undone. I wonder what is next. Answer: nothing. The lady unstrapping him is off to another task. OK, I'll improvise.

I pick the skinny fellow up and carry him in my arms. It feels like I am walking around with half a dozen two-by-fours; his arms and legs don't bend, his body only hinges at the hips. Though we have no language in common, we have a good understanding of what he wants me to do in under five minutes. He stares at something, I walk him there. He looks at something else, I go there. Thus we spend the next forty-five minutes. We have a surprisingly good time together; his face lighting up every time we reach the end point. I carry him past the little gate of the playroom into the temple area, which, given his positive shaking and encouraging sounds, clearly excites him. I am forced to take frequent breaks since it is hot and I sweat like a horse. Carrying a dead weight plank in this heat is not an easy task. He does not seem to mind.

Luckily, after a while I get him to relax a bit, and his legs start to fold at the knees. This makes my life much better as a semi-limber dead weight is much easier to carry. My new friend goes into a giggling fit as I dare carry him outside the Pagoda into the little side streets. Suddenly I realize I might just have corrupted him; I'm not sure how often he goes outside the confines of the temple area

A bit later, in the general area I place stick-man on a mat, it is time to switch to another victim of chance. Taking inventory of the rest of the family members I notice Alicia has leeched on to a long-term French volunteer. She sits at a table with slightly more mature kids, coloring in drawing books. She's happy. I'd seen Leendert on the walk-about, and he is trooping away, taking different kids for walks. The ladies of the Pagoda told us "exercise is good for them", and while I won't argue, I -yet again- don't honestly see the value. Suddenly, the atmosphere in the play room changes and there is a flurry of activity. Lunch is ready.

The kids are put into chairs, most of them tied in. Large bibs appear and bowls of food are distributed. For most it is a Pho with rice, but for those who cannot chew, a baby food version is supplied. I re-live feeding my own kids. I am lucky because the girl I am feeding is happy to bite and swallow. In fifteen minutes I am done. I look over at Heidi, and she is struggling; not only with the feeding, but physically too. I sit next to her on the tile floor and take over. Heidi's back is troubling her; the bus rides and the uncomfortable bed took their toll. After thirty minutes, only half the bowl is emptied into the child. A volunteer coordinator walks up and tells us to come and have lunch ourselves. "What about this child?" I ask. We're told this particular child is known as one of the slowest eaters of the group and that one of the permanent ladies of the orphanage will finish the feeding job.

We leave the play area and sit in a big room where we are served rice, soup, fried tapioca and some sour green chard. Dessert is fresh watermelon. Not bad. Given that it is a Buddhist pagoda, and Buddhists don't even kill mosquitoes, it is not reasonable to expect a nice piece of tenderloin!

The orphans are taking naps, and nothing will happen until two in the afternoon. Time off for the volunteers. A great moment for school work! Leendert works on vocabulary while Alicia completes a section of mathematics. Time flies. When the afternoon session starts back up it is much like the morning: playing, drawing, entertaining, and walking (and in my case sweating).

After two hours, a repeat of the morning meal routine takes place. Feeding time. This time Leendert too feeds one of the children. When Heidi tries to take over, the child lets her know in no uncertain terms that he wants Leendert to continue. The same happens when one of the local ladies attempts to take over. Seeing my thirteen year old son feed a handicapped child (of about his own age) is one of those images that will forever be burned into my memory. The combination of suffering and servitude somehow making it an indescribably painful and beautiful image.

By five almost all kids are fed, re-diapered, and the room is cleaned. This is where we say our goodbyes to the pagoda and return to the bus, two hours of Sai Gon passing by. We take quick showers and eat our dinners off the metal trays. It is basic but good: rice, fish and a Vietnamese spring roll.

Later that evening, kids asleep, Heidi shares with me that this volunteering frat house is not the place she wants to celebrate her birthday on Saturday. I nod in agreement. As Heidi closes her eyes, I sneak out with our computer to find a corner eatery for a beer. Quietly reflecting on the days' events, scanning the internet for something to do for Heidi's birthday I drink my drink(s). I negotiate the price of my beer down by twenty-five percent and see the Sai Gon evening routine pass by: vending scooters with food, old ladies selling lottery tickets. Walking home, hugging my computer, I feel blessed, happy I don't have to rely on other people to carry me as I make my way.

Teaching in Sai Gon

Today we have a change of scenery. The usual morning rush gets all of us to the front gate at seven, stomachs lined with peanut butter, jelly and a splash of instant coffee (and a box of juice in the case of the kids). Hai, one of the volunteer coordinators, goes with us to take us to our new assignment, teaching at a school. The good news is that it is just one bus to take, the downside is that it still takes an hour and a half.

By nine thirty, we arrive at the school and make acquaintance with the principal; a nice late-middle aged lady who has a rather good command of the French language. She is a bit nervous about her language skill and prefers to talk through our guide who patiently translates. We get an overview of what we can do teaching-wise. Not much later, we leave the principal behind and walk towards the first class. A quick word with (and introduction to)the teacher before we poke our heads into the room. Glancing around we see the class is open to the elements on both sides; the side walls have no glass windows just metal bars. It makes me wonder if it is to keep students in or people out. The room has nice tiled floors and long dark brown wooden benches. We present ourselves. Instantly, the blue-uniformed children stand up and recite a half-sung verse in Vietnamese. The low benches which form the seats for the students force them to stand and sit at the same time. At given moments in the choral the teacher interjects replies, which makes for a nice 'back-and-forth'. The chant takes about a minute, after which the students retake their seats. We exit and the same routine happens in the next two classrooms. That is the full school. Three classrooms, fifteen kids to a class. We walk past the building and arrive at a large open, canopied area. Three children mop the floor while our coordinator gives us background on the school.

The school is sponsored by the Catholic Church. Students are mainly from destitute and broken families (divorce, prison, etc.). The school provides a final safety net. The kids either come in the morning, have lunch and return home to work in the afternoon, or they come in after lunch for afternoon classes. The principal is a nun. Under her directorship, the school has steadily improved; the facility is upping its quality with donations and effort from volunteers. Pictures on the wall illustrate an impressive progression timeline. Discipline is a key element of this school, and the results are very good. Our coordinator explains that the kids we see cleaning floors are former students, and a testimony to the success of the school. The alumni return as volunteers just because they like the school and want to help maintain it. Quite impressive!

We hang around until the morning break which is announced by a heavy drum. The "dong, dong, dong" vibrates through the air and within little time students exit the classrooms and start playing on the courtyard. Some of them clearly have been tasked with setting up tables and stools for later. Sixteen tables (4x4) are placed on the clean tiled floor and aligned perfectly. The students charged with the preparation work remind me of soldiers in the Scottish military tattoo in Edinburgh. They walk in perfect lines, clearly a trained routine. They place each piece of furniture consciously, neatly and perfectly straight.

The kids playing have, to my surprise, no toys. Even the usually ever-present playground football is absent from the scene. Having nothing better to do than to run around, they play tag, or, busy themselves with playful karate. I say 'playful' but must say that I am amazed that with their fanatic kicks, none of them get hurt. It is also amazing that despite the running and racing around, not one of the light plastic tables or chairs is touched or otherwise moved from their perfect position.

About a quarter of an hour later "dong" calls for a return to class. The kids put on their shoes (in case they were barefoot) and stand perfectly aligned in the yard next to the school building. Looking at them reminds me of Leendert and Alicia in school in France, where classes would enter the building row by row; students wait patiently before being told to enter. Three classes, six rows – each row with the genders separated. A teacher decides the line-up is not good enough. A bit more straightening out is required; each student places their right hand on the shoulder of the pupil in front, thus perfectly spacing themselves. Only then are they called to class. Row by row they go in. Girls first. They walk up the steps one by one, take off their shoes, align them in a row, place their hands on their backs and enter the classroom.

Leendert and I go into one class, Alicia and Heidi disappear with the volunteer coordinator into the class next door. I consider myself lucky, as the teacher of my class speaks a bit of French. She introduces me again to the class and says, *allez y*, graciously stepping to the side. By the time I have said "hello class" she has pulled Myriam's Galapagos trick. She is gone! OK, I've seen this before…

The class has about fifteen kids, and their level of English is 'count to fifteen and recite the colors'. Leendert helps out. We entertain and work with the learners until the next break. I glance several times at my watch. The class is ninety minutes long, which is not only too much for the student's attention span but also for my creativity. I muddle through the last ten minutes like a boxer in the ring one round too many and am intensely relieved when the 'dong' finally marks the end of class.

We meet up with Heidi and Alicia, who reportedly had a good session. The students go to the covered area and eat at the square tables which were set up during the morning break. We are told our lunch will be served once the students are finished. The kids clean their plates twice; once of food, once with soap and water at a sink on the side. They store the tables and chairs behind a partition and disappear off to home.

We wander around a bit until the principal finds us and tells us lunch is ready. Returning to the eating area we see one table is set; the same small plastic tables the kids ate from. The same low plastic stools. We see meat, fresh salad, soup and rice. Wow! Actually, double 'wow'. We taste the lovely chicken soup and savor delicious fresh tomatoes. Not long afterwards the principal brings out dried shredded chicken in a bowl, which Alicia remarks "is just like the stuff you used to take home from your trips to China".

We attack the food like wolves and together with the coordinator truly enjoy the meal. The quality is far beyond what we get at the hostel. Finished, we pick up our plates and go the kitchen area to wash the plates. Some kids disrupt us and start making noise. Clearly I am doing something wrong… Our coordinator listens and translates. The kids are telling her we are their guests and we should definitely not clean up. It will be their honor to do so!

As this was the first day back from Tet, the school routine is not quite re-established. Many kids are missing in the afternoon, so it is decided to put all of them in one class. We teach all together, which turns out to be a lot of fun. Alicia and Heidi first play shop with them, afterwards I take over and go over fruit, games, house, kitchen and singing *Frère Jacques* in several languages. By three pm we are done. We sit with the principal and agree that for the next days a class will be maximum one hour long. We'll also align to teach the last hour before the lunch and the first hour after. This works brilliantly for us as (1) we avoid the 'oh-my-god' wakeup calls, (2) we get to enjoy the phenomenal lunches, (3) we have a nice break of 2 hours in the middle of the day when our kids can study, and (4) we are not back too late. Now that's a sweet assignment!

That evening Heidi books the hotel for the weekend. I had delayed the decision on what to do for her birthday. Not because I wanted to stay in the frat house, but I had been trying to find something special. Unfortunately going to Da Lat (by airplane) or floating on the Mekong on a riverboat did not work out; either timing or availability crashed those plans. Too bad. Luckily I made reservations for dinner which she doesn't know about yet!

The evening meal is served on metal trays under neon light. The kids play together and Heidi watches a movie when we get a real scare. Settling in our room we find that very loud karaoke singing fills our room. Karaoke is fun when you are doing its but it is arduous to listen to if not done well. Now, if it is done by a friend, it can be tolerable. If the vocalist is a stranger, it becomes difficult, especially if badly executed. What we hear is both strange and badly executed! The music seems to come from two houses over and it is impossible to ignore. Heidi looks at me with panic and a 'do something' look in her eyes. I decide to give it a half hour before taking action; though what action I'd take I'm not quite sure. To my great joy the sound dies down twenty-five minutes later… Disaster avoided.

The next day we have an easy wake up since our classes start later. We get dressed, have the peanut and jelly sandwiches like good volunteer drones, and move to the bus stop for an eight-fifteen departure. Despite the morning hour I seek shade while waiting at the stop and chug down my first bottle of water. We observe the loaded scooters cruising by.

Right next to the bus stop is a gas station, which provides delightful entertainment. After people fill up, they re-enter the traffic flow in one of two ways. They either drive against traffic for thirty meters, crossing three lanes and merge into the traffic going the other way, or they merge with the flow. The second option is unique. I notice that except for one westerner, nobody (and I mean nobody) looks left before merging into traffic. They simply ride along the curb for a bit and then squeeze in, assuming the traffic will create the space for them. They obviously live by the Hoi An rule book - assume that traffic behinds you adjusts. Miraculously, though, it works. Indeed, no 'near misses', it works very well.

We ride the bus like locals for the hour-and-a-half; Heidi and I use the time to prepare lesson plans. As we walk up to school the principal gives us a polite 'good morning', treating us like professors with experience and tenure. The teacher – spotting me - waves me over and indicates 'here you go, the class is all yours'. I have a *déjà vu*. Walk up and they hand over the reins. Each class finishes with a little "thank you teacher"-song, which I think should be introduced in all schools. Nothing like a sign of appreciation.

At lunch time Heidi and I get into the habit of crossing the street and frequenting the corner coffee shop. The first time, we use hands and feet to make clear what we want. By the second day the lady realizes we are hooked on her '*cafe-sua*'. As of day three, we can just sit down and she brings us our concoctions. At times I feel guilty that week. The patron lady uses the warm, quiet hours in the middle of the day for her nap. Typically, she is hanging a few inches above the ground in her hammock behind the counter; happily in la-la land when we want to leave to teach afternoon class. I figure the discomfort of disturbing her is better than running out without paying, but still it makes me feel bad. Most of the time a couple of loud "a-hums" or an 'accidental' running into a chair on my way up to her does the trick of awakening her. A sleepy smile, an exchange of dongs, a "see you tomorrow" means we get a friendly wave as she sees us off.

Surprise Support

The second week of school is routine; it appears that anything that happens more than twice during our journey is a routine. Over that number starts to border on the boring side. Typically, our alarm goes off early; its sole purpose to trigger the parents not to get too lost talking over their coffees, and forgetting to wake the kids. At breakfast, we learn that Cathy, a French lady will join us. As usual, Heidi and I spend the bus ride preparing for class. We arrive well before school and enter the local coffee bar and have a 'sua' before presenting ourselves on site.

A few minutes before ten we enter the schoolyard, and like a honey bees smelling sweet flowers the teachers pop out of their classrooms to hand over their responsibilities. Cathy joins the girls. Our class goes well, and while I talk, Leendert supports with corresponding drawings on the blackboard. At first I think we are flying through the lesson plan too fast, but we end up with surplus exercises which we can use tomorrow. Now that's a nice surprise!

The students have lunch and we eat second. It is an upscale version: we get a larger round table, the small plastic stools are replaced by metal, knee-high stools, and, to my shock, I observe the chopsticks have been replaced by knives and forks. Given that one knife still has a paper price tag on it, I fear we have influenced the set-up (negatively). By trying to accommodate us, some of the authenticity has disappeared. I guess it would be unreasonable to tell them to stuff their forks, just so we can feel more local.

After lunch I have a chat with the principal, asking her what improvement projects the school has planned. In all honesty, this was prompted by Leendert and Alicia. They mentioned that they wanted to offer their 'lucky money', which they received at Anh's Tet celebration - to the school. The nun points to a pathway which needs upgrading. Not quite within the kids' budget. I ask if the students have all the supplies they need, to which the disappointing response is 'yes'. Continuing my probe, she finally mentions that a bit of financial support to pay the teacher's monthly salary would be helpful. With little reluctance she informs me the wage level is three million dong ($125 US) per teacher per month.

And so another ethical problem is born. How much is right? Do I really want to donate cash? Can you trust a French-speaking Vietnamese nun? How does this stack up against the skepticism I have nurtured over the years towards religious organizations? I vividly remember the silliness of the Catholic influence in Cuzco only a few weeks ago. There, I reconfirmed my disdain for religion in general. And yet here, in the middle of Sai Gon, the church seems to do such good work! Time to ponder and reflect; I make a note to discuss donations with Heidi later in the day.

The classes in the afternoon are combined again, not in the least because five kids are sick at home. This reduces the total number of our subjects to under twenty, easily manageable in one room. Cathy, pronounced "Cat-ti", comes from France and actively seeks to help. Well, let me say she forces Heidi to take the back seat – literally and physically.

In her defense, Cat-ti applies her self one hundred percent. She desperately wants to do a good job. I cringe when she corrects the pronunciation of some of the students. In parallel, I admire the flexibility of the students. Cat-ti speaks exactly as one would expect a French person to speak. The words "angry" and "hungry" transform into "hangry" and "ungry", and is perfectly copied by the locals. The students let the words roll smoothly off their tongues. I wonder if it might be an aberration from French colonial times. I feel the urgent need to interfere and to jump back in as I hear them chant "ze hairport iz not far from ear".

The afternoon class-time whizzes by. Though we intend to have another 'sua' afterwards, bus 31 drives up just as we leave the school, so we hop straight on. Back at the hostel we overhear that Cathy gets a licking from the volunteer coordinator as she was not supposed to have gone with us. I guess a miscommunication took place somewhere. An hour later she knocks on our door and formally informs us that tomorrow she is back to her old pagoda project. "I vood ave liked to stay viz your projet, but alas, I weel not". I notice I am glad with this development, happy to be back to just the four of us. Today felt like an intrusion onto 'our' workspace.

That evening we lay on our metal bunk-beds, eat from the metal trays, and chat a bit with the other volunteers. We take turns showering having learned to do so early in the evening, before the warm water runs out. As the last one uses the tiny shower, paterfamilias goes outside and stimulates the local economy. Drinking some carbonated foaming liquid seems a good way to cool down the body from the inside.

Weekend away

Over the weekend we go back into the city. First and foremost because Heidi wants to spend her birthday in a slightly more comfortable place. Fair enough. Second, we need to sort out our Chinese visas. We have a simple breakfast in the hotel coffee shop and I venture off to find a travel agency. I find one nearby, but the visit does not go according to plan. What should be a quick drop-off of pictures and passports (a task easily delegated to me) becomes an ordeal. The travel agency tells me the passports need to go to the capital, Hanoi. This means they need the passports for at least twelve days. Oops, our Vietnamese visas run out in nine days; and it turns out there is no such thing as an expedited process. I am bombarded with questions. They ask if I know if I have the visa for Nepal? IF we have them, Heidi would know, not me. I run across the road to get Heidi. We hurry since the travel agency reportedly closes in fifteen minutes. We return, haggle, negotiate, beg.

In the end, we need to change our travel dates, cascading our planned trip by one week. It is an administrative marathon. We have invitation letters re-sent from China. We inform the volunteer group in Nepal that we'll be arriving one week later. Well after the formal closing hour of the agency we hand over our passports. They promise to get the passports back "probably a week on Monday". It is the "probably" which makes me nervous. An express mail delivery guy collects the passports and disappears on his motorcycle while we are still filling out some paperwork. What is most surprising is that the passports go with the mail courier, without details of our hotels or flight reservations, which I've always been taught is an absolute must for Chinese visas. Anyway, what is done is done, the passports are gone, and we are stuck. Stuck because we can't fly to China until the Tuesday after. Stuck because we realize that to check back into any hotel in Sai Gon we need a passport, which we no longer have. The hotel choice becomes simple; singular in fact. As we walk back into the hotel, we ask for a reservation for the following weekend. We explain the situation our administrative challenges and luckily, since they have our passports on file, they are happy to make the booking and take our Dongs for another weekend. I am sure the long blond hair of Alicia and her smile helped our case.

That evening we have a special dinner; Heidi's 'surprise' birthday dinner. Of course the birthday is no surprise, she has one every four years (yes, February 29th), so it is hard to forget. The place itself, "Blackout", is the surprise. The restaurant is not too far from our hang out, and we arrive exactly on time. We sit down, get the menu and are asked if we want a drink. We indulge, white wine for the parents, passion fruit juice for the kids. The menu is simple: seafood, meat, combo or surprise. The kids immediately go for "surprise". We join them, encouraged by the hostess who point out that it makes the experience more fun as we can than 'share' the experience. What experience you might ask? Well, let me tell you…

Around the turn of the century two guys started the first 'Dining in the Dark' experiment in Zurich, Switzerland. The title tells it all. One eats in complete darkness, hence the name Blackout. Visually impaired and blind staff serve and help you. The aim is to encourage interaction between the blind and the sighted. Putting sighted people in the dark should foster a better understanding, awareness and empathy for the world blind people live in.

Before we enter the main part of the restaurant, we must part with any light-emitting objects (phones, watches, etc). Next, we are told to put one hand on the shoulder of the person in front of us, and in a four-boxcar train setup we get guided through a zig-zag of curtains into a pitch dark room. And I mean pitch dark. Absolutely zero light. We are guided to a table, and one by one we are placed behind our chairs. We sit and talk nervously. The first five minutes I only seriously wonder about one thing... where the hell is the exit? How can I get out? My heart is racing and I have a light sweat appearing on my body even though I am in a well air-conditioned room. I feel genuinely uncomfortable. The chatting and laughing of the kids helps me through this phase. A stealth waiter approaches and tells us he has a plate with some *amuse-bouche* on it. "Please have some." Easier said than done. I don't know exactly where he is, much less the food. We also have no clue what's on the tray. Small, big, hot, cold, liquid, solid? The unseen waiter explains we should feel free to pour ourselves some water saying "there are glasses on the table, as is a pitcher with ice water". "By the way, your napkin is under the cutlery". Right! I ask Alicia if she could be so kind as to pour the water. Giggles all around. Ever tried to fill a glass from a pitcher filled with water and ice cubes in the dark? I promise your fingers get wet!

As my nerves settle, and we are guessing what we might be eating, I try to figure out if I should close my eyes or not. Physically there is absolutely no difference. Either way it is dark. Keeping them closed makes you feel silly, having them open sillier still.

Not much later the first dish arrives. It turns out to be a tray with several items on it. Given that smell, taste and 'touch in mouth' is all we can rely on makes us pay close attention, conscious of every bite. With no visual reference we experience the 'feel' of the food, the blend of tastes. The food is delicious. Both the main course tray and the dessert tray are fantastic. Both hold surprises, but between the four of us we think we can guess all but one. We'll have to wait till the end of the experience to find out how right (or wrong) we are. Time flies. After we finish our dessert we are guided back to where we came in: in train formation, hand to shoulder, hand to shoulder. We exit through the heavy curtains into the light and immediately close our eyes, the evening lights blinding us.

The meal took slightly more than an hour and we sit down to enjoy one last drink. Because I had indicated it was Heidi's birthday, they come out with a little cake; on the plate is written 'happy birthday' in chocolate. Nice touch. We eat cake and the hostess debriefs us on the menu. We thought we knew all we ate but one item. As it turns out we got at least three dishes wrong. Luckily we are half French and all-foodie. Had we been squeamish, I guess we might have been shocked to learn we ate *grenouille* (frog), boiled pig-blood, lotus root and eel. We are delighted with the experience. Strolling back, we try to find a good word describing the experience. Leendert comes up with the word "sombrellic" which we decide captures the experience nicely. A nice combination of *sombre* (dark), 'excellent' and 'terrific' (as in: great intensity).

Over an hour later I still feel a rush, that's how intense it was. I'd compare it to a good roller-coaster ride. Intense, parts scare you to the point you feel it in all your senses afterwards, and yet you'd be happy to do it again. The fact that the food was novel and had some unknown twists just added to the experience.

On Sunday evening, we grab the backpacks and take a taxi back to the hostel. We take a taxi not because we feel we are 'too good' to take a bus. No, the buses in Sai Gon stop driving at seven on Sunday evening. Bet you that will change in the next ten years! The fact that we know of what we return to - the basic metal bunk-beds, no springs but a piece of foam on slats, a noisy air conditioner (only after nine o'clock) makes the transition more predictable, though not particularly pleasant. Uncomfortably, we settle back in our habitat. Before ten everyone is in bed and the only light in the room reflects from my computer screen. Soon I get the request to dim the intensity a bit. Ah, the joy of living in one small room again!

The second week of Teaching

Regular family life in the hostel; reasonable wake up times, (cold) morning showers for those who skipped it the night before, peanut butter and jelly on white bread breakfasts. Instant coffees. The next day, a new batch of volunteers arrives. Unfortunately, the volunteer organization forgot to adjust the breakfast supplies to the new influx, creating a food shortage. Luckily, Heidi had the foresight buy some cereal and yogurt so we don't go hungry. We take the bus to school, prepare our lesson plans *en route* and shoot a couple of e-mails off over the ether. Luckily the school office has good wifi. We go into our respective class rooms and teach until lunch-time is announced by the drum. Totally routine!

We enjoy great lunches. One day we have a big pile of green beans and soup over rice, all complemented by some meat and tofu. While I am not a fan of tofu, and normally only order it consciously as part of a miso soup, the version we get here in Viet Nam is very tasty. I am always confused and don't know what to do with tofu. Its consistency is less firm than mozzarella but still rubbery; you can't really chew it, it is too slippery to press to bits with your tongue on the roof of your mouth, and swallowing it whole is not a good option either (I tried). More than once I have squeezed it between my teeth like jello. This is a good option, but it should be done quietly, making sure other table guests don't notice the sound it makes as it jets between your teeth.

On the return trips from school, we update a teaching log. There are no records or lesson plans for us, and we have learned that one of the trickiest things of volunteering is establishing what the students know already. It is a real downer if you try to teach them "heads, shoulders, knees and toes, knees and toes" when it is known. Likewise trying to work a theme way above their skill set is demoralizing for both the teacher and the student. By starting a teacher's log we hope that future volunteers will have a smoother landing and can hit the ground running.

Heidi and I consider doing something for the school beyond teaching. We are impressed by the island of stability the school provides for the students, so 'giving more' seems the appropriate thing to do. We decide to trust the nun, which is not a slam-dunk since just that day another article appeared in the world newspapers about young children being sexually mistreated by Catholic priests. Nevertheless, we decide to donate cash for teacher wages. As always the tricky part is how much? What is the right amount? We settle on paying for one teacher for the remainder of the school year. In parallel, I pre-discuss with the nun the proposal of the kids offering their 'lucky money' to the school. When, later that afternoon, the kids broach the subject with her she plays her part excellently "*des stylo-a-bille sont toujours bien appréciés*" (ballpoint are always much appreciated). Before dinner we go to the local ATM to pull out teacher's wages and buy pens for the students.

The next day at school, the principal is delighted as I hand her an envelope filled with wages. I have always been cautious giving cash to a cause, suspicious of how it will be used. However, I feel certain that not much will 'get lost' or squandered with this grass-root support. I have seldom parted with cash so easily and felt so good doing it.

As expected, the students get shiny eyes when our kids distribute the new pens. On top of the gifts, we also bring another volunteer teacher: Mathilde. Mathilde is a new arrival to the volunteer house who will take over from us. She will stay for over a month. She is from Geneva and speaks - to my surprise - impeccable English, no French accent whatsoever! Mathilde is introduced to the principal and joins the girls that morning. We have lunch as usual, this time with delicious fried fish and - of course - rice with broth on top. Not a day without Pho! Mathilde is introduced to *cafe sua* across the road. Heidi and I teach afternoon classes with her observing. Tomorrow she'll join my class, and by Friday she'll be ready to take over. We share our teaching log-book with her, which she appreciates.

That evening, after we shovel the lukewarm food from the trays into our bodies and retire to our room, Leendert entertains us with some clips of 'amazing facts' on YouTube. As his iPad circles from bunk bed to bunk bed we learn: A strawberry isn't a berry but a banana is (yes, really, look it up and be amazed); there are more stars in the universe than grains of sand on all the beaches of the world (wow, now how would one determine that?!); and the closest US state to Africa is… Maine! I also learn what happens if you throw a huge amount of water on the sun. What's your guess? (a) the sun gets hotter, (b) the sun cools down, (c) the sun would shine less bright? The answer is (a).

Okay, one more. The sour taste of buttermilk comes from (a) urine of a fungi, (b) urine of a virus, or (c) urine of a bacteria? Whichever you choose, it changes the way you think of buttermilk. The answer (c), bacteria.

By the end of the week I summarize the day in my diary using no phrases, only words. Again, an unedited version: *wake-up, peanut butter and jelly sandwich, heat, bus, school, class, lunch, cafe sua, class, more heat, bus, hostel, metal tray dinner, reading on uncomfortable bunk-beds, airco on at 9pm.* Of course some variations existed in the days. During one school session I attempted to supplement my animated lecture by having the students write (hey, they have pens now!). Big mistake. The range of capabilities spreads from the earth to the moon and back. Some are quite skilled; some barely know how to hold a pen. Waiting for the non-writers to copy diligently from the blackboard means the others are bored and spin out of control. Key lesson learned? Once over the tipping point of capturing and holding their attention, getting them back on the rails is close to a lost cause. Remember, I have no teacher in the class to keep a watchful eye, nor can I use Vietnamese voice commands.

In Pursuit of Chocolate

One other noteworthy event is when Heidi gets a mail from the local volunteer organization. Out of courtesy we had told them we donated money to the school. They wanted to ask how much, and provided their logic: "we want to know so we can adjust the budget we allocate to them". Wham! Wow! No! What a boomerang! The entire idea is NOT for THEM to allocate my money. This is our grass-root effort; our decision on where money is wisely spent. If they counter-allocate, our entire effort is undermined. No, no thank you very much, no can do. We purposely ignore the e-mail. I am glad I told the nun we would not disclose the amount, that it would stay just between us. Luckily, we never got a follow-up. Thinking back on it I realized there was zero benefit of telling the volunteer organization of our contribution, we should have just kept it under the radar and it would have never become a subject of debate.

The Last Day of School

Somehow it felt different waking up today. One reason is that the school requested us to come in earlier, advancing the alarm with more than an hour. The second is that a mosquito insisted on proving it was nocturnal, thus causing me a rotten night of sleep. As we are all together in one room, I dared not to turn on the overhead light to chase it down. By the way, if there is a smaller animal which can give more overnight agony, I have yet to meet it. In a half slumber I managed to scratch myself semi-awake several times. Consequently, I feel like a freight train drove over me. Combine fatigue with the adrenaline injected in my body because it is the last day of our project at the Vinh Son (pronounced like the French 'Vincent') school, and you get the picture. I am tired and energized at the same time. We set off – together with Mathilde - an hour earlier than usual. The bus trip is identical, hot, slow and with lots of stops.

As soon as we arrive at the school, the principal takes it upon herself to sound the big drum and she tells us that the kids are ready to perform for us; 'if we could please go to the *grande salle*' (the big hall). We make our way to the covered lunch area where we usually prepare for our afternoon classes. I notice the stage is different. The *Chuc Mung Nam Moi* (Happy New Year) signs are gone, decorative plants are placed in front of a stage and an array of small brown plastic stools are perfectly arranged for an audience. In the middle aisle five somewhat higher blue plastic stools are placed, obviously for our VIP convenience.

The classes empty out and the kids take their seats in the audience. We join them, taking the large chairs in front. The caretaker turns on a microphone system, testing if it works using the universal "testing one-two-three". From earlier encounters I suspect this is the only English he knows. The principal gives us a short briefing and hands the microphone over to a young student. I notice he is wearing the school uniform shirt, but for the occasion he has on a nice pair of jeans, rather than the usual shorts. He reads from a paper in Vietnamese, and I think to detect the word 'Alexander' in one of the opening phrases.

Once he is done, the principal translates into French what the boy has just shared with us. Words of thanks to the 'Alexander-family' for dedicating effort and time to the school, a wish that we might have fond memories of Viet Nam and the Vinh Son school in particular. As token of their appreciation we get packages of tasty cookies and nuts. Mathilde gets a bouquet of flowers as welcoming gift.

The caretaker starts the music, and we are treated to two separate performances. The first is performed by three student-couples doing a classic village dance. The boys in black attire and typical red/white or black/white headbands lead the girls over the stage. The young girls are beautifully dressed, as if ready to go out, including mascara. The second skit is staged by eight girls colorfully dressed in the traditional Vietnamese *Ao Dai*, the long silk dresses - cut on the side - worn over silk pants. Each dancer holds two traditional Vietnamese pointy reed hats, and accompanied by music they perform a lovely choreographed dance show.

Our applause at the end of the performance is heartfelt. We are truly honored by the show, and happily comply as we are asked to climb on stage to join the performers for pictures. More pictures follow, this time with all the teachers. To wrap it all up, I am asked to do a small 'thank you' speech. I honor the school, the leadership, the teachers and - of course - the kids. Big applause, and now straight back to class! One teacher, thus far unseen, joins for a while in 'my' class (funny how I already use that possessive pronoun). As I write the first words on the board the teacher interferes and corrects me. She explains to the kids that my writing is incorrect and shows how it is supposed to be. I didn't make an English mistake, no, it is how I write which she dismisses. I use block-letters instead of cursive. Darn! Why didn't I think of that before! The teacher smiles and tells me to carry on as she walks out. I continue, now writing in the style I was taught as a kid, 'cursive', as the French say *en attaché*. Instantly I notice there is a better understanding in my audience of what is written on the board. If only I would have known. Nice to find that out the very last day of school!

During lunch I print the documents we'll leave behind in a folder for Mathilde and the next volunteers. Using the caretaker's computer and a slow printer it takes a bit of time, so I join lunch late. Vermicelli spring rolls, soup with tofu (I am learning to appreciate it), fresh vegetables. We drink our last *cafe sua* across the road, and prepare for the afternoon class. The last class is a blast. We review all the vocabulary of the last two weeks and succeed in cementing the right pronunciation of some words. One of the students, who goes by the good Vietnamese name 'John', even accomplishes in his biggest challenge. We have been working with him on the word 'lips'. It is a tough word for him. While it took time, on this last day it has transformed from "slisp", "splis" and "spils" to "lips". He is as proud as we are; he smiles and gets applause from the class.

Now that I know better, I use my skill-set of writing in cursive only to be corrected again: "NO!" The kids scream as I write on the blackboard. It takes a while, but finally one of the students is willing to correct me. Turns out they learn to write the first letter free-standing, and the rest of the word cursive,… go figure! Old French school with an American twist.

As we are ready to leave for the last time one of the teachers walks up and congratulates me on my three wonderful children. It takes a moment before I realize Mathilde just became my oldest daughter.

After school, I stroll around the neighborhood in search of a 'Hot Toc'. I was told that a simple haircut (no massage or ear wax removal) should be 30,000 dong. This makes me happy, because I am still competing with Leendert for 'the lowest price haircut'-award; Leendert currently leads. I lost the honor in KL at $2.50 from my earlier Galapagos triumph. The first place I visit quotes 50k, and he won't move on price. I call his bluff and walk off. To my surprise he does not call me back.

For the next fifteen minutes, I enjoy getting lost in the small little roads around the hostel. Spotting a small shop with two dilapidated barber chairs and a couple of guys playing Chinese checkers in front, I signal I need a chopping. I open with an offer of 40,000 dong and a face of "don't mess with me, I know the going rate". A short internal discussion follows and to my delight the offer is accepted without further negotiation. The young lad doing the honors employs a Remington most likely left behind by the US army in the early 70's. I observe my surroundings: a broken mirror, a couple of little cages with birds. A rooster circles my chair, brushing my toes with its feathers, perhaps hoping something edible falls out of my scalp. The clippings of the day lay on the floor; I guess proof of 'lots of business' trumps a pristine looking place. The job is quickly done. The barber's chat limits itself to "where you from". My answer "Paris, France" only causes a puzzled look, obviously the detailed answer is far beyond the geographical awareness of the coiffure. I pay the agreed amount and return home to do a "nah, nah, nah, nah, naaah, na" to Leendert. The 'lowest price haircut-award' is back in my possession: $1.88!

That evening we have a dinner appointment with Anh, who we haven't seen since we celebrated Tet with her family. We invite our newest family member to join us, and Mathilde is happy to oblige. We eat in a restaurant specializing in the food of the region where Anh grew up. Hue food turns out to be tasty, like most Vietnamese food. I pick up the tab telling Ahn she only had the right to ask for the bill, and telling Mathilde that as my adopted daughter she should be quiet. The initial resistance dissipates quickly and they both graciously accept my offer to pay. Total bill for six people, including drinks, 670,000 dong ($28 dollar US). That won't break the bank. A lovely way to finish up our project, and a great way to introduce a new volunteer to a local.

Departure and a Sai Gon City goodbye

Early in the morning, the last peanut butter and jelly sandwiches consumed and the beds turned upside down twice to make sure we do not leave anything behind. As usual the last bag packed is the toilet-bag; it patiently holds out until all of us brush our teeth. With foam in my mouth I open the tap, only to find out there is no running water in the hostel. Oops. Fortunately we have just enough bottled water left to rinse. We see the absence of water as a clear omen that it is time to leave.

I insist we go local - no taxi's, just backpacks and the bus. We say farewell to the 'Peace House' which has been our home for two weeks. As an aside, the name is really a bit of a misnomer as the term "Peace House" is normally reserved by the Hanoi government for places taking care of victims of agent orange and those hurt in the American War. We walk to the bus stop in District 7, noting it is not hard at all to leave the hostel. I imagine it is a bit like leaving a lifeboat after a shipwreck, or the Apollo 13 moon lander right before returning to earth atmosphere; glad it was there to provide a safe heaven, but definitely a good thing to leave behind.

Perhaps it is the lighter Saturday traffic, perhaps there genuinely is a weather change, either way, the air feels cooler this morning. The ride to the city center is easy and comfortable. Once close to our hotel we jump out. Yes, jump. Buses don't really stop in Sai Gon. Unless you are over seventy years old, they only slow down a little (backpack or not). It is just after eleven when we arrive at our hotel and the receptionist informs us our room is still being serviced. We drop our bags and walk to the nearby

In Pursuit of Chocolate

coffee shop for a caffeine fix (*Cà Phê*) and a Slurpee for each of the kids.

It ends up being a relaxing day, the afternoon spent booking travel in China. The kids study and read until PE-teacher-daddy takes them down to the pool for a thirty-minute workout. The swim is good, and I must admit it looks rather cool to have the three of us do laps next to each other. I secretly enjoy knowing the other sun bathers are probably watching us lap back and forth, different paces, different strokes.

For dinner, there is a large push for the same pizza place we visited a week ago, but I resist. I walk the tribe in a different direction, hoping to find a restaurant which fulfills my desire for local food. Noticing nobody reacts to my suggestions passing the various Pho courtyard places, I set the direction towards more touristy quarters. Before you know it, we enter the non-local dining area. Zeros are added to the menu prices. Okay, I tried. Nothing I propose seems to hit the spot for the gang. In the end, I cave in and without telling them set a new bearing, this time for the originally requested Italian restaurant. My pigeon-gene seems to work, and soon we are homing in on the place I reviewed on trip-adviser only seven days earlier. Matteo, the restaurant manager, not only recognizes us instantly but also thanks me for the review. We are introduced to the owner and upgraded from a regular square table to a booth.

Dinner is lovely. Pizzas, a bottle of wine and some juices put all of us in a good mood. In fact, I notice that my tolerance for alcohol has diminished and bottle of wine has my neurons firing. Making matters worse, Matteo offers complimentary limoncello's (plural). Going back it feels as if I can't really walk a straight line. I do my utmost not to show the kids that the alcohol is affecting me (usually a solid sign that it is), but figure it isn't that bad since Heidi makes no remarks. It does feel strange and I feel embarrassed to be tipsy in front of the kids. I am happy the remainder of the evening is spent on i-tronincs, relaxing on the couches (oh how nice it is to be in a place with sofas and chairs!); we all savor the quiet family time.

Before leaving Viet Nam

A couple of noteworthy elements before we leave the Land of the Ascending Dragon and Sai Gon in particular. Consider this the Trip Advisor section. The city has a nice feel to it. While there is no doubt you are in Asia, the European (French) influence is ever-present. It is in the Main Post Office, a building designed by Gustav Eiffel, as well as many other buildings; there is an abundance of good croissants and coffees.

The town also has some unique shows. One of them is the acrobat AO-show. Having bought tickets in a small shop along the road one day, we were told to go armed with the receipt in hand and present ourselves at the Opera House. Both the place we bought the tickets and the ticket price made me suspicious. However, it turns out my skepticism was totally misplaced. Upon arrival, an usher in an AO T-shirt takes my receipt and asks me to wait for a moment. Within minutes he returns with our tickets and points us up the stairs to the side. We are offered tea and cookies, and step through French doors onto a side-balcony to enjoy a view of the Ho Chi Minh streets below.

Twenty minutes later we enter the theatre. It is a small but beautifully maintained opera house. Inside it is much like a small opera house like the *Volksoper* in Vienna: the building is well air-conditioned, immaculately maintained, and has nice red velvet chairs with carved woodwork. The show starts promptly at eight for a full house. For the next hour we are regaled by a well-choreographed show of skilled athletes performing mesmerizing routines. The show keeps us on the edge of our seats the entire time. The theme is based on traditional Vietnamese activities. They make extensive use of the traditional basket boats (*thing chai*) we saw in Hoi An. We are delighted to recognize most of the typical Vietnamese ingredients (think hats, bamboo, baskets, etc); it's a nice recap of our experiences in Viet Nam. The performers jump, dance, fly and roll over the stage. The raving reviews on the web are totally in keeping with the performance. Certainly a "must do" if ever you are in Sai Gon.

One afternoon we battle the heat and visit the Independence Palace. I had read that it was a nice icon of the American War time. We go despite this description: is there really such a thing, as a 'nice' icon of a war? The architecture is cubic, and though it has a bamboo motif, it has a western and modern feel to it. The footprint of the building is a "T", derived from the Vietnamese character for "good destiny", and the center part of the prominent front facade has the Chinese character for "prosperity" designed in it. There is a lot of symbolism. Despite the heavy concrete bamboo motif, it has a deceptively open and spacious interior. It is not unlike a purpose-built gallery for modern art. Once inside it is clear the interior has been left untouched for decades. It can best be described as a gem capturing the James Bond *Goldfinger*-era of decades ago. The decor of the large entertaining rooms throws you in a time warp straight to the 1970s. Textured walls and oversized lacquered furniture decorate the rooms, while large minimalistic wood cabinets are lost in space. It feels a bit like a show-room during clearance with 80% of the furniture already sold.

We work our way to the top of the building. The rooftop is a sight in itself. Originally designed by the architect for meditation, the president had a hard wood dance floor installed to make it a party space. And what a view! As we walk over the top terrace we see a Huey, the typical US army helicopter. It originally served for presidential transport. Also on the roof we spot two red marks. These are where the North Vietnamese pilot 'hero' dropped two bombs to announce the imminent attack and overthrow of the South Vietnamese leadership. What is not clear is how the bombs had such accuracy, but did no structural damage to the building (the winners do write history!).

The informative signs give an overview of the importance of the building. It was originally the residence of the President of the South, and many dignitaries visited during those turbulent times. Black and white pictures show the former president with other heads of state. Except for the sporadic jab, the information is neutral in tone and impresses on the visitor the important role this building played in history. Only after visiting the basement bunker do we run into a hard punch at the USA. In a small room (which most people unknowingly walk past) a cinema shows a video. The black-and-white film is worthy of being played in the not-so-subtle War Remnants Museum. It oscillates between film-shots of 'the brave North Vietnamese army' (usually in color with pleasant military march music) and images of US solders killing innocent people, bombing schools and hospitals (black and white; lots of war noises). Of course the film points out that the evil enemy was beaten by the 'brave man' of Viet Nam. The latter shot down thousands of American planes. They are the heroes. The men who incapacitated the American war machine. You get the drift...

In needs saying that for any geopolitical historian, Viet Nam is a treasure trove. The books I read during our stay were very insightful. One particular quotes stands out: "The North Vietnamese beat the Americans, but it is the South Vietnamese [think Sai Gon] who beat the Russians in the subsequent years". The headline is that while the Communist regime took over in 1975, slowly but surely the free market economy of Sai Gon has gained strength and dominance. Formally, Viet Nam is still communist, but the crumbling of the USSR - and subsequent diminished financial support to Hanoi - means things are changing - rapidly. Looking forward, it is not hard to imagine that the formal party power of Hanoi will continue to dissolve and the business-driven Sai Gon will gain in strength and influence.

On the lighter side, we sought out cultural entertainment. One day we set our sights on the famous Vietnamese water puppet theatre. Not wanting to miss the performance, we showed up ten minutes before the ticket booth opened that afternoon. We bought tickets for the late evening performance since all the other timings were already sold out. That evening, we enter the small theatre. About fifty old chairs rest on a slightly upwards slope. Moments before show starts, a busload of tourists filling the room. For the next forty-five minutes we are treated to a scene in front of a Chinese-looking house with bamboo curtains. From behind the curtains, various animals and puppets appear. In the front of the house is a large basin of milky water, about four meters by fifteen meters wide. The entire puppet show takes place in the water.

Along the sides sit musicians and storytellers. The dialog is in Vietnamese but the story is self-explanatory. Fishermen interact with dragons, butterflies, birds, kings and slaves. The painted puppets spend quite some time in and under water and accompanied by lots of splashing. The movement is intricate, but it feels like watching a kid's show and I spend most of my time trying to figure out how they move the puppets from behind the bamboo curtain. I conclude they either continuously switch places or handover the puppet controls very efficiently. Either way, the mechanics are impressive. As we walk home we comment on the performance. Clearly my obsession and trying to figure out 'how do they do that?" kept me more engaged than the others. Leendert quips that it was really '*langweilig*', apologizing for the fact that he could not come up with a better non-German word. Quietly I agree. Yes, it is unique, but why it is so popular is beyond me.

And we're gone

Now that hurts. The alarm clock beeps just after five. As I pry one eye open I notice Heidi is already out of bed and fully into her "gotta catch a flight"- mode. We fold the last laundry and create enough sound to arouse the kids. The backpacks are packed, and before six we hail a taxi. Sai Gon is still asleep, as is the taxi driver. His eyes blink often, his head nods as on a bobble-head doll while he maneuvers over the empty boulevards to the airport. We find the queue for China Southern and wait patiently. The check-in counters only staff up about ten minutes after our arrival. Noticing how slowly the row dissolves from the front I decide to try my luck with my old Skyteam silver card, stepping into the empty business-class line. To my amazement the lady is willing to help us. Considering myself the King of the Airport I wave the rest of the family over. We bid farewell to Viet Nam. The country certainly captured a place in our hearts!

China - Impossible to Capture

WE ARRIVE IN CHINA. AH, but not so fast. I might consider myself the "King of the Airport", but the check-in lady in Sai Gon certainly isn't the "Queen of the reservation system". As she types in our details and scans our passports, something obviously isn't quite right. Managers appear and paper work is re-checked. Blank stares at the screen and passports indicate something is amiss. It takes a long fifteen minutes before they share the dilemma with us. The good news is that we are all on the flight to Guangzhou, the bad news is that for some reason Leendert's ticket on the onward flight to Shanghai is missing. The senior service desk manager finally says not to worry: "you'll be able to get it resolved in Guangzhou". Slightly nervous, I accept this proposal, thinking I overheard him say that an upgrade on the onward flight might resolve the issue. For now it seems we are in cattle class, row 33, back of the plane.

We transit passport control and settle in a food court. Knowing we are in a former French colony and convinced that in China we'll be restricted to more local breakfast choices, I order a croissant with ham. As usual, the picture above the counter shows a delicious image: a fluffy croissant with freshly cut ham, nicely contrasted with a fresh glass of orange juice. As usual, what I get is completely unrelated. I chew on a lukewarm piece of rubbery bread with stringy bacon. Both the disappointing breakfast and the early hour contribute to me having a little run-in with the kids. It is about their slack approach and their lack of motivation to write in their journals and prepare blog posts. Authoritatively I decide that they "will not get any screen time until they have recorded some of our experiences". My aggressive tone and stance are disproportionate to the infringement, and Heidi gives me the 'evil eye'. I realize she is right, so I decide to blow off steam by walking the airport. While walking, I convert myself back into a more reasonable dad and, at an exchange booth, from a multi-millionaire (in Dong) to the owner of a mere $65 US.

A bus brings us to the airplane. As we walk the narrow aisle, we notice the seat rows go the regular 1,2,3 (business class), but then suddenly jump to 31, 32, 33, 34: Premium Economy. Wow, we did get an upgrade! We settle into row 33 and I demonstratively put the iPad in the pocket in front of me. It doesn't even touch my knees…ah, the luxury! The flight to Guangzhou is about 2½ hours. The kids study, I read a bit. Slurping an aluminum square of warm noodles, beef and veggies, I feel avenged for the airport croissant. Chatting with the kids and Heidi, I ask them about their expectations of China. We made it a game each time we entered a new country. We'd write down our preconceived notions. The aim was to capture in three to five words the place we were about to visit. Not surprisingly, most - if not all - times, we got it spectacularly wrong, something we could usually concede within 48 hours of arrival. For China, our words included: crowded, unfriendly, dirty, smelly.

Landing in Guangzhou we are bused to the terminal. I take great pleasure inhaling the fresh air. Well, perhaps not fresh. It is China after all. But at least it is 'fresh' in the sense that cold air envelopes my body. It is the first time in weeks that I am outside and do not have the Niagara Falls running down my back soaking my underwear. How pleasant it is not to have damp undies - to feel that one can actually sit down without leaving an embarrassing humid imprint on the chair!

We complete immigration formalities and soon we are inside China. We hand over our backpacks for the connecting flight, and get Leendert's boarding card, no questions asked. By the time we cross from one terminal to the next, it is boarding time. An unpleasant odor welcomes us on the plane. It is that 'too many people in too small a space' smell. In fact, add some incontinence to it and you are close. Although I anticipate the stench will reduce as we get deeper into the plane (as our nasal orifices get used to the smell), the opposite is true. As bad luck would have it, we are in the last row of the plane, right in front of the bathrooms. Bathrooms with toilet reservoirs which clearly do not hermetically seal. The plane is fully booked, so there is no way to change seats. Needless to say, we are truly happy once we can escape from the smelly metal flying cylinder on the other end of the flight. One of our preconceived notions was right!

We collect our bags, grab cash from an ATM, and are on our way to our friends' home. We take the Maglev Train from Pudong airport to Shanghai. Maglev stands for Magnetically Levitated, and it is an engineering marvel. The magnetic train flies at 300km/hr from the airport into the city, in eight minutes. Yes, two minutes to reach top speed, five at top speed, and one to come to a halt in the station. The ride is so smooth that the only way to tell the speed is the electronic display above the door. We arrive in town at 5:30pm, taking subway line 2 right in the middle of rush hour. At each station the wagons become more loaded. By the third stop people push themselves in, squeezing other commuters, who have no place to go. We hang on to a post, our backpacks and each other. We are glued tightly together for eleven stops. Leendert reports at one time he is not sure his feet are on the ground. Between station nine and eleven we reposition ourselves to make sure we can get out at Zhongshan Park station. We succeed, backpacks and all. Another preconceived notion - populated - is confirmed.

From the station we walk to our friends' house. The temperature is just a couple of degrees above freezing, so the first 'my nose is cold' is reported. Personally, I relish the fact that my undergarments are dry. On the short walk we make a stop to buy wine, sticking with Chinese customs not to arrive 'with carrots' (the fingers representing carrots), that is, empty handed. The reception at our friends is warm and soon we get the run-down on what to do and where to go.

Enjoying Shanghai

Over the next days we investigate various parts of town. We visit People's Square and the local markets close to it. The Flower and Bird market seem incorrectly labeled. They strikes us more like a jade/stone and a cricket markets, but for all we know we were in the wrong place. The market sells a wide range of animals: birds, cats, dogs, turtles and fish. A large number of stalls sell crickets. Individually boxed in small cartons, we observe them through the netting or see-through plastic. There aren't many people around, and the vendors invite us to take closer looks without being pushy. It takes a while before we realize the critters are not for consumption. Neither for humans nor for animals. It turns out they are for cricket-fights. Locals look at them closely, sometimes even poking them with little toothpicks to see how they react. It's a big business, and from what we learn, having a winner can be lucrative.

We stroll to the next market, which focuses on antiques. A couple of streets are lined with stalls selling real and fake antiques. What stands out most is Chairman Mao's presence. Chairman Mao's picture is available here on everything - plates, watches, chop sticks, posters, games, 3D posters and much, much more. My favorite moment is finding - between all the coins and tea-pots - a group of women playing Mah Jong. They play quickly, with a serene seriousness during the game and light-hearted banter, glancing up at us while "rebuilding the walls".

We visit a museum about the city of Shanghai, its history, its growth and its future. The five-story building houses a huge model of the city. A large part of the exhibition focuses on city planning and the environment. It provides a very hopeful display of the use of parks, solar energy and city planning. It tells the story of how city life has improved since 1990 - how the living space per capita has gone from six-and-a-half square meters to about seventeen square meters, and how the city is addressing the pollution issues. For example, three years ago fuel based scooters and motorcycles were banished. Today, they are all electric.

The guide books direct us to Yu Gardens, the old center of Shanghai. It is pretty, but does have a bit of a Disneyland feel to it. The 'wanna buy a watch?' gets thrown at me several times. My 'no thanks' is immediately followed up - 'what are you looking for?' While my mind screams 'the exit', politeness prevails and "nothing right now, *xiè xiè*". The latter means 'thank you' and is pronounced shyeh-shyeh. Our friends told us, the real Old Shanghai is behind this touristy part, so I navigate away from the masses and the flag-toting tour guides. Within two blocks we land in a totally different world. We pass from small shopping streets to smaller alleys. Had it not been for our friend's remark that crime basically does not exist against foreigners in Shanghai (due to harshly enforced punishments), we might not have been so adventurous. As it turns out, I'm glad we did. We enter a small street with food stalls and produce; shell-fish, noodles, fried and steamed dim sum. We stop at what looks like a small metal tumble dryer. The owner tosses hot coals under it and roasts peanuts. Next to him a man bakes a flat bread. He uses an old barrel as an oven. The drum sits on a fire and is, on the inside, covered with concrete. He sticks dough against the hot stones to make the breads. Looking up at us, he is clearly puzzled why we have strayed out of the tourist area. However, keen to make conversation, he speaks to us in Chinese. I say Chinese, well aware that to be correct one has to specify Mandarin or Cantonese in Chairman Mao's country. But since Shanghainese is a variety of the Sino-Tibetan Wu language, often referred to as Hu, and they are all Greek to me, I keep it at Chinese. Either way, the friendly resident holds out a floured hand with two RMB's in it. I catch his drift. Who says you need to study languages? Reaching in my pocket, I hand him two silver coins say "*xiè xiè*" and get a piece of flat bread with chives on it in return. Delicious! We devour the tasty bread as we walk further down the street.

Not suffering from paraskevidekatriaphobia we visit the Longhua Temple, the Temple of Gods on Friday 13th. I'll save you the Google effort: paraskevidekatriaphobia is the fear of Friday 13th. That word, by the way, is only trumped in this book by hippopotomonstrosesquipedaliophobia (the fear of long words). We take metro line 13 to line 4, and I realize that four is an unlucky number in China. It is considered unlucky for no other reason that four is nearly homophonous to the word 'death' in Chinese. Did we tempt fate? Arriving at the Longhua Station an eerie surprise awaits us. It is a brand-new tube station and there is not a single soul to be found. Not just 'a few people'. There are none. Did we morph into an alternate reality stepping through some type of membrane getting out of the metro? It is so quiet in the huge station that it is uncomfortable. Aware of the unique circumstance we take the camera out of the backpack and shoot photos. It is the first time we really need a selfie-stick, there is nobody around to ask to snap a shot of us! Not quite the image one has of densely populated Shanghai.

Above ground, we come to an intersection of two six-lane streets. We are no longer alone, but it is still very, very quiet. At the traffic light, we notice pedestrians wait for the lights to change. Not a car in sight, six lanes to cross; what to do? Do we teach the kids to obey the law or teach them to be critical and to not just blindly follow any rule, but evaluate if it makes sense? In the back of my mind plays the fact that there isn't a major metropolitan city in the world that I know off where those going by foot will wait and stand idly on the sidewalk to cross when there is no traffic. This part of Shanghai clearly is different. Except for one bent-over old-timer shuffling across, a pensioner who probably lived here long before the roads, buildings and traffic lights were erected, people patiently wait for the crossing light to turn red. When the yellow appears for the car lanes, the waiting people all start walking the first five meters of the road, anticipating the pedestrian light going green. The daredevils!

We buy entry tickets to the Longhua Temple at a small booth and enter the grounds. As the guard rips our stubs he points to packs of incense on a table. As I try to impress on him we are not interested but he insists and makes it clear that a bundle of about 15 sticks is included in the admission price. We each grab a pack and read a little sign in English on the table "it is not the quantity of incense you burn, but the intent and thought that goes with it". I doubt the distributors selling incense agree, and just to be safe rather than sorry, they pack the sticks in larger bundles.

Inside the temple grounds it is serene and tranquil. We are the only non-Chinese, and observe the other patrons' behaviors. The temple-goers light the incense with candles. Some of them hold several bundles of two foot-long sticks. The incense smokes heavily, not unlike a freshly lit cigar. The devout pray, holding the stick between their hands, the smoking part at eye-height. They bow, bending at the hips, and depending on the person the bowing happens slowly or at woodpecker pace. After the first set of bows the person turns one quarter to the right to repeat the bowing, then again and again, ensuring all four sides of the temple honored.

We cross the courtyard and light our own sticks, more driven by pyromaniac obsessions than anything else. Despite my desire to copy the bowing routine for a picture, I resist doing so. I feel a genuine respect for the people surrounding us who evidently feel fortune will be bestowed upon them and their ancestors by burning hard earned cash on incense sticks. We simply light, stare at the smoke for a while and dump the slightly burned sticks in the large open fire-altar. This is consistent with the locals, who pray a few minutes before releasing the partially burned sticks onto the red-hot coals. In one of the temples, the bowing in the various compass directions is explained. The visitors burn the incense to the Western King of Far Sight (holding a dragon in his hand blessing human beings), the Northern King of Virtue (holding an umbrella protecting human wealth), the Eastern King for Protection of Buddhist Territory in Heaven and Earth, (holding a pipa - a sort of guitar - protecting all living creatures), and the Southern King of Developing Merit (holding a sword protecting Buddhist Law). We learn the respectful way of entering and exiting a temple. Moving the feet over the high doorsteps -not stepping on them - the girls go with their right foot first, the men, left foot.

Watching our steps, we explore all the temples on the grounds. Along a central axis, buildings hold different temples with hundreds of lanterns hanging from the rooflines. Each structure is more ornate than the previous. Statues are everywhere - stone, marble, large golden Buddhas. One temple is appropriately called the "temple of the 1000 golden statutes". It is breathtaking and impossible to photograph. In each and every temple people kneel, bow and pray. A peaceful atmosphere envelopes the buildings, the small gardens, the statutes and the bonsai trees. Heidi remarks that if on the next part of our journey - where we will teach in a Buddhist temple - the feel is similar, it will not be hardship. Spoiler alert, somehow I don't think that the oldest and prettiest temple of Shanghai will be much like Nepal… but time will tell.

Slightly overdosed on incense, we head back to the metro. We rely on an old paper map and my memory to find the way to our next location. We stare at the subway map. Brightly-colored lines criss-cross on a white background with the names of the stations marked with Chinese characters. I try to match the names on the tourist map to the stations, repeatedly hitting the 'English' button on the electronic ticketing display. Every ten seconds it defaults back to Chinese characters just as we pinpoint 'you are here'. A local man looks over our shoulders. We step aside, assuming he wants to use the machine, but we're wrong. He came over to offer help. For the better part of five minutes we converse with him in hand signals, the map and the ticket machine. Together we figure it out. As he walks off toward the escalator, we thank him and drop our coins into the machine. I take one last glance on the map before we enter the subway system. As we go down the escalator we see our Chinese friend going up. This is strange. Is he lost? The opposite is true. As soon as he reaches the top of the escalator, he zips around and goes down again. Concerned about us, he had gone down, then returned in our direction, just to make sure we took the right train! He catches up with us and waves at the platform where we need to go. We thank him again, and enter the same subway car. A few stations later we all exit. I follow the signs for line eleven and as we go up the escalator we hear a ruckus behind us. The friendly man waves his arms at the bottom of the stairs indicating we are going the wrong way. We now have a dilemma. Continue the way I believe is correct, or return to the helpful Shanghai fellow? The all-knowing stubborn man in me charges ahead, leading the pack forward. We all feel a bit of discomfort leaving our friend with waving arms behind. As it turns out, the route I picked is fine. It leads us directly to Pudong – the international financial district. We are aiming for the Jin Moa building (next to the iconic 'Bottle Opener'). The aim is to visit the Hyatt bar named 'Cloud 9' on the 85th floor. Not sure which station of the subway is closest to the building, we gamble. We end up about two kilometers from the aimed destination, but the road is straight and graced by a wide granite promenade with little parks on both sides. Even better we cross a road with restaurants, one of which seems to specialize in dumplings. Leendert is in heaven.

We continue towards the Jin Mao building and find our way to 'Cloud 9'. It is quite a trek, switching elevators three times in the same building. Unfortunately, the bar only opens at five in the afternoon, but we can peek outside through small hallway windows and see that the view is spectacular and mediocre at the same time. Spectacular because we are up high and it is a relatively clear day, mediocre because a light smog hangs over everything. Alicia remarks: 'this is much better than the Burj Khalifa, in Dubai. At least from this height you can still see the cars'.

And so, in only a few days, the city of Shanghai destroyed our preconceived notions of China. In general it wasn't dirty, and though some areas were populated (and the rush-hour metro is crazy), the majority of the city felt spacious and clean. Last but not least, the locals were always friendly, helpful and kind to us.

To Guilin and the natural beauty of China

It's clear that "doing China" in a few weeks is about as silly as "seeing Europe" in a two week summer holiday. Shanghai and Beijing were a given, but anything in between was open. We chose to visit Guilin and Xi'an. Our flight to Guilin is outside rush hour, so we decide to hop on the metro back to the airport rather than the high-speed train. We take line number two, a straight shot to the airport - nice and easy. Or so we thought. As we plod along we notice the stop-and-go absorbs more time than we anticipated, and we are a bit nervous as we get shooed out of the metro "end of the line", well before the airport. We follow the crowd across and down the platform and continue our 'line 2' trip fifteen minutes later on a different train. Time flies. We had planned to be at the airport well before the flight, but the trip takes close to two hours and we feel the crunch. The moment we arrive at Pudong International, we dash. The metro line arrives right between the two terminals, and once in Terminal 1, the concourse for domestic departures is at the opposite end from where we enter. I run as fast as my backpack allows, closely followed by Leendert. We find the counters for Shanghai Airways with queues, but with our flight departing in less than sixty minutes, I ask (or rather pressure) a service agent to tell me how to accelerate the process. She points me to a separate counter entitled "Standby and Boarding Passengers". We go there, and as sweat runs down my face and body, I notice the desk is not manned (or womaned for that matter). A glance over to a service agent two counters down has the desired effect. He walks up and asks if he can help us.

A few minutes later, our bags disappear into the airport bowels and we wait for the boarding passes. The counter agent shakes his head and points around the corner. Not a word of English, but it is clear we can not get our boarding cards until we go to the indicated spot. We do, and learn that a security check has picked out Heidi's backpack. As she enters a small room, my nervousness disappears. Knowing three backpacks are on the way to the plane means we're safe. They'll never let the plane leave without the corresponding passengers. Once security is cleared, and Heidi's telephone has been identified as the security risk, we rush to the gate. The flight should have been boarding, but people stand around doing nothing. A paper sign in front of the gate informs us: "flight delayed

In Pursuit of Chocolate

due to airflow". Now, I do not consider myself a full-fledged pilot, but I do understand some principles of flight. One of those is the need for 'airflow'. If a pilot ever informs you there is an issue with airflow, buckle in, put your head between your knees and wrap your arms around your legs. Something unpleasant is about to happen. Trusting that something got lost in translation, we take a seat, and await further instructions. Luckily the airflow issue gets resolved and the wheels disconnect from the tarmac about an hour after the official take-off time.

It's a straight flight to Guilin. Actually, there is very little straight about it. Outside the normal up-and-down, turbulence shakes us in every possible direction for the majority of the flight. The bumps are enough for me to stop reading because my iPad shakes too much, the inflight service is restricted to a bottle of water.

Once in Guilin we find our driver standing patiently with a name sign. For a moment I think we landed in England. A fog grabbed hold of the airport. It is damp and a forecaster would have a hard time deciding if it is raining or not. We enjoy the gray wetness. It's been since Machu Picchu, four months ago, that we've seen rain. It is a kind reminder that our friends have lived through autumn and winter. Rain? Fine for a day (or two).

Guilin, with a mere 975,000 inhabitants is considered a 'village' in China. It is known for its beauty and attracts many (mainly Chinese) tourists. The van takes us over a three lane road towards town. There is barely any traffic and we enjoy the twenty-five kilometer trip to the city center. Although blanketed by the mist we can still make out the high-rise buildings, the cranes on the construction sites, the hills for which the area is known. The motorbikes we pass are unique, they have hard, colorful, fixed umbrellas. This puzzles me a bit. Surely, even if it rains a lot, this would only help when the bike was stationary. While moving at the pace of traffic, an umbrella can't help much. Maybe it's protection from the summer sun? We check into our hotel next to Elephant Trunk Hill on a typical city road with restaurants, general stores, liquor shops and banks. The hotel receptionist is friendly and speaks good English. We have two luxurious rooms, each with a small veranda and complimentary mini-bar.

We unload and head for dinner. We are lured into a nearby restaurant by a hostess standing in front stating "English menu". This is helpful, as it helps us steer away from the delicious looking 'boar male genitals' and 'bamboo rat' as a main course. It still is an adventurous meal since the duck, beef and dumplings we order are unique in their own right - lots of bones and unidentified chewy things, mixed with many vegetables we don't recognize.

The following morning, we have breakfast on the sixth floor of the hotel. The mist has partially cleared and we are high enough to overlook the canopy of trees lining the road. We sit next to the floor-to-ceiling glass and soak in the view. It is a panorama worth painting. The "karsten" intermittently pop up out of slowly moving mist. Karsten are limestone mountains, with steep edges and rounded on top (almost like pears planted upside down with only the bottom parts sticking out). The view is hypnotic and it takes a while before we attack the breakfast bar. Leendert dives into the dumplings, Alicia into 'steamed buns'. We ask if it is okay for us to stay to do schoolwork; it is. Paper, pens, I-machines and headphones are procured from our rooms and we take root. The morning flies. Three hours later we are asked if we want lunch. We decline since HWH is dismissed for the afternoon while we explore Guilin. We wander to the center square, passing a large pond with two pagodas. Once at the square, we find there is an enormous shopping market underneath it. Small shops, some only two by three meters are woven together with small alleyways in between. It is known as 'little Hong-Kong'. We attract attention as there is not a single Westerner to be seen. We landed in real China! Like groundhogs we pop out of the ground at the opposite end of the square and find ourselves in car-free shopping streets. We scout for lunch. We detect an upstairs restaurant, but it appears to have no access. After a full loop around the block and an unwillingness to give up, we follow some locals climbing steep stairs. We found it! We take a seat and give thanks: the menu has pictures.

We unwrap the shrink-film from our plates and do the same with the cups, glasses and sauce cups which were placed in a big bowl on the table. We stare at the menu to determine which dish to try. When the waitress nervously walks up, wondering what these white aliens are doing in her restaurant, we point at pictures. Holding up four fingers, we indicate we are ordering for four. Chinese words return our way. It is clear she understands about as much of us as we do of her. The awkward looks, friendly smiling, and nervous laughter results in two more non-English speaking waitresses walking up and joining the party. Communication does not improve. The tables around us enjoy the entertainment but cannot help. Lots more pointing and smiling takes place. Ultimately we succumb to entering unchartered waters and start nodding 'yes' at their suggestions, clueless about what the suggestions actually are.

Hot green tea arrives and we pour some in our glasses, sipping it carefully as we wait for our food. At the table next to us, a family sits down. They too unwrap the dishes, and when the tea arrives at their table, the mother washes all dishes and chopsticks with the hot tea in the big bowl before distributing them to the family. Aha, the first pot of tea is to do the dishes before dinner! Not much later, our waitress returns, empty-handed. It does not take long for us to understand the dish she suggested is not available. She points at another picture on the menu. More nodding, and all is good. Within minutes a big pot arrives and is placed on a hotplate integrated in the table. The pot of soup bubbles over the gas burner. We dive in; octopus, garlic, ginger, greens, clams, shrimp, and lots of other unidentified ingredients. The food is tasty and very spicy. I wave to our waitress. We are desperate to get some rice; hoping it will numb the burn a bit. I thought I knew the word for rice in Chinese, but I butcher the language and get only puzzled looks. This one will not be resolved by nodding. Finally, I walk to the table next to us, undoubtedly scaring the daylights out of the unsuspecting family; pointing at their rice bowl does the trick. This time the waitress nods. The rice arrives, and with it the spicy heat becomes bearable. We empty the pan along with two more pots of green tea.

The next morning, our guide, Andy Lee, meets us in the lobby. Andy is not his real name, but like most Chinese he grabbed the unique opportunity of renaming himself when working with foreigners. We exit the hotel and step into the Great Wall. Confused? Great Wall is a car brand in China. It is much like our four-wheel drive at home, but it is fully decked out (leather seats, air conditioning, a TV screen). To my delight, Andy is a safe driver, passing with care and managing our expectations. He is taking us to the Longji Rice Terraces, a 2½ hour drive. It is a dreary day, gray and misty, but Andy remains optimistic: "Once in the mountains the weather can be different, we'll be able to see the terraces, and if not we'll figure something out". I like his confidence. As soon as we drive a bit out of Guilin the karsten hills disappear from the landscape and make way for flat agricultural land; oranges (still on the trees), pomellos, a bit of rice, and a tree called 'Osmanthus' which carries a flower used for tea and numerous fragrance applications.

Once we get to the real mountains most vegetation is replaced by bamboo. Unfortunately, the fog grows thicker as we climb the range. We pass over the summit. Andy drives slowly, not more than 30km/hr, hazard lights flickering on and off. Once over the apex we arrive at the park entrance. Andy buys tickets and gets on the phone with colleagues who give him a fog update.

We stop at the first village in the park. It is a village of two hundred people, known for the length of the women's hair. Their hair is wrapped around on top of their heads, knotted in front if they are married. Their hair can be up to 1,8 meters long, well longer than their height and worthy of a mention in the Guinness Book of World Records. We wobble across a hanging bridge and try to ignore the ladies attempting to sell us postcards of Longji. For a fee they offer to unroll their hair. We decline. Andy makes another phone call as we finalize the plan for the day. We'll go up to the next village, take a cable car up a mountain and then decide if we walk the longer or shorter route back down through the rice terraces.

We take the cable cars up, Heidi and the kids go one car, I join Andy in another. The bubble has a bit of music playing inside, increasing the enjoyment of the twenty-minute ride. As the fog breaks, we observe wonderful snapshots of the rice terraces. Endless horizontal strips, some only two meters wide. The narrow fields follow the contours of the mountain. Small clusters of wooden structures are sprinkled picturesquely over the terrain. As we step out of the lift, we opt for the long way down; the route with the more impressive views. It does not disappoint. We walk for two hours over slippery stone paths, stopping from time to time to take a picture thinking 'this will be the best spot', 'no, this one will better', 'hold on, this is better…'. It will be a struggle to bring the number of pictures down to the only twenty (a number I randomly defined as the target per event). Along the way, we also learn some Mandarin; good morning, good afternoon, rice, tea and 'the bill please'. We try to copy the sound and intonation, which we know is critical.

Back at the car park, we climb back into the Great Wall and Andy drives us back Guilin. He scores with the kids by putting in a video in the entertainment system. How perfect, they watch Kung-Fu Panda. The return trip is stress-free and after we clean up, we return to the streets for dinner. We follow Andy's suggestion to a restaurant nearby. No English menus are provided, so I point to dishes on tables around us. The waiter anticipates well and speaks a bit of menu "Octopus", "goose liver", "flied pok", "steam vegetables and bun". Realizing I forgot to order rice, I beckon the waiter and ask for 'bee-fa'. He instantly understands, and a few minutes later rice arrives. Whoo-hoo my first order in Chinese!

At a table next to us, a family with an infant is enjoying their food. They glance over at us numerous times. Over the last days we have gotten used to it. Not many westerners come to this region, and we are quite an attraction. Alicia's long blond hair, of course, adds to the interest. At one point, the mother of the family walks over. In half-English she asks "for picture". We think she offers to take a picture for us sitting at the table. Wrong. She wants a picture of her baby surrounded by us foreigners! Happily, we oblige. We finish dinner and I ask for the "Mee-Táahhh" and lo and behold, the sound is passed on from one colleague to the next and within minutes our bill arrives.

The morning, Andy picks us up to for another excursion. He is very excited as we will first visit the 'Antique Village' of Langzi, "well worth the visit" he assures us. It reportedly has Ancient Folk Houses and is an exceptional Old Town. When we arrive, we are thoroughly underwhelmed. The settlement is a couple of buildings erected by a rich family two hundred years ago. It is completely dilapidated. A group of folks are attempting to do some restoration, but there is only so much one can do with old adobe dwellings. We take some pictures, not because it is stunning or pleasing, but more not to insult Andy, who obviously believes this is worth taking the long windy detour side road. The kids comment that "it's not built like the Inca's", and I realize that we've spoiled them with Peru. What I found most impressive in Langzi, (as in 'it made an impression on me'), is that some houses are locked. Locked not to keep tourists out because of the danger of collapse, but locked because people actually live in these houses. The village is not an open-air tourist attraction. The people we saw working in the front of the buildings were not restoring an 'Antique Village'. They were doing basic maintenance on their own homes. Homes without running water or sewage connections. At that instant, I'm intensely grateful for being born where I was, a feeling which only intensifies as I look over a wall and see three ladies hand-wash clothes in the small canal that passes through town.

Andy leads us back out of Langzi telling us we are on the way to the Silver Cave, which is "well worth the visit". With the experience we just finished and my recollection of having been dragged through many caves in my life, my expectation is low. Yes, I remember the first cave I ever visited with my parents. That was marvelous. But since then, every cave has more or less been a copy: drippy stones, up, down, bit of humidity, stalactite, stalagmite, little river, big river, some are cold, some are warm. My brain screams "Yeah, yeah seen it all before", and meanwhile I try to remember how many caves we have dragged the kids through ourselves. Once at Silver Cave, Andy tells us head to the entry, he'll get the tickets. We climb the stairs and I notice the place is designed for many visitors. Zigzag metal barriers fill a large surface. From up high, we see the huge parking lot down below. Luckily today it is quiet. Andy reappears and explains that he timed the visit on purpose right after mid-day, since "most Chinese are enjoying lunch, which means we avoid the crowds".

Still skeptical, I must admit that the cave is impressive. Multi-colored lights accentuate the spectacular natural formation. The colorful lights are a matter of taste, clearly appealing to the "bling-bling" the Chinese appreciate. We walk on and arrive in a larger cave; the "Grand Hall". I stand corrected, I have not seen it all before. It is stunning. We continue for two kilometers, yes, two kilometers, winding our way through the caves. A unique landscape of dripping stone. Some of the nature-sculptured walls are over thirty meters high and at least that wide. Even walking at a good pace, it takes us well over an hour to loop to the exit. Later investigations confirm Andy was right; during peak hours the place is too packed to appreciate its magical splendor.

The next stop is the Li River for a boat tour. Andy calls ahead, and when we arrive a captain is standing ready to have us embark his raft. The "boat" consists of eight large plastic tubes in the shape of bamboo, tied together. On top, wooden boards and two garden benches have been placed for our comfort. We plant ourselves on the seats and the captain starts up the engine. A long metal pole sticks out under the engine, and the propeller sits all the way at the end of the same stick. The propeller enters the water at least three meters behind the end of the craft. The engine is as noisy as my weed eater, but seems to have only half the horsepower. The raft fights the current and we crawl upstream surrounded by at least fifty identical floating devices. All moving rather slowly, all pushed by noisy engines. The good news is that the scenery remains impressive, albeit semi-cloaked in haze. A few days later we'd make another boat trip further up the same river. That time the boats are made of real bamboo, propelled by broomsticks and paddles, which we like more. The real bamboo boats only last six to eight months before disintegrating, which explains why we sit on plastic versions of the same shape. At the turn-around point we are off-loaded for ten minutes on an small island where 'tourist piranhas' try to shake money from our wallets "wanna buy postcard?", "picture with bird on a stick?". It takes some effort, but we are able to brush them off. The return trip goes quickly and, back on land, Andy ushers us to a spot a little way down the road. He asks us to take a close look at the panorama of the karsten behind the Li river and asks excitedly "do you recognize it?". We don't. He produces a twenty yuan banknote. The image on the bill perfectly matches the mountain range before us. We are standing exactly on the spot the image was taken for the bill. It reinforces that the area of Guilin is an important natural treasure of China.

Back in the Great Wall, Andy drives us to another local old village. As before, it is not too impressive, the stunning element still being that people live in the houses. An elderly Chinese man spots us, makes much noise and quickly disappears into his house. I figure he is upset about us roaming around his place and that he does not want to be seen. Boy, how wrong

I can be! Moments later he reappears and walks up with folded papers in his hands. Oh, no, not again. What artwork does he want us to buy now? Again, wrong! He shows pictures on plastic posters. Of course, he tries to sell us places to visit! No, wrong again! He talks feverishly through his two remaining front teeth nodding at Andy to translate. Andy explains the man used to be a guide. The signs date from when he still had his business. His 87 year-old legs can't take him up in the hills anymore, but boy would he have loved to show us the beauty of the surrounding area. Much laughter, and "please walk on past my house", discover the town,… Heidi wants to take a picture, but is not sure if she should. As we are about to turn the corner she looks back, camera in hand. She snaps a picture. The old man returns his two-teeth smile and a friendly wave. I think he is posing for her. Heidi snaps again.

Now, a guide would not be a guide if he didn't take you to a local show. Andy is a great guide. In the evening he takes us to the Sanjie-Liu show in the Water-Mountain theatre, an open-air stadium with three thousand seats. We enjoy a seventy-minute show, set on a large lake with the karsten mountains as backdrop. The show is created by Zhang Yimou, a famous Chinese film maker. In fact, unknowingly you may be familiar with Zhang's work. He was the Chief Director of the 2008 Beijing Olympic ceremonies; the one where a gymnast makes the final ascent to light the Olympic torch while appearing to run though air around the upper part of the stadium. The show is a grandiose event with six hundred actors. At its climax, two hundred and fifty people simultaneously walk and dance in outfits covered with little lights. The lights flickering on and off in sync with music. The coordination and the choreography is on a scale I've seldom seen. We're distracted by the people in front of us who find it more important to record the show on their phones and tablets than watch it live. The fact that they want to capture the show is okay, but when they are holding the devices high above their heads, blocking my view and forcing me to watch it 'live' on their 10-by-15cm screen it goes one step too far. Luckily, a couple of taps on their shoulder and telling them in English to lower the electronics has the desired effect.

Andy planned a bicycle trip for our last day. The temperature has plummeted from above thirty to fifteen, which has the strange effect that all the floors in the hotel are wet. The high humidity condenses on the stone tile floors. They are as wet as if the cleaning crew has just mopped the entire building but forgot to towel. The ever-optimistic Andy claims "this is great weather for cycling!" Everything in Guilin happens around the Li river, so the bike rental place too is right next to it. We select bikes. Heidi and I go for mountain bikes; the kids want to try a tandem. It takes time to find bikes with saddles which can be adjusted to our long western legs; the turning devices clamping the saddles of most bikes are rusted in place. After an initial wobble, Leendert and Alicia get in a groove on their tandem. Not a moment too soon either – the wide concrete roads come to an end and we find ourselves on a small slippery path. In my mind, I see the two of them drop face first into one of the rice paddies on either side, but in reality, Leendert zigzags masterfully through the hard crevices and muddy paths. Nonetheless, I am relieved when they make it 300 meters to the next slab of concrete. For the next two hours, we pedal along the river only interrupted by a few photo stops. We pass the spot where we took the bamboo boats a few days earlier and continue past Dragon Bridge to the Fuli Bridge. The latter was apparently our objective. Later I'd comment on TripAdvisor that a 'stone bridge' is just what one might expect; a stone bridge. The pleasure is the trip itself, the bike ride to get there. I could never imagine getting in a car to visit the Fuli bridge. It's a bridge. Okay, a bridge in a great environment, and, yes, it is rather high and looks frail while it is strong, but still, it is just a bridge.

One of Andy's last actions is to help us buy train ticket for the sleeper train from Xi'an to Beijing. He walks with us to a small hotel in town. Had it not been from him, we never would have found it. At the reception we present ourselves with passports and cash. The next day we collect our tickets, and while our names are misspelled, he says not to worry.

As we walk back to our hotel, we see a fishermen on a bamboo raft with a bird. We are in for a surprise show. Fishing with birds on the Li River is quite a thing to see. The big birds dive into the water (not unlike loons) and pop up a little later, returning to their masters. Voluntarily, they hop on a T-shaped stick on the raft. The fisherman grabs them by the neck and makes them cough up the fish they caught. A ring prevents them from swallowing the fish. Every so many 'catches' the fisherman opens the ring and offers the bird a fish to eat. A great motivational system.

The next day, we say our farewells to Andy and head back to the Guilin airport. The Guilin airport is going through some major renewal. At least I assume it is. For me it is unclear if they are building or demolishing at this point in time. Sitting in front of the gate, I read a newspaper which happens to have an article on the ten-year airport plan of China. The government aims to build 1600 airports in a decade. Yes, read that again; 1600 in the next ten years. This means they will open a new airport every two to three days! In the West, this would be impossible; local farmers would not want to sell their land, the environmental groups would object because some local animal species would be endangered, the local mayors would fight for their towns not to be subjected to the noise pollution. Having had one of my own Chinese factories ousted from an industrial site because the local government 'reallocated' the terrain, however, there is little doubt in my mind that if the Chinese Central Planning has decided on 1600 new airports in ten years, that's what will happen. Guilin is clearly on the list. For now, it does mean we are in somewhat of a construction site. There are a few small shops and only one restaurant is open. The menu has only Chinese characters on it, no pictures. Unfazed we walk up to the open kitchen and point at food. We all get a big bowl of noodle soup which has beef or pork, though we're unsure which. While eating we joke around that it probably is peef, bork or dog. After the meal we head on to Xi'an.

Xi'an - China's History & Culture

After collecting our bags in Xi'an airport we find our guide for the coming days: Helen. Helen is a lovely young Chinese woman with an outstanding command of English. We instantly like her. On the one hour drive into Xi'an city center she starts sharing information on the region. She explains that Xi'an is a minor town with a mere 8.8 million people. While I still try to wrap my mind around this fact, she continues "despite its smaller size, it is historically important because the old dynasties used it at their capital city". Helen explains it is her objective to give us a good feel for and appreciation of all there is to see and learn. She'll show us the town, the terracotta soldiers, the local life and – if we want – the local dishes.

As we enter town we pass an impressive city wall and are introduced to the Bell and Drum towers. In the past, these were used to let the citizens know the time; bell in the morning, drum in the afternoon. Time and again we see groups of people line-dancing on the side of the roads, in parks and on street corners. Helen enlighten us that "square dancing" is popular with older people to stay in shape and to entertain themselves in the evenings.

The next morning the sun is shining on us figuratively and literally. It is a beautiful day and we are all well rested and ready to go visit the terracotta soldiers. As we finish our breakfast we see Helen and her chauffeur drive up ten minutes early. We grab our daypack and hop in the van. Helen's first lesson of the day is how to casually say good morning. We practice "knee-chi-la-ma". The emphasis is on the 'chi'; any other way and the Chinese won't understand what you mean. The expression loosely translates into 'have you eaten today', perhaps indicating that breakfast was not a given in the old days.

The drive to the terracotta warriors takes longer than expected. The site is a fair distance out of the city, and while traffic is normally no issue on a Saturday, our schedule is messed up because the highway is under construction. The driver tries three alternatives. The first two lead to U-turns and sitting in more traffic, so it is just before noon when we arrive at the museum. We buy tickets, swinging from one ticket counter to another as 'the rules have changed'. Helen informs us children under sixteen are half price, but those tickets need to be bought at a different counter. With tickets in hand we present ourselves at the entry gates. The ticket ripper at the barrier shakes his head. Helen herself passed through a different turnstile specifically for guides and returns to ask what the hold-up is. She chats with the guard who informs her that while 'the rules have changed' the kids are too tall to qualify for half price. Thus we learn there are three qualifications which determine lower pricing: (1) age, (2) student, (3) maximum height. On the last, our kids, and, I presume, most western youngsters fail. I give Helen additional funds and she runs back to buy the correct tickets. Meanwhile I make two mental notes. First, I prefer the overt differential pricing policy of the Peruvians: one price for locals, one for foreigners. The reasoning is clear. If you have the money to travel all the way from abroad to Machu Picchu or the terracotta soldiers, you can probably afford the premium. Second, if ever I have/own/exploit an attraction park in the west I will introduce a pricing rule to get revenge: (1) age, (2) student, (3) minimum height of 165cm regardless the age.

Helen returns with the right tickets and we enter the site. It consists of large hangars placed over the discovery sites. We enter the first hall and observe a huge excavation dig. Long 'pits' are best described as trenches about three meters wide and about half that deep. They are filled with thousands of the acclaimed warriors, their horses and wagons. Note, I use the word 'warrior' not 'soldiers'. The delicate balance being that warriors are soldiers who engage in direct and close combat with the enemy. They have a high risk of death or physical harm, and there is an element of honor and glory that goes with it. Alicia, having studied Chinese history as part of Heidi World High, disappears off with Helen. Helen was a history major, and she is in heaven. For once she doesn't get the standard "how many soldiers are there?", "when were they discovered?" but she gets detailed questions from Alicia: Why did Emperor Qin order this project at age thirteen? Why are the soldiers facing east?, How come the weapons are so well preserved after 2000 years?, What's with the shoes?". Answers: Qin believed that at his death his armies would go with him to continue their service. An advisor convinced him that having replicates would do the same trick, allowing his reign to survive his death. This explains why each warrior is unique (representing a real person). The warriors face east in the directions of the regions still to be conquered to form one nation. The weapons are preserved because they were chromium coated (very advanced for that time). The shoe variations indicate the warrior's rank.

Through Alicia, we learn how to discern the level of soldier (by hair style, clothes and shoes), we learn about the nine generals, the horses, the amazing swords they had. To prove the latter, one clay general actually sat with his two hundred kilogram clay weight on his sword in the tomb for two thousand years, bending it. When they took him off, the sword straightened by itself and the edge was sharp enough to cut through twenty pages of paper.

We walk from one 'pit' to another, awed by what we see. Thus far two thousand unique warriors have been fully reconstructed out of a total of an estimated eight thousand discovered. The 'polychrome' coloring is stunning. The details are mind-blowing. It is not just different bodies and faces, it goes down to the detail of the hair, the facial wrinkles, the patterns in the soles of the shoes, the palm print details on some of the archers. The total site is a big puzzle, far from completion. We visit on a Saturday, so it is quiet. During the week, workers can be seen gluing pieces together, restoring the army to its former glory. It is amazing to realize that the warriors were only discovered - by accident - in 1975. Had the local farmers dug the intended well twenty centimeters to the side, the site would probably remain undisturbed today.

As Alicia bombards Helen with questions about the Jin, Han and Tang dynasties I notice people taking pictures of her. Chinese visitors come from all over the country, including regions less visited by white longnoses like us. As such, a tall blond girl competes with the warriors for attention. Over the last weeks she has gotten used to paparazzi circling around her. Some of the tourists try to discretely take pictures, looking one way while snapping shots in her direction; others walk straight up to shoot the picture, placing one or more of there family members around the light-haired stranger. While Alicia complains at times, I think she secretly enjoys the attention and the thought of being sent over the internet to a wider audience. Even though it is a bit of an annoyance at times, she is a good sport, mostly joking and laughing it off. I suspect that she is photographed at least as often as some of the less famous terracotta statues

On the way back we grab some cold noodles and drive to our next stop: the Huaqing hot springs. This popular historic park is packed with forsythia and cherries in full bloom. Sunshine and eighteen degrees add to the delightful walk through the recently rebuilt palaces. Helen enlightens us about this retreat. She tells the story of the various buildings, baths, ponds and the forty-two degree spring water. She also relates the life of the Emperors and their concubines. She glows as she tells the story of legendary Lady Yang. Lady Yang was (is) considered as one of the "Four Greatest Beauties of China". She was the favorite concubine of the emperor, and with over three thousand to pick from, that's indicative. However, the road to royal concubine was not straightforward. When the Emperor's preferred concubine died, a servant traveled far and wide to find a replacement. He found Lady Yang who was mesmerizingly beautiful. In Shakespearian fashion she was unfortunately also married to one of the emperor's own concubine's sons, who's mother had passed away. The emperor could not marry his own daughter-in-law, so a solution was needed.

Lady Yang was forced to become a Taoist nun to pray for her departed mother-in-law. Not much later, her abandoned husband, the emperor's son, was ordered to remarry. This liberated Lady Yang, and she entered the court to become the soulmate of the Emperor. All this takes place in and around 750 AD, and history is now filled with anecdotes, stories and tales of Lady Yang's beauty. One such chronicle is that flowers closed as she walked past, ashamed to be in the presence of her beauty. Perhaps the story is also so known and romanticized because of its sad ending. The emperor was ousted from the palace and he flees with his entourage. After a long journey, the soldiers turn on him and they pinpoint Lady Yang as the cause of all troubles. The emperor is forced to order her strangled, which he reluctantly does. Truly Shakespearian!

On the way back to town Helen gives us more Mandarin lessons and translates our names. A-lee-san-dur, Ghi-di, Leen-deert, A-lee-shia. She becomes Alicia's friend for life explaining that, in Mandarin, her name translates into "beauty, smart, elegant".

In the morning we pack up sweaters and raincoats and meet Helen downstairs. We drive is to the largest park of Xi'an. Why I would wake up early to go to a park is unclear to me, but we follow our guide like good little tourists. Helen is a great guide, so we trust her completely. In the park, we observe a large group of people line-dancing to music, the moves undoubtedly influenced by martial arts. At least a hundred people participate in the dance on a flat and wide stone pathway. We snap some pictures and walk further.

The sound of the music of the line-dancers is still present when we hear other speakers compete. This time the sounds are more classical but at the same time still Eastern-sounding due to the instruments used. In front of a large pond, still on the wide stone path, at least seventy-five couples are square dancing. They are waltzing away, circling around an imaginary midpoint. Some of the couples could be professionals, several are dressed-up for the occasion. More photos are taken. I notice that some couples and even individuals are dancing solo, away from the group, on side paths in the park, still in reach of the sound. One lady dances on her own, as if in a trance, oblivious to anything but the music.

We move deeper into the park, enjoying the lovely spring morning and trees in full bloom. At an intersection of two paths a choir is singing. Helen explains "these people, mainly retired people, are just getting together, no formal organization". A self-appointed conductor waves a baton at a choir so large, most cathedrals would be envious. "They are singing songs praising our great leader Mao and China in general" Helen says, before we are distracted by a 'toink-toink' sound. We glance to the side and see people standing in circles. In groups of four to six they kick what looks like a badminton shuttle with long feathers and a heavy bottom. Metal rings in the bottom generate the 'toink' sound. The game is best compared to "hacky sack" which was popular when Heidi and I went to university. As with the dancing, the people playing are not young; on the contrary, I would guess they are over fifty, both male and female.

On the side they sell the plumed objects, and Helen buys one. An older gentlemen tries to convince Alicia to try and play "jaing-zjeu" with them. Natural hesitation follows, but I tell her I will join, so she and Leendert are ready to try. Within no time we have a team of six. The aging Chinese are skilled, agile and patient with us. To my surprise I catch on quickly, and they ask "football, yes?" I have never played, and am not a fan of soccer, but for the conversation I nod my head. At one time I have the "shen-ze" (the plume) land on my head and, by freak accident, am able to keep it parked there in one bounce. The crowd goes wild, impressed by the trick and the white folks playing in general. The number of camera's clicking increases dramatically from a shy number of people taking a snapshot at first to nearly every phone-camera recording the event.

We have a blast. The gentlemen are good-natured and encouraging every time we make a good shot. I peel off layers of clothing as do Leendert and Alicia. The temperature is going up and this is hard work! We play for almost an hour, and I assure you it is a good workout. Being aware that we are at the risk of totally ruining Helen's schedule, we thank the pensioners for playing and Heidi exchanges e-mail addresses with Chinese paparazzi who – full of pride - show the pictures and videos they have been taking.

Thankful for the daypack with water, we walk on. The sound of the choir and the 'toink-toink' is slowly drowned out by yet more Asian music. A minority ethnic group is dancing in full costume. They are from the West of China, and the Kazak influence is unmistakable. It is a blend of Asian and Arab dancing; bright color, big robes, unique headdresses, all beautiful. More photos, of course.

As we exit the park Leendert remarks that playing games with the locals is the best thing of the trip so far. Of all things, kicking a toy around with strangers. Isn't it amazing how quickly one can bond with people despite age, religion, cultural background, and a total absence of a common language over something silly as a plume with a metal bottom? Leendert is less charmed by the prospect of our next activity - a museum.

The driver drops us off and Helen critically looks at the long lines at the ticket counters. She explains "the entry is limited, but normally in this season it is no issue". She tells us to follow her as there might be a better way in. We follow her into the Museum gift shop. She instructs us to browse and look interested while she has a word with the shop manager. Soon, she is back with a smile on her face. "I know the manager" she states, "we can go in this way". We walk upstream through the gift shop, which, as in any good museum, is the exit. We pop through security gates meant for employees and end up in the museum. It pays to have a guide!

The museum holds an extensive collection of local artifacts. The area was home to many of the dynasties, so it has a lot to offer. We make our way through creatively named 'gallery 1' (stone-age to bronze-age and the Qin Dynasty), 'gallery 2' the time of the Han Dynasty, and – no surprise - 'gallery 3' which covers the Tang dynasty. The exhibition is busy and it isn't always easy to get in front of the display cabinets. As usual, this problem dissipates deeper into the galleries as initial excitement wears off and people overdose on the information. It is striking to see how far ahead the Chinese were compared to our western culture in 3000-1500 B.C. Pottery, tools, weaving, writing - practices which would not come to us until Greek and Roman times. With Helen, we make surgical strikes on the truly interesting exhibits, skipping over many other 'stone age' spear points, broken cups, etc. Although we too wear out quickly, having studied different dynasties in HWH does allow us to contextualize. It makes it a rather manageable museum and a good stop.

For lunch, we head to "First Noodle under the Sun" to have the renowned "biang-biang" noodles. These are extra wide, wheat noodles, up to three meters long. The superstition is that long noodles are healthy; "long noodles give long life". Central China is a culinary cross-over point. The South is generally hot and wet (rice-based dishes), the North is cooler and dryer (wheat-based noodle dishes). Xi'an itself is the region where dim sum originated. Needless to say, we eat well. The biang-biang noodles are tasty, albeit hard to serve and eat. If you have ever served spaghetti and had to stand up, or hit the overhead light with the serving spoon and fork, you can imagine what it is like serving these three-meter-long ropes. Transferring one noodle from serving bowl to eating bowl takes skill, eating it is a tremendous logistical challenge.

The afternoon is filled with a visit to a Buddhist temple and the Swan Pagoda. On the way we pass a huge square with sloping terraces. Suddenly music fills the air, as does water. A wonderful display appears before us with at least nine-hundred individual fountainheads spurting water in a carefully choreographed water dance. The thirty minute show is artistically captivating and an engineering marvel. We carry on to the intended temple complex. Incense fills the air. One temple is particularly ornate, covered with jade bas relief, depicting the life of Buddha. Helen gives us a crash course of the life of the Buddha and the Buddhist philosophy; a helpful introduction for our next stop in Nepal.

By now the kids claim they are worn out. They are not excited when Helen says "let's go visit the city wall". Heidi and I hesitate for a moment, then make them come along. Helen explains we can bike on top of the wall surrounding the city, a twelve kilometer loop. On top of the wall we rent bicycles and to our delight, they have tandems. All at once the kids are keen to participate. The wall is the most compete surviving city wall in China. It is twelve meters wide, smooth and perfect for riding bicycles. I race the kids while overlooking the old inner city and the modern outer city. The kids hide in the corners of the ramparts. I pretend not to see them until they catch up. It's a blast.

The last day in Xi'an with Helen is as full as the previous days. After settling the hotel bill as Helen enters the lobby and we greet her with "knee-_chi_-la-ma". With a smile she responds with the same. Since we haven't eaten, we head to a market for some breakfast. Stalls along the main road sell fresh fruit, those in a side street offer anything you might want: noodles, buns, meat and vegetables. Helen explains that the street stalls will disappear soon. I ask her if they are being replaced by grocery stores and she laughs: "no, they will disappear soon, as in the next twenty minutes". She explains that officially, the street stalls are not allowed. They are tolerated until 9am, which is when the police start their shift. "Afterwards they get fined". One stall sells steamed buns filled with red beans or vegetables. They are passed quickly from hand to hand; hot-hot-hot. They are delicious and spicy. A few stalls further we pass an old lady behind a frying pan. I ask Helen what the small meatball-sized items are. She explains they are made of potato and carrot, and are eaten during weddings; more specifically in soup at the end of a wedding; "they give the guests the hint that it is time to leave". I ask if I can buy one or two. Helen convinces the lady to give us some for free. Although there is not a wedding in sight, we like them so much that we buy a bag full.

From the market we drive towards 'calligraphy street'. Helen has made an appointment for a calligraphy class. On the way I notice that most taxis have BYD on their trunk. Not able to place it, I ask Helen if it is a Chinese brand. She confirms it is "BYD is much like LG". Slightly puzzled I ask how so. "Well", she said "like LG stands for Life is Good, BYD stands for the car brand Build Your Dreams". Oh how far branding has come from plugging your family name on the label or emblem!

The calligraphy street is quiet, a combination of bad weather, Monday and early morning. We meander in and out the little shops because we are early for our planned session. As a consequence, Alicia has time to look at hand-painted fans. The sales lady is not very friendly and does not want to negotiate. She must figure we are uninformed tourists, unaware that we have Helen with us suggesting the 'fair price' range. Four shops further Alicia buys a box with small stone warriors. Leendert also wants a set, so they negotiate a good deal. From there we are off to the art museum and calligraphy class. An art student runs us through the recent paint history of China: peasant painting, cultural revolution painting, clay mask painting, etc.

In a dedicated art room, we sit behind a big table, four big brushes with sharp points and rough white paper in front of us. Our young instructor makes us write the basic eight strokes which compose the Chinese characters. She then teaches us the word for 'forever' [yong] which contains each of the strokes. From there we advance quickly to the ultimate challenge: writing 'Biang' - as in Biang-Biang noodles. The symbol for Biang is the most complex one in Chinese, it is constructed of fifty-two strokes. Our teacher also asks for our names and helps to translate them: Alicia (Daring, Beauty, Elegant), Leendert (Strong will, Prosperous, Special), Heidi (Flower, Elegant), Alexander (Pressure, Strict, Mountain, Success). All of us enjoy the lesson wishing we could spend more time doing it. There is something very social and bonding to sit down with the family and learn a new skill together. We get an appreciation not only for the text writing but also for the intricate paintings we see on the walls, black-and-white designs of bamboo. These ink drawings are one-shot only, "first time right" rules. Do it right and it is great, mess up one line and you must start over, there is no way to erase or paint over. No big deal if you are just writing your name, but if you have a two-by-two meter bamboo forest with a boat and perhaps some reflections in the water – which you have been working on for weeks – it is a different story.

After class, we are hungry, so Helen takes us to a nearby restaurant. I look at the picture menu and order food. I order a classic drink; warm Coca-Cola with ginger. I know what it sounds like, but I wouldn't have ordered it if it were awful. In no time, the jug is emptied. It nicely complements the cold duck, shredded squid and salad soaked in sesame oil.

After lunch we drive to the mausoleum of the forth emperor of the Han dynasty. This site was discovered even more recently than the famous terracotta warriors site we saw a few days ago. This site was stumbled upon in the 1990s when the road to the airport was constructed. Since then eighty-two more pits have been identified, covering a twenty square kilometer area. The mausoleum of the two-thousand-year-old emperor remains untouched out of respect for the tomb, but the 'pits' around it are fair game. So far, only the first few have been excavated. The project of unearthing still has decades to go. The current exhibition shows a large collection of statues of animals; pigs, dogs, goats, horses, etc. Unlike the terracotta warriors we saw before, the statutes of the people are small. They missing their arms. Helen explains that the statues used to have rich silk clothing. To position and dress the statues correctly, the arms needed to move. To make this possible, the limbs were made of wood. The wood and silk have long since turned to dust.

Three kilometers further, we visit the Empress' tomb. She was the only female emperor. Originally she was a concubine of the Emperor. When he died, his son broke tradition and took his father's concubine as his beloved wife. When he died, the Empress took the reins of the kingdom. She was a much respected and honored lady. The museum at the Empress' tomb is a empty of tourists, but very nice. Besides ourselves I count one other couple, and 12 security personnel. I'm not sure how that business model works. Helen, motivated by Alicia's questions, continues to bestow upon us the intricacies of the Qin, Han, Tang dynasties. By now we are able to distinguish them by looking at the statues and works of art.

At the end of the afternoon, Helen brings us to the massive train station. She walks with us through the security check and into the 'VIP' waiting room and we say our goodbyes. The VIP lounge is nothing to get excited about. I look around and think it is comparable to any cold train station waiting area. This one has seats which could have been transplanted from a 1980s airport of the USA. Luckily the wait isn't long, and before you know it we make our way down to the train. Not being able to read anything on the train ticket itself, we stop at every wagon asking the uniformed person is this is the right carriage. After four conductors wave us further down the platform, we find the right one. We are in the 'soft sleepers'; one cabin, four beds (up/down of course). For two reasons, we are unlucky with the communal toilet. First, it is not as nice as reviews suggested. Second, it is adjacent to our room, meaning every door opening and closing and every vacuum flush is acoustically enjoyed in our cozy little cabin. Overall, though, the train is nice, the beds are okay and the temperature is fine. The train travels between seventy-five and one hundred and fifty kilometers per hour and will bring us overnight to Beijing. I find the train a great travel option if you are not pressed for time. It is more spacious, avoids the hassle of airports, eliminates the risk of losing bags, and typically gets you into the destination's city center. To top it all off it is cheaper than a plane and you can skip a hotel night. Soft rocking and the ka-dang, ka-dang of the rails puts us to sleep that night.

Beijing - More History and Culture

Ka-bang! What the…..?? As I try opening my eyes, lying in bed, I stare into the eyes of a Chinese woman. I don't recognize her. A moment of pure fear shocks through my body. What happened last night? Tears blur my vision as my eyes are brutally attacked by the morning light. I realize the door is open, bright lights are on, and the face of a Chinese lady in uniform is at a hand's distance from my face. A rude awakening. Neurons fire and it begins to register that we are still on the train. Five minutes before my 06:30am alarm went off, a female train worker opened our locked door from outside, switched on the lights and dove in the hole separating the two beds Heidi and I sleep on. Her task: emptying the small trashcan under the table at the window. Okay. Cool, relax, all is well. In fact, all is very well. We all had a reasonably good night and we've arrived safely in Beijing.

We repack our belongings and take turns at the hole-in-the-floor toilet. The train pulls into the station ten minutes early and we find our way out. Kevin, our next guide, is waiting at the exit. We greet him and walk to the van. He will take us to our Airbnb apartment. Our new home has two bedrooms, a living room, dining area and a kitchen. The building wraps around a quiet courtyard full of singing birds. It is an oasis, one that certainly does not feel like we are in the middle of a city of twenty-five million. We freshen up and head straight back to Kevin.

In Pursuit of Chocolate

Kevin is a funny character. He constantly refers to himself by his own name; "Kevin will get you to the hotel", "Kevin suggests eating duck","Kevin likes Beijing", etc. Outside the apartment complex there are food stalls, and being breakfast time, we buy dumplings and steamed buns; "Kevin thinks those are good". They are.

Our first target today is the Great Wall, or, as it is known by the Chinese: the Long Wall. Once measuring almost enough to go around the world, its current length is 8,852 kilometers - the distance from San Francisco to Amsterdam. I show Kevin where I visited the wall years before, a slightly off the beaten track location, but "Kevin thinks that's rather far away". We negotiate. I insist I want to end up going to a more 'local' spot of the wall rather than the prime tourist places; "Kevin thinks that is a good idea" and takes us up the road to Mu Tian Yu. This jump-on point was just finished last year according to Kevin and not too popular yet. It has the feel of a new upscale shopping strip with a large parking, restaurants and souvenir shops, but it is not too busy with tourists (yet).

We buy tickets and are shuttled up the hill in a brand new bus. We go a bit over a kilometer and stop at the 'base station'. From here we have two options: walk up, which looks a rather mean climb, or take a chairlift. We choose the latter, and find ourselves sitting two by two in the fresh morning air on a ski lift, but without snow on the ground or ski-boots on our feet. Once landed at the top "Kevin thinks you should first to right, then left", and he leaves us to explore the wall on our own. "Kevin will meet you at one o'clock back at the shuttle bus area". So much for being an active guide. For those not familiar with the Great Wall, it is not like a wall around a town or castle. The Great Wall follows the mountain ridges and turns and twists like a serpent over the landscape. It is seldom flat. Most of the time you walk up or down a slope or actively climb stairs. At times the steps are steep enough to require using hands and feet. The wall took over a thousand of years to build (started 7th century BC and had a final boost between 1300-1600 AD). While impressive, it largely failed as a military deterrent. Many lives were lost building it, enemies like the Mongols rode around it, or gates were opened by traitors, making it one of the most useless military endeavors ever. One of the better quotes I read summed it up well: The Long Wall was about as useful to China as the Bible on a battlefield: it brings comfort, but it won't stop the enemy.

Walking the wall, I dispense little facts I read: over a million people died building the wall resulting in the nickname "the longest cemetery in the world"; despite the claim, you can't actually see it from the moon; it was created by connecting many sub-parts. Heidi and the kids listen with half an ear, enjoying the combination of cold air and the radiance of the sun. As we walk, we peel off layers of clothes. There are some other tourists, but it is far from crowded. In fact, we can take quite a few pictures with just us in the frame. We spend the better of three hours trekking the stone structure, taking hundreds of pictures; repeatedly telling each other what an amazing site it is.

To return down the mountain there is a surprise for the kids. We can take a toboggan; a summer sled. It is a long ride, over 1500 meters; fun, and much faster than taking the ski lift. Once back down "Kevin advises to eat lunch here", which we do - and regret. The food is mediocre and expensive. The restaurants cater for one-time tourists, so they are unconcerned about repeat business. Back at the car, I give Kevin feedback about the lunch location. He tries to make it up to us a few moments later by buying some strawberries from a road side stand. What a lovely springtime treat!

On the way back to the city we stop at a cloisonné factory. This is an art form crafting mainly vases and plates. A guide takes us through the process. First, flattened copper wire is bent into designs varying floral motives, dragons, lotus flowers, birds, and landscapes. Next, the wire is glued onto an object (like a vase). Putting the design on can take up to a week. The object is heated in a kiln to cure the shape. Then, ceramic colors are placed to fill in the spaces. Again, the item is fired to fix the colors. The firing is repeated (up to ten times) until all segments are filled. After coloring, the surface is still rough and some of the metal wire sticks out. Polishing is next. A man sits with a bowl spinning in front of him. Water drips through a small tube onto the object to keep it wet. He presses two pieces of black charcoal onto the sides. It is a slow process, but once he is done, the vase is perfectly smooth and shiny. It is a very interesting process. Were it not for the fact that we are backpacking, I am sure we would have bought a piece or two.

On the ride back to the capital we go to the 'birds-nest', the iconic stadium from the 2008 Olympics. The building, its surroundings and the swimming pool area are massive and impressive. We take the classic picture, all of us jumping, hands in the air. I have no clue where that started, nor why people do it, but it was something on my bucket list to do on this large square in front of the stadium.

As we stroll on, Kevin realizes he forgot his mobile in the car. This is an issue, since he needs to tell the driver where to pick us up. First he uses a phone from a security guard, next I offer him mine. Unfortunately, the driver doesn't pick up. Time goes by, still no luck. Our coats and electronics are in the car, the temperature is going down, we're getting tired, and my patience is beginning to run low. Kevin reads the signals and gets us a taxi ("Kevin is sorry"). He sends us on our merry way, promising to drop our stuff later in the evening.

Two hours later Kevin appears at the apartment. He points us to a 'Peking Duck' restaurant near the apartment. Isn't it funny how we talk about Peking Duck, while the town is called Beijing? Ever wondered why? And why is the airport code PEK, but we refer to the airport nowadays as Beijing International? The explanation is found in the Olympic Games. At that time, The Party decided to push the name Beijing. By and large it worked, but the iconic dish and the airport code still remain firmly anchored in the historic name.

Following Kevin's advice, we walk up the street and enter the restaurant. Thankful for the pictures, we point at various illustrations: soup, vegetables, and, of course, duck. As we sip jasmine tea, I look at the kids. It is clear we are paying the price for the overnight train ride and the long day. Leendert's throat hurts and Alicia looks tired. I pray the food is quick and good. Preferably in that order. Within no time, the Peking Duck arrives at our table. It comes on one platter in three forms: the crispy skin and fat, slices of dark meat, and white meat with a bit of skin attached. The lady serving us is excited to have foreigners in her restaurant. She grabs disposable plastic gloves and takes great pride in showing us how to take the thin pancakes, add the duck, sauce and other toppings and fold it closed. The sight and smell of the roasted duck as well as the lady's genuine energy makes our fatigue dissipate like snow in the sun. A total revival. We eat like tigers, devouring at least two ducks before returning home, ready for bed.

Early the next morning, Kevin finds us in the courtyard of the residence playing "jaing-zjeu", kicking around the feathered shuttle which we bought in Xi'an. Kevin waits patiently as we grab our gear. A short stop for steamed breakfast buns and we are on our way. Beijing classics are on the schedule.

First, we head out to the Summer Palace. In Beijing, a city of twenty-one million people, traffic is a constant, so it takes a while to get to our destination. We jump out of the van and enter the grounds. While not as busy as Tiananmen Square, it is still packed and our pictures are photo-bombed by other tourists. The wooden buildings are beautifully painted. They overlook an enormous lake, all created for the pleasure of the emperor. Yes, it is a man made lake. It is so large that a mountain, not a mere hill, was created with the sand dug out. We wind along a 728-meter corridor dedicated to the empress. It is called "Changlang" - the Long

Corridor – and is in the Guinness Book of Records as the longest corridor in the world. The empress would stroll here, getting her exercise while being protected from the sun and rain. We enter the residence, which is built on Longevity Hill. The buildings are impressive. However, since they are all in the same style, our interest wanes quickly, and I must agree with Leendert that to some extent: "if you've seen one, you've seen them all". The good news is that the buildings are on such a steep incline that the climb itself is fun. It culminates in a panoramic view over the lake towards 'turtle island', a man made island in the middle of the lake.

Kevin stays behind while we climb, not feeling up to the physical exercise, I guess. He awaits our return on a bench in the sun. As for Kevin as a tour guide, I am not too impressed. He tells stories about what happened at the time of the emperors, but he focuses on concubines, palace intrigues and repeats stories of superstitions about longevity. His stories do not score very high on my list. They follow a consistent pattern, only the names of the characters and the years seem to alter. Headline: Emperor has wife, beautiful concubine enters, tension, one of them dies, sadness for a while, wiseman is consulted, some natural phenomena takes place, new female enters the scene. Repeat. The benefit of having Kevin is that "Kevin knows the way", he comes with his driver and he has his phone with him (most of the time). This means we are dropped at the front gates of attractions and Kevin can quickly get our tickets and help us access the sites.

After the palace, we drive towards the Forbidden City and realize it is already time for lunch. Here, Kevin redeems himself for his lame stories. He brings us to a nice restaurant which is not an obvious find for foreigners. We look through the menu, but it is merely for form. The decision is made as soon as the menu is opened: Peking Duck, veggies, egg-fried rice and jasmine tea. Following Kevin's tip, we ask the waiter to 'barbecue' the remaining bones. They arrive on a plate with the rest of the duck. "Barbecued bones" means 'deep fry anything left over'. Effectively it is an improved version of KFC with remaining parts; sounds worse than it is.

After lunch we go to Tiananmen Square. We opt not to go to Mao's mausoleum. Waiting over an hour in a queue to see the old leader Mao preserved in his crystal coffin for twenty seconds is not on our bucket list. It is impressive, however, to walk over the largest square in the world, especially knowing its history. It is impossible to walk there without recalling the image of the student standing in front of the tank, defying the odds. I probe Kevin for his views on the Cultural Revolution and the Student Revolution, but get little feedback. The headline is that Kevin (as most Chinese) respects, no, idolizes Party Leader Mao. "Kevin knows

Leader Mao was a smart and good man". One fun anecdote he shared with us: Mao spent time meditating with a Buddhist monk. This wise Buddhist monk gave him the answer: 8241. No further explanation was given. This number was to be important for him. Subsequently, Mao named his personal guards '8241', figuring this would be a good start. Nothing specific happened. No big revelation until his death. Mao died in 1976, aged 82. He had been in power for 41 years. Proof enough for Kevin that the wise man was right.

There is no doubt that in the past (and today) Kevin and many Chinese still adore Mao. Somehow the atrocities of years of cultural revolution are explained away. Peasants were deemed 'pure and good'; the educated, intellectuals and people with family members abroad were not. Kevin admits that the latter were interrogated, imprisoned, killed or never heard of again, but that was only because some people misinterpreted the wise words of Mao. As for the student revolt (the kid standing in front of the tank) it was lucky the government crushed this uprising "where would we have otherwise been now? Kevin thinks it would have been a mess if the students would have taken over!". I still wonder if those were his honest thoughts or 'given' thoughts (realizing those might be the same).

Kevin's most valuable stories pertain to daily life. He talks about marriage and match-makers; the latter a consequence of China's one-child policy. During our visit, the one-child policy was still partially in place (being phased out as of 2015). Until then, most of China had strict one-child restrictions (with - in some places - the permission to have a second child if your first one was a girl). While I see the logic to controlling birth-rates in general, the unfortunate 'law of unintended consequences' raises its head. Let's not detail the various causes (they can be grim), one of the policy outcomes is a skewed population profile: the boy-to-girl ratio got messed up, became uneven. This means, in theory, that girls can be more selective when it comes to their mating partner. However, in practice, women are often pressured by their parents to get married focusing on 'the chocolate'. Realizing their girls are a scarce resource, a car, an apartment and money become a key selection criteria in finding a partner rather than other (non-material) elements. This is also where a marital matchmaker enters and an entire industry flourishes. Case in point? Kevin. He got to know his wife through a matchmaker. The agency helped him find and court his wife. After the agency helped him select his wife using an album with profiles and pictures, Kevin was introduced. He got four months of week-by-week instructions: 'have a drink with her (tea)', 'buy her a scarf', 'get her chocolates', 'invite her to your parents'. An entire script played out. Four months after the initial meeting, the wedding date was set. Two months later, the marriage was a fact. Traditionally, the groom's father pays everything, so it was tough on his dad. One year after the wedding their child was born. Kevin points out they were lucky: a boy. He mentioned it because he can't have another child; he could never afford it. Like so many of his peers, he works in Beijing while his wife and six-month-old baby are in a village two and a half hours out of town. He tries to see them every two weeks, or at least once a month. If all goes well and fortune is with him, he might get them to Beijing three years from now.

Loaded with this story, we arrive at the Forbidden city. Heidi and the kids are as impressed as I was when I first visited some years earlier. It is busier than the last time I was there, but the exception of the doorway in front of the emperor's seat and his bedroom, we can enjoy the site without feeling overrun. Kevin doesn't seem to know much about the palace construction or it's rich and fascinating elements. He can confirm and share juicy details on how concubines entered the palace and how one emperor died young due to his sexual activity, but that's it. I'd rather he pointed out the roof sculptures, how the (almost) heavenly number 'nine' appears everywhere on the site; 10,000 being the number of heaven itself. Having read up on the place, I point at the doors with the large 81 decorative nails: nine rows of nine nails. I explain the myth that the palace has 9999.5 rooms (the palace actually has 'only' 8707), how the emperor would be confined to the palace, how the big bronze vats are there not for decoration only, but to store water in case of a fire; how in winter they would light fires under the vats to prevent the water from freezing.

After several hours appreciating the Forbidden City with its golden roofs we rejoin Kevin and the driver. One more attraction has been planned before the day is over. We are booked for the Beijing Chaoyang Acrobatics World. It is a modern theatre and we delight in the performance. Ladies bending in every possible way balancing platters with wine glasses, incredible human pyramids, guys jumping forwards and backwards through hoops up to six feet high, a climbing acrobat putting chair-on-chair-on-chair all the way to the top of the theatre. Once on top, he does one-armed handstands. It gives me that uncomfortable feeling of being torn between watching or not; appreciating the skill but fearful of what might happen. There is also plenty of classic circus-like entertainment; a bicycle performance ends with more and more women loading themselves onto a single bicycle circling around on stage. By seven you think they are done, but they continue; eight, nine…finally ending up with twelve. For the final act, a round spherical metal cage is rolled onto stage. We hear the sound of a motorcycle. A door is opened in the sphere and a motorcycle drives in. The rider picks up speed and goes around and around, first horizontally, but soon doing loops upside-down. It would have been boring, weren't it for the fact that he is joined by a second bike, and a third, a forth and a fifth. How they succeed in driving around, crisscrossing one another without crashing, is unclear to me. Needless to say, when numbers six, seven and eight join, the audience goes wild. But the climax is still to come. The lights in the theatre are extinguished, with only the 'exit' lights remaining on. The motor rider's suits are lit up in various colors. The audience, awestruck goes completely quiet, stunned to silence as the eight bikes rotate about inside the metal ball with lights flashing. Afterwards, we agree that it's amazing what humans can do if we set our mind to it! It was a fantastic 'grand finale' for both the show and the day.

Shopping and Economics

The following days are dedicated to the last items on our China list. We start by going to a flea market. My interest in flea markets waned years ago. Many a weekend I strolled with my parents, and subsequently with Heidi, over markets across Europe. I have come to the conclusion that the only redeeming factor for doing so is the cup of coffee in the sun on the terrace afterwards. I am convinced that when we bought something at these markets, it was either driven by feeling sorry for the vendor who stood there for hours in the cold air, or because of the underlying sense that we'd feel silly returning home two hours later empty handed. And no, I am not swayed by the argument "if we go early we get the better bargains". No, even before the internet arrived, flea-markets were dominated by stuff even fleas would have little interest in. Digital platforms ensure that nothing truly valuable makes it to the tarp on the cobblestone square. Bottom line, I was skeptical going to a Chinese flea market. I caved to the family pressure, however, knowing that we had bought almost no gifts or memorabilia on the trip thus far. We were also planning to ship a box back to Europe, so why not? It was at least a good opportunity to see if Chinese flea markets are similar to the ones we know from home.

Kevin picks us up after we procure our morning steamed buns from the street vendor; the driver navigates us through morning traffic. It's a short drive, and I realize instantly this is not a flea-market as I know it. We stand in front of a large building. "Kevin likes this flea-market; Kevin will return to pick you up in ninety minutes". We enter the building and make a quick scan. It is quiet. Quiet the way a mall is still when the retail shops are closed and only the coffee shops and breakfast eateries are open. Inside, spread over several floors, hundreds of vendors have little stalls, often one table wide, comparable to a market in Europe. Not much – or anything appears second hand. Most is in 'original' packaging. The first stalls are filled with cloth; table runners, scarves, etc. Sales people jump on us as we are the only ones to jump on. Their luck – fat juicy Westerners! Luckily, we remember "*buyao xie xie*", the 'no thank you' we learned in Shanghai. This makes the vendors think we are 'local' westerners and subdues their eager approaches.

We came with the target of buying some chopsticks and iron dragon statues which we had seen, and liked, in Shanghai. We weave our way up and down the aisles walking from one section to the next. From the fabric section we enter into electronics; mobile phone covers, iPad covers, etc. One gadget grabs my attention: a Ipad cover with an integrated keyboard. The sticker price is 285RMB. Within seconds the "you my first customer"-price gets posted on the calculator. We're down to 180RMB. I look and hesitate. The sales lady hands me the calculator "how much you wanna pay?". I know it is too early for me to type any number in, so I fake walking away twice. As expected the price drops: 150...140. "Okay, final honest price" 100RMB, "if you say yes now". I smile politely and walk away, hearing what I believe to be a 80RMB. It might have been something totally vulgar as well. In keeping with our routine in these situations, Heidi and I split off as soon as I started negotiating. Intentionally, she looked at other stalls only to follow me about thirty seconds after I broke off the negotiations. It has the expected effect. When she joins me she says the vendor told her I can get the item for 70RMB if Heidi convinces me to come back. We agree to pass by on the way out.

We climb the stairs and find the second floor of the flea-market center to be the jewelry level. Gold, silver and especially pearls. The bling is blinding. Needless to say, Alicia and Heidi get stuck at a jewelry stand as Leendert and I make our way into the next section: Chinese souvenirs. That's what we came for! We look at some iron dragons; but they don't have the 'Shanghai' ones. We continue looking. In-and-out of stalls we go. We notice fans and chopsticks, knowing the girls will be happy as those, too, were on their shopping list. Meandering through, Leendert spots them first – the statues we are looking for. They have a sticker price of 915RMB, but, as 'special first customer' the dragon can be mine for a mere 750RMB. I smile, see the calculator appear and know to refuse to put an amount in. The usual price cascade happens, bottoming out at 175RMB. I walk on as I am joined by Heidi and Alicia who also have walked away from a potential purchase; a nice set of jade earrings and matching necklace. The difference between the kids when it comes to haggling is striking. Leendert is very uncomfortable with price negotiation, Alicia sees it as a game, almost a sport. We look at paintings, woodwork, and Alicia buys a set of chopsticks she likes. She also gets a piece of paper inscribed with the name of one of her friends. Leendert, meanwhile, takes pride in showing me all the stuff he does not want to buy: "Look dad, I really don't want that ashtray with Mao on it".

We negotiate the price of the dragon statue we like. Different places have the same model; identical dragons, five stalls apart. It takes a bit of time, but we end up at a rock-bottom price of 150RMB. I decide to buy two, one from each stall. Leendert inquires, "couldn't you have gotten a better price if you bought two from the same place?". And yes, I am sure that a better price was possible if combined. It also doesn't make sense to buy two identical items from different places with a price gap. "But dad, the one stall ends up 25RMB more expensive!". It's a five Euro investment I'm willing to make to allow for the discussion that ensues on economics later over coffee and juice. We talk about 'reasonable pricing'; about supply and demand. How seller brings the prices down, how buyers brings the prices up. We discuss the importance of 'bargaining', how leaving both parties with the feeling that a fair deal is reached is important. We reflect that you can negotiate and still not come to an agreement. Walking away without purchase and/or guilt is fine. Alicia is comfortable with it, Leendert 'gets it' intellectually, but still doesn't like it. On our way out, we circle back to the stand which offered the iPad-cover with key board. I end up paying 90RMB. See, by coming back I showed the vendor I really wanted it, and as a buyer I brought the price back up! Here endeth the lesson.

After the flea-market we go to the Heavenly Temple. This site is where the emperor used to go and pray. It is well worth the entry fee. We walk through the park over a promenade leading to a pavilion. The unique aspect of this temple is that it is round. It has the typical gold, blue, white and green painting on the maroon red beams. Alicia rolls her eyes, starts to hang on my arm and pleads "not another temple!". I have to admit, aside from the fact that it is round, it is remarkably like the other buildings we have seen. In fact, you would wonder if the emperor would not get sick of the same five colors, the identical constructions, the nine sides, nine steps, nine stones, nine golden knobs, the nine cross-bars.

The walk from the temple to the exit is over a wide and long elevated stone walkway. Truth be told, this elevated construction is more impressive than the Heavenly Temple itself. It's a long way to where Kevin and the van are waiting, so to entertain ourselves we horse around with the kids, imitating the "ministry of the silly walks" made infamous by John Cleese in Monty Python. Locals enjoying their stroll in the fresh air and sunshine try inconspicuously to decipher what these strange foreigners are doing, struggling between staring and not looking. We wonder what their conversations over lunch will be.

Lunch is back in the basement of the flea market. It is much like a food-court in a mall, but with a twist. Upon entry you by a "lunch card", on which you load money. Then, as different people choose their platters from the various places, the card is used for payment. This temporary currency makes me reflect. What is the story on the Chinese currency anyway? Is it Yuan or Renminbi? I had to look it up. The official currency is RMB (Ren-Min-Be), which loosely translates out of Mandarin into 'the people's currency'. The money used in China is Chinese Yuan (CNY). The Yuan is like a Dollar, which has Jiao (dimes) and Fen (cents). The overarching name is RMB, much like the US dollar is formally a Federal Reserve Note (FRN). So the RMB equates to a FRN, the Yuan to a Dollar. Either way, on our plastic card we have digitized Fen, rolled up into Jiao and Yuan. As we get our food no money exchanges hands, the card just gets swiped. All quite hygienic. I glance around as Leendert dives in his dumplings, Alicia in the beef noodle soup and Heidi and I munch on rice. The area is clean, well-lit and could have been any high-end food court in the world, were it not for the fact that none of the 'usual' western chains are present. Each and every one of the small kitchens is local. I realize this is a misnomer, with local I mean 'Chinese', which, for all I know could include Kasgar, in Xinjiang Province, well over 4300 kilometers to the west of where we are currently eating, so not too local.

After lunch it is off to the post office. Having bought a few little gifts over the last months, it is time to ship a box back home. The Chinese post office is in an old building. As advanced as the food-court was, the post office throws us back in time. The lady helping us is dressed in a dreadful green uniform, which was probably worn by her father twenty years ago. He must have been at least a size-and-a-half bigger than she is. Old glasses and an unhappy face stare at us. Luckily Kevin is helping to explain what we want to do. We pack a box carefully, buying a square meter of bubble wrap on the spot. As we hand her the box she opens it up and goes through the content with total disregard of privacy and no sensitivity to fragility. A triage follows on what we can and can't ship. Electronic chargers, lenses in saline, spare computer cables and a back-up disk are not allowed. Darn, this is worse than an American airport! We try to make her change her mind, to no avail. We repack, taping everything closed again. For the service of her security check, the bubble wrap and the box we pay and get a receipt. I see her toss the box on a pile of bags and boxes, and pray the bubble wrap will do its intended task. Next we go to the payment desk with the receipt. We get ready to pay for the shipment itself. What?!? Four hundred and forty yuan? Are you nuts? Here I am spending the morning haggling to get the last ten yuan off an iron dragon only to find the shipping is four time the price of the item! For a moment I consider negotiating, but remind myself of how this might be misconstrued into 'bribing or attempting to bribe a government official', a domain I prefer to stay away from as far as possible. We pay, get a receipt and leave. The receipt is useless, of course. Assume for a second the box does not arrive in Europe, what can we do? Travel back to China to make a claim? I think not. This at least gives me the opportunity to share another business lesson with Leendert: deck chairs and the Titanic. There is little use to find cheap products locally if the cost of shipping kills the value negotiated!

From the post office we walk to the old part of Beijing; Hutong. These quarters are where the Mongols settled in the late twelve hundreds during the Yuan Dynasty. Closely set, gray brick one-story housing creates a maze of small alleyways. Through the middle there is a river and lake, lined with hip bars and restaurants. The river is a man-made canal, dug for the emperor all the way to Guanzhou (near Shanghai). The canal stretches over 1600 kilometers and allowed the emperor an easy way to get to the sea, avoiding arduous road travel. We meander, observe and have a drink. Kevin asks if we want to go to a park to see the Drum and Bell tower. Heidi and I agree with a single glance. No thanks, I think we are 'guided-out'. Just drop us at the apartment and we'll be fine. As this was the last day with Kevin, we pay him. Bluntly "Kevin asks for a tip for the driver". If someone did deserve an extra payment, it was the driver, so I empty out my remaining cash. As they drive off, I am not sure if Kevin is disappointed with the amount, or if he will even share with the driver. I hope he does, and it is much like the post office receipt, there isn't much I can do to change the outcome now.

Back at the apartment. I play the feather-shuttle kicking game with the kids in the courtyard. Passersby smile at the sight of us. The rest of the late afternoon and evening we busy ourselves with useless things. It has been three days non-stop and on-the-go. We all enjoy the quiet time. We even agree that we are overdosed on food, so we skip dinner. A nice and relaxing evening is the result and we relish the fact that tomorrow we have nothing specific to do!

End gaming in China

We are now in the last days of March and take a recovery day. I know it sounds crazy, how can we need a recovery day? Trust me, the continuous overload of new impressions has a way of catching up with you. Now, having said that, as if on cue, with no need for the kids to get up early, they do. Someday, someone with more brains than me must explain how this works. If something is on the agenda in the morning, be it school, a flight, or some other event, I have to use a crowbar to get the kids out of bed. On a day like today, with nothing planned, they cheerily appear out of their bedrooms early, ready to go.

For brunch, we chose a place called Uncle Sam's. We order, grilled ham/cheese sandwiches, two kinds of burgers and a hot dog; for once no dim sum or rice. We have a conversation on superstition, since it holds such a prominent place in the Chinese society. Reportedly, after India, China is the most superstitious country in the world. I am not sure how this is measured, but we have certainly heard many stories on the subject. No matter where we were, people pointed out that a tree, rock, lake, or other piece of nature looks like a phoenix, dragon, lovers representing the afterlife, longevity, health or the emperor himself.

Even today, superstition is prevalent. The Chinese belief in 'invisible forces' and 'signs' is strong. Feng Shui ("wind-water") is a phenomenon which can't - and shouldn't - be ignored. Officially, Feng Shui deals with the 'invisible forces' which connect everything in the universe. The philosophy is very much alive and used constantly in architecture. Houses with the wrong doorway or compass direction are sold for substantially lower prices; having the right house number (6,8,9) commands a premium. People use Feng Shui to decide where to hang mirrors and other objects with special meaning (like forks) in doorways. The beliefs are so strong that Disneyland Hong Kong shifted its original building plans by several degrees, just to make sure to incorporate the right Feng Shui.

Leendert, usually a skeptic, says he believes in the connectedness. He mentions that even as we sit there he sees signs that embody our trip. Slightly surprised and perhaps concerned, I frown and look at him. I ask for an example. "Simple" he days dryly, "look at the sign on the wall behind mom and Alicia". I look up, the others turn. Above their heads is a metal sign which reads: 'Life is like a Road Trip – enjoy each day and don't carry too much baggage'. We have a good laugh and agree few signs would better embody our trip. We discuss our next stop. Volunteering in Nepal. We are all in, but do agree that after Nepal we'll take it easy for a week.

We decide on Siem Reap, Cambodia. How innocent we were. Cambodia, a country to recover? More on that later.

It had become a sport to find inexpensive flights and accommodation. Searching for reasonable fares from Nepal to Cambodia was not helped by the slow internet. To our surprise, we found that depending on the piece of electronics we used, the same hotel via the same site has significantly different pricing. That is the ultimate in profiling and dynamic pricing. Optimizing between gadgets, we book three weeks out, not sure how the internet will work in Nepal. Our expectations are low, so we feel relieved once this is done.

Dinner, by popular demand is down the street – Peking Duck one last time. We feel like locals as the lady recognizes us from two days before and she is keen to give us another wonderful dining experience. We skip the rice and have additional dumplings instead. Jasmin tea flows in large quantities. Typically Chinese, I have a beer right next to it; more out of respect for the custom than anything else.

Chinese Departure

It is a hard ending to Beijing. Early in the morning a driver awaits us at the end of our little alley. We are all a bit sad knowing we are nibbling on our last steamed breakfast buns. En route to the airport we do a quick recap of the last weeks, reflecting on what we liked the most. The last eighteen days were a huge success – the food, the places we've seen, the people we met, the history and the culture lessons.

We check-in, and as our luggage disappears we are told that in spite of both flights been with China Eastern, we have to reclaim our bags in Kunming and re-check them for the connecting flight to Kathmandu. As always, when you are early, the security checks go quickly. Today is no exception and before you know it we are in a coffee shop and the kids chow down on waffles. We board and have a great flight, one of those where everything aligns. No long wait, straight to the plane, ample leg room. Even better, the rest of my row is empty, so Alicia joins me, spreading out – real luxury.

While the kids do their routine "airplane homework", I dive into a book on Nepal I had downloaded the night before. Feeling a bit unprepared, I frantically start reading. The book is good, making it no hardship to pass two-and-a-half hours getting acquainted with Nepal. Long live Amazon ratings. We land on time and navigate the Kunming airport. Albeit a rather new airport, it certainly is not the most intuitive one. I consider myself no novice as far as airports are concerned, but this one has got me beat. We do find our bags, but the check-in for the flight to Nepal is tricky. We finally figure it out: go to the domestic counters! Really, for Nepal? Perhaps a bit of wishful thinking of the Chinese authorities? At least we have plenty of time, so even with the additional security check on Heidi's backpack and four queuing opportunities: customs, passport, boarding card/passport check, security check, we end up at the gate well in time for our flight

The terminal is new, clean, and misses only one thing; passengers. The waiting area is the size worthy of a European capital city, but if anyone would bet me that there are more than 200 people present, I wouldn't hesitate to take the odds. We sit down and order noodle soup. Nothing wrong with the kids' appetites. I take a couple of bites from Alicia's dish, treasuring the experience, anticipating lentils over rice - twice a day - for the next two weeks. That's my expectation of monastery life in the mountains of Nepal.

The second flight is also pleasant. A bit of schoolwork and videos for the others while I steam through my first book on Nepal. The book describes the story of a world traveler who becomes 'hooked' after volunteering in an orphanage in Kathmandu. It is a great preparation for our trip and an enlightening read on the recent history of the country. I was totally oblivious to the civil war which raged there between 1996 and 2006, the impact on families and the creation of a group known as the 'lost children'. A painful story about volunteering gone wrong. More on this later. Suffice it to say that as I finish the book, I feel I have at least somewhat of a base by the time we hit the landing strip in Nepal.

Nepal - Serene Reincarnation

WE LAND IN KATHMANDU AND reset our watches. Nepal is one of those places where the time zone is off, strangely off - not by hours, but by fifteen minutes as well. Go figure. I guess with the remoteness of the country, it matters little.

The arrivals terminal has a 1970s feel. Dark brown wood surrounds the customs officer, who works quickly and makes pleasant conversation. He compliments Alicia on her beauty and efficiently sticks our pictures on the forms. We chat with some other tourists as we wait for our luggage. Time ticks by, but no backpacks appear. When our flight number no longer appears on the old monitors, I go on a walk-about, concerned that our packs stayed behind in Kunming. To my delight I find our colorful backpacks sitting next to a carousel down the hall. It turns out our luggage had arrived a long time ago, just not where we expected it.

We proceed to the taxi area, trying to find a driver willing to take us to the hotel. Our hotel package includes the transfer and they told us to simply tell the driver that the bill would be settled upon arrival. The drivers are uninterested with this arrangement; they realize we are not the big catch they are hoping for. My bad for telling them upfront! We finally find a driver willing to take us and we are on our way. We stare out the windows, relishing our first glimpses into life in Kathmandu.

On trips to new places I always pay double attention at the beginning. Not only for security reasons, but I also find that first impressions set the tone against which subsequent observations will be calibrated. The initial impression of Kathmandu with its 700,000 inhabitants is that I believe I landed in India. Colorfully dressed people walk along small dusty roads, tiny cars honking as they pass even smaller cars and rickshaws. I notice a fair number of maroon-dressed monks and a heavy dose of Indian-looking people; green and red silk dresses, red and orange bindis on foreheads. With India less than one hundred and forty kilometers away, I guess I could have anticipated that.

The driver drops us in the tourist quarter of Kathmandu. We are welcomed with Nepali tea - heavy on milk, sugar and spices. Heidi and I check out the neighborhood and I feel a little unsettled as we roam. It's as if the Starship Enterprise has just transported me to a different planet. After almost three weeks of China, it is strange to see non-yellow faces, a high proportion of westerners and western food. We have landed in rich backpacker heaven. Stores are full of Cadbury chocolate, granola bars, Oreos, and peanut butter. Restaurants and bars serve every type of international food. The food selection is excellent and you can have pretty much any drink you might fancy; including cocktails. Not quite the lentils and rice I expected! We enjoy the evening, happy not to suffer from altitude sickness, which I anticipated in Nepal. Turns out Kathmandu is at 1400 meters, so we all feel fine.

The (almost) two hour time difference means we are up early the next day. While the time zone change was recorded on our watches, our body clocks clearly didn't get the memo. Even Leendert and Alicia are ready to roll. After breakfast, we ready ourselves for our next stop, Pokhara, and try to find a working ATM as we are not sure if we'll have easy access to cash in the smaller town. I solicit two machines, but neither one rewards us with bills. Rats! Time is running out and we have a flight to catch! We quickly return to our hotel and order a taxi. We want to leave well in advance since the traffic can apparently be very unpredictable. I decide to worry about cash at the airport. We hail a taxi and a small Suzuki appears. I doubt we'll all fit in.

But miracles do occur. We fit - barely. Two backpacks are crammed in the hatch of the small vehicle, the rest of us pile inside with the remaining bags stacked on our knees. If only I had space to take my camera out, I would have taken a picture of Heidi and the kids. Three-wide, sitting in a tight, tight space. We pass through roads never meant for a car, the alleys are just tiny. At one passage, the car has less than a hand-width of space on either side. Not holding an absolutely straight line would mean scraping the wall. If I stood on this little street, I would be able to touch both walls at the same time. Now that's small!

We have a chatty driver, who gets us to the domestic terminal quickly. He tells us that 'local flights are like buses, if you show up fifteen minutes before the flight you are okay'. Nice one, we now have two hours to kill. The departure building is being renovated and is a total construction site. There is nothing to do. What's worse, check-in is done only one hour prior to flight departure. Since we have our backpacks with us, we are effectively stuck. We sit on the floor, Alicia makes bracelets, Leendert watches world champion finals cricket on an old overhead TV. He doesn't know the rules of the game, but it is movement on a screen, which will do. I go in search of cash.

A helpful local tells me there is an ATM just outside the terminal "go out, to the right and ask the military guard to let you in". A little puzzled, I do as instructed. I walk out of the airport building (or rather room) and see a metal gate. Behind it, two military guys hang out of the second-floor window, smoking a cigarette. After stating my business, the gate opens. Looking around the courtyard, I see no sign of the promised bank machine. Figuring this parking lot is unlikely to have an ATM, I am about to walk back out when the guard motions to the left at a hole under a slanted concrete staircase. I point, he nods and indicates I should duck and go under. Wow, the second miracle of the day. I see an ATM. It is positioned like a broken-down vending machine, cast away under a staircase. Next to it sits three car batteries. On top rests a black modem. Suddenly it dawns on me. Due to the construction, they had to find a safe and dry place for the cash dispenser; the Military base provides the safe environment, the staircase a dry one. Five minutes later I re-enter the ticketing area smiling, with cash in my wallet.

We eventually check in, make our way through security and watch the gate information. It is messy. The timing and gate number of our flight moves continuously (both backwards and forwards). Finally, forty-five minutes after formal take off time, we are taken to our 18-seater propplane. The flight is under half an hour, a short hop straight over a mountain range. We fly because it saves us from at least seven hours of agony on a bus - reportedly a hair-raising experience. The flight is smooth and as we touch down we find ourselves in a damp and misty land. Low hanging clouds can't seem to make up their mind if they want to hover fifty meters above ground or blanket the earth and transform into a complete fog.

Our contact from the Nepal Volunteer Council meets us at the Pokhara airport. He is friendly, albeit quiet. He chats little as the driver navigates us through town and down a country road. Every five hundred meters, the surroundings become more basic and the houses more spread out as can be expected in a impoverished, rural area. A side stream along the road serves many purposes, including sewer. We drive along a river valley and spot a large, well-maintained building on the mountain side. It turns out that this is the monastery we will call home for the next weeks.

Entering through a big gate and working our way into 'the office' our guide informs us that the headmaster is absent. Luckily a 'lama' (the nomenclature for any teacher of the Dharma) in orange-red attire shows up and helps us out. We inscribe our names in a big volunteer log book. Obviously we are not the only ones placed here. There is a bit of discussion between our contact person and the lama (in Nepalese I presume), and they agree on giving us 'the family room' (the only word I can discern).

As we are guided through the building we pass well maintained classrooms before arriving at the dormitory. Red and orange cloth hangs in front of the doors, hiding the entrances. I keep my fingers crossed as the curtain is pulled to the side and we open the door. It is amazing! We walk into a small sitting room, complete with carpet on the floor, a sofa and two comfy chairs. Wow, that was unexpected! On either side of the room is a bedroom with its own bathroom. The bathrooms have sit-down toilets and showers! After the hostel in Sai Gon, this feels like we landed in heaven. Never mind that electricity will be available on a sporadic basis. Never mind that the weather best predicts if there is warm water (sun-yes, clouds-no). Never mind that is has no heating. Secretly, I am glad we took showers in Kathmandu this morning; the forecast for Pokhara is rain and clouds for the next 4 days!

Our contact explains how things work. Tomorrow at nine we should present ourselves at the headmaster's office. He will tell us about the daily routines. Meanwhile we should know that there is no such thing as a class schedule; timings change depending on prayers. For instance, a plane-crash in Europe might mean an hour extra of praying - or two. "Oh, and, by the way, next week are exams, so timings will be totally different than normal anyway."

As for the volunteering assignment itself, he tells us it is best to address this question to the headmaster "perhaps there is garden work or assistance in the kitchen needed". I am slightly disappointed, since we'd been told we'd teach like on our previous stints, but I tell myself not to be picky. Who am I to decide how volunteering time is best spent? "Breakfast is at six-thirty right after morning prayer" he tells us. "Don't worry, you will be awake, as the drums and flute will sound an hour before that". Wrapping up he says that we are invited to join religious study, prayer and meditation classes every evening; and "oh, before I forget, expect dinner at six in the evening". With those words he leaves us to ourselves, and we settle in. As we wave him off, I see the clouds lift a bit. We catch our first glimpse of the snow-covered Annapurna mountains. Wow.

The rest of the afternoon passes quietly. I watch the young apprentice monks play outside; a bike, a stick, a single roller skate. An older lama walks by with small headphones and a mobile in his hand; it's a strange image - the monk, leaving all possessions behind, wearing simple robes, but carrying an iphone.

At six sharp we present ourselves at the kitchen. No activity. Only a large pan covering two gas burners silently awaits action. We come across a person and inquire about dinner. "Normally around seven" is the response "but it depends". It feels like 'island time', so we retire to our room for another sixty minutes. Meanwhile I adjust my expectations of this volunteer project. If little support is actually needed, I will use the time for quiet and slow reflection and perhaps subject myself to some Buddhist teachings.

At seven we return to the kitchen, and while on our way, a bell sounds. Little red and orange robes appear from everywhere. Short-haired monks pop from behind the curtains and race to the mess hall. As we enter, an elderly lama points us towards the kitchen. As soon as we walk in, the kitchen staff indicates we should walk through. We exit the backside of the kitchen and see other westerners collecting around a big pot in a covered area. People sit on low benches and eat their dinners. It turns out it is a 'full house' at the monastery tonight. Besides other volunteers there are paying guests in the monastery as well. People traveling through use the monastery guest house, an additional source of revenue. We quickly connect and chat with several of the volunteers. The food is good. Basic noodle soup with vegetables. The temperature has gone down and it is still damp, so the warm food tastes twice as good. By eight we are back in the room, we read, relax and turn in for a good night's sleep.

Life in the Monastery

At precisely five-thirty a slow drumbeat wakes us. Over the next minute the beating slowly increases in pace up to a fast paced bong-bong-bong. It is the call to prayer for the monks and serves as the wake-up call to us tourists, no snooze included. We get ready for the seven o'clock breakfast, but notice we have neither electricity nor water. The former goes off while we're getting dressed, the latter had disappeared during the night. I can adequately live without hot water, but to be totally without H2O is more challenging. We use wet-wipes which appear magically out of Heidi's backpack and freshen up before going to breakfast.

Breakfast is served in the same spot we ate dinner last night. We sit on the benches around low tables in the near dark (no electricity here either) and help ourselves to circular breads resembling naan. We spread spicy tomato salsa on the bread and drink a milky cup of Nepali tea with it. I wonder if the Nutella and peanut butter which sits in the center of the low table are for communal use or if one of the guest brought it for him/herself and forgot to put it away. As for peanut butter, some brand should consider creating a global commercial: "Peanut Butter: The Breakfast for Volunteering Champions". Clearly there is a distinct segment.

As promised, we present ourselves in the principal's office at nine. No one is to be found. A monk receiving tutoring nearby tells us the headmaster will be in at ten. We return at the indicated time, but again, no one is there. I linger a bit, go for a stroll and try a while later. Someone is in the office, but not the principal. "He went to town but should be back in thirty minutes" I am told. All this travel and I still struggle to slow down. I notice it still irritates me that appointments are not 'fixed'.

Meanwhile, the rain arrived. While the room has no water, rain and thunder fill the air. I retry the headmaster one last time and find him in his office. He asks my expectation for the volunteering and I tell him we were hoping to teach. "Give me five minutes and I will check for you." In parallel I collect the family. A few moments later, reassembled in his room, we talk a bit about the monastery and the schooling. There are about one hundred students, 80 in grade school, the rest in 'college grade'. We learn that the Buddhist school is actually Tibetan. Almost all students come from the three Tibetan refugee camps in the area. The schoolmaster himself was born in Nepal, his parents escaping Tibet in 1959 when the Chinese took over. He has no Tibetan passport, nor Nepali passport but considers himself one of the lucky ones because he had an "RC". Of the 30,000 refugees, a mere 4000 were issued a Refugee Card (RC) in 1995. This card is renewed annually, with much paperwork, and serves as a travel document giving him mobility.

After looking at the schedules, he offers us three morning classes; two physical education classes, one English class. The English is in session and he proposes to walk us over so we can get acquainted. There are about twelve students in the class, no teacher, and no apparent activity. We get introduced, and the schoolmaster wishes us "good luck", turns around, and walks out. Boy, doesn't this feel familiar? It's just like the Galapagos and Sai Gon! The concept of providing a "landing strip" is clearly not part of the volunteering mechanics. We spend the next half hour trying to establish what course material the young monks have to cover for next week's exam. Answer: all 124 pages of the book. Okay, that's a challenge. How to cram an all-pages review in, over the next four days? We'll have to try and answer that question by tomorrow morning.

At exactly one o'clock the school bell sounds and we are all off to lunch. It's delicious. Rice, lentil soup and a veggie. There are no afternoon classes and the weather remains rainy, so we spend the rest of the afternoon in our room. We're still without running water, so I improvise and use a bucket found in one of the bathrooms to capture rainwater. Given the rainfall, plenty of water flows from the rooftops onto the courtyard so it's an easy task to fill the toilet tanks. I refill the bucket one more time as backup. At least this way we can do the necessary when necessary, without smelling up the place. We also head out and join the group for afternoon tea. Since there is no heating in the room, the warm milky tea tastes good, and we cradle the mugs in our hands as we sip the spicy drink. Huddling close together we enjoy the fried pita-shaped bread served alongside.

We make conversation with other volunteers whose hair length correlates to the time they've spent on the road. The monks must think that American and European men almost all have long hair. A mother and daughter both have braids long enough to sit on. Most of the volunteering visitors are 'taking a year off'. Some [like Frank] are here to find some 'inner peace' before figuring out what to do in life. He spends time meditating before going back to Europe. Thus far, he has figured out that he does not want to work very hard. Given the length of his hair, it's taken him some time to draw this conclusion. The image of a surfer comes to mind; dude, like, no way man, work nine-to-five, that's crazy!

Monkeys pass by and roam in the morning and evening, daringly popping into the kitchen to steal food scraps meant for the cow. Long-term volunteers remind us to close and lock all doors and windows when not in the room. Reportedly, these four-handed thieves are known to take a liking to clothes, shiny things and anything which you might value and leave in your room unattended. We also get details on when and where the Buddhist evening teachings take place.

A few hours later I drag the entire family along for Buddhist class. They are reluctant, but at the appointed time we sit down on the upper floor of the temple, shoes off, cross-legged on cushions. We stare through a glass wall at the top part of a two-story tall Buddha. We are in a semi-circle with seven other pupils when suddenly chanting sounds rise up from the floor below. Clearly that is where the real monks are starting their prayers and lessons. I notice Frank has already taken the full lotus position. A monk - in typical dark red robe attire - appears and takes his place in front of us, cross legged, on a slightly elevated wooden box with pillow.

He starts rocking side to side, his head doing a Steve Wonder-move while chanting indistinguishable words which I assume to be Tibetan. We endure about five minutes of this mumbling chant. Next the monk takes a little booklet to guide his teachings; a book we can buy for a buck-and-a-half at the small on-site drinks/candy counter in the courtyard. This evening he focuses on the first paragraphs of the text. He starts by reading out loud in Sanskrit, something which blends well with the sounds of the singing from down below and the smell of incense which lingers in the room. He subsequently translates the text to English, undeniably struggling between a verbatim version and one that makes sense. A discussion of the subject matter follows. During this open dialogue a question is posed on the age of the participants. Heidi and I learn we are at least twice the age of any of the other students. In fact, all other participating members are much closer in age to Alicia and Leendert than to us. We feel like dinosaurs.

The monk touches on several subjects but the key teaching today is around the importance of making and breaking promises. The headline is to make many, many promises. In fact, make as many as you can, he says. You commit and use the process of reflection to get closer and closer to the moment of breaking the promise. Ultimately, you catch yourself just before breaking the promise. Yes, read that again. It is profound. He also covers the importance of not being attached to material things, the importance of moral code and mental discipline. This segment of the teaching I like. He points out the irrelevance of religion to these fundamental beliefs, which resonates with me. He also points out that Buddhism is a philosophy, not a religion - even more resonance. But then he loses me. He shifts the discussion to the afterlife and reincarnation. He attempts to prove the existence of reincarnation. Nice try, not even a thread of traction. Reflecting afterwards with the kids I realize that if one does away with the caste system, the monks, guru's and reincarnation, I think I could become Buddhist. Too bad those elements are a rather fundamental part of the philosophy. The session ends with Q&A, and some of the previously demonstrated Stevie Wonder singing. Completing this lofty experience we get back to our room nicely fatigued and ready for bed. Reveille is set for 5:30am.

The first day of regular Monastery life

Boing-Boing-Boing, rise and shine; time to get up! Heidi, the early riser in the family had already moved to the living room area. I hop out of bed, having enjoyed only the last half hour of laying diagonally in bed in a slumber. The beds are constructed for short Nepali visitors, and while I am short for Dutch standards, my heels touch the base-board of the bed while my head banged against the wooden cubbyholes of the headboard throughout the night. Without baseboard it would have been okay, my feet would have simply stuck out, but with the boards on either side, I was boxed in - not conducive to a good night's sleep.

I get dressed, glance out the window and join Heidi. The Nepali morning is glorious, and we go for a stroll. Outside we stare for the first time at the Annapurna mountain range. The cloud cover disappeared overnight. Against a blue sky, snow covered peaks contrast perfectly like on a postcard panorama. The air is crisp, but not necessarily cold. It helps that there is practically no wind. We observe the reflection of the sun on the snow caps and I think of Chamonix back home. At seven, the 'clang' for breakfast vibrates the air. We take a few quick photos of the stunning view and return to our room to collect the kids. As we make our way down for breakfast we get an 'oh, wow' from Leendert and Alicia as they observe the stunning mountain view.

Downstairs we look into the two breakfast pans. The usual bread in one, a lovely bean soup in the other. This simple meal, combined with the sweet warm milky tea is an excellent way to start the day. After a third cup of tea, Heidi World High goes into session. I finish my book on Nepal while the kids work though math and English. Teacher mom continues to impress me with her dedication and continuous support to help the kids; the kids meanwhile impress me with their enthusiasm and willingness to do the schoolwork.

At ten we have to teach our first class: health. This grade 1 class is taught from a book. We learn that there has not been a teacher for an extended period, and try to take a quick measure of (1) the material to cover (2) how much of the content has been learned, and (3) the command of the English language. The good news is that the level of English is high. The classes are primarily based on level of study, not age, so while there is a large age range, the students are academically similar. Flipping quickly through the school book gives a fair impression of what content the students need to grasp. It is not rocket science. On the contrary; the elements they need to master are the basics on personal hygiene, health and safety. We use the book and cover washing hands, brushing teeth, washing clothes, drinking purified (or boiled water), healthy eating, no smoking, no playing on the road, and crossing roads using painted cross-walks. I particularly love that last one, as I have not yet seen a zebra crossing in this country.

Time flies, and before we know it we are off to the next, 3rd grade, class. Generally, these kids are older and perhaps because of it they seem clearly less interested or, for that matter, devoted. The book they have is fifty percent the same as first grade, which probably explains their low interest. Upon finer inspection the book does seem to have some more depth. We find that especially when we focus on the safety and health part it is easy to engage with the young monks. We see it as a compliment when fifteen minutes into class even the two older kids in the back of the classroom put their board-game away and start to participate. An hour later the 'clang-clang-clang' rounds up the lesson and we are off to English class, grade-2.

This is the same class we were introduced to yesterday, so we had established we could work with them on vowels and adjectives. The latter proves to be tricky for them, some of them just guessing the answers to the questions we pose. In fact, the adjectives fill the full hour. With the three classes done, our teaching for the day finishes. Overall, we feel good about the classes. What helps is that these kids are clearly used to volunteer teachers and there is somewhat of a curriculum to follow. Having finished the school day, we walk down the hill from the monastery. Reportedly, a local bar/restaurant down the road has internet. We amble along the road, get honked at (the local way of offering rides), and find the targeted restaurant. We order drinks and get the WIFI code. Two disappointments: first my beer is ridiculously expensive, second the internet is excruciatingly slow. Even up and downloading simple e-mails is a challenge. Actually, the beer is only 'relatively' expensive. Paying six times more for a coke than a local beer seems exorbitant, especially knowing that in most of Asia, beer is normally the price of water. Then I ask myself: what I am complaining about? A half liter of beer for $2.50 is not really a killer expense, is it?

Back in the monastery, our apartment is still devoid of water. I walk up to Lobsing-la, the head master. Lobsing is his name, the 'la' part is the respectful way of addressing someone in Nepal. On hearing about our drought issues he walks me down to the affectionately called 'water monk'. The monk promises to take care of our issue. For a moment I reflect back on yesterday's evening session around making promises. However, I am soon sidetracked as Lobsing-la uses the opportunity of my presence. "Since you asked if you could help out…, [me nodding]… the windows of the lunchroom need cleaning" he states. "If we wouldn't mind?". Really? A moment for reflection. We don't clean our own dishes after meals for ladies come in to do that, but Lobsing-la would want us volunteers to clean the windows? Really? A bit flustered I accept the bag with rags and Mr Proper. I know I can have the kids help out, and reflect that "it is probably good for me" in The Karate Kid kind of way.

I don't get the slightest push back from the kids when I suggest they help me clean the windows. As soon as we finish our tea break, we attack the windows with water and soap - me on the outside, the kids on the inside. They stand on the inside benches so they can reach the top, me on my tiptoes on the other side. Double-sided synchronized window cleaning is always fun. Waving at one another separated only by a thin piece of glass, trying to figure out which side of the pane has the last streak, invariably creates smiles. There are a lot of windows to clean, so after forty-five minutes I suggest we do part two of the window cleaning later in the week. No push back there either. When we arrive in our room we learn from Heidi that the water monk has been successful. Oh joy, running water. We can flush toilets! Even better, we can take showers! Okay, they will be Spartan military showers since there has been no sun, but we are so happy to have water at all that we can almost ignore the temperature.

It seems the gods are with us that afternoon. Even the electricity comes on. We charge the electronics and attempt our luck at the Internet connection. That turned out to be one step too far. A short visit to the "IT-monk" informs us there is no wifi in our building, only in the guest house across the courtyard. Yuck! Nevertheless, we get two of our machines 'authorized' and walk to the other side of the monastery to test the speed. Not great, but it works. Score!

Dinner that evening consists of the usual noodle soup. As we enter the communal corner we hear a big bang, and the electricity goes off again. As it is dinner time and pitch black, a backup generator fires up about one minute later. Complements of the "generator monk". We learn the generator is only used at crucial moments, dinner being one of them. After our meal I walk to the little shop in the courtyard. It's open one hour a day and sells drinks, candy and the Buddhist book called 'Parting from the Four Attachments'. I acquire the booklet so I can read along in the evening class and pick up my reading glasses in the room. The others stays behind. One Buddhist session was apparently enough for them and with smiles on their faces my kids tell me "we still have lots of homework to do dad, but you go ahead and tell us if we missed anything".

For a moment I fear the evening session will be a 1-on-1, but then Nina, an eighteen year old volunteer shows up as well. The monk does his 'rocking'-singing-mumbling kick-off thing, and we talk for over an hour. Tonight he does not use the book since it is just Nina and myself. In ninety minutes he puts on an impressive monologue, and I get to practice staying zen. He covers death, reincarnation and - to really draw me out - uses population growth as proof that human kind is improving. The underlying assumption is that humans are at a higher level than animals (which one could argue about), but following that logic, the fact that we have a population boom, proves more 'beings' are returning at a higher level. I bite my tongue at first, then take the Buddhist approach, detach and enjoy the moment. I even succeed at smiling as he explains there are people out there called CEO's and Directors. He imparts on us that these people work all the time and that they only think of money. He also reveals that all these individuals are unfulfilled and unhappy. It only missed the "all the time" at the end.

The last part of the evening's teaching concerns death. Our monk shares that we should spend more time thinking about death; "especially on our birthdays". I agree with the former. Death has the ability to calibrate everything, to ground us and make us realize that truly everything is relative. However, the second part puzzles me - why birthdays? He explains: "Buddhists celebrate death on birthdays because with each birthday-celebration we are getting closer to death". I'm not sure I share his excitement on how profound this thought is. If you ask me, Christmas, Eid, Thanksgiving, mid-summer-night, any day really, is closer to the inevitable. To me, it seems much more appealing to spend birthdays as carefree celebrations with food, drink and laughter than contemplating the non-sense of life overall.

As we end the session I can't help but think it is a bit perverse and scary to have this thirty two year old monk 'teach' the impressionable youth on the pillow next to me on 'life'. A youth who came all the way from Europe, now taking her inspiration from an individual who has never been out of Nepal, never worked, nor carried the responsibility of a child, or has had to worry about where his next meal came from (for monks meals are provided through alms by the community). Amazing.

1st of April

What a day. This morning we all had the opportunity to meet with a great master of Buddhism, a direct member of His Holiness Dalai Lama's entourage. His presentation was inspiring. Actually, it was more than that. The simplicity by which he explained the purpose of life, the logic of the wheel of life - and how we can live a life of full detachment and joy - was not only well timed for us, but also for the kids. We got the chance to meet 4:1 with HH Sakayamaya and all felt excited. As a result, and by joint decision, we decided to extend our time in the monastery with 4 weeks and to enroll in Buddhist meditation class. Leendert is especially very keen on doing this. I have seldom seen him so enthralled to do something. What is more, the attentive reader will have noticed the date of today. Today is April fools. Just in case you had not caught on yet.

Reality is that we had our usual gong wake-up, pita bread and soup for breakfast followed by HWH. Our health and physical education class started at ten o'clock, and since the robed little fellows knew most of the material, we split the class in three parts. First, we reviewed the basics needed for next week's exam, then we let them read in smaller groups, and finally we did some physical activity. Leendert and Alicia took the lead on the last part, playing a fun game. The game works, albeit differently than the kids had planned it. It teaches our young ones how tricky it is to give good instructions.

The next class was somewhat of a copy-paste, but with older students. I start by asking them what's the most important muscle of the body, clearly hinting at the heart. Instead we get a unified answer shouted at us: "the brain". I guess that was to be expected from Buddhist monks-to-be - and they might be right! We propose the heart as second most important muscle, not wanting to start a debate on "who's first, what's second". We quickly insert a section in the lesson plan on heart rate and exercise. It is fun to ask them about heart rates. They have no notion of beats per minute or blood circulation. We have them take their resting pulse rate, make them exercise with some burpees, and retake the measurement. When asking them why their heart rate has gone up, they look puzzled. We teach them about circulation and blood as an oxygen carrier to the muscles and brain. They really seem to enjoy the improvised presentation.

After our English class we lunch on the usual rice-soup-veggie combo and decide to skip the planned window cleaning. Instead we go into town to look at options for the weekend and to find an internet connection. With exam week next week, Heidi and I are rather disappointed with the volunteering. Snobs that we are, we decided we are not getting our money's worth if we can't teach and work degrades to window-washing. Remember, we pay dearly for being allowed to volunteer. We decide to consider 'sunk cost sunk' and invest in a trek. We head to the "Lakeside" which is, as the name suggests, bordering on a mountain lake. The area is full of shops, offering the full range of branded adventure-travel gear to serve everyone from the casual hiker to the professional climber. We bargain with some trip organizers to get a feel for options and pricing. As often in tourist towns, they all offer the best deals, and, after discount, quote exactly the same price for the same service. Having done our research, we locate a cafe with wifi. The restaurant also offers pizzas, so we're in heaven. The kids enjoy food while the parents do bits and bytes on their computers. Oh it feels so good to be connected again! The inflow and outflow of data is therapeutic. We upload to our travel website, download TV shows. The influx of binary code into my computer makes me sigh with relief. I feel like a Tour de France rider in the third week after a secretive blood transfusion, updated, upgraded and ready to go again. The browsing, the deleting and filing of the e-mail box is so rewarding!

For the return to our sacred dwelling I negotiate a good deal with a taxi driver. He elegantly circumnavigates both the moving traffic and stationary objects. We pass cows lying in the middle of the road, which Alicia counts with great delight. Amazed, we observe these animals happily laying around, quiet and peaceful as the Buddha himself, despite the madness of traffic around them.

In the evening I go for my usual punishment. I am in Nepal, in a monastery, so by golly I will participate in the Buddhist teaching and explanation sessions. Luckily there are a few more volunteers present compared to the previous night. Following the monk's ritual 'rocking' chant, we learn about learning and meditation. The highlights are that we all have been animals in previous lives, we just don't remember and that animals have a soul while plants don't. For clarity, the latter two facts are proven by the fact that several Buddhist guru's (not just one, but numerous) can mind read. They have unequivocally proven mind reading is possible with animals but not plants. Consequently, animals have souls, plants don't. Solid argument, case closed! As you can imagine I find very little knowledge nuggets in this particular evening's teaching. In fact, the most entertaining moment is generated by a fellow participant, one who is deep in the lotus position and clearly in the 'zone'. He shares that he agrees with the monk on the reincarnation cycle. He sometimes sees proof in his cat, and [I quote] "it clearly tries to climb out of being a cat in order to deserve to become human upon death". At this point I get tears in my eyes and I wonder if the cat might be the higher life form compared to the speaker. Secretly I am happy the kids did not come along to get exposed to these particular teachings.

A week of helping and other activities

It never ceases to amaze me how quickly things become 'normal'. Given the dynamic state of our lives this seems to hold true even more. In only the few days of our monastery residence, the vibrating sound of the accelerating drum has become not only expected at the ungodly early hour, it is almost pleasing to my ears. Figuring you can't be in a Tibetan monastery on a mountain in Nepal and not attempt to understand the orange/maroon lifestyle, I have now started reading books on Buddhism.

By the second round of the drum roll, I put my book to the side, get out of bed, dressed, and ready to pull the kids out of dream land. The clang-clang-clang breakfast call supports us and indicates to the young ones it is time to move if they want to see breakfast. We make it in time and find pita bread with a jar of jelly in the usual space. Wow, what happened to the lentil soup? Where is the peanut butter? Major routine break here!

While we prepare for class we motivate Leendert and Alicia to prepare another game for the Physical Education class. The last time was a bit messy, so we ask them think through the session. We help them discover how best to explain to a group what to do and how to present. Reluctantly, they accept the challenge to practice.

The classes go well. Heidi and I tag-team between reading, revisions, and doing group crosswords on the whiteboard. About whiteboards: who on earth invented this concept? My experience is that the number of times chalk failed to write on a classic chalkboard is inversely related to the number of pens one needs to write on a whiteboard. Dry markers have a ridiculously short lifecycle. In fact, I suspect that up to 50% of the time they fool you by only working for the first few letters, then fading quickly. I'm convinced they work perfectly for three to five letters, only to make sure you do not toss them out immediately. They fool you in making you think they will magically recharge themselves once you have put the cap back on placing them point down, in a jar. Of course they don't find a second life. It just means that you end up with a cup full of non-performing markers. That's not all. White boards also have a shiny glare. This to make sure that the unlucky ones who sit in any window- or light-reflecting spot can't read half the text that's written. Oh, but I'm not done yet! Whiteboards seem to have the uncanny ability to attract permanent markers. Even if you test it, it leads to embarrassing moments. Ever done this? You put a small dash on the whiteboard and try to quickly wipe it with your finger, hoping the colored dust particles stick to your extremity. They don't. So quickly you lick your finger hoping the permanent marker is semi-permanent. Of course it isn't, and you can only blush while a smear on the whiteboard and a stained finger remains. You hope someone has extra strength window cleaner close by to take care of the mark you made.

Perhaps I am crazy, but wasn't the old blackboard (now often green or blue) much better? Did you ever have a failing piece of chalk? Think about it, can you give me any other object that works on four sides after it breaks? Wiping the classic blackboard? Not an issue. A sponge and water. And if you ask me, few things in life are as pristine as a blackboard at the end of a school day, right after it has been washed with H2O, ready to go for the next day. Whiteboards on the other hand always have smudges, even after they are wiped. Did the switch really happen because of dust complaints? I am convinced we have lost the plot on this one. I don't know many people with chalk allergies, but I can name many a frustrated a business manager almost going of the deep end because of 'dead' dry-markers. Their level of frustration measured by the speed at which they throw the pen in the plastic trash-can in the corner of the room; lower levels of frustration means pens end up in a jar. Okay, thank you, my tirade on white boards is over, I am better now, thanks. Perhaps I should reflect on whiteboards and pens in my next meditation class and practice detachment.

Later that afternoon, enjoying our afternoon tea, we see a monk pass with a football. Leendert and I go in pursuit and end up leaving the monastery grounds through the big gate. Right next to the temple boundary is a football (soccer) field. We are invited to join the game. Over 45 monks, one other volunteer, and the two of us on a dusty sandy pitch.

As it turns out, football with the monks is challenging on several fronts. First of all, they are all bald and all wear the same robes; dark red and orange. Beats me how you can see who's on your team (or not). Second, with this number of people on the pitch, the best you can hope for when the ball eventually does come your way, is that you rid yourself of it as quick as the side of a pin-ball machine - immediately. Hold on to the ball for more than ½ a second and six monks descend upon you. Third, given that they wear long robes, if three monks stand around you, legs apart, they have effectively zoned off any area you can play the ball to without it being caught in their nets. A derivative of the robe-effect is that trying to follow the ball itself is next to impossible. Pieces of cloth always hang between you and the ball, obstructing any clear views. Last, there is a health-risk playing with these monks. Their footwear is either slippers or Croc-like, loose fitting shoes. I estimate the odds are one in five that the kicker loses his shoe as he kicks, meaning that when you see an object coming at you from behind one of the cloths, the first thing you need to discern is if you are about to head a ball or some plastic clog. Oh, and before I forget – these guys have no fear. They clearly believe some divine karma protects them, so when they come at you, don't stand in their way!

After the game we return to the room for a shower. Wow, what a pleasant surprise, there is warm water! It is drip-drip-drip warm water, but combined with the drop-drop-drop of cold water, and it makes a reasonable dribble (or is it drobble?). Either way, it is nice to wash off and enjoy the shower.

Teaching goes well over the next days. After the morning boing-boing-boing and clang-clang-clangs, waking up, drinking milky tea and eating pita bread we teach our classes. We are used to the students by now, and they to us. In the afternoon, Heidi tutors one of the student-monks. The fellow is super nice, chatty, but unfortunately is not endowed with the sharpest of minds. The good news is that he knows it and seeks help. In a small pagoda surrounded by Tibetan prayer flags I sit next to them as Heidi runs over the imperfect future tense (or the semi-perfect past future tense – or something else way beyond my comprehension). As the monk learns, monkeys pass within arms-reach. Undisturbed by these long armed animals walking, climbing and swinging, the tutoring continues. I am impressed with both the monk's concentration and Heidi's patience I notice the weather is changing. Funny phenomenon, the weather in Nepal. Many days seem identical. Clear sky and sunshine in the early morning provides incredible views of the snow-topped roof of the world. By mid-morning clouds, nestle around the peaks and by noon the cumulus have taken control of the skies. Drops of rain come down around tea-time for about thirty minutes, after which the clouds retreat and dissolve. Before dinner, rays of sunshine cast long shadows on the hilly terrain. When I return from my evening lectures the sunlight bounces via the moon onto the snow-capped mountains. The pale light reflects on the silhouetted peaks against the black background of the immense universe. This scene makes me feel like a small insignificant speck of reincarnation.

While in Nepal, I do the usual reading on and about the country. As remarked before, we have been introduced and sensitized to the dark side of Voluntourism. Reading the book *Little Princes: one man's promise to bring home the lost children of Nepal* triggers it, and subsequent reading, research and discussions confirm details of some of the most perverse situations. The vast majority of Nepali orphanages are filled with kids who aren't orphans. They are children from the mountain regions (or very small villages) who are poached from their parents by traders promising a better life for the kids. Under the pretense of providing education and housing, the parents allow them to be taken. For this pleasure, they pay the traders what little they have (e.g., their goat). The kids are taken to the city and kept in "orphanages". These places make the living conditions of Charles Dickens' Oliver Twist look like The Ritz. Tourists are subsequently bussed in and shown the "atrocious conditions" these kids have to endure. Donations flow. None of the funds make it to the kids or the parents. For the model to work, the kids must be kept in deprived surroundings. One particularly bad case stands out. A group of visiting donors were shown how their funds were used for a new school and improved living quarters. It was constructed right next to the 'dump' where the orphans currently lived. Clearly there was hope for the kids for a better life. It was not to be. Once the building was finished, the trader turned the new construction into a hotel. He moved the orphanage down the street, since he don't want them next to the hotel. The new place was a dump of course, and the process restarted. Headline? Beware and research before giving to a good cause!

During the weekends, the gongs and bells continue to ring, there is no escape, no sleeping in. We take the opportunity to observe a morning prayer session. Just after six o'clock we are outside the temple, enjoining the view of the mountains. While normally the temple is open for those interested to observe, today a guarding monk tells us that we have to wait for a moment as the monks will perform a 'Special Puja' for a family in need. A 'puja' is done on daily basis and is an expression of honor, worship and devotion. We learn that today's puja is much more than the routine bowing. As we stand in the crisp morning air, novice monks exit the temple, leaving the older monks behind. The robed children hang around at the doorway, having been ousted from the ceremony inside. Five minutes later they –and us foreigners- are allowed back into the temple.

The center room is ornate only marred by 'please no pictures' signs. The older monks sit on the inside aisle, the young ones in the row behind. Large pieces of red and yellow felt are placed in front of each monk. Less than five minutes later the monks put on special robes, take the piece of felt and stand up. The felt turns out to be a high hat. From the side it looks a bit like a large tear drop, not unlike the shape the hat a smurf would wear, but flat on the sides. With these on – chanting - the monks leave the temple and move in procession for a tour around the campus.

Once they complete the loop they scatter, some bring part of their special robes to their rooms, the rest leisurely reentering the temple. It was a bit anticlimactic as we wanted to see the temple rituals, but we did get to see a unique procession with the special robes. The special 'puja' also means the monks will – exceptionally - eat breakfast in the temple. We conclude that rather than sitting in a temple watching monks eat breakfast, our time is better spent eating ourselves. We collect the kids and meander to the kitchen area to indulge in lentil soup and breads.

No classes are held on the weekend, so we set out to explore the neighborhood. No map, no clear directions, only the memory of what one of the other volunteers told us a few days before: "Cross the road, over the bridge with the Tibetan prayer flags, start climbing and you get to a stunning view". How hard can it be? We cross the metal grid cable bridge which is extensively decorated with the typical square weathered blue, white, red, green and yellow prayer flags. Note the order, it is not random. They represent the five elements: blue symbolizes the sky and space, white symbolizes the air and wind, red represents fire, green is water, and yellow the earth. The flags are used to promote core values like peace, compassion, strength and wisdom. In the old days the Sutras (prayers) were written on the cloth banners so they could travel along and be dispersed in the region. It is a misconception that the texts are directed at the gods. In fact, the devout believe the mantras will be taken by the wind and spread everywhere, thus bringing good will and compassion to everyone.

We pass a small town and see women stooped over, carrying a heavy load in bags on their backs. The bags are held in place by a rope which runs over their shoulders and loops across their forehead – hence the leaning. An old retired lady uses this system to carry five cinder-block bricks up the concrete steps of a house under construction. As her crooked old legs mount the stairs of the residence I see a man - maybe her son - on the second floor. He has one hand in his pocket, a mobile in the other, and seems to be giving directions to an older man - perhaps his father - the brick-layer. The scene provides light entertainment at first, but soon ignites a discussion on what 'helping out' might mean.

We aren't sure which path leads to the promised viewpoint, so we guess a few times. The path goes from gravel to sand, from wide to "is this the path or a deer track?". Ultimately we climb a steep section which mountain goats might have found challenging. I'm not sure of the distance still to go, so I ration water. I am cautious since the other volunteers told me it took them 2½ hours to reach the top. The kids are fine, but Heidi battles a head cold which makes it rough going. After an hour and a half, we sit down on the graphite-colored lookout enjoying the 360 degree view of the peaks around us. The views are indeed stunning. We eat a piece of bread topped with a piece of KitKat in celebration for getting to the top so quickly. I lighten up on the water restrictions. For good measure I even let the kids dive into the Coke I hauled up the steep slopes. We take a few pictures and politely brush off four "where you from mister"-youths trying to offer us guidance to the 'bat cave' or the 'nice new hotel' on the mountain. We do share our cookies with them, and in return they become our selfie-stick, ensuring we get nice pictures. The way down is easy and fast, not only for the most obvious reason, but also because we take the formal path we should have been on in the first place, rather than the 'self discovery' bush trail we took on the way up.

Back in the village we see some taxis, the usual small Maruti Suzukis. We grab one after negotiating, pretending not to be in-and-out tourists. For the equivalent of five euros we'll cruise into Pokhara. We explore the town and go for a second session of visiting agencies offering rafting trips and treks. We learn about walking poles, guides, porters, and the need for some better cold-weather gear if we intend to going up into the mountains. We shop for the essentials and book a rafting trip for the next day. Unfortunately, the minimum age for the big rapids is sixteen, so we book the 'easy' ride. I hope it is not too lame, there hasn't been much rain lately.

Later that afternoon we play another game of football; volunteers against the monks. The students are ready; fluorescent soccer shoes (with cleats), soccer jerseys and shin protectors. The opposing team is on old trainers with no special gear. For the first forty-five minutes there are only the three volunteers and five kitted out monks, so we play 'monk(ey)-in-the-middle'. The light drizzle turns to pouring rain, but nobody seems to mind. Soon, my only pair of shoes is drenched. The rain stops and more monks appear, fully decked out. One has a dress-hat he doesn't intend to remove. It's clear that free time for the students means football. Some of them are extremely skilled. Teams are formed, and the number imbalance means some monks join the volunteer team.

We play two games, each well over an hour. My body is spent, I am bruised and bleeding due to close encounters with some of the fearless monks. I could really do with a hot shower. Unfortunately, the lack of sunshine means I have to make do with a cold one. It takes some scrubbing, but I get the mud and grit out of most crevices. The warm afternoon tea tastes extra good. Pure joy in a cup.

The next day, the first reaction from the kids on our pre-breakfast wakeup call is lukewarm at best. However, self-motivated movement is detected soon after we remind them that today is 'rafting day'. In no time they are up, dressed and ready to inhale breakfast. Over spicy potatoes with pita I chat with the other volunteers. We take inventory of the assorted injuries resulting from yesterday's football match. I have a bruise giving me an additional kneecap, a lightly twisted ankle and a sore elbow. It is clear who played yesterday. Each of us is moves less fluidly than usual, after being tenderized by the game.

The rafting organizers are supposed to pick us up at nine-thirty and we arrive at the bottom of our hill, our rendezvous point, on time. It's not much before ten when we still stand there and my phone rings. The connection is horrific and my phone emits incomprehensible English

In Pursuit of Chocolate

through static and cracking. I default to a beacon signal, repeating name and location over and over again until the phone connection is lost: "Mr. Alexander, bottom of the hill at the monastery, Mr. Alexander bottom of the hill..."

It must have worked, because a few minutes later a Tata four-wheel drive maneuvers to our side of the road. The driver looks at the receipt I've taken out of my wallet, nods approval and we jump into the Tata, settling in back on makeshift benches. Two other passengers move closer together so we can all squeeze in.

A kilometer down the road the car makes another stop. We crunch together even more as a new passenger enters. We drive only a few kilometers up the road. It is closer than I assumed, which increases my apprehension regarding the lameness of the descent we are about to take. A safety briefing follows, which I assume is over the top. I guess for good form it needs to be done. We learn how to rescue someone overboard, how to get back into the boat, how to hand a paddle to someone in need, and how to grab the rope if needed. We are offered wet suits, which Alicia and I decline. An extra kayak joins for security as we take to the water; six people in a raft plus the guide. And we are off. The idea of staying more or less dry is just a dream. For a moment I wonder if a wetsuit might have been smart. The rapids are perfect; some parts are gentle, but some are really challenging. We get stuck several times at bigger drops and are deluged by cold mountain water. I am glad we aren't on the big rapids. If these are the lame ones, I don't want to know what 'extreme' looks like.

We see one of the other rafts lose a passenger, and the earlier practiced safety technique is put to good use. Apparently the training instructions were more than just form. As we are the downstream raft, we pick up the loose paddle and the two flip-flops of the man-overboard which rapidly floated our way. The total ride takes about one hour, which is perfect. As luck has it, the end-point of the rafting experience is less than a kilometer from the Monastery, so we decide to bid the crew farewell and walk back. I expect we can make it back just in time for lunch. As we walk in we notice the lunch pans are still on the table. We serve ourselves rice, veggies and scrape the bottom bits of lentil soup out of the pan. After the effort on the river it tastes twice as good.

When we return later for afternoon tea, we are in for a shock. All the monks are bald, all their hair is gone. Perhaps because of the full moon and the Buddhist rituals which go with it, but clearly today was haircut day. Or rather, head-shave day. Where before it was tricky to keep the monks apart since they all wear identical clothes, the children now have the same non-hairdo as well! The next surprise comes when I return to our room. I find an agitated Heidi and Alicia. We had a break in! The sliding screen of our window was opened, the bedroom is a mess. We scan the place – iPad, headphone, watch - most precious items are still there. You'd think that the second floor of a monastery with no balcony would be safe from burglaries. Certainly not there! Darn monkeys! Down below on the grass we see the spoils. A plastic bag and a host of small items scattered around. These long-armed animals know that food is usually in plastic bags. Too bad for this culprit, he only got bottles of earwax remover and 'swimmers ear' drops. He must have been disappointed as he drank those down! Although one never knows what is missing until it is needed, we are fairly sure no valuable items have gone missing. We take the Buddhist approach, detach, take a deep breath and play a game of Yahtzee (okay, that last one was our addition). The next shock is a double shock.

The first shock is that I don't win the dice game. For the first time during the holiday, I have to admit that this game is not a game of intelligence. Second shock, suddenly it feels like someone drops a fully loaded 36 foot container on top of our building. Everything shakes, lamps rattle. An earthquake rocks the building! None of us have consciously experienced an earthquake before. The last one we encountered happened when we were in Peru, but we were isolated from it as we were riding in a taxi. This one we definitely felt. We find it rather eerie and thrilling at the same time. Looking outside the monks continue playing in the yard, oblivious to the quaking. By the time we get to dinner we are still between excited and shaken up. Interestingly, dinner is uneventful - noodle soup and no mention of the earthquake. For the locals, this was no big deal: "just a small trembler", "happens all the time".

Daily life and the unwelcome guests

One morning, a few days later, I wake up from strange background noise. It is not the drums, nor the bells. It is the knocking on the window. He? Knocking on the window? We are on the second floor! What the…. I open the curtain and am confronted by a monkey staring straight at me, one foot away. In surprise I jump backwards on the bed. He is unfazed, only upset that today he can not just slide the screen away to ransack the room and plunder some more toiletries.

Heidi grabs the camera to record the incident. She laughs at me because it is my second animal shock of the day. During the night I had woken up 100% convinced a monkey was poking my feet. It was so real that I jumped out of bed, turned the overhead lights on, and scared the living daylights out of Heidi as I violently removed all sheets and covers from the bed. I even lifted the mattress to look under it. Heidi, realizing it was monkey-paranoia, quietly remade the bed said: "Is it over? Can we get back to sleep again now?". She slid between the sheets and continued her beauty sleep. For me, it took me over an hour to get my heart to slow down and fall back into unconsciousness.

Anyway, after disappointing the monkey by not letting him in, I visit the headmaster 'Lobsing-la'. He turns out to be an overloaded manager with the unique characteristic of being task-oriented, detail-oriented, and having absolutely no skill in social interaction. A ruthless combination. We've been told that in the near future he will get more support, meaning responsibilities for the school (and volunteers) will be transferred to someone else. This, no doubt, is good news for all involved.

The reason for my visit to Lobsing is to inform him of our plans to take a four day trek. Given the exam week, there is little teaching we can do. Rather than cleaning windows, I explain to him we think discovering the mountains is a better use of our time. I do a selling job on him. He immediately dives in to rabbit holes and the detail, never really looking up from his desk. I propose our trip for Thursday through Saturday night and moving workdays around. I spell it out for him "This allows us to be around for the grading of exams on Wednesday, and to grade the Sunday exams when we return." He checks paperwork, schedules and a calendar. Though I am not sure he fully understood what I said, he agrees to our plan. "Yes", and "of course, we can leave our stuff behind in the room for those days". This is great news since now we don't have to worry about storing our stuff while we are on our hike. By staying the Sunday we also have an additional day of a roof over our heads.

Having the formal approval of the principal, we go to town and confirm our trek. We grab a taxi but get dropped at the wrong side of town. Being stingy I make the family walk to the area where we need to be. "Good practice", I claim. The walk is long. Very long. The sun is hot in that unique convection way. In the shadow it is downright cool, but once you get the direct hit of the sun, it is like an altitude exposure. While it is more than uncomfortable, I stay the course, making the family walk. I see it as an acid test for our upcoming trek. Several times I reset the 'we are almost there mark'. Over forty minutes later, I reach the true "we're fed up" moment; a combination of the heat, street noise and pain in our ears caused by the constant honking and tooting of Nepali drivers. Nepalis have this urge to continuously use the horn, making roadside walking very unpleasant. We are all happy when we finally arrive close to our destination, sit down and slurp a cold drink.

We book the trek and buy gloves, poles, and hats. We need to buy new hats because we either forgot them in China or we lost them to the monkeys; we are not sure. Later that afternoon a Suzuki Maruti taxi takes us back from town to home. The driver tells us we should be happy to have done our shopping today since a nationwide strike is planned, "Tomorrow will be impossible to get in or back out of town."

That evening, I return to the Buddhist lessons. I read a couple of books on Buddhism, and I played around with meditation, so I felt I was getting a slight understanding of what it is all about. But today is not going to be the day to get converted. My cross-legged friend talks about the space where the 'special spiritual person' finds joy. I perk up, interested, only to crash soon after. He explains, the "joy spot" is in the "non-externalistic, non-nihilistic space". I wonder where this exactly is. Inquiry offers me the explanation that it is in "one non-specific spot". Note, not several, but one non-specific spot. Instantly, I am reminded of my time in Catholic boys school. The priest had stated 'God is everywhere'. This invoked the question: 'also in our backyard?' The inevitable answer was 'of course', to which the immediate response was "impossible, we don't have a backyard". Needless to say this didn't go over well. In hindsight it probably was similar – or close – to the non-existent spot just described by my monk-teacher. I wondered if a non-existant backyard could qualify as non-nihilistic space. As my mind wanders back, the monk explains that the infamous place can be considered a negative space: "it isn't an object, nor is it nothing. It simply is". I have seldom gotten close to understanding these concepts without an inappropriate amount of alcohol and right here, in a Tibetan monastery, sober as can be, I certainly can't grasp it. Half disappointed, half frustrated I cross the courtyard back to the room. I look up at the darkness into space, real space, a huge expanse of nothingness. I feel small and lost though I know exactly where I am.

As it turns out, the evening becomes even more trying. Two mosquitoes decide to keep me company. I understand the Buddhist's respect for all beings, but whoever deserved to be reincarnated as mosquito – whose sole purpose in life seems to be to propagate, suck blood out of others and make them itch – probably deserves to be more than just manhandled. From that perspective, I did them a favor; I gave both of them another shot at being reincarnated. The evening gets worse. Further into the night I have a re-occurrence of my monkey-paranoia. Half awake, I definitely feel a monkey on our bed. It is pulling and scratching the blankets. Grabbing a flashlight I flick it on and scout around. "I swear I felt it" I say to Heidi who stares at me confused, wondering if I have gone mad. She gets a little fed up with these middle-of-the-night episodes. Listening carefully, my senses engage like a sonar. With the overhead lights on I troll the room. I find the culprit. Under a side-cabinet sits a large gray rodent - fifteen centimeters long without tail. Clearly this vermin had been sitting on our bed, probably enjoying my body heat while rapidly scratching the blanket on my back. I ponder what to do next. I have no trap, nothing to catch it with, no clue what to do with it even if I catch it. Killing a mosquito is one thing, but having bloodstains on the carpet from killing a sentient being might not be wise in a Buddhist monastery. While sitting on the bed pondering my options, I hear the rat-mouse take off into the other room. Keen to know its point of origin, I follow. Coming out of the well-lit bedroom into the adjoining dark living room I lose track of it. So much for finding where it resides (or hides). I close the bedroom door. Problem solved, for now. We'll deal with that one in the morning.

Unfortunately, the episode fully awakens me. Neurons firing, I cannot return to sleep. I lay awake for a long time, not sure if it is due to my fear of "Mickey's Return" or just a general awake state after the bombardment of fright, lights and walking barefoot on the cold bathroom floor. A miserable two hours later, the daily gong sounds and rouses me from my slumber. I prop up a pillow behind me and grab one of the books I am reading. Then I realize something is missing. Noise. It is totally quiet in our room. No beep, honk or toot travels up from the road below the monastery. How strange. The road sounds had become 'white noise'. It is almost eerie now that they are gone. Due to the strike, all traffic in Nepal has come to a screaming halt. We learn that anyone who takes the risk of driving has a high change of being stopped and having their car set on fire. This appears to be enough of an deterrent for people not to drive. Go figure. The silence is deafening. After the days of constant background noise it is a relief to listen only to the sounds of the (young) monks playing in the yard outside.

We continue prepping the students for exams. As we sit with a couple of young monks we notice they are memorizing the responses to exam questions by singing the answers. Almost like American soldiers in boot-camp copying the chant of the drill instructor, I hear them sing. We listen to them chanting: "we comb our hair every morning", "we wash our hair with shampoo", "we cross the road at the zebra-crossing", "we spray DDT to kill the sand flies". I don't know if I should laugh or cry. The nonsense of the first two are driven home as an older student walks around with a pump-operated flask squirting cream onto each monk's head, a gift to sooth the razor burn on their bald heads from the clipping a few days ago. As for the third quote, when asked, they admit there are no zebra-crossings that they know of in the area; and I can confirm there is not one within a thirty minute flight! The last remark is wrong on so many levels I don't even want to explain. DDT, really? Promoting killing sand flies with DDT in a monastery knowing the Buddhists' respect for life?

After dinner one evening (surprise, surprise - lentil soup), I find myself conflicted as I help a couple of students with their exam preparation. My toes curl as they are taught one gets AIDS from kissing and general physical contact like a handshake. Now what do I do? Do I help them pass their exam, or teach them what I believe to be correct? It gets sillier. They have to learn to distinguish between the "straight arm position" and the "forward position" of a gymnast on the parallel-bars. Really? They don't know about oxygen, blood and heart rates, but Olympic gymnastic positions are relevant? I take a deep breath and I remind myself that these are the lucky kids, they get an education. I detach, and meanwhile I seriously wonder if we as a society and as volunteers in particular can't do better.

Mercifully, for the rest of the week the nights are uneventful. Closing the bedroom doors keeps Mr. Rodent out. We eat the pita and spicy sauce for breakfast, giving us and the monks pre-exam energy. The exams start at nine on the ground floor of the temple, often allowing us a last minute revision with the students. The temple itself morphs every morning into "exam auditorium". The monks sit on square pillows as if on little islands, taking their exams.

Exams are taken together, regardless the grade. The students are spaced out, their names indicated on white papers on the ground in front of a pillow. I get flashbacks to taking exams in Belgium in the school canteen. The difference is that in Belgium you could hear a pin drop; here it seems each student is murmuring or singing to himself. Some ask assistance of the teachers, others are talking to one another while scribbling their answers down. A student asks me for a rubber, showing that in Nepal the Brits provided language education (no erasers found in this establishment).

We walk around the exam room, hands on our backs, clarifying questions as required. Most kids ask assistance with the aim to confirm that they have the correct answer. It is actually arduous not to spill the beans as they seem to guess even on the simple yes/no questions. It is tough to resist when they plead with their big brown eyes searching for our confirmation; 'We should write on the walls?…. Yes?… [they look up, trying got read my face] … No?….[another look with begging eyes]'. With a poker-face I answer: "Yes, that is indeed the question" and walk off quickly before caving in.

On some questions we do help out for consistency. The English teacher has some dubious questions on the exam like: 'What are the causes of alcohol?'. Now, I ask you, do *you* know the *causes* of alcohol? I think it is a tough question, especially for a 10-year old novice monk.

Personally, I think the cause of alcohol is a noble rot and fermentation, grounded in the more basic 'cause' of people looking for an escape medium, amplified by the 'cause' of companies aiming to make money, and supplemented by the 'cause' of governments attempting to maximize tax revenues (some Scandinavian countries being the obvious exception to this rule). The answer the teacher is looking for, however, is 'stress and pressure from friends'. The attentive reader probably realizes that the intended question of the teacher was 'what are the reasons people might drink alcohol?', rather that 'what is the cause of alcohol'. I suspect the English teacher's English is not that good, but he had access to a thesaurus and tried to impress.

After exams, we walk to the little town across the bridge. The dusty village consists of two cross streets and one intersection. Shops extend one hundred meters in all four directions. The shops are more like two-by-three meter stalls packed with clothing, pharmaceuticals, and food. There are several hardware cubicles selling basic tools, home-improvement paraphernalia and piping. There must be a specific market segment they target, because all three advertise 'healthy paint'; I assume it means water-based. A few restaurants and several tailors complete the shopping zone. The tailors are most picturesque. Four guys crammed close together sewing suits using foot-operated machines.

Heidi points out that I have to retract a previous claim. I said there are no zebra-crossings in the region, but we actually detect one. Now, I would like to qualify that a little. Detect is the operative word. Undeniably, one of the streets has evidence of wide parallel white stripes. But in my defense, the stripes were likely painted when the bitumen was originally put down. I estimate this happened in the 1970s making the lines partial and very, very faint. It barely deserves the name zebra-crossing. It is also about two hundred meters from the only intersection in town and connects nothing to absolutely nothing. The question therefore is IF it qualifies as a zebra-crossing at all. Let's be fair. If something is old, misplaced and has zero functionality, would you still call it by its original name? An old unused castle is 'a ruin', an old abandoned ship 'a wreck', old clothes are 'rags'. I therefore think that I can stick to my guns; this is not a zebra crossing. An old, unused zebra-crossings should be called something else. I rest my case.

We meander around looking for a T-shirt. We only find polo shirts. No simple T-shirts here. It clearly is not a tourist area; no 'I [heart] Nepal' or 'Yak,Yak,Yak Nepal'. No "my parents went to Nepal...."-shirts. Not even shirts with the unique Nepali flag are available. I end up buying a cotton polo and negotiate a thirty percent discount. In all honesty there was more on the table, but the shopkeeper was pretty, had a lovely smile, and seven dollars did not seem unreasonable. Call me a softie!

Back at the monastery I attempt to meditate. I say attempt, since I am accosted by one (or two) mosquitoes making concentration next to impossible. Remembering the 'respect for life' and 'all sentient beings' I am able to take the double-bite rather than flatten the buzzing insects with brute force. I even manage not to scratch for a while, but it does mean that I have to abandon my session long before becoming one with the universe. Maybe next time.

Over noodle soup we talk with a senior monk about Nepal, Tibet, and the monastery in general. He has a deep baritone voice with a silky smoothness and gentleness to it. We ask about the monks' names. At the exams, we noticed that many monks carried similar names; Kunga and Dhondu being some of the most popular ones. He explains that as the students become monks, they leave their old clothes behind (and start wearing the saffron and maroon), they leave their hair behind (hence the bald heads) and they leave their name behind. A new monk is thus assigned a new name. Often the new name reflects the one of the 'naming' monk; hence the repetition.

The Poon Hill Trek

When we wake up the next morning I cross my fingers, praying for healthy happy kids. Today we start our trek. We, the parents, had an absolutely ghastly night. Hideous mosquitoes tormented us. I spent part of the night on the couch in the living room, trying to lure the animals away from Heidi hoping she'd get a good nights' sleep, but as it turns out it merely served to give me additional bodily discomfort. In fact, by daybreak it turns out the kids too had midnight battles. But a plan is a plan.

We pack all the gear we need on the trek into two backpacks, figuring the porter will take one, I the other. The weather forecast promises blue skies so we decide to take Leendert and Heidi's backpack. We leave my bigger, heavier and waterproof pack behind at the monastery. At eight there is a knock on the door and our guide 'Raj' presents himself. We finish packing and leave 'base camp'. It feels strange to put on backpacks and walk away from the monastery. Somehow in the short time we have been there, the place has crawled under our skin. It feels a bit like leaving home, like leaving a warm blanket behind. I can not imagine what it must be like for a monk after completing years of study to leave this sanctuary and enter the real world.

In front of the gate is our transport. It is one of those small vans you typically find in Asia. We cram the backpacks behind the back seat. While doing so they ask the kids to hold some sleeping bags which threaten to fly out while they slam the back door closed. We squeeze in and Raj informs us we'll pick up our porter on the way.

Not much past the Tibetan Refugee Camp we stop and a skinny fellow enters the car. He squeezes in on the back seat next to the kids. His name is Rodrup. He clearly has no command of English and I can hardly imagine him as a porter. Leendert, our thirteen year old, who could be a model for a Giacometti bronze himself, looks bulky compared to the fellow seated next to him. No way this smiley guy in his trainers, jeans and a T-shirt can be the porter!

The drive to the starting point takes over an hour. For every kilometer we progress the road gets worse. Initially the road narrows and potholes become more frequent, but soon paving intermittently disappears altogether. At times the asphalt becomes too narrow for our petite vehicle and we bounce from hole to hole. Hobbling along the patchwork of bitumen and gravel we climb over ridges and plunge back into valleys. I am surprised the road is in such bad state since it leads to the number one starting point for Nepal's trekking tourists. It is abundantly clear why tourists come here. The views are so magnificent that I ask the driver to halt for a photo-stop halfway. Soon we arrive at the launch point and unfold ourselves, popping out like a "jack-in-the-van". We stretch our limbs and accept a cup of sweet milky tea while the porter takes inventory of our bags. As we extend our walking sticks we review our water situation: two 1,5 liter coke bottles with purified water, two 1 liter flexible packs and Alicia's waist pack with two 600 ml Mountain Dew bottles. That should do for starters. As a backup, Heidi has a filter and tablets.

I look and see Rodrup grabbing a piece of old string, ready to tie the backpacks together. I signal him to stop, indicating I plan to carry half our payload. It takes an intervention from Raj to make Rodrup understand. Rodrup looks puzzled, confused that I would carry a backpack myself. I, in return, look puzzled at him, thinking he should realize his body is too skinny to attempt carrying both packs.

Moments after finishing our tea we are on the path to Ulleri. The path is wide, a gentle upwards slope, at times a bit steeper. Raj has our permits checked and registers as we cross a metal bridge covered with the prayer flags and enter the national park. As we start our ascent, we are glad to have brought sunscreen and hats. A few four-wheel drive cars pass us filled with time-restricted tourists who do only a short hike, starting higher up the mountain. Mules make their way down the hill hauling empty gas-bottles. An hour into the walk Alicia starts dragging her heels. We worry because we still have a long, long way to go. It takes us a while to realize what is happening: the heat is getting to her! We slow down a bit, cool her down and make her drink water. She quickly improves.

Raj halts us at our designated lunch stop. Apparently, we are making good time, as it is only eleven-thirty and we are the first patrons of this little restaurant. Peeking inside, a very rudimentary country kitchen. Dark beams at (my) eye level hold up a second floor, presumably bedrooms. A tiny old lady holds a knife too big for her stature and chops garlic. There is little cooking equipment – a couple of pans and pots, a few spoons and knives. The entire place feels like a hut, the kind I built when I was a kid. Luckily, the way the kitchen looks has absolutely no bearing on the tastiness of the food it produces. I am also relieved to see that we can buy bottled water. It means we overdid it with the tablets and filter bag, but we can drag less weight while stimulating the economy along the way.

We eat and head back to the gravel path. After another short hour, Raj asks if we want to stop for the night, or push on. We look at each other. Really? At two-thirty? Stop already? No thank you, we'll push on. He tells us it will be a challenging stretch in front of us, "so normally it is foreseen for the tough second day". We ignore the warning, say 'go', and continue. After a while we cross a magnificent hanging bridge leading us to a slab-stoned set of stairs. Raj informs us that this is where the climb really starts; "It is uphill from here. Uphill for 3700 steps".

Not surprisingly, Alicia starts the count 1-2-3-4.... Within minutes Heidi's body gives her feedback that her cold from the last two days has not quite left her body. She is thankful for the forced breaks we get when a mule-caravan comes down the mountain path. We learn to stand on the mountainside of the animals. As Raj explains "it is preferable to be wedged between the animal's cargo and the mountain rather than getting knocked over the ledge". I look over the edge and feel no need to debate.

The scenery going up is wonderful; both the nature and the colorful people in it are to be admired. It is fun to observe the various tourists in all their degrees of preparedness. It is even more fun to contrast them against the locals who go about their daily business. Most of the tourists are armed as if they are making the last push to the summit of the Himalayas: 'Everest here we come'. Unlike us, they are equipped with sunglasses (with leather side covers), flashy all-weather-proof gear (from the top Alpine brands of France and Germany), walking sticks (light weight, some with shock absorbers), and hiking boots (in the most trendy fluorescent colors). It would not surprise me if the latter has GPS trackers and electric heaters in them. Most of them sport a little daypack. We get peeks at the contents of their day packs as they take their breaks. I am sure they consider it the bare essentials; altimeters, gels, goo's, sugar tablets, granola and power bars, and first-aid kits. Their porters carry all the rest.

As for the locals, we found they could be split in three groups: those trekking goods up and down the mountain, those who live on the mountain, and those who help tourists. The latter has two sub-groups: the guide, mainly for hand-holding, and the porters for the brawn. The porters are loaded double high, double wide, with a strap over their foreheads carrying the massive payload on their stooped backs. I regret not having my camera at hand at one particular moment. It would have been the shot of the day. A porter passes us and the group of fully kitted-out Asians in front of us. He overtakes the kaleidoscope of branded clothing (traveling at double the speed), carrying three adult size backpacks. He could have been Rodrup's twin brother, weighing in at forty-five kilograms tops. The best off all? He zips past us and the expedition team in front of us while dressed in a T-shirt, old shiny Adidas training pants and flip-flops!

I can't help but laugh at the scene, proud that we only invested in walking sticks; for clarity, no shock absorbers. For untrained people like ourselves the walking poles are more appreciated every step we ascend. Heidi continues to struggle, compliments of the 'hangover' of her cold. She continuously apologizes for her climbing speed. Clearly, she is oblivious to the fact that most mountaineers around her are suffering from the steep climb as well and slowing down considerably. In fact, as a team, we out-pace most others, principally because we take no long breaks to dive into daypacks for snacks. At last we arrive in Ulleri; Alicia informs us that the number of steps was indeed 3741, and that since we started in the morning we walked and climbed stairs for 4 hours 31 minutes and 21 seconds. Nothing like being exact! The bad news? Our 'hotel' did not get our booking, so we need to go a bit further. For a moment I think we are about to lose Heidi. She looks at me pleading "make it stop". But there is only one option; the climb continues. Fortunately the next 'hotel' is only about seventy-five steps up. Now, seventy-five steps might not sound like a lot to you, but trust me, by the time we take the last steps to the entryway of the hotel, we feel those last steps alone equaled climbing to the top of the Empire State building starting from 5th Avenue. I am ecstatically happy to learn that this hotel has space and that we can rest and recuperate.

The 'hotel' does need a bit of explanation. The rooms are basic. Actually they are basic–basic. The sleeping quarters have linoleum floors, two side-by-side wooden framed beds, sheets, old wool blankets, and one shaky small side table. At the end of the hall there is a squatty-potty; opposite is a room with a communal shower and a regular toilet. It reminds me of the set up of the mountain huts of the *Alpenverein* in Austria. We quickly settle, and sit outside on the terrace enjoying the view over the mountains. Soon, I find myself with a beer in hand while everyone takes turns for a shower. We were the last guests to arrive, so the shower is available. After all the sweating, the luxury of a warm water shower reportedly feels amazing. It is a luxury we have missed in the monastery.

Having downed my beer, I grab my stuff and enter the shower/toilet room. I open the taps, happy to indulge in the bliss of warmth which I have been denied for weeks. I wait for the warm water to arrive. No luck. I test if the Hot and Cold are reversed. Nope. A few minutes later reality sets in. The warm water is gone, it ran out. The option before me is between "cold" and "freezing" glacier melt. So again, a cold military shower it is. As I return to the room, my teeth are chattering and my lips are dark blue. I get heartfelt compassion from the entire family. It turns out Leendert had hot-hot water (needing to mix it with lots of cold), Alicia added a bit of cold water, Heidi took a lukewarm shower using only hot, and that's where the warm water ran out. I am chilled to the bone, but at least I am clean.

We go down for the evening meal. On plastic garden chairs we enjoy the food and - especially me - the hot tea. I cradle the cup in my hands, slowly warming up. Finishing dinner, the kids and Heidi devour a big bowl of rice pudding while I try the millet-based 'local wine'. It is served tepid in a large glass mug which is its only redeeming factor. It smells like *eau-de-vie*, tastes like lighter fluid, and has a long aftertaste. In order not to insult the chef, I end up pouring half the concoction in my tea mug by the end of the evening.

Despite the cold, there is a cozy atmosphere and we socialize with the people around us who are also bundled up in coats. We play cards and dice. Yawning and feeling tired after the third game I glance at my watch. Only eight o'clock? It feels like midnight! We make plans with Raj. He suggests leaving early as we have a long day ahead. Knowing we have climbed the hard part, I suggest a slightly less ambitious start. It takes a bit of doing, but the seven a.m. proposal moves to a much more reasonable eight-thirty before we retire.

As in most mountain huts in the world, by nine p.m. everyone, and I mean everyone, is in bed. The site is closed. Not a single light remains. Grateful for the slightly insulated walls and double soft plastic floors I close my eyes. From previous mountain stays I know that insulated walls will keep the noise down from people's snores. The soft floors of this building, which has a foamy material under the linoleum, will do the same for the sounds of midnight toilet visitors as well as early birds insisting on being the first ones on the trail. Ah, sleep at last! No mosquitoes, no monkeys, no rodents, no noise; only fresh mountain air.

Day two of the trek

It is no surprise that, given the early bedtime, Heidi and I are up at the crack of dawn. We peek past the flimsy curtains and take in the mountain view. The clear sky, the cool quiet of the morning, and the light of the early morning make the sight even more majestic than the day before. We stare at the hills and the valley we hiked through only twelve hours earlier, silenced by its overall beauty. Slowly the hut comes to life, with dimmed noises of travelers going through their morning routines. We dress and have our breakfast outside. Halfway through our meal, we are interrupted. Right off the overhang platform an event begs our attention, and our camera. An upward mule-caravan encounters a downward flow of like-minded stubborn animals. The issue is that their respective loads; bags of onions, bags of cement and empty chicken cages prohibit them from passing one another on the narrow path. Major traffic jam. Ever tried to make multiple donkeys go backwards and have them parallel park? Trust me it is a sight to see. It provides great morning entertainment! It takes the herdsmen over fifteen minutes to de-bottleneck the path, but they eventually prevail and continue on their respective ways.

Gulping down the last swallow of tea we saddle-up and Raj leads the way to Ghorapani, our next stop. We take our initial steps. Just as my muscles are trying to get used to forward movement again a harsh reality sets in. It isn't just forward movement we seek, it is upward movement as well. The climb continues. Raj imparts on us we will only go up 1100 meters today. I am dumbfounded, realizing that had we not pushed on yesterday after lunch, we would have had to make the climb of yesterday plus what is in front of us right now. I am sure that the previous day's 3700 steps plus today's challenge would have done us in.

The way up is impressive with flowering rhododendrons surrounding us. The loop over Poon Hill is the most popular trek in the area. It is made by sixty percent of all walking tourists coming to Nepal. I can see why. It is simply stunning. Thankfully, two hours into our walk, Raj halts us for our first stop. My legs are happy for the break. At a simple restaurant, we order two cokes and a flask of tea. Without showing it, I am upset about the six-hundred rupia we are charged. "That's extortion", I think initially. It is only after reflecting that I realize how unreasonable I am. All those supplies need to be carried up!

After finishing our drinks we pursue our path. Rodrup brings up the rear - always happy, always smiling. I suspect part of his smile is derived from having to carry only one backpack. His English vocabulary is extremely limited. Rodrup mostly utters repetitively the names of the mountain ranges we will pass, pass or have passed. Sometimes he dares to speak another word of English, but unfortunately they add little value: "cow", "highway", "bus", "local", "nice", and "beautiful" seem to be the only six English words he has mastered. I do take a liking to him, though he sometimes gets in the way. Literally. He is as camera horny as Leendert is shy. Rodrup has the uncanny skill of jumping into the scene at any and every occasion we take a picture. I estimate he photobombs over half our pictures. In hindsight it is part of his charm.

According to our official time-keeper it takes us 3 hours 44 minutes and 12 seconds of active walking that day to reach Ghorapani. We arrive around two-thirty. We conquer the last six large steps into the Moonlight Hotel with difficulty, our legs complete jelly. Again, the word 'hotel' needs some explanation. Had we deemed the hotel the day before as 'basic', today's guest-house proves things can always go downhill as you go uphill. The building is a wood frame structure. I suspect that the blue paint on the outside contributes to keeping the plywood building standing. A quick glance at the thin walls make it clear that the establishment will only give limited weather protection. Seeing how the window frames are barely attached to the structure and how insulation and inner walls are missing, I wonder how qualifies as a hotel. No doubt, the big bad wolf could knock this structure over by accident, farting.

Further inspection of the Moonlight Hotel -and our bedrooms- confirms a more basic set-up than the day before. Two beds in a room, no sheets, just a duvet, nothing but very thin ply-board between the rooms. Definitely no in-room heat or insulated floors. Oh Boy.

We dump our bags and return to the main room. I scan the room and see a recycled metal oil drum as center piece. The drum was probably hauled up here way back when, to provide fuel. A metal chimney now sticks out on top of the barrel, the pipe disappearing through the roof of the building. A little door is welded in the bottom of the drum, providing a place to shovel firewood into the makeshift furnace. Three low benches are strategically placed around the contraption. I guess that's what is meant by central heat.

Casting my eye around the room I see a couple of very well equipped Koreans. I know they are well equipped, because it is cold enough inside the room to merit them wearing their new branded coats and other paraphernalia. Clearly, the furnace is not in operation. It's going to be a cold afternoon. At another table in the corner sit three fashionable Chinese girls from Guangzhou. They eat the 'mixed spaghetti', which they report is very tasty. We observe one commonality between the Chinese and Koreans on a trek in Nepal. Each one is attached to their mobile phone device (in isolation), talking and texting to people far away, listening to music, ignoring the people and the environment around them.

I decide to take a shower before eating since I am chilled from my sweat-damp shirt. My turn to go first! The shower shed is not exactly what I had hoped for given that Raj had promised the hotel would have warm water facilities. The Moonlight Hotel has a shared shower in a small area just off the common room. The lady running the hotel comes with me to connect two rubber hoses, creating the water supply. Obviously it is not used often. She turns knobs on a gas-heater and shows me the settings. I gather a towel, dry clothes and a whole lot of courage before entering the shower shed. The bottom of the walls have big gaps to the outside and cold mountain air blows past my ankles through the space. The floor is slanted concrete, and standing barefoot on it, I suspect this slab has permafrost. There is a single twenty watt light bulb dangling from a wire which provides some light as well as a safety risk. Raj was right. There is warm water. He never made commitments on water pressure or quantity, air temperature or safety. Not plentiful, but warm droplets fall upon my head. Unfortunately the frozen floor gets to my inner core quicker than the water drops reach my windblown shoulders. Brrrr. It is not my lucky shower week! Ultimately, only Heidi and I brave the shower; we let the kids off the hook, fearing pneumonia.

For lunch we order the mixed spaghetti the Chinese recommended. We supplement it with a Nepali pizza. This is opposed to a Napoli pizza, noting that changing two letters gives rise to a totally different creation and experience. After that, the kids watch a movie on the iPad in their bedroom. They cover themselves with blankets and all the sleeping bags available in an attempt to stay warm. At four in the afternoon the oil-drum receives the much needed paper, wood and a match. Slowly, the temperature in the common area crawls up. Most of the heat dissipates between the cracks in the walls and the openings around the outside door, which doesn't close completely. Suddenly I realize why it is called the Moonlight Hotel; even when you are inside you can always see the moonlight through one of the cracks!

The smell in the Moonlight Hotel also deserves mention. It is an interesting blend of scents. The smells from the kitchen are very pleasant. However, the overriding smell is caused by the eight short wash-lines hanging on the ceiling of the common room. The lines serve to dry sweaty socks, shirts and towels of the patrons of the eight-room hotel. As the pieces of cloth dry they absorb the fragrance and smoke from the heated oil drum, and give off a pungent odor which make my old running shoes smell rosy. It's a good thing the building is not air tight! We pull the kids from their room to join us in the coziness of the common room. It happens under protest: "but if we stay here our bodies will warm up the room". We drag them out and end up playing cards and dice games. Looking outside, we see the mountains disappear in clouds. Not much later a big hailstorm dumps ice on the roof and spectacular lightning bolts light the sky. We order dinner; pretty much a repeat of our spaghetti and pizza lunch.

After our meal we invite our guide and porter to join us playing games. Rudrop takes a particular liking to *"dobbelen"*, a Dutch dice game. Not hampered by his continuous misunderstanding how the game is played, he tosses the dice with full commitment and stares at them with glee. Every throw his eyes light up as if he opens a Christmas gift. He smiles and yells two of his six English words at each roll: "nice", "beautiful". His infectious laugh adds to the fun. Even after an hour of play his understanding of the game equals a number not to be found on any of the dice; zero. It matters little, we coach him several times to a win: "Nice!"

Meanwhile, Raj insists that I try the local wine again. The volume and temperature of the beverage is similar to the day before, but this time the smell is less repulsive and a taste barely existent. I'd qualify it as 'drinkable', but having said that, it takes little effort to pass on the offer of a refill. Since we'll climb Poon Hill tomorrow to see the sunrise, we all go to bed early. As usual in mountain dwellings, the lights are off well before nine o'clock.

Not much of a night that was! First of all it was cold. And if I am cold, it means the rest of the family must feel they are trying to sleep naked in an igloo. On the other side of our paper-thin wall, one of the Korean guests snored in the highest pitch I have ever encountered. Sleep did not come easily. About the time I finally drifted off, the first climbers pass outside. Eighteen minutes after four o'clock they set off the hotel dog. This caused a chain reaction. The dog agitated me, but what's more, it set off the Koreans. The Koreans are well-equipped to sleep in the cold, but ill-equipped to keep their voices to a whisper. They also don't have shoes which allow them to walk quietly, nor do they consider walking quietly on socks until they reach the front door. Consequently they send decibels and vibrations through the entire hotel, waking others, who figure they may as well get up. In other words, by a quarter after four, Heidi and I are both awake, up and about. By four-forty five we rouse the kids; it's time to see the sun rise on the mountain!

Fearing the cold, we layer our bodies like onions. With small headlights on our heads we look like coal miners following our guide into the darkness. The lack of sleep combined with her remaining head cold make Heidi struggle with the conditions and the altitude. Leendert too battles a headache. There is little wind, so we soon start to strip layers of clothing (this is good news - at least better than the alternative of being cold). After a while Alicia and I decide to climb at our own, faster, pace and leave Heidi and Leendert to follow behind. It doesn't take much more than half an hour to reach the top of Poon Hill. There we wait, getting cold again.

Now I have to get something off my chest. What is it with people and their urge to wake up at ungodly hours to see the sunrise (typically in the cold)? Be it a temple in Angkor Wat (Cambodia), the Bromo Volcano (Indonesia), Poon Hill, or whatever other place. I just don't get it. It is almost a group hysteria to get there in time, and invariably it is a near non-event. Guess what folks, about 365 days a year the sun comes up; and for the those interested, it sets about as often. It would be worth the climb, the agony of the hour, the discomfort of the cold if, for once, the sun decided NOT to rise. But, on this day too, the light appeared, the sun came up. Hallelujah!

First, the sun rays start to light the horizon skies, then the top of the mountains, and finally it brings the awaited convection heat to our stone-cold heat-craving bodies. Snap, snap, snap. Picture, picture, picture. More pictures, all in attempt to miss the photo bombers. Not easy but we succeed. We get one shot that makes it appear as if we were on the top of Poon Hill on our own - even without Rodrup! Now, let's get our butts off the mountain into the comfort, or in our case the semi-comfort of our hotel. Breakfast awaits.

I compare the euphoria of the early sunrise on one of these peaks to the one I felt as a kid leaving church. More often than not it wasn't the sermon that was so inspiring and made me feel better when exiting, but rather the getting up off the hard wood benches after that long hour. Likewise, the rising sun on Poon Hill puts an end to the misery of the dark, cold, and standing around, instantly filling people around us with joy as they commence cruising down the mountain. I am convinced that it is this relief and perhaps selective memory (erasing discomfort), which triggers people to later tell their friends "oh, you must go, it is definitely worth it!"

Be that as it may, we have three interesting moments on the Poon Hill summit; first of all Raj secures us warm cups of Nepali tea. Seldom has tea tasted so good. No need for a piece of chocolate! Second, we run into a young Dutch couple we met in our hotel two days earlier, giving us people to chat with, and third, the view. Oh **WOW** the view! The view of the mountain range is incomparable to any other mountain view - at the crack of dawn or not. What we'd consider mountains in the French Alps would simply be rolling hills against this backdrop. The Mont Blanc would be nothing more than an insignificant blip against these Nepali peaks.

Back to the hilltop. The Dutch girl we met is freezing, her mind on frostbite, she tries blowing heat into her fingers. As we cradle warm tea mugs, Heidi, her true self, gifts her gloves to the girl stating "we won't need them on the next part of our trip anyway".

It is not long before we are confident the sun will continue its climb, so we can take the steps down to get to our eggs, toast and cereal. Back in the hotel, as we repack, I notice our room looks as if a chicken was chased down and murdered. In the darkness of the morning I had not noticed it before. Now I realize the sleeping bag I was using was of such low quality that it shed at least fifteen percent of its content overnight. Down is everywhere; on the floor, in my shirts, attached to my socks. The good news is that it is easier to pack. The sleeping bag is much less bulky this morning!

We tighten our shoes and get on our way to Ghandruk. For a few minutes we walk down hill, and then it is back up, and up, and up. The legs of the parents are screaming while the kids appear to be in great shape. They race up the hill appropriately singing songs from the "sound of music". Every so often they kindly wait for us. The ugliness of this game of catch-up is that as soon as we have reached the same point to relax, they are off again, having had an extended break. Ah, where have the days gone where we dragged them along and resisted the pleas: "carry me"?

As we take a rest and cast a glance back, the view the mountain range is again mind-blowing. The silly part is that we have climbed back up to about 3210 meters. Effectively the same height of Poon Hill. Had I known that, we could have skipped the Poon Hill climb, been at this spot on our own and shot the most amazing pictures without dozens of photo-bombers. We also would have been on our way one hour earlier, well ahead of the other tourists!

For the next hours we walk through the most stunning rhododendron forest. It is mystical, almost fairytale-like. For hours we trail through high-altitude red-blossoming trees. Some trees are so big you can't wrap your arms around their trunks. This blooming jungle, partially covered in moss, invites us to take many photos. I feel like an addict. Time and again I hear myself say "okay, one more", "this is really the last one", "we have enough now, but one more won't make the difference", "this one is too good to pass up". Long live digital photography!

Advancing I notice that slowly the kids start imploding, their young energy burning off. Raj suggests we do one more ridge, but Heidi and I insist we have lunch first. It is a good choice. The kids visually revive as the food re-energizes their bodies. Before you know it we are back on the road down. Where the steps up the last few days took effort, the steps down are introducing an entirely new experience. Aches appear in body parts previously not felt, bones and ligaments objecting to being used as shock absorbers. I can assure you, a twenty-minute stairway of big steps down towards a riverbed does not go in the category of a comfortable walk. We conquer another ridge, and Heidi 'triangulates' with the kids; they are getting fed up with walking. She keeps them busy counting steps in sets of twenty five. Soon we all participate, alternating who gets to count. It makes us forget about the laborious task at hand or in this case the 'laborious task at feet and knees'. We use the opportunity to teach the kids about problems; how to tackle them. "How do you eat an elephant?" Answer: "One bite at the time". See, if you have a problem you break it down is sub-problems, small steps; solve each step and you can do miracles. The distractions are partially successful as distance passes under out feet. Secretly, I wonder if I should have transferred more weight to Rodrup's backpack last night. Not only my legs, but also my shoulders, are beginning to show signs of resentment to the backpack's weight and the rubbing of the straps.

While traversing the woods Raj and I discuss our next destination. I let him know that the last 'hotel' was far below par for the money we pay and insist on the next place being better. Tonight must be one with warmth and hot showers; I specify water quantity and pressure. Soundproof walls may have been mentioned. Laying into him several times results in him making phone calls as he walks effortlessly down the steps. He reassures me it is all under control.

Going up and down the path, we leapfrog the same people time and again: the Koreans, a couple from New Zealand, the Chinese spaghetti girls, the Dutch couple. The Chinese girls are fashionably dressed; shiny bling-bling hats, trendy shirts. They have their phones attached to their backpack playing loud music, no earphones. Really? Here? In this setting? Do we really all need to hear the latest in Chinese pop music in this incredible forest? I am glad we outrun them on one of the steeper parts, leaving the music behind.

After the steps up of the last two days, the majority of the trek is now downhill. We follow a stream, which, at times, turns into a waterfall. I don't know how many steps we hike down, how often we step onto an uneven slippery stone demanding full attention and muscle strength. On the way down the walking poles turn out to be a life saver.

Well into the afternoon we feel a rain drop. We don't have rain covers for our backpacks, and since we left the waterproof backpack behind given the forecast of sunny days, I pray it is only a short rainfall. It's not to be. Soon real rain sets in. Raj indicates to Rodrup to run ahead, to find shelter with his backpack. Like a scared gazelle, the skinny fellow disappears down the path, seemingly unaware he is carrying the bigger of two backpacks. In no time he disappears from sight. We put our raincoats on, and I use my coat as a cape, covering the backpack. We continue trekking. The next thing we know, the heavens really open up. Then it starts hailing. Not little grains of ice, but pea-sized spheres of frozen water. Raj scans and finds a tree with a big canopy; we huddle together around the trunk and partially escape the bombardment from heaven.

As soon as the hail changes back to rain, we hit the trail again. The conditions are treacherous. If you step in the puddles your shoes get drenched with ice water, if you step on the large flat stones you risk breaking your neck since the platform is filled with small ice marbles. About ten minutes further we find Rodrup in the shelter of a tea house. Leendert is tucked under my baseball hat and under the hood of his raincoat, in total isolation. Obviously something is wrong. I ask him how he is, and his non-response ticks me off. I force him too look up. He's crying. He's hit rock bottom. He is cold, tired and "just wants to sleep". I kick myself for not having paid more attention. The early lunch we took was not good enough. He had a small pizza, not half the amount of carbohydrates he needed for the walk we are making. We try to make him eat an energy bar. He refuses. We have little choice but to push on.

In Pursuit of Chocolate

At last the rain stops and we tramp on. I cannot imagine what this place must be like during monsoon. Right now, after only forty five minutes of rain, the path we walk has become filled with puddles. Streams plummet down the mountain and cross the trail. We attempt to avoid puddles, trying to keep our shoes semi-dry.

Ghandruk, today's target, is still a solid distance away. The final twenty painful minutes are nothing but big downhill steps. It's not unlike those big steps you take down in a sports arena or on bleachers in a stadium, each one of them doable but uncomfortable. The difference? The steps are not horizontal concrete and the rainfall cascades down the stairs transforming the path into a river. I call it lovingly "the route of a thousand waterfalls". We give up trying to keep our shoes dry. We've reached the tipping point, that point where you simply don't care anymore. We, and all those around us, have the same mindset by now. Sod it. If we're gonna get wet, we're gonna get wet. No more evasive moves, straight line down from here on; puddle or not. The good thing is that it is not too cold and there is next to no wind.

Finally, we reach Ghandruk. Our official timer informs us we actively walked for 5 hours 30 minutes and 24 seconds, a new record. We enter the 'hotel', and I am happy to see that my assertiveness to Raj has had the intended impact; two nice rooms, beds, blankets, each room with it's own bathroom with shower (even a towel!). And yes, the shower has pressure and enough warm water for all of us. We undress and hang our clothes to dry. Heidi convinces Leendert to take a bite of peanut butter. Within minutes the fat and protein do the trick; his batteries recharge. A second spoonful almost gets him back to normal. The third gives him the strength to shower.

The food in the restaurant is similar to the other places we have been. However, the meal is much more pleasant because the room is nice, cozy and warm. Heidi and I dive into Dahl Baht (lentils), the kids into pasta and pizza. Soon after, the kids ask to go to bed. It doesn't take long for them to fall asleep, and we follow soon after.

And so we get to the final day of our trek. How nice it was to sleep in a bed of regular width, with sheets, and without cold wind flowing around our heads. But how I dislike barking dogs! It started just after one o'clock and it just wouldn't stop. It barked and barked and barked. It was not until well after two that quiet returned. Trust me, that makes for a long, agonizing hour. Honestly, if not as an owner, as a neighbor wouldn't you do something about that? Anyway, outside the barking intermission, we all slept soundly. In the morning, we find that our clothes are, against expectations, mostly dry. Long live wool! Only our shoes are still drenched. We crunch away on breakfast and tea at a leisurely pace, having pushed Raj's timeline back again.

By nine we set off on the way to the bottom of the valley. The first hour-and-a-half is nothing but steps down; big steps, little steps, uneven steps, slippery steps, wobbly steps. Were my calves painful before I woke up, they now are screaming. There is no relief, and pride prevents me from transferring weight to Rodrup. Several donkey caravans pass us and I am thankful for the short break it provides as we press our bodies to the mountain side.

We see an elderly couple sitting in front of their dwelling and Raj informs us that both have bad cases of diarrhea: "if we have something?". 'We' don't, Heidi does. She's always prepared. Given that we have no stomach issues and that the retirees are in desperate need, Heidi dives into her medical kit and pulls out the required medication. She even administers the first dose; "It goes under your tongue, like this", she shows them: "Just let it melt away". Raj helps to translate the rest: "Tonight one more dose. Tomorrow morning the last one". As Heidi offers her compassion, I conclude that the best medicine is the one you can give away.

Leaving the locals in front of their hut, we lean on our poles and continue down the steps. It is with great joy when we finally take our last step down and plant our feet on a level gravel road. From this point on the route back will be on a relatively flat, wide, country road. Back on the semi-flat we set a quick pace, keen to return to our starting point. We see the first car in three days. It looks out of place. Entering the small town which is our end point, we have lunch in the very first reasonable restaurant we see, glad to give our legs a break. While waiting too long for our food, Alicia reports we actively walked 3 hours 28 minutes and 46 seconds that day. It sure felt longer! Lunch arrives and it is quickly devoured. Standing up slowly, we complete the last four hundred meters of the trek. I am sure this sounds like no distance given what we have completed in the last four days. To me, however, these final steps are pure agony. The long wait in the restaurant gave the lactic acid in my calves a chance to settle and my calf muscles feel like blocks of steel. I walk the last part feeling like a penguin and am intensely happy when we arrive at the pick-up point. I look around at the faces. The scene reminds me of the Norman Rockwell drawing of "Going and Coming". I recognize the two sets of smiles - those keen to start their walk, innocent, full of joyful anticipation, and those smiling painfully, happy to have completed the trail, relieved to have crossed the finish-line. I am in the latter category, fearing my legs won't recover quickly, if ever.

The final segment of our escapade is spent back in a small taxi van. It is an hour of restricted movement. We drop a smiling Rodrup and drive the last kilometers to the monastery. At the gate I ask Raj the tally on the 'extras' he paid along the way. This to cover the cost of some of the cokes, beers, and extra tea which were not included in the original price. Heidi and I had calculated this to be about 1000rps a day max. He offers to calculate in detail, but we accept his $40 estimate, which is close to our guess. I tip him a days' salary as I did with Rodrup. And with that we say our goodbyes.

Whereas before the monastery seemed nice but basic, after the recent days it feels like a luxury resort. It felt as if we were coming home after a long holiday, we walked in and inspected our house. Monkey check, check. Kids play in their room, check. Start doing the laundry, check. No running water, check. Stroll around in search of the water monk, check. All is back to normal.

I chat with the water-monk and he invites me up on the rooftop to inspect the installation. Painfully, I follow him up the stairs. As he expected, monkeys have played with the reservoirs. The big black tank feeding water to our room is empty. Showing compassion, the water monk gives me a key to a room in the other building; "they do have warm water there today" he says, with a proud smile. I thank him, and relish in a much-needed warm shower.

At precisely seven that evening the oh-so-familiar clangs call us to dinner. To our surprise, there are no familiar faces around the big pans. The long-term volunteers are gone. Following 'exam week' there is a formal holiday, and they escaped for a little trip. The people now present are short term visitors using the monastery guest house for an overnight stay. We enjoy the familiar noodle soup and give the newcomers nuggets of wisdom regarding the region and life in and around the temple. Back in the room we read and watching movies on iPads. We are truly content and part of us regrets that we will fly back to Kathmandu tomorrow to complete our Nepal experience.

It is strange how a place so unfamiliar only a week before can feel so much like home. The smells, the sounds, the light switches, they all are so familiar. We sleep well, and as I sit behind my computer in the morning, I catch myself with a smile on my face when the vibrations of the 'wake-up-gong' resonate in my ears.

Just before seven we wake the kids. I still walk like an invalid, the muscles in my lower legs hard as rocks. Breakfast is the usual chapati, the bread I have called pita bread for the last two weeks. It is only fitting that on the last day of our stay in Nepal I start calling it by its real name. Today they serve my favorite version - with spicy tomato sauce. We have an easy morning, spending most of it correcting last weeks' exams. To our delight we see everyone did really well. We pack, strap on our gear and lock the door behind us.

We drop of the corrected exams and the room key with Lobsing(-la). He is as detached as usual, focusing on some minutia which occupies his brain for the moment. Despite having our backpacks on, I'm not sure it registers with him that we are leaving. It is a blessing that the 'monk with the voice' sees us out. He thanks us for our contribution, and reiterates that we are always welcome. While saying this solemn goodbye he gives us a slow double handshake. His intensity is captivating, and I am glad he did not ask me for another donation as I am not sure I would have been able to resist!

A customary Maruti taxi waits in front of the temple, and we fold in. Although it rained this morning, there is a short dry spell, and I click my backpack on the roof rack to make the trip more comfortable. Not that I have much choice, trying to pack it inside the car would have been next to impossible. We take the shortest route to the airport. This means little roads full of potholes. I am sure that avoiding the big road and cutting the corners saves our driver a couple of drops of petrol. Likewise, I have no doubt that the wear and tear on his vehicle which bounces from pothole - to rock - to puddle - to asphalt ridge - does more damage and will cost him more in maintenance in the long run than his current petrol savings.

We check in and go through a light security check. Just after three the boarding starts. Unfortunately it turns out it is not our flight. Ours is delayed, but no one seems to know why or by how much. One roll of Oreo cookies and two coffees later we still wait patiently. Two rolls of cookies and three coffees later we step aboard our plane. It is the same plane we saw before; obviously a bus-service Pokhara to Kathmandu, simply hopping back and forth. Regrettably the overcast prevents us from seeing the top of the world one last time. As we cross through the clouds it is a moment of reflection. The monastery has provided us two great weeks; we walk out richer in religious and cultural experience and with fond memories of mountain tops. The cost? A few t-shirts and lost toiletries – our sacrifice to the monkeys.

The next day is spent in Kathmandu. A crazy and busy tourist town. The main road can vary from one-direction-into-town and three lanes out, to three-in and one-out. This does not count two wheelers. The number of vehicles next to one another is dependent on the circumstances.

On the road we cross cows, a truck with a broken axle, a beggar in the middle of the street with a broken leg (I wonder how he got that?) and a fruit cart. In town, we indulge in the things we have missed the past two weeks. After being more or less vegetarian for fourteen days, we devour steaks and burgers. We enjoy fresh fruit and warm showers. I even take a bath to give relief to my still-aching legs. The town is in a festive mood as it is celebrating New Year. Yes, again a New Year. This time the midnight clock welcomes us into 01-01-2072. Not only is Nepal fifteen minutes off to the hour, it also stubbornly maintains its own calendar. It is our third New Year celebration in four months.

Despite the lactic acid in our legs we explore Kathmandu by foot. Using the hotel map we explore. It is hard to know what is an official road and what is just a path. While directionally knowing where we need to go, the next hour-and-a-half can best be described as "purposely being lost in Kathmandu". As adults, we bathe in the wonderful surrounding of the small streets, the Hindu shrines, the tiny open-to-the-elements butcher shops. We soak up the atmosphere of the lilliputian passages, so small two tricycles can't pass. We smile at the sight of monkeys on the temple roof, the teeny barbers shops giving haircuts and shaves. Shops whose door frames are so low they only reach my shoulder. We inhale the smells, listen to the sounds the assortment of bells on small temples, taste the dust of the streets and blink at the visual overload of the brightly colored dresses of the women. The kids are dragging along, being tolerant of our enjoyment but clearly thinking 'okay, just another place, what's the big deal?'.

Often, the minuscule roads we enter seem to dead-end, only to surprise us with an open gate at the end leading to the next courtyard. We have to duck to get out of what seem like inner sanctums. At one point I'm not sure if we walked through someone's private dwelling as we exit through an opening suspiciously looking like the front door of a Hobbit-sized house. From the friendly smiles, the 'Namastes', and the 'chocolate mister' uttered by the kids in the small squares, we know we are off the beaten track in quarters not often visited by non-Nepalis. The density and crookedness of the roads provides such a maze that I need to use the sun to guide me in the right direction. Slight paranoia sets in as I am aware that I don't have the hotel's specific address. The roads are so scaled-down and the overhang of the six-story buildings block the sky so the sun, my reference point, can hardly be seen. I turn left and right purely on gut feel. About to throw in the towel, I realize I can use signs to a larger hotel chain as reference point. When we finally re-discover our hotel, we ask the kids if they want to continue to explore the town. They shake their heads - the past two hours have given them their fill. We hand them the room key and head towards

Thamel. Soon the concentration of foreigners increases, as do the sizes of the shops. We are accosted by people ready to make us a good price on anything touristy, and thus it takes us less than ten minutes to know we, too, want to go back.

That afternoon, we settle the bill of the hotel, drink one more Nepali tea and head to the airport. The driver explains the roads are empty because it is New Years Day. All official institutions and offices are closed. Fine by us! The airport check-in, customs and security is smooth. AirAsiaX runs a good show. Heidi booked the 'comfort row', which means bulkhead seats with ample leg space. As some of the locals board, it is clear from their puzzled and scared faces that an airplane is new to them. Most are standing a bit lost in the aisle trying to figure out where to go. I point to seat numbers on numerous ticket-stubs and show the corresponding numbers posted under the luggage bins. I receive grateful nods and thank yous.

Push back is early, and the flight-deck informs us that all is on plan. KL has thunderstorms and 28 degrees centigrade "but it should not affect us". I cannot imagine what it must feel like for the novice Nepali traveler to land and enter Kuala Lumpur airport. After short two weeks in Nepal walking through the KL mall-like airport feels like we landed on a different planet. The immense shops, bright lights, the dust-free, shiny, level square stone floors, the floor-to-ceiling glass walls and the s p a c i o u s n e s s... is simply overwhelming.

Cambodia - Hit Hard

THE FLIGHT FROM KUALA LUMPUR to Siem Reap is just over two hours and despite flying east, we gain an hour. In other words we set our watches back as we land. We sat in front of the plane, so we are off first, something you appreciate in places like Siem Reap where you get a 'Visa on Arrival'.

We jot our names on the immigration forms and copy the same data onto the customs declaration and visa application. We hand our paperwork to the first in a row of Immigration Officers. She takes the paperwork, the pictures and performs a check, stack, staple activity then hands the pile to Immigration Officer Number Two. From there the passports pass, one by one, from officer to officer, ending up with Number Seven, who's sole task is to ensure the passport is handed back to the right person. I look at the visa. Darn. Cambodia is one of those 'visa sticker' countries. This means a full passport page is sacrificed for one country's admission. A few more of these and we'll run out of pages!

The good news is that we got to the visa counter first, so the entire process takes only ten minutes. I fear that those leaving the plane last will be here for a while, in spite of the large number of officers. In other countries, the process was slow not because the lack of systems, but the lack of people. Here, the lines are created because the officers work in sequence. At least here one sees people working, which somehow makes it less painful.

By the time we get through immigration, our bags have been tossed on the belt. We exit the airport and a friendly driver stands with a sign in hand. As usual our name is butchered, but we recognize it nonetheless.

Our first impressions of Cambodia are - for lack of a better word - festive. The driver begins by wishing us Happy New Year. Wait - what? At first I have some serious doubts about his level of English, but the matter is soon cleared up. Today is Khmer New Year, the biggest holiday of the year. He informs us we have just entered the year 5259, and there will be three days of celebration. The new year means the harvest season has ended and the rainy season is upon us. For the new year, Cambodians clean their houses fanatically, preparing for family visits and, if possible, a rush to their hometown. The city will host numerous special events. There are two Guinness Book Record attempts: the largest cake ever made, and the largest number of people dancing at once. The driver hopes to participate in the second one.

Our hotel is on a dusty road a bit out of town, but it feels like an oasis. We sit in the open reception area overlooking the pool. The only solid structure we see is the reception counter with an adjoining office. Not unlike what's seen in Fiji or Hawaii, the set-up itself is the clearest indication that the temperature is good year-round. It also is evidence that rain typically falls vertically (unlike Scotland where horizontal rain probably has it's own special name).

This lovely boutique hotel has only eight villas, two connected rooms per building. It is small, brand new and quiet. Just perfect. After being on the go and having slept in seven different places in as many days, the idea of not packing and unpacking for a couple of days is very appealing. Especially in a place like this. After the rather rudimentary living in Nepal, we have landed in luxury land. The rooms are spacious - teak chairs with big pillows on the front patio, large beds filled with pillows, a walk-in shower (with hot water!) so big it doesn't need a door, tea making facilities and a bowl filled with colorful tropical fruits. Heaven. Within minutes, bathing suits are on and the overflow pool in the center of the small complex has pulled the youngsters in. We follow, laying on oversized lounge chairs with a coconut in hand - a decapitated nut which holds at least a liter of fresh natural juice. Wow that tastes good!

A feature of all resort hotels like this one is the overpriced laundry service. For vacation travelers needing to wash one shirt or press a dress, I am sure that's fine. To us, long-term travelers who haven't done laundry for a week, the high rate-card doesn't fly. We know it is usually easy to find local cleaning services and we are willing to explore. A quick internet search shows that there are several laundry places between the hotel and town, at almost walking (but definitely biking) distance. Pricing is by the kilo, varying between one and three dollars, depending if you want your wash done individually (meaning it won't touch someone else's garments). For comparison, the hotel charges three dollars to wash one pair of sock. Our total bill would have been seventy dollars! Yeah, no. Being reasonable, I pass by reception and throw out a hook, testing if they are interested in doing laundry at more reasonable pricing. Not even a nibble.

Not discouraged, I request a bike the hotel has for its guests. Ten minutes later I bump down the sandy path, a backpack of dirty laundry strapped on my back, the helmet (offered with the bike) left behind. As a Dutchman, I cannot wear a helmet unless I am on a racing bike or careening down a mountain. On top of that, I am vain enough not to want a bright-red baseball-like helmet on my head while pedaling down the empty, sandy streets of Cambodia. That perspective doesn't change even as I turn onto the parallel road of Highway Number Six into Siem Reap. Now, let me qualify 'highway' to avoid confusion. It is a two-lane asphalt road with occasional traffic lights. The closest laundry shop is closed, but the next one is open and has a lovely display of clothes hanging out on lines in front of the store. With a *Sues-Dei* I greet the people in the shop. In spite of the holiday, the owner and his wife (or perhaps the owner and her husband) happily accept the opportunity to work. I unload our dirty garments into a plastic bucket, which is weighed on a small scale. The shopkeeper points to the wash 'menu' asking me when I want it back. It is New Year, four o'clock in the afternoon, and he offers me express service "all done in under 3 hours, sir". I tell him I am happy to let him take until tomorrow. He calculates and hands me back the receipt. The wash will be ready tomorrow afternoon for a whopping bill of $2.50. Yes, one pair of socks washed in the hotel is more expensive than the week's wash for a family of four in this place. With a *or-koon* (pronounced 'awe-koon') I wave goodbye, mount the bike and head back towards the hotel. As I pedal, I see the Khmer families sitting together and barbecuing along the road, I realize I got a receipt for weight, but we never itemized what I left behind. We didn't even count the pieces. I don't even consider looping back. First of all I have a high trust in people, second, even if I lose a shirt, it still is a good deal!

The afternoon is spent relaxing. The toughest decision is choosing whether to lay on the lounge chairs next to the pool, or those half-submerged in the pool. To end the day, we have dinner in the hotel. We are the only ones doing so, probably because the restaurant pricing is in line with their laundry charges, made for short-visiting guests. We enjoy the Khmer cooking in general, but the Phat Tai is somewhat of a disappointment. In fact, I wonder if something is off. It smells like a dubious shrimp, and I know from personal experience that it only takes one crustacean to ruin a perfectly good evening. Leendert couldn't finish his food so I switch plates, leaving mine on the side. When the waiter inquires if all is okay, I make a remark about my dish. He is gracious receiving the feedback and goes back to the kitchen. Minutes later he returns and admits that the cook tried to make a Phat Tai not having the right ingredients. He apologizes on the cook's behalf and asks if I want something else to compensate "free of charge of course".

Not all relaxing days are stress free

The night was wonderful. With big beds and fresh sheets it is like sleeping on a cloud. I feel mediocre, probably because I nibbled on the dubious shrimp, but the grumbling in my stomach stopped soon after I broke a good sweat. I felt infinitely indebted to Heidi who told me to stop eating as soon as I said I did not trust the food. We sit outside, enjoying the quite morning hours and the sunrise while overlooking the pool reflecting the sky as a spotless mirror.

After breakfast, Leendert and I get into a pleasant philosophical debate. Via a story on Cambodian history and Pol Pot we move to the concept of *Je pense donc je suis* (I think, therefore I am). Perhaps not an obvious jump, but if you know Pol Pot studied in Paris, where Descartes came up with his Latin *cognito ergo sum*, it is not such a big stretch. We reflect on the location of our innermost self, the "I" of our being. Where is "I"? Where does it reside? In my heart, my brain or somewhere else? And where on earth does it go when I go to sleep? Does it stay on earth? How does it find me when I wake up? How can we influence it? It is one of those conversations that makes you acutely self-aware and gets you lost at the same time. After about an hour, Leendert is so self-conscious he needs to stop. Truth be told, so do I.

I decide to get on the bike to collect our laundry. I ask Leendert to come along for some exercise. He does so, grudgingly. Riding to town he complaints about the heat. Each time I slow down to let him ride besides me, he moves his legs even less, falling behind time and again. No matter what I try, he won't ride next to me. I plead, encourage and beg. No success. With droopy shoulders he flatly refuses, 'how much longer do we have to do this?'. Almost falling of my bike from the lack of speed and perhaps influenced by the heat, I reach the point where I get mad. I decide not to wait for him and speed up. To my surprise he stays behind, not caring at all. I guess he is getting older and is staking out his independence. Soon he is so far behind he has lost sight of me. As I stop at the Laundromat,

I see him ride on. Being in his own world, he never saw me stop.

I take my time paying the bill and wait for Leendert to return assuming that at some point he'll realize his is on his own. He does not. I wait. I wait. I reflect on the comments I'll get from Heidi if I return without him. Knowing he typically does not pay too much attention to where we go, and the roads are a bit tricky around the hotel I realize that he probably would not be able to find his way back. Seeing no option, I ride in pursuit. A few blocks further I find him at an intersection waiting. Seemingly unfazed, he just stands there, assuming something will happen. Rather pissed off, I tell him to follow me, suggesting that if he wants to return to the hotel he better stick with me. On purpose, I ride back above average speed. He stays behind, but close enough that he can follow all the way home. Once back I tell him he has just succeeded losing his computer play-time for today and tomorrow. He walks outside and sits down mad. I do the same inside, scared about what might come at me through his teenage years.

To take my mind off things I walk up to reception and order a tuk-tuk to go to Angkor Wat. The young man behind the counter tells me the trip will cost twenty US dollars. I glance at him over the rim of my glasses giving him a stern stare. Really? Twenty dollars? I'm not asking him to wash my socks! I am already dealing with an "I'm mad" hangover because of the incident with Leendert, so I don't need this fellow to charge me a full day tuk-tuk price for a simple ride to Angkor Wat! My looks and subsequent remarks have the desired effect; a manager is called from behind a wall, and he re-negotiates the price. Okay, a driver will take us out there, wait for us and take us back to town for twelve dollars. I agree, mentally noting that I just negotiated a savings of four loads of laundry.

A quarter of an hour later we step into the tuk-tuk. The design of the Siem Reap 'taxi' is new to me. Technically it is called a moto-remork; a perfect translation from French: "motor trailer". And that is precisely what it is. A two-wheeled canvas-roofed cart is hooked onto the back of a motorbike which pulls the contraption. The seat at the rear of the trailer is wide, deep and comfortable, the front seat is narrower but also seats two people easily. Knee-to-knee we ride out over the sandy pathway. Heidi, with her usual charm, tries to unfreeze Leendert who is still not recovered from our clash. As always, she succeeds, and I admire her for it.

The tuk-tuk brings us to the ticket office a few kilometers outside of Siem Reap. We learned that if we buy tickets for tomorrow after 4:45p.m. today, we can access the site today for free. Since that is only fifteen minutes from now, we wait until the appointed time and buy our three passes. Three because children under twelve (like Alicia) can go in for free, provided they proof their age by showing a valid passport. Although we don't have Alicia's passport with us, they say that is no issue for today (the park closes at five-thirty) and they let her in.

We continue our route, learning that what is referred to as Angkor Wat is not a building or two, but a huge park with roads leading to the various temples. Despite the fact that we are getting close to formal closing time we are surrounded by locals making their way to the temples. Rows of cars are stuck in traffic. Our tuk-tuk driver weaves through the cars and passes over the shoulders dropping us right next to the entry. The place is packed with partying people. Then it dawns on us. It is the New Year celebrations. Obviously Angkor Wat is the place to be! The driver drops us off and tell us where he'll meet us one hour later. We drown in people. We make an appointment with the kids where we'll meet in case we lose one another. Submerged in music and surrounded by crowds we cross the main bridge and enter one of the most iconic complexes of Angkor Wat. It is simply stunning. We walk around for an hour, impressed as is all it is proclaimed to be. Tonight we only see one temple, but it is a great taster for the days to come.

As the sun turns into an orange ball over the horizon, people dance in front of large beer stands, presumably erected solely for the New Year festivities. According to Alicia, the locals are doing *'la danse des canards'*. It is a weird and out-of-place sight. You might not know the French term, but my bet is that you know the dance. It is probably one of the silliest dances in the world. People place their hands on the hips, flap their elbows and take small steps forwards, sideways and backwards; preferably in group, if possible in sync. Originally created by the Swiss composer Werner Thomas, the song - and the silly steps and arm movement that go with it - has over three hundred and fifty versions. Originally called the *Tchip Tchip*, it clearly taps into some universal and rudimentary dance gene. Under normal circumstances, it lays dormant but when the conditions are right the gene is activated. I will admit to having been infected once or twice in my college years.

I suspect the dance might have outpaced wrist watches as the number one Swiss export product. The dance and song combination is known all over the world, its name translated to many languages. Usually it associated with a reference to birds; the English call it the Chicken Dance, the Germans *Vogelktanz*, the Japanese *Okashi Tori* (sweet bird), the Spanish *el bale de los pajaritos*. Over the years I noticed the *Tchip Tchip* goes well with large volumes of alcohol and that having dance skills is absolutely no

In Pursuit of Chocolate

prerequisite to enjoy the sound or movement.

Here in Cambodia, a group of guys at one of the larger beer stands is in a particular good mood. Listening to the well-known tune, they move around flapping their elbows. As we pass, they attempt to have us join them. Had I been on my own I might have done so, but since we have tuk-tuk waiting, we walk on. I can see the relief on the faces of the children. Clearly the *Tchip Tchip* gene either develops later in life, or is suppressed in children when parents try to participate.

Our tuk-tuk driver is at the appointed gate and zips us into town. The warm air blows around us and gives some respite from the stagnant heat. Over the noise of his two-stroke engine, I ask the driver to take us to a local restaurant, specifying I want him to avoid the touristy area. He says he will, and I hope he understood me through his helmet. When he stops in front of a restaurant he says "this is where I sometimes eat". The restaurant is still way upscale from what I intended, but it looks nice and we are swayed by his personal accreditation. Soup, spring rolls (both fried and fresh) and other local dishes are ordered. Two of the dishes are served out of coconuts Each of us claims to have ordered the best dish on the menu. I guess our driver did okay. We pay fifteen dollars a head, which I find overpriced, but since we are in a tourist town I probably shouldn't expect much else. Walking back from the restaurant to the town center we pass the typical local restaurants where we had wanted to eat. Having said that, given the quality of the food we just had, it is hard to complain. We take note of the location of these local-looking places for the coming days; perhaps we'll want to enjoy the real local 'off the grill' or 'out of the pan' dishes they advertise.

Before grabbing a tuk-tuk back to the hotel we get some cash. An ATM provides us with American Dollars. Although the Cambodian Riel is the local currency, the second currency in the country is the US Dollar. The truth is that in the more touristy areas the dollar dominates and one typically only sees the Riel appear in change. I am reminded of my old economics lessons from University. In Econ 4-'O'-whatever, the "money supply" was explained. I have a flash-back to Monetary Policy, Milton Friedman, John Keynes and others. Suddenly, I remembered M1, M2, and M3 (different money circulations). At the time, it surprised me that most physical dollars are not traded within the US boarders. High volumes of dollars are used abroad, in illegal deals south of the border, and in Asian countries. What I only realize now is that the previous sentences had commas. Linking Opium wars of the past to Asia, and perhaps movies, I assumed the dollars were used in Asia for illegal transactions. Now I realize the greenback is merely a stable currency of trade, not unlike when they were originally introduced in the US in the 1860's (these promissory 'demand notes' which were unique in that they were printed on both sides, the backside green - hence the nickname).

With dollars in hand we hop back in a tuk-tuk to the hotel, but not until I negotiate him down to $4, telling him I know the way. He accepts easily. I know we are overpaying him by at least twenty five percent, but since we are with four and a bit out of town it seems reasonable. After night falls, we splash in the pool, enjoying floating while looking up at the stars. Drifting in the warm water with no air or light pollution, we stare into the immense darkness of the universe. It isn't until mosquitoes find us that we return to the coolness of our rooms.

Angkor Wat - What a site

After a peaceful night, Heidi and I spend the first hours of the morning exploring the internet on how to navigate the Angkor temples. We have a moto-remork ordered for ten, so we aren't in a particular rush. This turns out to be a good thing. We both search the net, finding it frustrating. As mentioned before, Angkor Wat itself is only one building in the complex, and a very impressive one at that. This is the largest religious complex on earth - four times the size of Vatican City. Yet what is referred to as Angkor Wat is actually much more. It is an immense national park which was the center of the Khmer Empire in the twelfth century. Historically a city, it had many temples spread out over acres of land. That said, as famous as the site is, none of the two million visitors who visited just last year has left us a good description of how to visit the various temples. We find itineraries that are helpful if you are Mr. or Ms. One-Day-Tourist. We're not. We have several days at our disposal and want to go a bit off the beaten track.

Opting to concoct our own route, we grab a paper map. We mark the particular locations to visit but find it tricky to decipher the time it will take between various temple sites. Depending on which report one reads, the travel times vary dramatically. Annoyed, I vent my frustration to Heidi. As we discuss the plan I also realize how only ten years ago, before the internet robbed us from both patience and willingness to discover, we ....well... discovered. We just went to a place and 'figured it out'. Now we expect to know everything before arrival. I'm convinced that in the future people will speak of the AI era, as opposed to BI era; After Internet and Before Internet. In this AI period, search engines have take over

In Pursuit of Chocolate

our willingness to explore; we just 'look it up' and sheepishly follow the highest five-star rating from the masses, assuming that is best. It probably isn't. Knowing more does not always improve the situation, it kills the emotional thrill, just like knowing how a magician does the trick kills the magic of positive bewilderment.

Be that as it may, we piece the day together, at least enough to be able to give instructions our tuk-tuk driver. Around nine I open the curtains in the kids room. I tell them that in an hour we'd be roaring down the dusty path pulled by the Honda engine, so "it's time to get up for breakfast". Alicia gets dressed…in her bikini; "But mom promised we could swim first". The statement comes with a little pout, her head tilted off to the left. It's the kind of look no self-respecting dad can say no to. Minutes later I find myself in my *lederhosen* swimming trunks (a souvenir from our Austrian life) rinsing the sleep out of my eyes while being pushed under.

We all feel pretty well rested, except for Heidi. I notice she takes it easy at breakfast, mainly ingesting medication to avoid frequent bathroom stops (you catch my drift). At the agreed time we find our driver up-front at reception. We explain the tour we'd planned. He nods both understanding and approval, but suggests a few practical changes; pointing at the paper map he says "if we loop this way, we can time lunch in an air-conditioned restaurant and avoid the tourist buses". We accept his alternative and plop ourselves in the trailer.

The tuk-tuk takes us into the park, and since we have the tickets in hand from the night before, we avoid the queues going in. We zip past the iconic Angkor Wat Temple which appears on the Cambodian national flag. Translated the 'Capital Temple', it is a prime example of Khmer architecture, and lit by the morning sun it is hard to find superlatives which truly capture the view.

We visit Banteay Samre, East Mebon, Pre Rup, Banteay Ksei - each and every one truly impressive. Our expectations were high, but these constructions are unrivaled. Even Machu Picchu might have to bow to Angkor. The parallels are clearly there; both are huge construction marvels, ancient, from rich historic empires long since gone and re-discovered from the overgrowth of nature. But where the awe from Machu Picchu came from its amazing the placement on the mountain tops, Angkor has to rely only on the Khmer people built. Honestly, between the two, it is a toss-up which I'd tell you to go to if you had to choose only one.

The hardest thing about tourist places like these is…well…the tourists. They are noisy, at times disrespectful and often have the innate ability to appear in the most horrendous reflective clothing, lingering right on that spot you are trying to take a picture of. Not only that, they seem to inadvertently work in cahoots. As the pink-hatted lady exits a shot, invariably the overweight, fluorescent-yellow-trousered one makes her appearance. Argh. Luckily, the research we did provided us with the best 'stay away from the crowds' itinerary one can hope for. With a bit of patience we end up taking some great shots without being totally photo bombed. It probably also helps that the Cambodians themselves celebrated New Year the day before, and are recovering at home.

One of the truly unique features of the Angkor site is that one can not only see them but climb all over. I am sure that over the next ten years much will change, but for now, it is possible to walk and climb over the temples, the ramparts, the ledges. Some parts are not for the faint hearted nor for out of shape people. Climbing the steps of the steep buildings often requires hands and feet. Standing on top, near unprotected edges lead to multi-level drops. We relish every corner and crevasse, walking over edges which would be deemed so dangerous in the USA that even after signing waivers you wouldn't be allowed on them. No doubt, if the kids ever return, there will be specific paths to follow, ropes placed with 'no entry', and railings erected. Boy are we lucky to be visiting now!

Lunch is at one of the few restaurants in the park. Sitting around the table we reflect. We anticipated temple fatigue, but none of us are suffering. So far each temple has been sufficiently different that we are pulled in, anxious to explore and enjoy the sites. The toughest thing is the heat. Climbing temples in the tropics is no mean feat. We drink lots of water, have fresh coconuts, and drink, drink and drink some more. As the day progresses Heidi's internal sewer system does not untangle itself, making the air-conditioned lunchroom - with proper toilets - a welcome stop. The kids and I enjoy lunch while Heidi sticks to a watermelon juice and iced tea; even white rice has zero appeal.

Once we are re-energized (and somewhat cooled down), we get back on the trail and visit Ta Keo and the world famous Ta Prohm. The latter has been used for movies like Tomb Raider. It is well known for the way silk-cotton trees have overgrown the buildings. Like the other temples, this dazzling building is in the process of being restored, one stone at the time. It is a tricky balance because the trees and strangler fig that engulf it have become such an unique feature that restoration is done while trying to maintain "a condition of apparent neglect". An interesting concept. Restore, but don't restore completely. Also interesting is that much of the restoration seems to be sponsored by foreign nations. China's sponsoring sign is up at one temple, India has a notice board at another, and so on. We complete today's circuit, knowing we have another two days to spend in the compound.

Quietly sitting in the tuk-tuk we observe life along the roads. We see many Cambodia families having picnics, hammocks tied everywhere. If hammocks aren't available people swing and hang on thick jungle vines. The only thing ruining the otherwise picture-perfect scenes is the plastic trash on the ground. Perhaps a left-over from the New Year celebration, but still a real shame.

Arriving back in Siem Reap, Heidi makes good on a promise to the kids. She takes them to a fish-tank pedicure and massage place. Sound confusing? Let me explain. In this set-up you sit on a bench and puts your feet in a large glass fish-tank. Instantly, pinkie-sized fish swim up and start nibbling on your feet and toes, considering the calluses a gourmet dinner. The slogan is 'feed me your dead skin'. Alicia and I go first. Keeping both feet in the water is horrendously difficult, especially for those who are ticklish. I am one of those. A good number of the fish decide that the bottom part of my toes is especially tasty. I feel tortured but have tears of laughter running down my face. Meanwhile, I feel sad for the Chinese couple sitting next to me. From the moment my feet land in the aquarium it was clear my Dutch skin was tastier - or at least more plentiful - than Chinese skin. While the young man continues to get somewhat of a biting, his girlfriend only has the odd fish nibbling on her feet.

It takes the better of five minutes to compose myself and resist the urge to kick the fish or pull my feet out. Luckily, one gets used to being tickled after a while. Now more at ease, I start looking around. Behind us is a tank with bigger fish - two to three thumbs long. After another five minutes I try my luck. I swivel around on the wooden bench and place my feet in tank number two. The bite is harder, but having passed nibbling 1-'oh'-1, I am able to keep my feet in the bath. Clearly one can get used to anything. By now the entire family is sitting side by side on the bench offering their feet to the swimming callus removers. Skin-a-la-European evidently is a tasty dish. Our cleaning massage lasts for about half an hour. The bill comes to eight dollars; not bad for four pedicures!

Our moto-remork takes us back to the hotel. Heidi immediately crawls between the sheets while I join the kids for a quick dive in the pool. The kids and I eat dinner while Heidi sleeps. Halfway through the starters, we are suddenly in the dark. No electricity in the building or anywhere. A minute later the lights are back on, thirty seconds later back off. They cycle intermittently. Candles appear on the table and the waiter explains that electricity is not something they can depend on this far out off town. The lights continue to flicker, but are off far more than on. The candles give reasonable light making for a romantic scene. The only issue is the heat. Without electricity, the fans stop blowing, making our core temperature rise quickly.

In the background we hear a thump-thump-thump bass beat which overrides the American country music spilling from the hotel speakers. Not good. It definitely ruins the 'romantic' atmosphere. I inquire with the waiter. He explains that in Cambodia it is lucky to get married on the first day of the New Year; "There is a wedding party going on about one kilometer up the street". They obviously like loud music. My mind is with Heidi, and I pray she is well in dream land by now. Hearing music in the background when she is trying to fall asleep is a catastrophe. Soon I get my answer. Heidi joins us at the table, but clearly not attracted by the food. Even the earplugs were not able to block out the thumping. The waiter anticipates the problem and says "the good news is that we are out of town. In town music can play until very late. In the countryside, where we are, parties are only allowed to go until ten p.m." I guess the farmers need to get their rest. As promised, around ten the music winds down. We all go to bed happy.

Siem Reap - Not as relaxing as planned

Early in the morning we learn that wedding parties in the region are multi-day events. While there is a noise curfew in the evening, nothing prevents parties to starting back up early in morning. At six am, the penetrating boom-boom-boom restarts. It contrasts harshly against the quiet of the morning. In fact, since we are only separated by a flat field, it feels like we are living in a speaker box. Yuck!

Thankfully Heidi feels better, her stomach somewhat settled. We have a coffee on the comfy couches in reception and run into the hotel manager who inquires; "how is your stay?". He's interested since the hotel is new and he is looking for feedback. He asks, we answer. He gets the full run-down. We start with the positive, the rooms, the friendly staff, the pool. Next we lean into him about the background music, the laundry pricing and the fact that the restaurant is well overpriced. We have an interesting discussion about the restaurant, him saying that given the low number of guests, the premium is needed to make it viable. I point out that we (and other guests) travel into town since it is still far cheaper than eating in, even including the tuk-tuks out and back. I also mention that the first night the food wasn't that good and that the electricity is about as dependable as that of a monastery in Pokhara. The manager takes it well and takes ownership for the issues, except for the wedding music. That is an issue he unfortunately cannot address. However, for the other inconveniences and in thanks for the feedback, he offers a meal in the restaurant in the evening. We happily accept.

We have breakfast and Heidi slowly starts to reintroduce solids to her body. We spend the rest of the day taking it easy. The kids are in Heidi World High, alternated with some dips in the pool. We try to ignore the wedding music, and are glad that day two of the wedding is usually in a restaurant in town after which people leave for home. Around midday I escape the sounds by jumping on a bike, a backpack full of dirty laundry on my back. As I make my way out of the door Heidi calls after me "try to find a message play". I stop my bike and walk back; "say what?". "Try to find a massage place" she repeats herself. I nod and am about to ride out as she stops me again. "Here, find this place" she says as she hands me a coupon. I pocket the paper coupon and head out.

Biking in Cambodia in April is a challenge. It is all about finding the right speed/heat balance. As any Dutchman will tell you, wind is your worst enemy on a bike. It is unseen but takes disproportionate amounts of efforts to battle. Nine out of ten times, it's in your face. This is actually true since your own speed creates headwind. Note, unlike in The Netherlands, headwind in Cambodia is good; it provides a bit more cooling for the distance traveled. Pedaling along, I think of Reaganomics. Yes, Reagonomics and the Phillips curve. The basic thought behind that principle was that by lowering taxes the spendable income of the average American would increase. With more disposable income, they would spend and thus inject cash in the economy. This would create an economic boom. The boom, in turn, would result in more tax revenues, filling the tax hole. Simply put, less gives more in the end; more less. The trick is finding the right equilibrium and not overdoing it. Back to the bike ride. The concept can be perfectly re-applied to biking in the heat of the day in Cambodia, but in reverse. Reducing cycling speed means one's core temperature will not rise as fast (that's good), but also that you generate less headwind for cooling (that's bad). Riding slower also means that total travel time goes up, so you will be longer in the heat (that's bad). So while slowing down takes less effort and avoids the body temperature to rise, slowing down too much doesn't cool enough. Again, it is a matter of balance. The trick is to find that magic spot of equilibrium on the curve. The point where if you pedal harder you heat up, if you ride slower you heat up.

As I contemplate and aim to find the right speed I can feel the dryness of the road dust on my teeth and the back of my throat. I look around for a coconut to slurp down in order to replace the liquid that has evaporated from my skin while trying to find the 'coupon' massage place. Both have momentarily perfected the skill of hiding. I zigzag through the city center of Siem Reap. Finally, I find a cute collection of small little passages with restaurants, bars, clothes shops and bakeries well laid out in a grid form. There is an undeniable French influence in this town, including the look and feel of the restaurants. Sadly, there is also the good French habit of awful sign-posting. Even when I ask locals they do not know the address of the massage parlor. It takes some doing, but I finally find a drink stand *and* the massage place. I book a session for the entire family late in the afternoon. Having completed the task, I ride home, ever so careful to find the right speed/heat balance.

I swim with Alicia and Heidi and we start our 'where do we go next' searches. Even if one knows the destination in general, finding the right hotel is not always easy. We research until it's time to go with a moto-remork to the town center. Before the massage, we want get some food into the kids; a chicken quesadilla should do the trick. Next we head to the spa. For 1½ hours we get a Khmer massage and are kneaded, oiled and have our extremities pulled on. A Khmer massage combines normal massage with pressure points, and I enjoy the session. Compared to western prices, it is a bargain. For the combined six hours of massage we pay $70. For good form the girls polish the afternoon off with a pedicure while Leendert and I wait in a restaurant having virgin Mojito's and beers respectively.

Since it is dinner time, we decide to have a burger in the same place we snacked earlier. To our surprise, Alicia doesn't take a single bite. She is not feeling well and goes down hill quickly. She looks pale in the tuk-tuk and back at the hotel she wants to go straight to bed. Heidi makes a quick check and indeed, she is running a fever. Not good. On the up-side, the wedding party behind our hotel has stopped, on the down side, another has started up not much further away. Again, as per good Cambodian tradition, the deafening speakers produce the same base-beat which filled our surroundings for the last two days. Note to travelers: avoid the first days of the Cambodian New Year! Heidi and I are to the point of seriously considering relocating to a place not prone to music. The continuous beat is simply not acceptable for four more days.

But then we are interrupted. Alicia walks in, boiling hot – trash bucket in her hand, saying "my head hurts", and "I really do not feel well". We lead her to our bathroom. She is hotter than I remember ever having seen anyone before. We attempt to cool her down with wet towels, but it is as if the water evaporates from the towel as soon as I place it on her. I grab a small towel out of the freezing compartment of the fridge (our trick for traveling on hot days). No use, it's impossible to get her temperature down. As concerned parents we are thinking cause, emergency measures, local doctors. A quick research on the internet: how are Cambodian hospitals? Then Alicia throws up. If there is anything that gives more relief to the human body than when it throws itself in reverse gears, I have yet to encounter it. Within five minutes after filling the bottom of the bucket Alicia's temperature is coming down. Another five minutes and her body goes limp as she dozes off. For the second time on the trip, that one day that we eat international food and she gets food poisoning!

We surf and determine that Cambodian hospitals are better avoided, so we are semi-nervous and take turns keeping watch. I take the first shift, Heidi moves to the bed in the other room. I sincerely hope Alicia rid herself of all that was necessary. Sitting on the bed looking at her I realize how even an atheist or agnostic converts instantly, willing to pray and plead with Jesus, Mohammed, Buddha or any other deity the moment their child gets sick. You never know, right? In cases where the pain is really bad, parents will even asks the appropriate almighty to take the suffering and agony from the kid and place it upon themselves; happy to take their child's place. I am no different. At 23:30, with the new wedding party music going outside (I guess they are just within the city boundaries), I make my prayer wondering what happened to that nice and relaxing day we planned.

And you know what, praying works! The gods listened! Sort of. One of the gods must have had a sense of humor! Alicia's illness takes over my body. However, the Almighty never informed me that suffering is infinite, and there is enough suffering to go around. Giving me suffering does not reduce the load on Alicia. Before midnight I am in bad shape. Really bad shape, fever spiking and all. I will spare you of the details of the delusions, the shivering, the sweating, the buckets, and the toilet escapades. Let it be known that by mid-morning the next day Leendert followed suit, and we had three people down. Luckily another quick prayer I made was heard: "please dear Lord, do not let Heidi get this same bug!"

The next two days were a pretty sad sight. Suffice it to say that it was a good thing we had connecting bedrooms and two bathrooms. At one instance queuing actually took place, and trust me, that pushes many boundaries. Heidi, the angel from heaven, turned out not only to be schoolmaster and teacher extraordinaire, but an excellent as a caring nurse as well. Two days went by excruciatingly slow despite the fact that most were spent in a state of sleep or half slumber. Except for Heidi, no one left the room for two days. Room service was waved off at the door, we only took the fresh towels. The diary entry of these April days were short. And I quote "bed-sleep-toilet-bed-sleep-toilet-be..- oh, no toilet again….".

Siem Reap - Relaunched

The good thing about being sick is that it makes you appreciate getting back on your feet. By day three we are not back one hundred percent, but we are willing to give breakfast a shot; green tea, dry toast and an egg. The staff, happy to finally see guests back at breakfast have little to do and try to make our stay pleasant. Each of us gets a cup with butter (on ice), two kinds of jam, croissants, '*escargots*' (the rolled French pastries) and fresh buns. The vast majority remains untouched. We feel still frail and dry toast is about all we can manage. Back to the room we take a break, yes, a break. It is stunning how exhausting the first meal of the day can be, especially if you haven't had one in three days!

The food gives us strength and combined with being fed up seeing the inside walls of the hotel room we are willing to plan an afternoon activity. Heidi finds something which doesn't take too much effort, a pottery class. A moto-remork takes the kids and me to ceramics class. Heidi, having been on duty for the last days, prefers a break at the pool. Fair game. To my surprise, at the Art Gallery, the tuk-tuk driver gets paid by the owner. The cost of the ride was included in the price of the activity. Nice.

As the kids plop down on red plastic garden chairs behind swiveling potters-wheels, I have my credit card swiped and realize why the Gallery was happy to pay the driver. Any apprehension I might have disappears quickly as I see the kids smile and learn the art of pottery making. The wheels are foot operated, counter clockwise, with their right foot. The instructor insists the 'counter clockwise' direction is important. I watch and wonder. Would spinning the other way exacerbate the Coriolis effect? Would it therefore be different on the southern hemisphere? Would being left or right handed not be of greater importance? Curiosity gets the better of me, so I look it up on the internet. Apparently the counterclockwise movement is standard in the western dominated cultures. In China and Japan they go clockwise. And while cultural habit thus seem to be the main reason, other arguments float around. One is that using the right foot to push the wheel is easier, another, more technical kinesiological explanation states that for most people the right hand is best suited for the fine motor skills (right handedness), and thus preferred for the outside of the object. We learn everyday.

Whatever the reason, the instructor has the kids spin the wheel counterclockwise and shows them how first to make the clay into a ball and smack it down in the center of the pivoting plate. This in it self provides great entertainment. Nothing like slamming a piece of wet malleable material on a hard surface. Next he shows how to wet hands frequently while making the ball into a blob, into a tall blob, into a tall blob with a hole in the top. Then comes the tricky part; raising the edges of the rudimentary ashtray-looking object into a bowl. Moving the wheel with you foot as your hands shape the walls of the object is far from easy. Once the edges are raised enough, the top is cut with a metal wire for a clean edge. To complete the piece, it gets a work-over with a wet sponge to make it completely smooth; a steel wire is passed under the object to pry it loose from the spinning plate. *Et voilà*, done. The kids get several tries. The first three times the teacher jumps in at critical intervals, offering a helping hand, making it look easy. By try number four and five they are on their own.

Being youngsters, their creative minds start flowing and they attempt making something a bit different. Leendert seems to have his mind set on something like the Tulip Vases seen at Chatsworth but struggles to get the clay to do what he wants. Clearly the vases from the Duke of Devonshire's residence is one step too far, something he is not quite willing to accept. Frustration builds. Meanwhile Alicia, seeing her brother do something different, doesn't hold back. Her construction keeps going off center, her creations return to a mangled blob of twirly clay time and again. Without the instructor's helping hand, making pots is not easy. Each renewed attempt means more water is added, which unfortunately causes the relatively dry clay to get softer and muddier, making it harder to handle. This doesn't help the process or the mood. It takes more than half an hour, but then both cave in. Fuming with frustration, they return to basics, to what the coach showed in the beginning, simple bowls reappear.

I am delighted to learn this isn't the end of the session. Finishing with two grumpy kids frustrated with their own lack of skill and dumbed down creativity would not be good. Luckily there is decoration to be done. With a wooden skewer, drawings are made in the -still wet- clay of the urns just created. Samples of Angkor floral designs are shown and copied. Not totally unexpected, by the second bowl creativity takes over again. For a moment Leendert threatens an aboriginal design (dot-dot-dot), but luckily – from a time perspective – decides against it. They apply themselves full-heartedly for the next hour and the results are a nice blend of local design and their own creativity. At the end of the session the kids can choose which one they want fired. The finished product (if not broken in the oven) will be brought to our hotel the next day. The selection is made and we hop in a taxi back to Le Trèsore D'Angkor where we find Heidi in good shape. At last, with the family fully recovered we can book our follow-up tour of the Angkor Wat temples. It also means that we can go into serious planning mode for the travels of the upcoming weeks.

How nice it is the next morning to have the entire family at the breakfast table, enjoying food again. We meet our moto-remork driver 'mister Thoeun', who was happy to see us after our absence of the last few days. Reviewing our proposal, he reverses the order by which we'll visit the temples. We bump down the driveway to the main road when Leendert decides to count cars. Toyotas to be specific. This brand seems to have a powerful grip on the Cambodian car market, or at least in Siem Reap. I help him out. I count the total cars, Leendert keeps track of the Toyotas. At least at first. Soon he switches to counting the non-Toyotas, as that is easier. A positive spin-off of our exercise is that it offers Alicia a chance to practice her math; she gives interim updates calculating the percentages. By the time we reach the Angkor Wat gates, Alicia does the final math: 76% of all cars are Toyotas if you include the Toyota-owned Lexus brand. That is a cornered a market if I ever saw one.

Entering the park we enjoy the smells, the hot air and the sights of Cambodian life on wheels. Over the last months we have become accustomed to what can be transported on two-wheelers; stacks of banana-filled boxes, piles of woven baskets, fridges, hunks of meat, cages with chickens. Today we see a guy transporting pigs on his motorized bike. Notice the 's'. Not 'a' pig, not small little baby pigs, two fully grown pigs. They lay on the back of his bike, feet in the air, bound together. I am amazed his vehicle can carry the weight as much as I am stunned he is able to keep the balance. As a second, similar, bike passes I am astonished to notice that it is actually live transport! Not meat transport, the pigs are wiggling as the driver cruises up the road. I guess it'll be fresh pork chops for lunch.

About thirty minutes into the park we arrive at Angkor Thom. For those wondering why the 'Angkor' returns in so many of the names it is the Khmer name for city. The Angkor Thom site consists of Bayon Temple, Baphuon Temple, and at least eight other named – but less well known – temples. Upon entry into a complex, we show our entry pass.

For Alicia, we need to show her passport. Kids under twelve go in free, but given her height, the locals don't take her age at face-value. 'Yes, here is the passport' and 'Yes, Alicia is allowed in for free', 'yes she is tall for her age....'. The guards can't get over that this 11-year-old is way taller than them.

Bayon temple is as stunning as the sites we saw a few days before. While Khmer temples are similar in some ways, each and every one is different enough to feel unique and thus fun to explore. We continue to the next. It is a short hop to Baphuon, an immense temple at the end of what must be a two hundred meter long elevated pathway. The path is supported by hundreds closely placed columns, four-wide, all the way to the temple entrance. Given it is April, the hottest time period of the year, sweat is rolling down our backs. Walking to a drink vendor, I realize I left my wallet in the backpack with Mr Thoeun in the moto-remork. Tough choice. Do we survive without water for the next half hour or do I go to the spot where he is waiting for us to get my money? I decide on the latter, making haste, not wanting to miss too much of what the others see. The walk reinforces how large this complex is. I thought I could pop out and back quickly, but the walk is close to a kilometer. I find Mr Thoeun laying across the back seat, eyes closed. As I grab my wallet, a bottle of water and a coke out of the cooler, he opens his eyes, startled to see me. I explain my early return, consider asking him to drive me back the 300 meters to an entry path, but decide against it. Walking back, I realize that at the pace I am going I sweat more than I can possibly rehydrate my body, so I slow down. This has the benefit that I pay closer attention to my surroundings. The 'elephant terrace' I am passing consists of meters and meters of bas relief sculptures. Incredibly detailed, absolutely stunning.

Heidi and the kids wait patiently and thirsty in front of the temple entryway in the shade of a big tree. I buy a big bottle of water from a vendor and tell them I am a bit surprised they waited for me. "You ran off with the entry tickets and Alicia's passport, so we had little choice". They aren't upset. They enjoyed the surroundings and the break was pleasant. Walking up to the guard we ready ourselves for the "yes Alicia is..."-routine, but only Heidi gets stopped. Her shoulders are not covered, and it is an active Buddhist temple. Oops, her pashmina too is in the backpack with Mr Thoeun. I offer to run out and back one more time, but Heidi chooses to sit this one out and watch us climb the stone edifice.

The temple buildings are tall with steep sides. By the time we make it to the top, we are totally drenched. Leendert and Alicia slurp down the water. We make the tour on top, take pictures, and climb down. As I do so, I reflect again that in other places you would have to sign wavers, attach yourself to safety lines, wear helmets, knee protectors, declare to be sane, capable and able, and to understand that - due to the beating sun (for which the owners do take not responsibility) - the stones might be hot. Here in Cambodia a local guy just mentions it is wise to hold on, as some steps are very slippery. They are. I reiterate, climbing these ancient buildings is not for the faint-hearted.

We re-join Heidi and walk towards the Leper King Temple, passing the extraordinary wall of sculptures. Along the way we buy more water. One bottle is emptied immediately, a second survives less than five minutes before disappearing down our throats. Hydrating is a losing battle as you climb the temples in this season.

We skip at least ten more buildings, only viewing them from a distance and head out of Angkor Thom. As we navigate through the North Gate, passing live elephants and their masters on their way in. Not much later we get to the extraordinary Preah Khan Temple. It is built on a pattern of a cross, one axis 250 meters long, the other 200. As we pass the center point, a guy in a police uniform pro-actively starts telling us about the building, the historic facts. He takes us to spots we would other wise have missed. He points out the library, the dance hall, the prayer area. He offers to take our pictures - from the best vantage points - and effectively gives us a private tour. As we leave him I give him two dollars for his unsolicited effort, figuring he makes more money in tips than our driver does carrying us around. If he gets four or five customers an hour, he probably nets forty dollars a day. That would be twice Mr. Thoeun's income; on top of his civil servant salary, and no cost in petrol or anything else. Not bad…and definitely worth the two dollars I gave him. Leendert later makes an astute observation about this guide; something he seems to have in common with all the Cambodian people. They don't seem to talk about 'Cambodia' but always refer to 'my country', as if – almost – ashamed to call it by its name. We wonder why.

During lunch we replenish our liquids. I down two coconuts. The juice drinks easily and perks me up. We open a discussion with the children about the volunteering we are doing. We ask them what they liked about the assignments; what they didn't. Trying not to lead them, we ask open questions. It turns out they like teaching more than other support work, that they prefer living with a family more than being in a hostel with other volunteers. Both kids are quite explicit that they prefer to be in a place where they can communicate with the students. We like their logic and agree with their perspectives.

The unfortunate part is that our recent research (where the four of us could be placed) only showed projects which were not teaching, in hostels, typically working in orphanages. We conclude that if we don't find a 'right' assignment we'll skip the plan to do one more project and just continue the travels. It felt good to have this adult conversation and make the decision together with them.

While eating dessert and drinking a coffee we check around the table for 'temple-fatigue'. None of us suffer. Even the kids are happy to see two more, as we had planned. The next temple on the schedule, Neak Poan, is walking distance from the restaurant. We take a long boardwalk across swampland. The water is dirty and it stinks. Leendert quips that it is so smelly that even the water would like to escape. Approaching an island in the middle of the swamp we spot two fishermen. Really? Fishing? In this water? I am glad that an hour before, in the restaurant, I changed my mind and didn't order fish soup!

Neak Poan itself is a round construction and looks like a large basin, effectively a round, empty swimming pool. If Neak Poan was in any other setting, it would be awe inspiring and not pale compared to the fountains of Versailles. But here, against the backdrop of the other temples we have seen, it seems small and insignificant in scale or structure. Somehow the fact that is was built on an island placed in a man-made rectangular water-pond stretching nine hundred meters by three and a half kilometers doesn't impress us. Maybe we do have temple fatigue after all!

As we hike back over the boardwalk we pass a man with a wooden leg. His replacement leg is no more that a round hardwood post sticking out from under his tied-up pants, pirate-like. It's a painful image and a stark reminder not to walk outside the formal paths in Cambodia.

The five years of Pol Pot's Khmer Rouge regime not only killed twenty five percent of the Cambodians (yes, a quarter of the population), but maimed many in all the years since. One has to travel just a bit in Cambodia to see the many landmine victims.

Back at the moto-remork, Mr Thoeun tells us that rain is coming. He just got off the phone and his friend told him Siem Ream is very wet. Unfazed, we continue our tour to the last temple of the day: Ta Som. Coming from Northern Europe, we are not going to back down because of a bit of rain. I'm glad we didn't cut the trip short. I won't give you the superlatives, but it is worth the visit to see the intact state of this last temple; the carvings, the decorations, the faces and the depicted scenes. What is even better is that on the way back we see the wet roads, but completely missed the rain.

Riding towards the hotel I notice that along the road there are many shops that have storefronts lined with bottles on metal racks. Square Johnny Walker whiskey bottles seem popular, but other glass containers and even plastic bottles are recycled to distribute a yellow liquid. Puzzled, since I do not see this country as an olive oil or apple cider place and I know rice wine is less yellow, I ask Mr. Thoeun what is on the racks. He informs me it is "petrol for the motor cycles". "The engines take pre-mixes, so people buy petrol and add the oil to it so they can fill up the tanks in one go". Good thing I asked about the content rather than buying a bottle and sipping it all evening thinking 'when in Rome…'

More lasting impressions

Some days just turn out differently than you expect. Today was one of those days. We have a car booked to take us to Banteay Srei and the Roulos Group. These are temples a bit farther out, but are still part of the Angkor Wat complex. Heidi wants to stop at a landmine museum on the way. It seems a bit morbid to me, but why not.

We take it easy this morning, dragging our heels a bit and we end up climbing into a sedan mid-morning. The trip out to Banteay Srei is almost 40 km and after days of moto-remork, the luxury of a leather seated four-wheel car with air-conditioning feels like business class. The roads are not bad but we do bounce into a pot-hole now and again, grateful for the high quality shock-absorbers. We observe the familiar sites along the route; pigs on scooters, whiskey bottles with petrol, a family of four on one motor, no helmets.

Just before Banteay Srei our driver pulls over. A small sign points to a little house indicating 'landmine museum'. The ten meter path towards the building's front door is lined with large airplane bombs, standing straight up. A printed sign at the entry door gives the history of the museum. We read the story: Aki Ra, founder, was taken at the age of five when his parents were killed, and trained into the Khmer Rouge as a child soldier. He spent time with the Khmer Rouge Army then was captured by the Vietnamese. There, he could choose between being shot and joining the Vietnamese Army. After a moment of reflection he joined the Vietnamese. The following years (up to 1998) he ended up fighting in the various wars that ravaged his country. As a child a large part of his work involved placing landmines.

Entering the building, our tickets are checked by an uninterested girl playing with her I-phone. We enter the first room, which is filled with banners of texts and photo's. I fear it is going to be a long and uninteresting read. While getting a feel for the place, another westerner walks in, clearly not a visitor, asking us where we are from. We summarize our life story as best we can. He introduces himself as Bill, and makes pleasant conversation. Then he starts to tell a story. A story that lasts over an hour. A story which captivates us. We find ourselves mesmerized, perplexed, interested and in total awe. Aki Ra, a child laying landmines turns into landmine remover extraordinaire and a beacon of hope for many Cambodians.

Bill educates us on landmines and Cambodia. Through his questions we learn much. Did you know that: (1) Most landmines don't kill? They are designed only maim so that someone has to take care of the victim, hurting the enemy twice. (2) Landmines don't 'click' when you stand on them? The clicking sound is totally a Hollywood invention – good for movies, as a suspense builder, but not a single one exists that makes a pre-noise, they just go 'boom'. (3) The aim of the landmine clearing efforts is not to remove all landmines? No, that would be a silly proposition. Assume there would be two landmines left 'somewhere in Cambodia', the cost of removing those last landmines would simply be too high. The aim is to remove them from heavily used areas. (4) Only two years ago a landmine was found in the USA, dating from the civil war? (5) In 2013 on average three people are injured by landmines in Cambodia every week? Can you imagine the uproar that would cause if that happened in the West? (6) In Cambodia alone there are between 4-5 million landmines still in the ground? Note: Bill admits this is a WAG – wild ass guess - but who cares if they are a couple of percent off? (7) Landmines hurt more 'friendlies' than enemy soldiers? This mainly because of the post-conflict injuries. (8) Only one country accurately kept track of where they placed landmines? Answer: Germany. *Punktlich* but rather handy for clearing fields afterwards. (9) Russians invented, designed and placed the only landmines without metal? Wood and nitroglycerin based explosives avoid detection with metal detectors. (10) That except for a few countries (including the US) most countries have signed treaties not to make, distribute or use landmines from now on?

But back to Aki Ra. He started to clear mines out of concern for the plight of children. Young children often stumble on the mines while playing in the fields. So Aki Ra got on his knees with a large knife to clear the fields around his town. He detects the mines by pushing his knife through the sand. Mines are funny that way. Push from the side and nothing happens, but you must stay away from the top part. And thus Aki Ra started. He trained others, and together they cleared fields. By the time we visited the landmine museum they had cleared more than 50,000 mines. But clearing mines was only the beginning for Aki Ra. He also began to take maimed and abandoned children into his home. He fed them and educated them. That effort grew into an orphanage and school. The humble beginnings of eight kids at home only got the ball rolling. Today it is a landmine relief effort that also runs a group of schools of 1200 students and 25 landmine removers. Bill tells the story how he got in touch by accident, after being asked to donate to the cause. He gradually became more involved until he sold his home in California, and moved to Siem Reap with his wife and dog, helping out full time. His passion is contagious, his explanations so down to earth you have to like them.

Over time, Aki Ra's work was noticed. He was so successful that it became an embarrassment for some government groups in Cambodia. The Cambodian government gets money and equipment from other countries, but Aki Ra's team cleared a like-for-like area at ten times the speed of the government team and at a fraction of the cost. Totally embarrassed, an attempt was made to use formal systems to shut Aki Ra down. A formal complaint was filed against his organization because he was not licensed to de-mine. He was not formally trained, and clearly not equipped (using knifes to find the mines rather than detectors), endangering people. Note that in all the years of clearing mines Aki Ra only lost one de-miner. Not to a mine. The gentleman was bitten by a snake while in the field, and rather than going to a hospital insisted in getting medical help from a village shaman.

Finally, there was an impasse between the government and the organization Aki Ra created. There was no escape, he needed formal training. Bill helped collect the funds to send Aki Ra to a de-mining training with the Royal Army in the UK. It was a big trip for Aki Ra. Concerned, Bill called to the UK academy four days into the training, asking to speak to Aki Ra. He wanted to know if he was getting passing grades. The reply he got was that Aki Ra was not available. Bill insisted. The surprising answer came back "No sir, he can't come to the phone right now, he's the one teaching the class at this moment".

After Bill's informal presentation we chat with him for a while and say our goodbyes. In the car we continue on the road to Banteay Srei. It is quiet at first; we all have that feeling of walking out of a movie theater after seeing an intense and impactful film. It takes a moment to return to reality. No pun intended, but we were all seriously blown away by what we had seen.

In Pursuit of Chocolate

It takes twenty minutes more to get to Banteay Srei. It's nice. No, it's more than nice. While perhaps smaller than the colossal temples we have climbed before, the carving in the sandstone is exquisite and the detail remains grand despite its age. It makes us wonder how the rest of the Angkor complex must have looked in its glory days. While the site is captivating, I notice the landmine experience lingers in our minds detracting us from the pure beauty of the shrine.

We refresh ourselves with cool towels presented by our driver on a shiny platter. They are glorious. The temperature is 37 degrees (98 Fahrenheit), and it feels like being inside an oven. We skip lunch and trod on to the Roulos Group. Spread over three locations, the first is rather uninteresting (scaffolding and piles of rubble mainly), the second is quite nice but far from impressive, the last one makes up for the last two. It is back in the 'wow' range: big steps, a large tower, fine carvings and a great view from the top. As we descend we comment that Angkor has been all we had hoped for, and yet internally we quietly remark to ourselves we are done. We are templed-out. It's like working in the chocolate factory; there eventually comes a point of overdose.

The driver to drops us off in town at a restaurant for a late lunch. Bill mentioned that the storms from yesterday knocked out the electricity in Siem Reap and the waiter reluctantly informs us that without power in the kitchen they can't cook our food. We leave to find a sandwich or some street food cooked on open flame. We walk and walk. Finally we see a shop with a French name a la 'Le Pain du Jour'. We enter and ask if we can eat. The 'yes' makes us sit down. We grab the menus, double check with the waitress that they can cook and we order food and drinks. Three sips into our drink the lady returns sheepishly. She regrettably informs us 'no electricity, no food'. I am not happy. Is this a way to force drink sales? I make our displeasure known. The waitress walks back to the kitchen and the cook/owner comes out, "sorry, sorry, let me see what I can do". He crosses the street and a generator starts chucking. A switch on the wall is moved, and what do you know? Fans above our heads turn. The electricity only stays on for five minutes, but that's enough to make four tasty *croque monsieurs*.

Before heading back there is one more stop to make. We want to off-load extra things and send them back to Europe - the warm coat we bought for Leendert in Nepal, a bunch of adapters and some other electronics, small gift items we picked up along the way. There is also an envelope with some legal papers to be sent. Inside the DHL office we prepare a small box with the items. For security purposes the box is packed on a dedicated table with a camera hanging over it. This is the way DHL tracks and ensures nothing goes 'missing'. The box is weighed; four kilos in total. The attendant looks up the price for the shipment to The Netherlands. One hundred and eighty four dollars! Are you nuts? We're not shipping gold here! I look at Heidi. If it wasn't for the emotional value of the items, especially the ceramic bowls the kids made, I would have tossed it all. In fact, I try to convince Heidi to lighten the load, to toss out all that can be easily replaced. I lose. Next is my envelope; admittedly a thick one. The yellow uniformed man behind the counter weighs and calculates. Eighty four dollars. Yes, 84 US dollars. For a moment I consider defaulting to the regular Cambodian post, but then I remember reading that it is a bit like gambling. The official Cambodian website for the Siem Reap post office reads as follows:

> *The main post office of Siem Reap is located at the river side on the Pokambor Avenue. Open daily from 7h00 am until 5h30 pm. You can post your postcards here but it can take a while before they arrive. They offer general post office services and also parcel sendings. If you need to ship something valuable or you want to make sure it arrives you can better use one of the international shipping services.*

We stick with DHL, bite the bullet and pay the exorbitant fees for peace of mind.

On the road again

It's easy to recognize when the kids have had a good night's rest. They don't need rousing and are awake before I am. I find Leendert reading and while Alicia's eyes are closed, her smile gives away that she is in a 'pretend sleep'. Today we are leaving Le Trèsor D'Angkor, making our way south towards Phnom Penh. Having been in the same spot for over a week means we can order breakfast without looking at the menus. We know all the options by heart.

The longer stay has a knock-on effect that packing takes longer. When traveling short stops, stuff tends to stay close to the bed you sleep on. Having been in one location longer means things have spread over the two rooms. Disciplined by now, we know better than to 'just throw things together'. Each of us packs what's his or hers. This is the surest way to ensure all pajamas, swimming goggles, and toothbrushes come along. The good news is that we're traveling by car, so we can pack with extra loose bags. Nothing like having the trunk of the car to throw things in!

We split the trip to Phnom Penh in two parts stopping halfway in Kampong Thom. As slow travelers, we don't need to make the five hour trip at once. Not being brave enough to drive ourselves down a two lane road in a place we barely know, it seemed a better option to get a driver. Sam, from the hotel in Kampong Thom, waits at reception at the agreed time and leads us to his Lexus. I am glad the 'Luxus' referred to in the confirmation was a typo. As we climb in, our Siem Reap hosts bid us farewell, accompanied by many bows.

Sam obviously knows this road. He weaves expertly between the traffic and potholes. He knows where there are small bumps, and where there are big ridges. It is good to be in a big car. The road is a mish-mash of sand, stones, asphalt, puddles, people, criss-crossing tuk-tuks and slow-moving cows. What we see on the road is sometimes impressive. In fact, it is admirable what Cambodians can pile into a car, even is they aren't attempting to set a new record. My favorite is the Toyota Camry transporting twelve people. Twelve? Yes, twelve. Four in front – including someone sitting on the left side of the driver; six in the back seat –four across and two on laps; and two sitting in the boot, lid open, feet dangling out.

The drive is not particularly picturesque. The landscape is mostly arid, and unexpectedly flat. And when I say flat, I mean Dutch flat. Equate it to Florida; the highest point is going over a bridge. What is also striking is that for two hundred kilometers, we never pass through an uninhabited area. For almost the entire stretch there are homes placed along the way. Sometimes up to one hundred meters apart, but I bet there wasn't one kilometer without a house.

Now, don't get me wrong, it is far from urbanized. There is one row of stilted houses on each side of the road. It is like two long chains of houses, with the road threading them together. The two-hour drive provides us a snapshot into Cambodian life as it passes by our windows. Kids on bicycles far too big for them. The bikes are so big, the kids can not sit on the saddle but have to stand while riding. I notice an inordinate amount of amputees, mostly on crutches. There are literally hundreds of roadside stalls selling the basics: bamboo-canes filled with rice, petrol-filled whiskey bottles, green coconuts and colorful garments. Competition must be murderous!

Almost all houses are placed on high poles, with open space below. Under the one-room dwellings is a space to keep animals, have a dining table, and hang multiple hammocks. There is no doubt in my mind that Cambodia has the most active hammock-population in the world. We observe different types of 'hammockers': the 'hands above your head'-types, holding the rope which holds the hammock up; the 'one leg out'-type, and the 'cross-sitting'-type. I notice that the older, perhaps more experienced folks seem to combine one and two together: hands up, foot out.

Around midday, Sam stops at a roadside restaurant. It is a flat roofed open area with tables and benches for at least a hundred guests. Wonderful smells surround us. We are the only foreigners in the open area. We plop ourselves down at a big table. Soon a lady walks up and takes Heidi by the arm. She makes it clear that we need to follow her to the kitchen. A simple plywood and bamboo wall separates the dining area from the kitchen. Rather than a menu, they simply show us what they have. Lots of pointing at frying pans, nodding at ingredients and group smiling. We think we order two noodle soups, two Lok-lak's (which have become a favorite) and the only drinks we recognize - cokes and sprites. The dishes are hot, tasty, and full of flavorful fresh ingredients. It costs us twelve dollars including Sam's meal. Now that's the way we like it!

After the break we continue our route south. As we approach Kampong Thom province Sam checks if we want to see the temples of Sambor Preh Kukh. This was part of the original plan, but scheduled for tomorrow. Sam suggests that we might as well do it now, since we have made good time. We agree and he detours to the site. My expectations are high, having read raving reviews on blogs, the internet and brochures. The ruins are five hundred years older than what we saw at Angkor Wat, dating from the 7th century - the period when the Koran was first published and Europe was in the Middle Ages. So when Europe went dark, the brick temples were erected by a pre-Angkor society, one civilized enough to send a first emissary to the court in China.

Full of anticipation, we turn off the main road and make a stop to buy entry tickets before driving into the site. I see one tour bus depart. Other than that we are on our own. The Sambor Preh Kukh complex consists of three areas and Sam indicates where we should go. Water in hand, we start our exploration. Perhaps we are a bit spoiled, but the ruins do not justify the praise on the net. Yes, when one considers the brick constructions are very old it is impressive, but given what we have seen the last days, this is not even in the same league. We look at stacks of crumbling bricks. In all honesty, it's about as exciting as staring at Hadrian's wall, which I never really thought was worth the travel out into the north of the UK. Today's stop is nice because it breaks up the trip, but were it not for that, I would tell people to happily skip this stop.

In all fairness, I might be influenced by external factors. The 38 degree heat makes it a warm walk, but what's worse is that I feel I am walking in a plastic dump. It looks like the day after an open air pop-festival. Plastic bottles, styrofoam buckets and plastic bags are everywhere. It seems we landed on 'Trash Island', that maelstrom in the Pacific ocean described as the 'Pacific Trash Vortex'. The problem with plastic is that you don't know when it was dumped, but my gut tells me it is more than the result of the new year celebration. If not, it is a rather embarrassing to charge tourists to visit the dump. We loop around quickly. I try to convince the others of the historic beauty, attempting to generate awe for the age of the bricks, but fail miserably. Within thirty minutes we climb aboard the Lexus, politely telling Sam the site is "indeed rather unique".

The last stretch to our hotel is short. The Sambor Villa is a nice oasis albeit 'animal rich'. We are in the jungle, so mosquitoes, ants, and lizards happily cruise and buzz around us. In our room a giant can of bug-spray on the bedside table invites us to take personal action. We do. We enjoy the pool, followed by a relaxing time under a ceiling fan, drinks in hand.

We have dinner in the hotel as we have driven around enough for one day. This turns out to be a good choice. We're entertained by the light show - a result of the electricity going out and generators kicking in several times while we survive on candle light. In addition, the walls and lamps are full of little geckos. Alicia counts twelve. One huge gecko pops its head from behind a beam. This particular one is an impressive lizard; I estimate well over forty centimeters. The waitress smiles at us as she walks up and says there are three of these harmless big ones around the restaurant. The 'harmless' puts Alicia at ease but the 'monster' is large enough that she prefers to switch seats, sitting away from it.

The food is another reason to celebrate staying here. Each one of us claims to have made the best choice - having tried a bite off each plate, I would be hard pressed to pick one over the other. We concur that this is the best dinner we have had in a month. As Heidi takes the kids to their room to tuck them in, I hear a familiar 'boom, boom, boom'. Another wedding is underway. The drums and music are happily pounding away and given the flat countryside, it again feels like they are right next door. I hope for a good night of sleep fearing Heidi's earplugs might not do the trick tonight!

Our room is lovely. As we go to sleep in our four-poster bed we spray one more time and pull the mosquito net over us, ready for a solid night's sleep. It is not to be. The stage is set by an over enthusiastic frog with an incredible sound capacity. While it is outside the room it might as well have been croaking on my pillow. It's amazing how much sound such a small animal can make. The good news is that by midnight frogs go to sleep, as do the wedding guests. Ah, sleep at last.

But, no, Act Two. The scene opens around 4:30. Loud thunder, lighting and the start of light rain. The thunder slowly rumbles away, making space for Act Three. The heavens work themselves into a crescendo of rainfall so great that the gutters can't deal with it. Unfortunately the roof between our bedroom and bathroom is "v" shaped and a perfect place to trap the overflow. Upon inspection, the loud cascade of water is not just outside, but also inside our room. We save backpacks, computers and other electronic paraphernalia, and I construct a run-off system with a reed carpet, two towels and a chair. It works partially; at least 90% of the water drains into the bathtub. Not bad for midnight engineering. By moving our four-poster bed we also manage to find a dry-spot in the middle of the room. Heidi walks across the path and checks on kids. Luckily their room weathers the storm without leaks. Returning to our room she reports that between our rooms the water is ankle-deep.

After another small nap, we pack up the room and have breakfast. Our intent was to leave around eleven, enjoying the hotel pool in the jungle. However, the blue tiled pool has turned cappuccino-colored overnight. The staff confirms that last night's rainfall was extreme, even for them. They had never seen the water rise so quickly, paths and garden become one big puddle. The pool-boy scratches his head while another staffer takes a picture of the swampy looking square. It will take quite an effort to clean that one up.

Sam, our driver, shows up in a different car. He explains he can't take us today to Phnom Penh because he has other engagements, but a friend will drive us. Our new driver doesn't speak a word of English, and I never catch his name. No matter, he likes to drive fast and appears to be somewhat safety conscious, which is nice given the challenging roads. Part of the road is stone, part asphalt, part puddles and potholes caused by the rains. Luckily the driver understands that sandy roads with small ridges are better conquered at high speeds, the wheels never entering the dips, allowing the shock absorbers to cushion the vibrations. This avoids our fillings popping out of our teeth.

The route is a repeat of yesterday. The only exception is that large parts of the road are under water and the arid landscape seems to have loved the rain. It actually appears much more green and lush than yesterday. The construction has not changed. Simple wooden houses on poles and occasionally a gold-plated shrine-like building, monks living in huge pagoda's.

It takes three hours to reach Phnom Penh, and we are grateful for having split the trip in two. Once in Phnom Penh we use the iPad to direct us to our hotel. Long live electronics. Our driver didn't have a clue where to go and since we didn't have a language in common, that could have been an interesting communication challenge. We zigzag through town and arrive at the Anise Villa, a small boutique hotel off the beaten track. It's a lovely place, big beds, leak-free roofs and Khmer Massages. Always ready to learn new things, Heidi and I book a 'Khmer Massage'.

Now for massage novices out there, let me help you. Massages come in different flavors and forms. They vary in location, from a specially designed chair face-front in an airport terminal, to soft double towels with candlelights and the sounds of waves in a swanky resort spa overlooking the ocean. They vary in intensity, from soft caressing to pressing fingers deep into muscle tissue. They vary in body parts used to give the massage: hands, feet, elbows. They vary in physical attributes used, oil (with or without scents), hot stones, wet towels, bamboo sticks. They vary in how the muscles are attacked; stretching, pulling, twisting, or long stroke rubbing or 'kneading'. And, last but not least, they vary on which part of the body is treated; back, shoulder, legs, arms, hands, and feet, and of course the popular 'happy end' part. Between the permutations, a full menu can be made, Swedish Massage, Deep Tissue Massage, Thai Massage, Aromatherapy Massage, Sports Massage, etc. We go for the Khmer Massage, which, according to the brochure is supposed to leave me feeling relaxed, sleepy and 'floaty'. It does most of what I expect, and it is totally in line with my wishes of the Asian massages. It's a good treatment, a blend of most of the above elements but without the candles, elbows, deep tissue pain or happy end. After all the time spent in the car seat, it's a welcome way to loosen the muscles.

Settled-in but getting Unsettled

The next day we get out of bed with no rush whatsoever. It's a school day, so nice and easy. We enjoy a lazy breakfast and stay in the air conditioned dining room, nestling in with pc's and homework books. While Heidi teaches, I drown myself in the various options of our onward travel and the history of Cambodia.

School stays in session until two o'clock when we decide it's time to poke our noses outside the hotel. I hand Leendert the map and ask him to navigate us to our destination: S-21. No, these are not map coordinates. S-21 was the name of the Tuol Sleng prison, also known as the Khmer

Rouge Killing Machine. The name leaves little to the imagination. The original building was constructed as a school in 1962, but for the four years, eight months and twenty days of the Pol Pot regime, it became the site for horrific torture. Today, it has been transformed into the Tuol Sleng Genocide Museum.

Phnom Penh is laid out in a north/south and east/west way, and Leendert directs us to the site. Once there, we spend ninety minutes walking through four old concrete school buildings. White and yellow square tiles cover the floor. The former classrooms are mainly empty, but they are haunting. The first building holds old metal bed frames, one in each room, shackles still attached. Each room has a faded and stained photograph on the wall depicting a corpse on the cold steel strips which form the bottom of the bed. The picture is a real image how the Vietnamese found the site as they gained control over Cambodia at the end of Pol Pot's regime. Despite the number of visitors walking through the corridors and rooms, the solemn quietness is striking.

The top floor of this building is dedicated to the pictures taken while this horrid place was in operation. There are mug shots of those who passed through the facility. Pictures were taken upon arrival, before the prisoners were packed in the former classrooms. We see only an excerpt of the 14,000 people who passed though these torture chambers - chambers from which only seven prisoners survived.

The second building holds individual prison cells. On the first level, the small cubicles are made of stone, the second floor has wooden cells. Again, the shackles and chains are on the walls; scratches on the walls make it painfully real. The third level of this building is filled with more pictures of those passed away. By this time, Alicia has had enough. I can't tell if it is too gruesome or because it is rather boring; photographs of faces and lots of text are not interesting for an eleven-year-old. I can't make up my mind which reason I would prefer.

The next building continues along the same lines. More painful pictures of the tortures and cabinets filled with instruments and devices used. Some cabinets display the clothing of the prisoners. Possibly for theatrics, the Khmer uniforms are neatly displayed, while the clothes of those who perished are all dumped in a glass cabinet. They are dumped randomly as if in a laundry basket, exposed through the side windows like debris sunk to the bottom of an aquarium. It feels disrespectful. By this time Leendert also bails out, in his case clearly because of the confrontation with such ugliness. Heidi and I leave them on a bench in the shade of a tree as we continue our path, disgusted by what we see, but drawn to it at the same time, trying to make sense of it.

The following building has more pictures and panels of stories of people who were persecuted but somehow avoided becoming one in the statistic of the two million people killed. This was the story of the survivors. This part of the exhibit also explains why the world turned a blind eye. Some of the excuse was geopolitical, but a large part was because the world was misled and masterfully deceived. In a stark contrast to the display cabinets with skulls, these displays how Swedish observers (themselves socialist red at the time) were given a tour of the country. They never suspected that anything so atrocious was going on - they were only shown the good parts. To them, the Pol Pot regime seemed a successful experiment of social equality. They even strongly promoted it in the western world and the UN for years after.

In the last building, two more subjects are broached. First, the faces and names of those involved in S-21 as guards. The testimonies are shocking with very little regret in them. The headline is "we did what we were told and would be killed ourselves if we'd show any objections"; "at the time it made sense". The book "The Lucifer Effect" comes to mind, one which explains how groups and individuals behave in certain circumstances. The strongest defense I read is that most of the guards were recruited and brainwashed at an age of thirteen or fourteen - barely the age of Leendert and Alicia - an age where one can hardly expect a strong moral compass. Several of the guards overtly claim to be victims themselves, holding themselves blameless in the texts shown on these walls.

The second part covers the court cases against the Khmer Rouge leadership. Pol Pot himself died in 1998, the same year the Cambodian government pardoned members of his core team (Leng Sary, Thirith and others). However, in 2007, seven years before our visit, these leaders were arrested and incarcerated. The trials dragged on. On 26 July 2010, a tribunal found Kang Kek Lew (Comrade 'Duch'), the person responsible for sites like S-21, guilty of crimes against humanity. He serves a life sentence. Leng Sary, Pol Pot's second in command, died in March 2013, before he was sentenced. Thirith, the sister-in-law of Pot who was very active in the regime, escaped punishment as well - she was suffering from Alzheimer's and deemed mentally unfit to stand trial in November 2011. The recentness of the dates impacts us deeply. Both Heidi and I are shaken by the exhibit, it's raw format, the basic signage, and the crude pictures. Shivers run down our spines as we collect the kids and walk to the exit. As a final reminder of how recent the history really is, we see an older man in the courtyard sitting at the table signing books. He is one of the three living survivors of the prison. We try to have a discussion with the kids on society and human kind, but the combination of words 'human' and 'kind' seems out of place. We notice neither child is interested in engaging with us, and we are happy to let it slide for now.

Trying to move our minds to happier things, we explore current Phnom Penh. Leendert takes the map and leads us to the Russian Market. It is a covered market place with many stalls crammed into too small a place. We've seen many of these places on our trip and it is in the process of closing for the evening, giving us an excuse to quickly move on. The next assignment for Leendert: find food and drink. Through the hustle of the streets we walk randomly, observing the people. I notice that each and every person smiles back as I smile at them. I have never been in a large city and experienced anything quite like it. Even the moto-remork drivers smile back as I wave them off. Now why would that be?

Just as the kids are getting cranky due to the long walk, the hunger and heat, we spot a restaurant. Their specialty is Cambodian BBQ. It's a large, open air space and completely empty since it's still before six o'clock. The hotplate on the table in front of us is fired up. We're the only customers, and it's clear they don't get many tourists here, so we get the undivided attention of the four staff members. They are eager to please, bringing meat, shrimp, vegetables and drinks to the table. They pour my beer over a big block of ice and open can after can of coke to top up the kids' glasses as soon as they take a sip. The head waiter underestimates my BBQ-ing skills and insists on cooking our meal, hovering over our table. It is an odd sight, the four of us alone in this huge space with a waiter cooking our food. As we get to the end of our meal the restaurant fills up, pulling the staff to other tables, leaving us to savor the food and the moment.

The following days have a similar pattern. Heidi World High is in session in the morning, the kids impressing me with their dedication to learning. Next, we nibble a quick lunch before diving into the cultural activity of the afternoon. Today, it's the Royal Palace. A moto-remork takes us through the busy roads to the palace located at the edge of the Mekong River. Once inside a young man in a purple shirt with a 'guide' badge pinned on his chest walks up asking if we want a tour. My pre-visit research has prepared me well, so I could go without a guide, but I guess the ten dollars means I can offload the "look at this kids" effort and contribute to a good cause - supporting the Cambodian economy.

Before entering the grounds we buy a t-shirt. Since the palace has temples, Alicia's shoulders must be covered and the pashminas we took along won't do the trick. The Cambodian economy is supported with another three dollars.

The guide is friendly and takes us into the complex. The first stop is a flowering Banyan tree, which he claims is quite unique since the flower only lasts one day. Reportedly, the Banyan tree is the one under which Buddha was enlightened, hence its significance. We march on and are shown the Throne Hall and the quarters where the king still lives. An open ornamental building is referred to as the 'dance hall'. In the old days it was only lit by moonlight. As we stroll from one building to the next our guide explains the difference between a 'temple' and a 'pagoda'. The former is the prayer building itself, the latter the entire complex of buildings including the surrounding lands. Hence a temple, a place of worship is always part of the pagoda.

Our next stop is the main attraction: the Silver Temple. We remove our shoes before entering the elaborately decorated building. I remember to enter the temple left foot first. The inside is stunning. Over 5000 floor-tiles, each made from over one kilogram of silver. While the Pol Pot regime destroyed a part of the temple, most remained intact, since even the Khmer Rouge was awed by this place. We see cabinets full of gold and silver sculptures. Most are royal gifts. The objects fade to insignificant ornaments, however, against the backdrop of two centrally placed statues. The first one is a fifty centimeter high meditating Buddha made of one block of jade sourced from Burma. The second, even more impressive statue, is a life size gold Buddha weighing ninety kilos, encrusted with 2086 diamonds. Two huge diamonds are part of the sculpture – one of 25 karats, the other 20. The most amazing part is that we can walk right up to the statutes without security guards, ropes or glass cases keeping us at a distance. As we descend into the court yard, the guide points out that the steps are made of imported Italian marble, impressing on us how it demonstrates the richness of the place (as if the diamonds, gold and silver had missed the point).

We pass more of the royal family's paraphernalia: the kings' costumes, shoes, carts and elephant riding seats and finally bid farewell to our guide. We work our way to the exit, avoiding the cheap souvenir shop. About those souvenir shops – I understand the urge to make an additional buck, but is it really necessary to force me to walk thought the shop at the end of exhibits? In the old days you'd enter a museum or expo and, when finished, you'd be on your merry way. Nowadays, you are forced to walk past picture frames (we ship!), postcards, themed pens and stuffed animals before reaching the final exit. Marketeers know the first and last impressions matter most, right? Do they really want my lasting impression to be negotiating with my daughter why a particular gift or stuffed animal is not in the category of 'must have'? The IKEA like set-up which forces one to weave past all the goods, the payment counters and the coffee shop is not a step forward if you ask me. Please, just signpost. If I want a memorabilia or if I need a drink, I'll find it!

Having 'part one' of today's local culture experience covered, I swiftly more to 'part two'. We walk around the block to visit the National Museum. It takes a bit of effort but we find the unassuming building. I had hoped for some relief from the heat, but it is an open-air building without windows, a/c, or fans. Looking at the kids I hear myself promise ice cream when we are finished. It's kind of funny since the kids don't even like ice cream!

I tell the kids they need to get at least five dollars of pleasure out of the museum. They do. The main attraction for them is the goldfish in the center pond. Heidi and I diligently walk the tour of the buildings, scanning the displayed sculptures which form ninety percent of the displays. We recognize several pieces. These are similar to what we saw in Kampong Thom and Siem Reap with the signs 'Replicate – The Original are in the Phnom Penh Museum'. On the one hand they look out of place, on the other hand it is nice to see the collection in one place. Having seen the various temples we appreciate the overview.

No more than 45 minutes later we exit the museum. I'm glad the 'gift shop' with books and sculpture replicas is limited to two cabinets near the exit. We skip the ice cream, looking for a café for a drink instead. We have somehow landed in the neighborhood of hostels and bars. White folks of all ages, often covered in long hair and tattoos, drink beer out of large mugs. The signs market cheap lodging, cheaper drinks and pool tables; 'happy hour any time'. I'm keen to find an escape route taking arbitrary lefts and rights.

As luck would have it, we walk into barber alley. One hair-chopping place after another. Leendert needs a haircut, the prices are displayed (no negotiation), and, worst of all, it only costs five thousand riel! A dollar and a quarter! And so Leendert regains the award for 'the cheapest haircut on the trip'. Darn!

The next day, with the excitement of the new location gone, it takes a crowbar to remove the kids from between the sheets. If it wasn't for "breakfast is only until nine-thirty" I might have failed. One kid takes over the air-conditioned breakfast room with math books, the other lays on a poolside lounge chair doing English, a mango smoothie by her side. Life could be worse. In no time, it is afternoon and our driver arrives. Today we are visiting the Killing Fields.

Our driver is a small, quiet man who is barely large enough to look over his Toyota's dashboard, even with his booster seat. He prefers shortcuts to main streets and has an uncanny ability to find roads with bad pavement which his weary old shock absorbers have long since forgotten how to master. At one point I am convinced he is taking us for an unnecessary detour. Were it not for our fixed price agreement, I would have been concerned. The path goes from bad to horrible to worse. There is no way the tour buses come this way! The only possible explanation is that the better roads are a longer distance and he is optimizing his fuel. Thirty minutes later, feeling like a James Bond drink (shaken not stirred) we arrive at the Killing Fields. We are in the village of Choeung Ek. This is where the victims of Tuol Sleng prison disappeared to in nightly convoys.

We buy our entry tickets and take the audio guides. Unlike normal museum headphones, these are of very high quality and work well. Both ears. We walk up to the single construction on site: a Buddhist stupa commemorating the thousands of people who died here. The buildings from the Khmer Rouge days have disappeared, but panels with photographs and the voice in our ears paints the picture of the not too distant past. It is eerily quiet here. Partly because everyone walks with headphones on, but I also suspect the place itself forces the utmost respect for the dead.

We walk past marked-off mass grave sites and stare at the pits where bodies and bones of some 17,000 people were discovered. Signs along the path ask you not to step on the bones. Bones? Yes, human bones. Rain washes away the top soil, exposing bones, teeth and clothes of those perished. Even today. It is almost as if their bodies are lifted out of the ground giving testimony to the atrocities which took place here. It is surreal as you walk over the path, avoiding human remains, the way you would traverse a kitchen floor barefoot when you know a glass just broke, careful not to step on anything.

The stories told through the headphones are painful, the more so because the narration is done by people who were part of the extermination teams. They tell about the activities which took place. How they themselves were involved. The Killing Fields are best described as a human butchery. Bullets were too expensive. One can hear the horror, the hurt and the agony in the voices of the prosecutor-presenters as they recount their tales.

Walking around one gets a dark emptiness inside and feels enraged at the same time. Nothing prepares you for the emotion you feel as a father standing next to your eleven year old daughter, staring at the tree against which babies were slung to crush their little skulls. The 'killing tree' was used to murder the infants in front of their mothers, right before they too were killed and tossed into the mass graves. Pure evil, pure horror.

The tour ends where it starts, at the sixty meter high Buddhist monument. Shoes off, we enter. Trays and trays of skulls. Each marked with a colorful dot sticker. A legend explains the color-coding of the five thousand plus skulls; it marks how the individual came to his or her end: 'hatchet', 'hammer', 'axe', 'cut throat,…'

Before leaving the grounds we stop at a little museum next to the parking lot and watch a short video. One more time the story passes in front of us. Even after reading about it, seeing S-21 and visiting the fields, the video is impactful and shocking. Words can't fully describe what we experience as we see it. As we walk out, our driver takes us back through the same roads we came. The kids comment on what they saw, but, strangely enough, appear not too affected. We learned later that this was their coping mechanism - they were deeply shaken by the place. Heidi and I try to explain their questions and the overall madness as best we can, attempting to rationalize it and put it in historic context. Tough job. For most of the way back I stare out of the car window, wondering about everything and nothing at all.

We barely have time for a snack before a moto-remork appears for our second excursion of the day. Were it up to me, I would have skipped any further activity. I am emotionally drained. But it was booked, so off we go. We tuk-tuk through town, along the water, past the palace and arrive at the riverside. A boat will take us on our Sunset Cruise on the Mekong river.

The shipmate is our guide for the evening and provides interesting commentary as we make our way up and down the river. Clouds fill the sky blocking an otherwise picture-perfect sunset It is a welcome diversion after our day. We are happy to sit on the deck and enjoy the scenes along the river. Chatting with the other passengers we learn that one fellow is living in America, but is Cambodian. It is his first time back to his home country, having left, by pure luck, two months before the Pol Pot regime took over. He was nineteen at the time, lost most of his family, and is now on an trip with his son through Cambodia. I thought our visit was emotional, but it pales in comparison!

We pass to the other side of the Mekong to observe a 'floating fisherman village'. Sitting on big pillows, beer in hand, it feels decadent and intrusive the way we pass close to these people's homes, taking pictures of their day-to-day routines as they pull in nets, wash their hair in the river and cook their meager meals.

Criss-crossing back, we see 'boat-people'. The guide explains these are different from the floating village. The village people own small sheds built on floating bamboo. The boat-people, by contrast, are poor. They live on boats one-and-a-half meters wide, perhaps eight meters long, an upside-down "U"-shaped tarp the only protection against the elements. They tie the boats together forming a makeshift village. The boat-people-village forms a stark contrast against the brand new Sokha Club Hotel built right behind them. The huge hotel just celebrated its grand opening. Our guide tells us the boat people will soon be forced to move to the other side of the river. The hotel owners have expressed concerns about the image and the impact on their investment. The fact is that the patrons have complained because their rooms overlook the poverty on the boats and that is not what they want to see on their holiday. I can only shake my head.

And so another intense day swoops by. I feel settled and unsettled at the same time; what a day of extremes this was.

End gaming as we pass day 200 of our trip

The last days in Phnom Penh follow similar routines. Morning school and afternoon activities in town. We make several 'educational' stops. The first is at the 'Daughters of Cambodia'. This organization aims to extract young girls between fifteen and twenty from the sex-trade by teaching them alternative job skills. The information cards and texts on the wall explain it is a tough battle. The girls are often sold by their parents into this 'slavery', but, relatively speaking, they are making an 'okay' living. The building consists of three parts: (1) a shop where craft items are sold. These items come out of the organization's sewing shop. (2) A foot massage and nail parlor – for women only; and (3) a coffee shop/restaurant. The girls decide to get their toes polished while Leendert and I watch a video on the 'Daughters' organization and head to the coffee shop. We read the comments on the wall and in the menu. An amazing one-in-forty girls in Cambodia is sold into the sex-trade. It strikes me how much more that sounds than two-and-a-half percent. One in forty! Knowing the young girls serving us our drinks and food came out of that environment drives the case home. Leendert and I discuss the subject as we wait for Alicia and Heidi to return. We reflect on how the effort of the Daughters of Cambodia is noble and apparently effective. We also discuss how one should try to stop girls from entering the system in the first place. As usual, there are no easy answers. There is an entire system in place, including the very shady, very profitable sex-tourism. The good news is that the organization has a very successful track record. The education and training they provide not only prepares the girls for a profession, but also gives them back their self-worth. They report that ninety-eight percent of the women going through the program do not return to the sex-industry.

With the nails of the girls well polished, we are off to location number two. This place was recommended by our hotel manager "Friends" consists of a shop and a tapas restaurant. It is just around the corner. The shop has a collection of handicrafts made by orphans. Small items like wallets, computer bags, purses and pencil cases made from re-purposed materials like bicycle tires are displayed. The signs on the walls are gripping. They plead in different languages for people - tourists - NOT to visit orphanages. The point is driven home by large posters showing kids in glass boxes as if on display in a museum, white folks standing around them taking pictures. It reminds me of what we saw in the Pagoda in Ho Chi Minh City. Buses of people coming by to take pictures, donate a few dollars, thinking they have done well while throwing oil on an open fire.

While there is less hardship today, the number of orphans is still growing. But 'orphan' is the wrong term. Orphans are children without parents. Today, in Cambodia over three-quarters of the children in the homes have parents! The issue is that the parents believe their kids are better off in the 'orphanages' than at home. The Friends organization puts effort into helping families understand that the children are best served by getting trained and becoming self-sufficient rather than being in a 'house' and effectively becoming street kids, as a segue into the sex-trade. The mission of this organization is 'to close the tap' rather than 'mopping up'. We enter the second part of the establishment - the tapas restaurant. Half the waiters wear blue shirts the other half yellow. It is the distinction between 'teacher' and 'trainee' and they work on a buddy system. While we're not hungry, we support the effort by ordering tasty tapas. Both trainees and the chefs are doing a great job!

The next stop is by special request of Heidi and Alicia, a women's workshop with a very similar theme to the two we just visited. A few days earlier Alicia had seen these earrings which she really liked. She convinced us using a three-pronged approach: (1) please, please, please - which has little effect (2) 'it is for a good cause', better, and (3) 'it reminds me of the landmine museum in Siem Reap', okay, sold! I am sure you understand the logic of the first two arguments, the latter might not be as obvious. It is actually very simple. The earrings are made of scraps of landmines, but you can't tell by looking at them. It seems like a nice little souvenir. It is supposed to be a quick stop, so Leendert and I stay in the tuk-tuk sending the girls in with my wallet. Oops. Mistake. Should have given them the exact change. I feel something is up as the time it takes for them to come out is more that is needed for a pre-determined earring purchase. We wait, and the tuk-tuk driver smiles – nothing like knowing he will get paid for waiting!

Finally the girls exit the workshop building. The smile on Alicia's face is proportional to the bag she is holding. Clearly she is not just carrying an earring bag. 'We got some extra stuff' she smiles. One of the additional acquisitions I fully support; it is a nice little booklet with a funky cloth cover- one to take notes in (or little girly secrets…). The second item I cannot help making fun of. They bought a photo-album booklet. Yes, one of those booklets with sleeves to put pictures in! Are you kidding me? What is the chance of us ever printing pictures? And if so, when on earth does one look at them? If it wasn't for the fact that it supports the local women and the Cambodian economy I would not only have made fun of the girls, but forced them to take it back.

The day before we leave Phnom Penh we go into town one more time to visit "the central market". It is a big x-shaped building packed with a huge collection of stalls. They have anything you might need. Clothes, leather, kitchenware, food and other day-to-day stuff. We have tried to get Leendert to buy a new shirt, and he does take a look at polo-shirts but finally convinces his mom he doesn't need any, "I've got three shirts, that's more than enough". The past months have proven that he is right. Provided you wash often, the only reason to have more shirts is really not much more than vanity. How much does a person really need? What a difference between boy and girl shopping!

I enjoy our afternoon walks and rides - the noises, the quick smell shifts from grilled meat to freshly cut Durian. I even enjoy the hustle and bustle of rush hour traffic. We stroll along the Tonle Sap River observing the daily routines and shopping behaviors of the locals. We plop down in a brasserie on Sisowath Quay for a drink. Sinking deep in the big rattan cushiony chairs we share a plate with fresh fruit. There is quite a lot of traffic along this touristic thoroughfare, spilling exhaust onto our fruit platter. Our conversation is continuously interrupted by vendors, poor folks and landmine victims selling small items, or asking for alms. Am I mean for saying that? Even thinking it? Is it morally incorrect and deplorable to feel interrupted and be annoyed by people trying to make a living? What makes me feel worse is that despite waving them off time and again, the Cambodian friendly smile is returned each time as they back off. No judgment, no pleading or begging.

On our last evening in Phnom Penh Heidi and I optimize our dollars by squeezing in drinks during happy hour. The kids are in the pool as we enjoy our strawberry mojitos. The Anise Villa has been good to us and we end up talking to the manager complementing him on the quality of the hotel and the food coming out of the tiny kitchen. He mentions that the chef noticed the kids seem to take particular liking to the Lok Lak. He asks if they might want to learn how to make it. Within minutes, both kids are in the cramped kitchen, camera, paper and pencil in hand to take down the details. Needless to say, now that they know how it's made, it tastes even better.

And so our journey winds to an end. The next morning we pack our backpacks and climb into a taxi which is ready to take us to the airport and sends us on our way. We spend a few days in Bangkok and a week of 'beach holiday' - the final stage of our journey. We had planned it this way, way-back-when. The thought at the outset of our trip was that after all the travel we'd enjoy a week of sand, sun and luxury. Looking back, it was our least favorite part of the trip. We were traveled out. We wanted to go home. Were it not for the fact that our flights to Europe were fixed, I think we would have returned a week early. The five star hotel could not compete with the thought of our own bed, own fridge and home-cooked meals. Joy and happiness was back home, perhaps with a cup of tea and a cookie at the kitchen table.

Closing the Book

WELCOME TO THE LAST CHAPTER. If you got this far, you're probably a completer-finisher. The good news is that you are about to feel joy. Only a few pages to go!

We started out at the kitchen table with my mom and an observation of how a small square of chocolate created happiness; the innocent boy on the plastic chair observed that 'more' is often better; 'having a lot' doesn't guarantee happiness. The delta, the improvement and 'change of state' was proposed to create happiness, all subject to the curve of marginal returns. The logic? The more you have, the more you need to create the same "kick"; to have the same 'utils of happiness', if you will.

Part 1 of this book provided a picture of a family enjoying life; of two individuals running up two different career ladders while somehow balancing family commitments. It was a thrilling phase, one of growth and new experiences. Not necessarily obsessed by collecting more, we certainly worked hard to gain the wealth which buys 'freedom' and 'independence'. We made conscious decisions to forego some family-time; prioritizing fun, funds, and collecting experiences instead. Following that early stage, we jumped on a different s-curve and re-centered on our family. We settled in Vienna and were comfortable, well-balanced and in line with our wishes and expectations.

Then came the T-junction. One of those external events which flips the world upside down. In a short period of time, we stopped running up the corporate ladder. In fact, the ladder abruptly disappeared. No one fell, no broken bones, no big catastrophes. Perhaps we had bruised egos as we faced the unforeseen change in circumstances, but that was all. We found ourselves with a big neon sign flashing on-and-off in our heads: "Now, what do you do?". As often, necessity is the mother of invention. We looked for new opportunities. We explored what to do next and took the plunge.

What if I gave you a year? One full year. Assume you have your health and the financial means to spend $50 per-day-per-person. Yes, that was the budget we lived on - all included: the hotels, flights, guides, immunizations, visas, volunteering, clothes, donations, food and drinks. What would you do with that year? Try to stay away from the thousands of reasons flying through your head right now telling you why you couldn't do it. Assume you are. Assume you must stop what you are doing today and do something else. Now: *What would you do with that year?*

We decided to travel, to homeschool and to volunteer. The objective was to be together and to give the kids (and ourselves) an appreciation for all they had; to impress on them that what seemed normal and natural to them might not be so 'standard'. We wanted to make them understand that 'having a lot' does not create happiness, that 'joy' and 'being content' can be found everywhere. It is not necessarily related to wealth. Four backpacks were our medium, volunteering was our chosen route.

The third part of this book provided nine stories - snapshots of different places on this globe. It depicted different situations which gave us many moments of joy, and, in some instances, made us very angry or sad. They always made us reflect. For completeness, I must divulge that we visited many more places than described in these pages. Those, too, contributed to our journey. They each had their own history, cultural sites and people making lasting impressions.

One example, in Laos, we ended up, totally unplanned, in a grass roots volunteering project for a few days. A young American had come to Laos intending to become a monk, but he ended up starting a one-classroom school. The small building grew into a dormitory for three homeless kids. He used all of his personal money and inheritance to improve the life of locals. He convinced friends back home to support some of his students to go to university abroad. Meeting him instantly filled us with hope and warm feelings.

The trip cemented how fortunate we really were, and are. It helped us understand that joy is not just 'having it all', but that happiness is first and foremost a mindset, an attitude. Since our return, many people have asked "what was your favorite place?", or "what was your best experience?". Simple question, hard to answer. How do I compare squid-fishing with my daughter on an Australian island with teaching English on the Galapagos with my son? How does one compare Machu Picchu with the Terracotta Soldiers, or cruising down the Mekong river? How does feeding children with hydrocephalus in a pagoda rate against driving a race car on the Sepang racetrack or seeing the Petronas Tower in Kuala Lumpur or the Burj Al Arab in Dubai? How does sitting on a boat to scuba dive in Fiji compare to donating money to a school in Sai Gon? How does walking over human remains in the killing fields of Cambodia compare to flying over the Nazca lines of Peru?

Not long ago, a friend asked a substantially different question. He inquired "Do you believe more or less in the basic good of people?" Again, a simple question, hard to answer. I am an optimist at heart. I am not sure I changed my view on humankind. I can say that as we traveled we were confronted with extremes on both sides.

Everywhere we went, we saw happy, sad, remarkable, draining and inspiring people. Their mood and well-being, more often than not, was totally unrelated to their physical or financial fortunes. Travel not only showed us the world, but also imparted on us both the horrors and the beauty of people, and the lives they live. But like Disney movies, you can't expect to have one without the other.

As a family, and individually, we reflected and learned. We learned to appreciate the sense and nonsense of so many things. Perhaps what impressed us most during our journey is the resilience of mankind, and how fine the line is between joy and distress. How arbitrary is it. How haphazard the condition into which one is born, and gets to live, really is. How fortunate we are.

Some of us can choose where we are on this planet, but for most of us, it is a result of where our parents happened to live. Some people can choose what they want to be, but for most it is luck if education is provided, double luck if it is good, triple luck if one can choose a profession afterwards and make a living. What most people do seem to be able to choose is *how* they will live. Choosing one's attitude cost nothing, but has a huge impact. It impacts you and the environment around you.

The story comes to mind of the guy who was always -and invariably- remained positive. His standard reply to "how are you doing?" was "if I'd be any better, I'd be twins". Always. No matter what happened, he'd have that attitude. I like that. I wish I could create that in a potion, distill and distribute it. It's an illusion to think one can live up to that standard one hundred percent of the time, but the real question is can you approach it?

Some people dream of traveling the world. It is on their 'bucket list'. For us, before we started our trip, we were living our bucket list. When the opportunity of the journey was thrown upon us, it came unexpectedly. A choice presented itself and we did not shy away from it but embraced it; despite all the 'friendly advice' and the comments from the "nay"-sayers.

It had never been our long-term latent desire. We hadn't seriously planned it for months or years. We were helped by many people supporting our choice, encouraging us. I realize that were it not for the external events forcing the issue, we would never have done it. I also realize that many of our friends today could do what we did - if only they chose to do so. It is not a financial matter. You can rent out your house, buy a smaller house, cheaper car, smaller boat, etc. It is only a choice, it can be done.

Please do not conclude that my advice is to sell up, jump on a boat, plane, train or buy a Winnebago and go explore and travel the world. In fact, I am not even an advocate of volunteering in general. *Au contraire*. For us, volunteering was a medium. We did it as part of the education for our children and, as it turned out, for ourselves. It may have been shamelessly selfish, but we saw benefits <u>for us</u> volunteering, trusting that any good that came of it for others would be icing on the cake.

Today, we have a deeper understanding and appreciation for the sense and nonsense of volunteering. Since our trip Heidi wrote a book entitled *So you want to Volunteer*. It is a workbook aimed at people considering embarking on a volunteering experience. I can't but recommend it. I believe it might demystify the field a bit and help ground those who are 'driven to volunteer'. For those deciding to volunteer, I have only one recommendation and wish: do your homework. Research and ensure you 'do no harm'. Think of your contribution in the greater scheme of things. Reflect before you choose your route, understand the real contribution you are making and how you impact the overall system.

So, where does this all leave us? I assume we all pursue joy and happiness. I've come believe that happiness is not something you pursue, but it is more something you decide. Choosing your attitude is a powerful thing! To us it is clear that joy is not likely to be found in the 'gathering of chocolate', nor does it magically appear in a trip around the world with the family. Such a world trip can bring, but will not guarantee, pleasure on its own, nor will volunteering.

Our trip was great, beyond great. And if I were thrown back in time and given the same choice again, knowing what I know now, I'd make the same decision. And yes, I'd travel with backpacks. And, yes, I'd home school the kids. I'd volunteer. In a heartbeat. Ask Heidi or the kids, and I think you'll find that they will say the same. For us it was phenomenal, splendid and amazing; superlatives actually can't do it justice. Once we thought about the world trip, we fortunately couldn't unring that bell.

The real key question on our plate today? The same as before, and probably the same as yours….. "What do we do now?"

Alexander van 't Riet

Appendix

USA

The State Fair drowned us in a superfluous amount of lights, colors and foods. In a way, it is indicative of what happens with the curve of marginal diminishing returns. In order to impress, the next ride or food offer needs to be more, bigger, better or harder, crazier, faster. It illustrates nicely the 'chocolate race' the western society is in. From a little local market we remember the musician, the hula hoops and craft shops, from the big State fair, we walk away numbed by overdose. Where a small piece of chocolate next to the cup of tea at my moms kitchen table stood out a real treat, no single ride (or food stand display) at the fair seems to impress. As we think back, we realize the cacophony and general exuberance provided a sense of overload. It was a great experience for one day, but as it turns out, it was representative of what we were trying to get away from on this journey.

GALAPAGOS

We went from extreme to extreme. From the explosion of lights, food and pandemonium of an American State Fair to a minimalistic setup on one of the most remote islands in the world. We taught English and appreciated nature. It showed us human agility. In two weeks we adjusted to a new reality. We calibrated to simple sleeping arrangements. We worked and made friends in a totally new and chaotic school environment. We met loving, caring people and faced ethical dilemmas. We enjoyed nature and realized that on a small island everyone knows everyone. We ran into school politics and had to organize our own lesson plans. It made us appreciate the basics: fresh water, variety of food, good schooling and all the luxury we take for granted. As we left the islands and landed in the modern Quito airport, we looked at it with different eyes. It felt that the shops, the flashing lights and the advertisements were bombarding our senses. How scary that must have been for the seventeen year old traveling with her baby. She who had never left the island!

We exposed our kids to another way of life and how some people lived. We had a platform to discuss things with them and, hopefully, contributed to the community. We volunteered, taught, and 'taught the teacher'. But it raised questions. How much did we contribute? Did the kids in our classes learn, did they advance because of our presence? Did we make a difference, or had we just had a long excursion in the most impressive zoo of the world?

PERU

Peru is magnificent. The nature is unbelievably varied and it is culturally rich. We again saw the extremes. We ate a 5-course meal overlooking Machu Picchu. We ate out of plastic cups and bowls which rats call home at night. We loved or at least appreciated both. It is strange how more then 500 years ago Inca's could live in such wealth while today so much poverty is present in that same region. For the kids, the different living conditions really hit home. They saw the poverty of people living in plastic covered sheds on the cold mountainside with no electricity, no running water. The contrast with the Belmond Sanctuary Lodge touched them deeply. Living with a local family gave us tremendous insights: you hear the local stories, see real day-to-day lives, eat local dishes, dance salsa in the living room. On purpose, these chapters covered a lot of repetitive food stories. That's because it struck us how food variety is such an indicative measure of wealth.

Taking Spanish lessons was a good move. It gave us another look into the local life. This time through the eyes of the teacher. It allowed us to have simple conversations with the non-English-speaking locals we met. We developed a deep appreciation for the teachers in our school. Yes, we gave some kindness to needy students and received hugs in returns; but then again, any child responds to care and thoughtful attention. Was tracing "O's" useful? Was cutting out Christmas trees and knitting scarfs helpful? Did we improve the world by marching the streets? Honestly, I don't really know or even care. The bigger contribution was to the teachers, the heroes of this story. I have to believe that for the short time we were there, it gave them a breather. We came out thankful, they received a helping hand and a smile. Only winners here. Lastly, our time in Peru impressed on me how precarious prosperity is. In virtually no time the Inca Empire was destroyed and much knowledge was lost, to a large extent in name of religion. It is nearly impossible not to dislike the historic Spanish for their presence in the region. By deduction, I feel embarrassed about my own country's colonial atrocities (let's be honest, the Dutch were not much different, we just focused on the other side of the world). The good news is that not all history is lost and there is still lots to see in Peru. Our stay in the Andean Valley gave us many contrasting experiences, the combination of the two provided much joy. It proved again that variety is the spice of life!

AUSTRALIA

While we didn't volunteer in Australia, it was still an important part of the trip. The journey worked in harmony with the children's education, and it is an interesting place to calibrate against. To me, the Australian continent holds that unique combination of extremes of being totally civilized and Western, but with a twist of unruly ruggedness, being kept in check by nature. For non-Australians there is always a certain nervousness traveling around because of the prevalence of jellyfish, sharks, venomous spiders, crocs, snakes and bush fires. The Aboriginals lived in harmony with that nature, accepting its constant reminder that it can overpower you, and modern Australians give the impression of immunity to these fears, totally unaffected by nature's obvious dangers. It seems they all have a family member or acquaintance who died, was maimed, or nearly didn't make it because of an incident with nature. What's so unique is that, without exception, they are so casual about it. One classic story is the disappearance of the prime minister Harold Hold in 1976. Harold just 'vanished' during a morning swim. I am sure that in the US, conspiracy theorists would have stories of crooked governments or aliens. In Australia, the formal report simply explained "that the failure to find his body could be due to an attack by marine life, the body being carried out to sea by tides, or by having his body be caught and wedged in rock crevices". Options galore. Yup, "could happen to anyone, no big deal mate".

Our time in Australia was not about volunteering. We focused mainly on the educational aspects; both school and cultural. It fit nicely because there were ample opportunities to calibrate our appreciation for what we have. Somehow Australia inherently possesses that schizophrenic joy seen in glamping. Roughing it during the day in nature, but enjoying a hot shower and a clean bed at night; enjoying a good kangaroo steak and staring at gorgeous fireworks knowing a spider can bite you anytime. Joy came from seeing the most amazing beaches, swimming at the Great Barrier reef, battling a Huntsman spider, peeling coconuts without tools on a remote island, being thankful the bush fire turned, and catching, cleaning and cooking squid.

As always, the biggest impressions were made by the friends and family who welcomed us in their homes. The gift of their hospitality and willingness to host the four of us was heart warming. I always like the Australian greeting "G'day mate". I never know if it is a statement of fact, a wish for fortune on what is yet to come, or a specific instruction. All in all, we could certainly summarize our time down under as "G'month mate".

CRUISE

Perhaps I went a bit overboard. I know many people feel a cruise is a great way to enjoy sun, different locations, excellent food, and light entertainment. Yes, the food is superb. Yes, the service was very good. Yes, the staff was friendly. That said, eating and living in a top restaurant for two weeks in a row clearly wasn't for us. We didn't see the joy in laying on a deck chair day after day. The cruise not only wasn't a big hit with me. It felt more like a floating prison. In fact, I'd rather face the lizard, huntsman or some other reptile in the bush of Australia than the 55-year old overweight tattooed lady ready for battle at the cruise ship buffet.

It's interesting how a place filled with luxury, a place that has everything in entertainment, all the food and drink you might want, is the one spot that scored so low on the pleasure scale. For many people, a cruise represents that ultimate holiday luxury experience. It is the "all you can eat" chocolate bar if you will. As we left the ship behind, I felt I parted from the epitome of joyless consumerism. Jean-Paul Sartre's work "*l'enfer c'est les autres*" came to mind. Were it not for the transport it provided from Sydney to Singapore, I would have gladly skipped it.

VIETNAM

The Viet Nam weeks made a tremendous impression on us. We saw the good, the bad and the ugly. It was an emotional roller coaster, one with much joy but also with confrontational and insightful moments. Many compare-and-contrast essays could be written.

The beauty of the country is stunning, the culture truly unique. It provided a smörgåsbord of experiences: the food, the silk paintings, the lanterns, the boulevards, the bike rides through rice paddies, the hospitality of the locals. We saw dazzling green landscapes and gripping art. We were mesmerized by young students preforming a delightful dance show demonstrating the rich heritage of a nation, and we were humbled by the efforts of the teachers and seeing our son feed a handicapped child in the pagoda.

Viet Nam was a study of contrasts. How can a grand pagoda, built with such enormous funds and so rich in golden decorations have young children live in its shadows in such depraved conditions? How can this wealthy shrine, despite the massive donations, have only one large common room for so many children and such meager conditions for sick children to live in? How sad that this pagoda provides the only safety net for the unfortunate. And how utterly painful that it needs to be staffed by untrained volunteers from abroad like us!

Allow me to be even more controversial and confrontational and share one thought that kept sneaking into our minds. Should some of these children, especially the ones who suffer severe hydrocephalus, really be kept alive? Should they be condemned to staring at old ceilings from substandard bed until their frail bodies give out before the age of fifteen? Is that fair, right, acceptable? Should we feed them and clean them, knowing that for their entire lives they won't speak, play, sit, laugh or interact with another human; all because they missed out on basic healthcare at birth? And, perhaps most difficult of all, is it bad for us to feel joy for the health which was gifted to us and our children? And bad, because if it wasn't for their suffering I'd miss the awareness of joy in being healthy.

The historic battlefields of Viet Nam in their own way, too, forced moments of reflection. We studied the recent decades and saw how winners write history. Reading through the aftermath of the First Indochina war and subsequent events we realized it was hard to detect one single villain, even with the luxury of hindsight. We were forced to lead my daughter away from displays of war atrocities which made us feel embarrassed to be part of the human race. Having been confronted with both sides of the "American War", it became obvious we grew up with a different set of truths than did the Vietnamese. Perhaps neither one is completely correct. As a derivative, it is harsh to understand years later that many lives were lost and ruined for political opinions only. It is slightly perverse realizing that formally the country still claims to be communist, a huge contributing factor to the war back then, while today it moves naturally to an entrepreneurial and open society. Today, its free-market attitude is alive and vibrant. No doubt the country is both politically and economically thriving.

One other insightful moment came when we donated money to the local school. Despite the fact that I dislike the Catholic church and so many of the dogmas it stands for, we handed a wad of cash to a nun. A nun we barely knew. But we looked in her eyes and saw the gratitude as she realized she could make the payroll to the end of the school year. Her reaction was delightful and brought joy (and a deep-down good feeling) to our hearts. In fact, that day the smiles of the kids in the class seemed shinier as they repeated our words, wrote carefully and tried to overcome language barriers. To us, true joy.

So many intense, conflicting, emotional, and, yes, insightful moments. Viet Nam; what a fantastic roller-coaster!

CHINA

China broke a mold. Entering the country we had preconceived notions. Within no time these were shattered. The sites we saw: the Great Wall, the Forbidden City, Shanghai, Guilin, Beijing, the terracotta warriors were simply amazing. We loved the food, the people, the culture. Whereas I had to overcome reluctance from the family to go to China, having been there, they'd jump on a plane tomorrow if I asked them to go.

We did no volunteering work (it was not allowed), but through the guides, we got a peek into the Chinese life. When traveling with a local guide on multiple days, you build a certain rapport. This allowed us to get much richer commentary and a deeper understanding of the environment. We ended up playing games in a park with the locals. Staying in an AirBnB also added a different dimension. Somehow living in an apartment, having to buy food in the shops and on the street market is so much more insightful than staying in some nondescript hotel chain.

NEPAL

The Nepal experience was, yet again, unforgettable. Not much comes close to living in the serenity of a Buddhist temple surrounded by refugee Tibetan and student monks. The lessons we taught and the lessons we learned provided a lovely balance. We helped the students prepare for exams; they taught us about the simplicity of life and the benefits of detachment. The time in the mountains impressed Buddhist teachings on us which drove home the message that happiness has no time line, no target. Ignoring the reincarnation and some other parts, I have to admit that Buddhists are on to something. Thinking back on it, the Beatles song "Let it be" resonates well with their approach. When reflecting on our Nepal time the feel of that song captures so nicely the general thinking at the monastery. Just let it be.

Perhaps underrepresented in the chapter is the profound impact the book 'Little Princes' made on us. It describes and illustrates the story of the orphans of Nepal. It opened our eyes to the sad exploitation which happens at the dark fringes of the volunteering industry. It showed that good core volunteering work is a not an easy concept. Yes, medical and dental support are easily categorized as good, but even with those, one has to beware. It's key not to make the area dependent on foreign aid alone. It is essential that the aid does not undermine local economies. Volunteering raises all sorts of questions. The law of unintended consequences ruthlessly applies. Don't get me wrong, volunteering done well is a good thing; both for those receiving, and especially for those giving. Notice the order. By effort and luck, we always landed in good projects. When asked by people about volunteering today, I find myself answering with duality, sending a mixed message. Yes, definitely do it, followed by a host of qualifiers and disclaimers. Our Nepal experience was not very fulfilling from our side. I think we were unlucky because the exam week prevented us from "doing" more. But as so often, there is an upside to every downside. In our case the upswing was the unforgettable trek we completed '*en famille*'.

The trek through the mountains to Poon Hill contrasted nicely with the enclosed life in the monastery. It was physically tough and in the open. The sleeping arrangements were basic and closer to nature's elements than I found comfortable. The result? Pure bliss later when we stepped in a shower which had water, double bliss if we'd stand in a shower without permafrost, devoid of cold winds blowing around us, triple bliss if warm water came through the hose. Nepal, yet again, re-calibrated us. It made us realize that we had little to complain about. How bizarre that against that perspective I insisted on having a nicer hotel the last day of our trek!

The short stays in Kathmandu allowed us to soak up the sights, the smells, the culture. It's a good thing we did. Only days after we left the city, in April 2015, an major Earthquake hit Nepal. It killed over 8,000 people and injured more that 21,000. Historic buildings of Kathmandu would be no longer, thousands of people became homeless in an instant.

We were relieved to hear - in the days following - that no one at "our" monastery was hurt. Little damage was done. I know they spent a lot of time praying the following weeks. I also knew they'd be okay; as I am sure they would detach and "Let it Be".

CAMBODIA

Of all the places we visited Cambodia probably held the strongest blend of extremes. The incredible Angkor Wat temples, which show what mankind is able to construct, shares the same ground where the annihilation of a quarter of the nation's population took place by an indescribably ruthless regime. Incredibly, it is such recent history. Even more impactful is to realize that, as a nation, the people either went along with the atrocities, or were killed. It's strange to consider that when you look at middle-aged people. I have to believe the current population is more than a little scarred by the events. Perhaps it is even the reason why they smile most of the time. They are glad it is over. While in Cambodia I read the book *Pol Pot - Anatomy of a Nightmare*. It is probably one of the best geopolitical books I read. It was not necessarily a pleasant read, and perhaps a scary reminder of what can happen and how fast, but if you try to understand the background and the events of Cambodia, a must read.

S21 and the Killing fields made deep impressions on the kids. So much so that for a long time it was next to impossible to talk about it. But it did not just impress them. As parents and educators we also faced challenges explaining what happened. In fact, even today it's difficult to place in context. The contrast of the always smiling Cambodians with the daily reality of land mines and injured people is insightful. The grand palaces, historic temples and impressive nature against the sex-trade, poverty and basic living standard makes for an intense blend. While Cambodia is not necessarily a country to spend months traveling in, I would definitely recommend visiting. In fact, from all the South East Asian countries it probably switches with Vietnam between the number one or the number two spot to go to, depending on the day you ask me.

www.ingramcontent.com/pod-product-compliance
Lightning Source LLC
Chambersburg PA
CBHW070533010526
44118CB00012B/1122